THE DEFINITIVE

Prince Valiant

COMPANION

From the Library of

Hal Foster

Proceeds from the sale of this book benefit

The Friends of Hal Foster Society.

THE DEFINITIVE

COMPANION

Revised Edition Compiled & Designed by:

Brian M. Kane

Revised Edition Text by:

Ray Bradbury
Brian Walker
Brian M. Kane
Arn Saba
Bill Crouch
Virginia Irwin

Revised Edition Edited by:

Kim Thompson
Gary Groth

First Edition Text by:

Todd Goldberg
Carl Horak

First Edition Edited by:

Don Markstein
Rick Norwood

Associate Publisher:

Eric Reynolds

Publishers:

Gary Groth
Kim Thompson

FOR HAL

The author would like to gratefully acknowledge the help of the following people,
without whom this book could not have become a reality.

Paul Baresh, Maria M. Barga, Robert R. Barrett, Ray Bradbury, Lucy Shelton Caswell, Katherine Collins (formerly Arn Saba), Bill Crouch, Nicolette Dobrowolski, John Fleskes, Lucy Foster, Robert Foster, Gary Gianni, Jack Gilbert, Todd Goldberg, Adam Grano, Tom Grindberg, Gary Groth, Calum Johnston, Katherine A. Kane, Richard Kelly, Jay Kennedy, Sven H.G. Lagerström, Mary (née Foster) McAskin, Cullen Murphy, Joan Murphy, Meg (née Murphy) Nash, Rick Norwood, Robert Porfirio, Sean M. Quimby, P. Craig Russell, Marie (née Foster) Sasaninejad, Mark Schultz, Rodney Smith, Kim Thompson, Charles Vess, Brian Walker, Sid Weiskirch, Al Williamson, and Cori Williamson.

Art on page 4 appears courtesy of Jack Gilbert. Art on pages 8 and 103 is shown at its actual size, and appears courtesy of the Ohio State University Cartoon Research Library. Art on pages 6 and 45 is shown actual size, and is from the *Hal Foster Papers*, courtesy of the Special Collections Research Center, Syracuse University Library. Art on page 48 is shown at actual size, and appears courtesy of the Hal Foster Estate.

CONTENTS

Introduction by Ray Bradbury 7

Foreword by Brian Walker 9

Introduction to the First Edition by Todd Goldberg 11

A Prince Valiant Story Index 13

A Prince Valiant Color Gallery 73

Of Mead, Whiskey, and Brandywine: The Artistic Bloodline of *Prince Valiant* 89

The Man Who Draws *Prince Valiant* 99
   (Originally presented in *Everyday Magazine* in the *St. Louis Dispatch,* February 6, 1949)

Hal Foster: Drawing Upon History 103
   (Originally presented in *The Comics Journal* #102, September 1985)

Hal Foster's Induction into the Society of Illustrators Hall of Fame 130

From Prizefighters to Princes: The Classic Art of John Cullen Murphy 131
   (Originally presented in *The Comics Journal* #253, June 2003)

John Cullen Murphy: Goodnight Fair Prince 143
   (Originally presented in *The Comics Journal* #264, Nov/Dec 2004)

Frank Bolle: The Ghost of Camelot 145

Gary Gianni & Mark Schultz: The Adventures Continue 147

The Friends of Hal Foster Society 160

THEY ENTER, AND IN THIS, THE HOLIEST SPOT
IN ALL CHRISTENDOM, REDEDICATE THEIR
SWORDS TO THE SERVICE OF JUSTICE AND RIGHT

INTRODUCTION

It's very simple: You fall in love and you stay in love.

I fell in love with the work of Hal Foster in the late spring of 1932 when, while drawing *Tarzan*, he introduced Tarzan to dinosaurs, which was the madness of my life.

Several months later Tarzan encountered ancient Egypt, which was another great love that began when I saw pictures of the golden mask of Tut when he came out of the tomb when I was a child. This led me to collect Hal Foster full-time during all of 1932 and 1933.

I was delighted when I was asked to write an introduction to those special dinosaur/Egyptian episodes of *Tarzan* much later in my life. When the book appeared with my name on the front with Hal Foster's, I burst into happy tears.

When I was in High School my love for Hal Foster increased because he then invented *Prince Valiant* and I collected it every Sunday for the next twenty years.

When I had my first book published, *Dark Carnival*, I sent a copy to Hal Foster telling him that I loved him and that he was doing work in the illustrated comic sections of the Sunday newspaper that was commensurate with the fine work of N.C. Wyeth, who illustrated the children's books for Scribner's. That impressed Hal Foster so much that he sent me two full-page Sunday illustrations of *Prince Valiant*.

I still have those giant placards, illustrated by Foster, put away in my office. I will never in my life give them away or sell them. They are part of my loving existence.

Even as it made me super-delighted to write about *Tarzan* a few years ago, now it delights me to be upfront in this book about *Prince Valiant* and Foster because his incredible talent remained absolutely tops all of his life. I'm so glad that I was able to write to him on occasion and tell him that.

That's about it. My love remains complete and I hope that the reader will enjoy what follows.

Ray Bradbury
March 22, 2007

BUT IT IS KING ARTHUR'S REACTION THAT SET THE WESTERN WORLD TO TALKING. FOR AT TH NEWS OF THE BETROTHAL HE CONVENES THE KNIGHTS OF THE ROUND TABLE. AND TO ITS NEWEST MEMBER, PRINCE ARN, HE SPEAKS THESE WORDS:

FOREWORD

A PIPE AND A PEN—Remembering John Cullen Murphy

John Cullen Murphy was my godfather. He first met my father, Mort Walker, at the Salmagundi Club in New York in 1950, the same year that both of their strips, *Big Ben Bolt* and *Beetle Bailey*, were released by King Features Syndicate. Soon after this initial encounter, Mort and Jack became neighbors in Connecticut and our families began a long tradition of celebrating July 4th together. Jack's wife Joan helped my mother make her decision to convert to Catholicism and the Murphys served as my godparents when I was baptized in 1959 at the age of seven. Although I eventually abandoned the Catholic faith, Jack and Joan continued to take an interest in my spiritual life and were always good role models.

In December 1973, during my senior year at Tufts University, I wrote a research paper entitled "The Comic Strip as a Communicative Art Form." I interviewed my father, Dik Browne, Garry Trudeau and Jack Murphy and developed a deeper appreciation for the art of cartooning. Having recently returned from an extensive trip through Africa, I was thrilled when Jack presented me with a spectacular *Prince Valiant* page (#1855, August 27, 1972, see page 140), which featured a panel that realistically depicted a lioness taking down an antelope in full stride.

A few months after my graduation from college, my father asked me to help clean up an old mansion in Greenwich, Connecticut, which was to be the first home of the Museum of Cartoon Art. The Museum opened on August 11, 1974 and the following year we mounted one of the first major retrospectives, *The Hal Foster Exhibit* (June 8 to August 31, 1975). We borrowed many important pieces from the collection at Syracuse University, including the very first *Prince Valiant* page. Al Williamson also loaned some original pages, most notably the famous episode in which Val battles "half a hundred hardy Vikings" at a bridge with the "Singing Sword" (#71, 6/19/38, see page 74). Hal Foster made the trip to Connecticut from his home in Florida for the opening. I stood beside the great man as he gazed upon this historic page for a long time. He finally looked at me with a smile, shook his head and said, "I worked my ass off back in those days."

When the Museum moved to the Ward Castle in Rye Brook in 1977, Jack did a pen-and-ink drawing of the building that was reproduced on all of our stationery, business cards and brochures. He attended many of our special events— exhibit openings, guest lectures and fund raisers—and his love of the art form was evident in the conversations I shared with him at these gatherings.

Jack and Joan attended my wedding in 1981, and were also regular guests at the Annual Champagne Croquet Open, a party which my wife Abby and I hosted for many years. In 1985, Jack was so inspired by the white hoop skirts and straw skimmers, set against the lush greenery of Pinetum Park, that he raced home to grab some art supplies and returned to capture the scene in a beautiful watercolor painting that hangs in our home today.

Over the years, on numerous occasions, I remember stopping by Jack's studio, which was behind his house in Cos Cob, Connecticut, to pick up or drop off artwork. The smell of pipe tobacco permeated the air. Costumes and props were scattered in the corners. A partially completed *Prince Valiant* page was always on the drawing board. Jack would greet me with a smile, welcoming the brief interruption from his grueling work schedule.

On November 4, 1999, the Connecticut Chapter of the National Cartoonists Society presented Jack with the Legend Award for his 63-year professional career. Most of the Murphy clan were there to pay tribute to their gentle patriarch. Jack's oldest son, Cullen, showed pictures of his dad posing for himself, dressed as both a Viking warrior and a wench.

I attended Jack's memorial service after he passed away on July 2, 2004. He was eulogized by all of the speakers as a warmly affectionate, remarkably intelligent and abundantly talented husband, father, friend and artist. Although he was honored as the Best Story Strip Artist of the Year six times by the National Cartoonists Society, it is a glaring oversight that John Cullen Murphy never won the organization's highest honor, the Reuben Award. He will go down in history as one of the great masters of the cartoon art form. I will always remember him as a gentleman and a scholar.

Brian Walker
September 1, 2008

A Prince Valiant Companion

Art by Hal Foster
Text by Todd Goldberg and Carl Horak
Edited by Don Markstein and Rick Norwood

Above: Cover to the first edition.

INTRODUCTION TO THE FIRST EDITION, 1992

by Todd H. Goldberg M.D.

Prince Valiant, one of the finest works ever to be produced in the comic art medium, was the creation of artist Harold R. Foster (b. August 16, 1892, Halifax, Nova Scotia; d. July 25, 1982, Spring Hill, Florida). Foster, often called Hal, was a man with little formal education besides art school. He reportedly led an adventurous early life, began a commercial art career in Winnipeg, Manitoba in 1910, and moved to Chicago in 1921 to get more art training at the Art Institute of Chicago and Chicago Academy of Fine Arts. After several years as a successful commercial artist and serious painter, Foster entered the newspaper illustration field in 1929 because of the lack of advertising work during the Depression. It is said that he did not take syndicated cartooning seriously until 1931, when his first feature, Edgar Rice Burroughs' *Tarzan*, became popular and elicited much fan mail. Realizing the pleasure his work gave to the public, Foster began to work more painstakingly and made the *Tarzan* page an artistic as well as commercial success. In order to reach his full artistic potential, Foster needed an outlet of greater scope, and in 1937, the 44-year-old artist left United Feature Syndicate and *Tarzan* to work for King Features on his own epic creation, *Prince Valiant in the Days of King Arthur*.

In *Prince Valiant*, Foster gives us the beautifully illustrated story of a believable, admirable young man who grows up in an exciting, exotic environment and becomes involved in many of the major events of medieval history and legend. The culture of the early Vikings and Britons comes alive amidst the grandeur of Arthurian mythology.

As a work of comic art, *Prince Valiant* stands high and alone because of its high quality and distinctive format. Foster was nearly as good a writer as he was an illustrator, making *Prince Valiant* a total work of art in both its literary and visual components—a very rare feat for comics. However, it must be understood that *Prince Valiant* is not exactly a normal comic strip in the usual sense of the term, because word balloons are never used, and the words and pictures are not truly combined to work equally and synergistically to tell the stories. Foster's text was generally his major storytelling tool, with drawings serving mainly as beautiful embellishments. We can therefore almost consider *Prince Valiant* to be a massive illustrated novel presented in a comic art-like style.

For over forty years, Prince Valiant grew up before our eyes, met many fascinating friends and enemies, lived through exciting adventures all over the world, married, and raised a lovely family which is still growing. In this publication we summarize the major events in the lives of "Val" and his compatriots and family and point out important facts in the development of the strip, as well as placing the stories in historical perspective. We hope that this "index" will not only serve as an important reference tool and monument to Foster's genius, but also capture some of the excitement, charm and verisimilitude of the story of Prince Valiant.

The stories illustrated in the *Prince Valiant* pages were said at times to have been derived from an "imaginary" set of "Chronicles" preserved from the Middle Ages. The historical background of these ancient times is quite interesting and needs to be discussed at the outset in order to place the stories in context. In the *Prince Valiant* strip, historical events are actually generally described relatively accurately but are quite intentionally rearranged or moved to fit the time scheme of the stories. Foster, as we will see, set his stories in the middle of the 5th century, one of the most colorful and eventful eras of early European history. At this time, the Roman Empire had begun to dissolve and had abandoned the British Isles. England then began to suffer many attacks from the Saxons (Germanic tribes from Eastern Europe) and the Picts (early inhabitants of Scotland).

The beginnings of Arthurian mythology seem to lie in that period, in the tales told by the early bards of Britain and Wales during the Saxon invasions (5th-6th centuries A.D.). These tales may have been based partly on the exploits of a real Celtic tribal chief who helped the ancient Britons hold out against the invaders, but also are similar to characters and situations from early Celtic mythology (the term "Celtic" refers to an iron age European tribal group and to the language and peoples descended from them, chiefly in Brittany, Wales, western Ireland, and the Scottish highlands). Such heroic legends, enriched further by tales from the continent (chiefly France), developed into the classical Arthurian romances of the 12th to 15th centuries. Geoffrey of Monmouth's pseudo-historical *Historia Regum Britanniae* (*History of the Kings of Britain*, 1136) and Sir Thomas Malory's *Le Morte d'Arthur* (ca. 1470, from French sources) are the classic early English versions. Modern readers might be more familiar with such works as Lord Tennyson's *Idylls of the King* (1842-1885), Twain's *A Connecticut Yankee in King Arthur's Court* (1889), Terence Hanbury White's *The Once and Future King* (1939-1958), and of course the numerous plays and movies based on these books. An interesting review and sampling of Arthurian history and literature may be found in *The Arthurian Legends: An Illustrated Anthology* by Richard Barber (Littlefield & Adams, 1979; Dorset Press, 1985).

Among the most well-known and important Arthurian myths are the Quest for the Holy Grail (probably derived from a Celtic myth of a magic cauldron which the gods fought over and grafted into the Christian tale of Jesus' cup from the Last Supper), the romance of Sir Tristram and Queen Isolde, and the romance of Launcelot and Guinevere. Perhaps surprisingly, these tales are all mentioned but briefly in the *Prince Valiant* series. The Wizard Merlin Ambroseus, another famous Arthurian character who may have been based on a real Welsh bard who was in the service of Kings Uther and Arthur during the Saxon invasions, does feature prominently in several *Prince Valiant* stories.

Finally, it should be noted that although Foster included many myths and historical events and allusions not from the 5th century in the Prince Valiant stories, all of British mythology is historically dubious, so that Foster's slight rearrangements of history and legend are not

inappropriate or without precedent. For example, "knights" actually existed in England only from about 1066 to 1300 (though the honorary title of course still exists), and the code of chivalry also did not really develop until about the 12th century. In fact, the entire "Golden Age," romantic outlook of Arthurian mythology is sheer fantasy—an obvious example of writers attributing their own contemporary attitudes and ideals to previous cultures, which may have actually been quite barbaric. Foster merely added his own anachronistic elements; indeed, he always was said to have proudly claimed that he had condensed many centuries of European history into Val's brief lifetime. It certainly makes interesting reading for us!

A PRINCE VALIANT STORY INDEX

by Todd Goldberg, Carl Horak, *&* Brian M. Kane

Story synopsis and commentaries for pages 1-2246 are by Todd Goldberg and Carl Horak. Story synopsis and commentaries for pages 2247-3783 are by Brian M. Kane.

1: INTO THE FENS
Pages 1 (13 February 1937) – 4 (6 March 1937)

King Aguar of Thule and his family are driven from their homeland of Thule and forced to settle in the Great Fens of Britain. Young Prince Valiant (shown only as a small boy in pages 2-4 and not assuming the leading role until page 3) begins his career of adventure as he grows up in the rugged swamplands.

2: THE PROPHECY
Pages 4 (6 Mar 1937) – 11 (24 April 1937)

The main storyline begins as Prince Valiant (first nicknamed "Val" in page 4) investigates the source of a mysterious light far out in the swamplands and encounters Horrit, the witch, and her son Thorg. The witch, who is introduced in page 9 and reappears many times in subsequent years, foresees a future of "high adventure, but nowhere contentment," for the young teenager (who will be haunted by this prophecy for much of his life). She also predicts great sorrow, and Val returns home to find that his mother has died.

3: THE HOME-MADE KNIGHT
Pages 11 (24 April 1937) – 15 (22 May 1937)

Val leaves the great marshes to seek adventure and fulfill Horrit's prophecy. An encounter with Sir Launcelot, the greatest knight in Christendom, inflames Val with the desire to become a knight. The pauper prince begins by capturing and training a wild horse.

4: THE TRIAL OF SIR NEGARTH
Pages 16 (29 May 1937) – 20 (26 June 1937)

Wandering inland, Val meets Sir Gawain, a famous knight of the Round Table who is to become his lifelong friend. The young prince learns about knighthood and helps Gawain capture Sir Negarth, a robber knight. On the road to Camelot, where Negarth is to be judged by King Arthur, Val and Gawain slay a great sea dragon that had unhorsed Gawain. Val visits the marvelous city of Camelot and meets King Arthur, Queen Giunevere, and Merlin Ambroseus for the first time (page 19). At the trial, Val convinces the King to pardon Sir Negarth because he had helped save Gawain.

5: FROM THRONE ROOM TO DUNGEON
Pages 21 (3 July 1937) – 22 (10 July 1937)

Just as Horrit had prophesized, Val meets the King and Queen and becomes Sir Gawain's squire at their suggestion. The hotheaded youth gets into a fight with other squires and is thrown into a cell. A battle with the Northmen breaks out, but the heartbroken Val is forbidden to participate due to his apparent lack of self-control.

6: THE FAKE QUEST
Pages 23 (17 July 37) – 38 (30 October 1937)

Sir Osmond and Baron Baldon, two officers of the palace guard, pick Gawain as the victim of a ransom plot. They decoy him and Val into accepting a false quest: the restoration of eeriwold Castle, which is held by a "terrible ogre," to the Lady Morvyn. Gawain is captured in an ambush and taken to another hidden castle, but Val escapes. Disguised, the Prince enters the castle, discovers the plot, and helps Gawain escape. Val and the wounded Gawain return to Camelot. King Arthur interrupts the Tournament of the Queen's Diamonds to lead his knights to punish the kidnappers.

7: THE MAID ILENE
Pages 39 (6 November 1937) – 55 (26 February 1938)

Sir Gawain and his squire ride at adventure to rescue the parents of the maid Ilene from imprisonment in their own castle by an outlaw band. Val falls in love with the slim, pretty blonde (Val's first love is introduced in page 38). The quest is interrupted by a battle with an evil red knight, whereby Gawain is wounded and is left to recover at a nearby house of an old hermit. Alone, Val disguises himself as a demon, sneaks into the captured castle, and frightens the Ogre of Sinster Wood and his followers. The superstitious ogre dies of sheer terror, and Val soon clears out the remaining outlaws. Ilene's father, the Thane of Branwyn, is liberated. As a reward for his service, Val asks for Ilene's hand in marriage, but the Thane informs him that Ilene has already been promised to Arn, Prince of Ord. Val vows to fight for Ilene.

8: THE SORCERESS
Pages 55 (26 February 1938) – 64 (30 April 1938)

Gawain is carried off from the hermitage by the evil half sister of Arthur, the sorceress Morgan Le Fay (this recurring nemesis is introduced in page 56). When Val rides to Morgan's castle, "Dolorous Garde," to confront the witch, he is given drugged wine and put into a cell. After weeks of horror, Val escapes and runs to Camelot, seeking the advice of Merlin, the wizard, and advisor to the King. Merlin's magic spell forces the sorceress to release Gawain.

9: ILENE ABDUCTED
Pages 64 (30 April 1938) – 85 (25 September 1938)

Val returns to Camelot with Gawain and is shocked to hear of the impending marriage of Ilene to Prince Arn of Ord. The heartbroken boy leaves for Ord to fight for the hand of Ilene. When Val encounters his rival (Arn is introduced in page 67), their conflict is interrupted by news that Ilene was kidnapped by Viking raiders while on her way to Ord. The princes forget their quarrel and ride to rescue her. They are stopped by some of the Vikings. Armed with Arn's charmed Singing Sword, Val stands alone on the bridge at Dundorn Glen to delay pursuit while Arn rides on to free their beloved. Val battles valiantly (of course) but is captured and becomes a prisoner along with Ilene. Arn follows the Vikings with an armed

ship. When Arn and his knights catch up, they win the ensuing battle, but Thagnar, the rover chief, escapes with Ilene during a storm. Val and Arn leave their ship to seek Ilene on foot. They are horrified to learn that she and Thagnar have been killed in a shipwreck! Dejected, the two weary, heartbroken princes return to Camelot. Arn gives Val his Singing Sword (in page 85) to be used in King Arthur's service and returns to his home at Ord (he is seen again 10 years later; see Story 37).

COMMENT: *Cutout "stamps" picturing the main characters were an added feature on the corner of the strip logo starting with page 83 and ending with 329.*

10: THE SAXON INVASION OF BRITAIN
Pages 86 (2 October 1938) – 103 (29 January 1939)

Val craves knighthood and fellowship at the Round Table, but Arthur says he is too young. In order to impress the King, Val enters the Great Tournament. Embarrassed when he loses a joust with Sir Tristram, one of England's greatest knights, Val leaves Camelot and returns after two long years to his old home in the mysterious Fens. Val again sees his father, the exiled King of Thule, who now has only a small swampy island and a few faithful warriors. Val secretly plans to help Aguar regain his lost kingdom but is interrupted when he learns of a pending Saxon invasion of England—the tenth and greatest. Val rides to Camelot to warn Arthur and helps the King's Council of War develop battle plans. With but 10,000 men, Britain faces an army of 20,000 Saxon warriors in the Fens. Using flames, smoke, and arrows, Val drives the invaders directly into the hands of the King's men. Amid the wreckage of the battlefield, Arthur makes the resourceful Prince Valiant a Knight of the Round Table (on page 103).

11: THE BARGAIN
Pages 104 (5 February 1939) – 107 (26 February 1939)

Val's proud father, King Aguar, recruits King Arthur's aid in recapturing Thule and sets sail from Britain. The oppressed people of Thule (apparently the site of modern Norway) rally to support their exiled King. A battle is not necessary, for the old, sick tyrant King Sligon has tired of his difficult life and trades back the kingdom of Thule for the tiny, peaceful island in the quiet English swamps. Aguar quickly reorganizes his government.

12: CLARIS
Pages 107 (26 February 1939) – 111 (26 March 1939)

When Sligon said he wanted peace (Story 11), he was so sincere that he left his wife and daughter behind. Little Claris schemes to become the bride of Prince Valiant and future Queen of Thule, but accidentally falls in love with a man named Alfred. Lonely Val asks Claris to marry him but lightheartedly gives her up when he realizes she loves Alfred.

13: THE CAVE OF TIME
Pages 112 (2 April 1939) – 117 (7 May 1939)

Bored with his peaceful new home of Thule, Val rides from his father's castle in search of adventure. He takes refuge from a storm in what he believes is an empty cave and is startled to find a beautiful witch woman who gives him a potent drink. Going deeper into the cave, Val wrestles with an old man who is a personification of Time, and the young Prince suddenly is turned into an old man. The witch woman restores his youth and Val rides away in a fit of terror.

14: ANDELKRAG, THE UNCONQUERABLE
Pages 118 (14 May 1939) – 127 (16 July 1939)

Val learns that Rome has fallen to Attila the Hun. All Europe has been burned and pillaged by the Huns, and only the city of Andelkrag still stands. Val slips through the besieging Huns and joins the gallant defenders of the city. For months the fierce might of Attila persists, and the walls of Andelkrag finally crumble just as the food and drink runs out. As death approaches, the women commit suicide and the men march out from their burning fortress to meet their fate as brave warriors. One battered survivor—Prince Valiant—leaves the smoldering ruins when the fighting ends.

15: THE LEGION OF HUN-HUNTERS
Pages 128 (23 July 1939) – 169 (5 May 1940)

For years the Huns have pillaged Europe unhindered, and now Val decides to recruit a large band of soldiers, knights, refugees, and bandits united by a common hatred of the Huns. A series of daring raids on the barbarians takes place. ("Pandaris," #140-152: Val and an impudent thief named Slith travel to the walled city of Pandaris when they learn that the treacherous false Duke Piscaro is letting Huns pass through the city in order to attack Val's Hun-hunters from the rear. Val and the real Duke, Cesario, restore the city to freedom from tyranny and from the influence of the Huns.) Val and his aides next seek a plan whereby their army of 7,000 can halt the 20,000 Huns sent to clear and important pass and open the way for further onslaught of Europe. Using a daring strategy based on the story of the Trojan Horse, Val's band slips into the Huns' base and takes over, leaving the Huns without food in the barren mountains. Val's army soon meets the Huns on an open field and defeats them. Finally, Val has shown the world that the Huns are not invincible, and they become nothing more than petty raiders. ("Girl Trouble," #159-168: After the battle, Val carries home a wounded soldier, Hulta, who turns out to be a beautiful woman in disguise. Slith falls in love with Hulta, who is soon installed as the new ruler of the conquered lands, and the two decide to marry.) Val declines suggestions that he lead a war of extermination against the hated Huns, explaining that he pledges his sword only in the cause of justice and freedom, and wars of aggression would be but breeders of future wars. Finally, after a banquet in honor of the marriage of Slith and Hulta, the hour of parting comes.

COMMENT: *The Huns were a real warlike tribe from the East that invaded Europe in the AD 300s and 400'. Their invasion attempt was halted in 451 in France at the Battle of Chalms-Sur-Marie. They attacked Italy (as in Story 14) in AD 452 and then were thoroughly vanquished after the death of Attila in AD 453.*

16: THE ROAD TO ROME
Pages 169 (5 May 1940) – 187 (8 September 1940)

Val, Gawain, and Tristram, who fought side by side against the Huns, cannot bear to part and decide to take a trip to Rome together. They stop for a night at a tavern where three gamblers, masquerading as noblemen, entice Gawain into a dice game and fleece him. ("The Giant," #172-178: Some idle time on his hands, Val undertakes a quest to rid the countryside of a troublesome giant who has for years demanded tribute of slaves and supplies from the villages, but our hero is surprised when he learns that the giant has secretly organized a refuge for freaks and outcasts.) The knights resume their journey down the road to Rome, which leads down from the snowy Alps to the marshy plains bordering the Adriatic Sea. On the way, the comrades help a small local tribe establish a city (later to be known as Venice!) far out in the sea, away from a menacing band of Huns. As the leisurely journey continues, the three fellows of the Round Table encounter much ruin and decay, for the Empire is crumbling. Near Ravenna, Val helps an Oriental jewel merchant recover some stolen gems. As a reward, the merchant gives Val a charmed necklace, whose wearer supposedly can never be bound by chains. Tristram, Val, and Gawain finally arrive at Rome; riding beside Flavius Aetius, last of the great Roman generals.

COMMENT: *The approximate dating of Val's saga is explicitly indicated in this story for the first time, when page 183 mentions that the fall of the Roman Empire at Ravenna (which occurred in AD 476), will be about 20 years later. This and the depiction of the fall of the Huns in the previous stories places these adventures in the 450's AD (see chronology).*

17: VALENTINIAN'S JUSTICE
Pages 188 (15 September 1940) – 199 (1 December 1940)

While Val, Gawain, and Tristram sightsee and gallivant, intrigue, jealousy and treachery bring ruin to the Roman Empire. Emperor Valentinian III, jealous of General Aetius' popularity and achievements, sends his assassins out after Aetius, caring nothing for the fate of his empire. The last of the great Roman generals thus falls, and with him the last hope of the Empire. Sirs Tristram and Valiant are witnesses to the sordid deed and are promptly arrested by the emperor's private assassins, accused of the murder, and imprisoned. Gawain, who has been busy seducing Roman ladies, is also arrested. Just as the evil Emperor is about to put his prisoners to death, the friends of Aetius rebel and permanently put an end to their Emperor's misdeeds. When the three knights see the Emperor fall, they leave Rome immediately, knowing they might be blamed for the killing. Pursuit comes swiftly, but the pampered Roman guardsmen quickly find that they are no match for these turbulent sons of storm and hardship. The three friends part, for their only chance is to try to escape singly. Tristram chooses to ride North, back past Rome, and follows his heart back to fair Isolde in England (see Story 28). Gawain rides westward toward the sea and sails to Marseilles. Val rides South on the Appian way towards Naples and escapes from the Roman soldiers by hiding in the crater of Mount Vesuvius.

COMMENT: *In this tale, Foster, rather than relying on superficial, sweeping overviews of events, shows cleverly how individual idiosyncrasies and relationships can determine the course of history. This story is based on true historical events—the murders of General Flavius Aetius in AD 454 and Emperor Valentinian III in AD 455, though Foster places it several years before the plunder of Rome by the Vandals (Story 30), which actually happened in 455 also (see chronology).*

18: FIGHTS FOR THE SINGING SWORD
Pages 199 (1 December 1940) – 246 (26 October 1941)

At Naples, Val finds a ship bound for Sicily and pays his way aboard, hoping to return to the North. A terrible storm drives the ship past dread Scylla and Charybdis and the burning Mountain of Etna, but the Captain guides the ship safely into a nearby bay. There, Angor Wrack, the Sea King, sends his warriors to obtain slaves, and they return with Prince Valiant, many wounds, and the Singing Sword. Val is chained among the hopeless galley slaves. Using the sharp edges of the charmed necklace of the Oriental jewel merchant (Story 16), Val cuts through his chains and escapes from the pirate ship in a small lifeboat. After days of drifting upon unknown seas, Val awakens from exhausted sleep to see, bending over him, a beautiful, smiling, longhaired blonde girl whose loveliness he will never forget. Then he sleeps again, and upon awakening he finds himself again drifting on a lonely sea, but now the boat is loaded with provisions. An explanatory note is signed by "Aleta, Queen of the Misty Isles." Val suddenly decides that from now on, instead of wandering around the world in search of adventure, he will dedicate his life to finding the mysterious Queen whom he saw only in a dream. The search ends abruptly when King Lamorack of Tambelaine takes Val hostage. ("Sombelene and Melody," #212-223: Enchanted by the beauty of Lamorack's two daughters, Sombelene and Melody, Val temporarily forgets his search for Aleta and idles away the days with the two princesses. When the evil Angor Wrack comes to wed the Princess Melody, Val seeks to settle old scores. First, he contrives the elopement of Melody and a young fisherman named Hector and then, with youthful overconfidence, tries to regain the Singing Sword by force. He fails, and an angry King Lamorack sentences him to death. Armed only with a knife, Val is thrown into a pit where a hungry monster lives. After escaping and swimming far out to sea, Val is picked up by a fishing boat and learns from the sailors that his enemy Angor Wrack had married Sombelene (who had admired Wrack's ruthless masculinity) and sailed on a pilgrimage to Jerusalem.) Val forces the fishermen to sail in pursuit of Wrack and the Singing Sword. After a long trip, Val reaches Jerusalem, where he meets Princess Sombelene, now the wife of his enemy, and she convinces him to try to regain the sword without killing her pirate husband. Far out in the desert, Val finds his enemy. As the men fight, an angry group of Arab slave dealers, whom Val had previously encountered, take both Val and Wrack prisoner and steal the Singing Sword. Again Val uses his sharp-edged charmed necklace to help him and Wrack get loose. The two stealthily steal back their stolen swords and escape. Angor Wrack begrudgingly allows Val to hold on to the Singing Sword temporarily. When the angry Arabs follow and attack, Wrack is injured and Val is captured. Wrack is taken back to Damascus by his wife, who was following. The sword is once again taken away from Val, and he is sold into slavery. Belshad Abu, a pompous Syrian merchant, buys both Val and the sword. Pretending to make love to his master's daughter, Val slips into the harem and tricks the girl into getting the sword back and taking him away. They ride through the desert, where Val gains some armor and freedom and deserts the confused girl. ("Belsatan's Magic," #238-242: Val speeds westward along the Euphrates, enjoying his newfound freedom. He meets Belsatan, a supposedly evil djinn, who is actually an eccentric, jovial magus. Belsatan tries to use Val in a scheme to get rid of his pretty but nagging wife, but the wizard soon becomes lonely and summons his wife back.) Val is finally able to resume his difficult search for Aleta, Queen of the Misty Isles, but first he has some unfinished business with Angor Wrack. The disputed ownership of the Singing Sword is finally settled when the white-haired pirate agrees to let the troublesome lad keep the sword permanently. The quarrel behind them, Val and Wrack become friends. Val rests at Wrack's house in Jerusalem and celebrates his 18th birthday with Sombelene and her pirate husband.

COMMENT: Val has had quite an excitement-filled life for a boy of only 18! Extrapolation from Story 30 (which is taken as a reference point, 455 AD [see chronology]) places this story in roughly 451 AD, so Val was apparently born in approximately 433 AD. This very long adventure was a turning point in Val's career because of the introduction (in page 208) of Aleta, a woman whom Val was never to forget. Foster claimed to have used his wife Helen as the model for Aleta! The historical authenticity of the Jerusalem episodes (especially pages 224-225) is noteworthy; Foster dots the landscape with accurate drawings of the Holy City and its famous religious landmarks. By this time, Foster's artwork was finally beginning to reach its polished maturity; the drawings were somewhat cruder in the first few years of the strip, as in the earlier Tarzan pages.

19: THE MISTY ISLES
Pages 246 (26 October 1941) – 253 (14 December 1941)

Angor Wrack fits Val with a small ship, and Val resumes his quest by sailing for the Aegean Sea (which is apparently where Foster conceives of Aleta's home as being located). On the way, the Prince tries to lead his crew against several bands of fierce Corsairs. The frightened sailors maroon Val on an island and sneak off, but the wind blows them back again. Val reboards, not knowing that while the rascals were away they had stumbled upon and plundered a helpless village in the Misty Isles. A storm damages the ship and again blows it back to the Misty Isles, where the vengeful villagers kill the crew. The horrified young Prince does not realize how richly his men had earned their punishment and thinks the islanders to be violent and evil. He at last meets Aleta and, thinking she must be a cruel Queen, denounces her and runs away, his romantic dreams shattered. Fleeing with misguided fear, Val stumbles upon a well-stocked boat, which he does not know has been planted by Aleta. He is surprised to find another cryptic note from the lovely young Queen. Val sails away from what he thinks is a cruel place, and this time he has no wild desire to return. Aleta secretly weeps at the strange boy's departure.

20: HOMEWARD BOUND
Pages 253 (14 December 1941) – 289 (23 August 1942)

Val's romantic dreams have turned to bitterness, and he feels a great longing for his windy, northern home. In the boat provided by Aleta, Val sails into the busy port of Athens. There, he meets a tall, fat, boisterous, red-haired Viking named Boltar (introduced in #253, he became Val's lifelong friend.) The two reminisce about their homeland, and Val decides to sail with Boltar and his pirate crew towards distant Thule. ("Rumors of Gold," #256-263: The ship sails westward on the Mediterranean. Val is annoyed when Boltar's crew takes a detour southward in search of treasure. They follow the African coastline south. Boltar glides his ship up a jungle river toward the location indicated on a treasure map. The search is canceled when Val and his men run into huge, monstrous African animals that fill them with terror. The Vikings quickly sail out of the jungle and resume their northward journey.) After a month of traveling, the pirates stop at a seaport in Gaul for supplies and repairs. There Val learns that Sir Gawain is being held prisoner in a nearby castle by Guy Haakon. Val gives all his hard-earned store of gold to ransom his old friend, but the treacherous Haakon sends his horsemen out to recapture them. The two knights are unable to reach Boltar's ship before it leaves the port, but they are pleased to find that Boltar had laid waste to Haakon's castle before going. Penniless and afoot, the two knights encounter Dame Gilbert, and glib Gawain so pleases her that she invites them home and gets them horses. ("The Siege," #269-275: Soon after leaving the Gilberts, Gawain and Val accept an invitation from the fat, jovial Sir Hubert, who wants the knights to aid him against assaults by his enemy, Hugh D'Arcy. Hugh's nephew, Raoul D'Arcy, loses his heart to Hubert's young daughter, Clair, sneaks into his enemy's castle, and is captured by Prince Valiant. When D'Arcy's forces ram their way into the castle, they become trapped in a cul-de-sac and are killed by falling debris. Although Hubert has won the battle, he loses both the D'Arcy castle and his daughter to Raoul. Val and Gawain stay for the wedding and a week of enjoyable boar hunting before they must leave.) Our heroes pass by a humorous battle between two inept, aged knights ("The Battle of the Behemoths," #275-277). ("The Curse of the Blacktower," #277-287: Lady Anne of Gaiforte seeks aid in finding her missing husband, Robert. Prince Valiant and Sir Gawain go to search the haunted ruins of ill-famed Blacktower, stronghold of Gaiforte's long-dead enemies. There they find that the missing Thane is a prisoner, but they, too, are trapped by a strange madwoman, who tries to set fire to the Blacktower. The knights escape from their cell and rescue sick Robert just before the evil tower crumbles.) After returning Robert to his wife and restoring the friendship of Robert and his former enemy Givric, Val and Gawain begin the long northward journey across Brittany towards Camelot. When they reach the English Channel, they encounter Boltar, who is embroiled in trouble with Sir Launcelot. Launcelot happily greets his fellow knights and has Boltar sail them to England. After three turbulent years of adventuring across the world (actually 3 1/2 years in real time; since Story 10), Prince Valiant comes once again to Camelot.

COMMENT: *This large story is one of the first uses of a plot device which Foster was to use (and perhaps overuse) many times again: Val makes a long journey and encounters adventure, intrigue, and/or romance at each of many stops and detours along the way.*

21: THE ROMAN WALL
Pages 290 (30 August 1942) – 311 (24 January 1943)

Val's joyous reunion with his friends at Camelot is cut short by tidings of war. Britain's security is threatened by an alliance of Picts and Vikings. King Arthur sends Sir Valiant to examine the old "Roman Wall," to see if it can again be used to defend the northern borders of the realm. Alone in the wintry countryside, Val searches for and finds the long wall, which was built from sea to sea by Hadrian to hold back the wild Picts of Scotland and which was abandoned when the Romans left Britain (in A.D. 412) to defend their own capital against the Barbarians. Julian, grandson of a Roman centurion left behind to guard the wall, helps Val with his investigation. Val passes the wall, enters Scotland, and finds the reported Viking invasion base. The Vikings discover the spy and question him under torture. Gawain, who had lazily remained behind, catches up and recklessly rescues what the cruel Northmen had left of his young friend. When Arthur learns of Val's mistreatment, he angrily leads his warriors northward. Soon, the armies of King Arthur and Horsa the Viking, face each other near the Roman Wall, neither side daring to initiate an assault. Thundaar, champion of the Vikings, challenges the best of Arthur's knights to single combat. After the brute kills an inexperienced young knight, Val angrily steps forth and defeats the strong but clumsy Viking. Val then leads a troop of reckless young horsemen against the Viking supply lines, taking vast quantities of stores, which Val lets fall into the hands of the Picts. When the hungry Vikings find the Picts eating their food, they fall upon their allies. The powerful alliance breaks down, thanks to Val's strategy, and Arthur's army is able to stand by lazily as the enemies of Britain slay each other.

COMMENT: *The Romans ruled Britain from AD 43 to ca. 400, and Hadrian's Wall was built in the AD 120's. The wall was intended to protect England from Scottish warriors, and it still stands between Carlisle and Newcastle-Upon-Tyne.*

22: MERLIN SOLVES A PROBLEM
Pages 311 (24 January 1943) – 317 (7 March 1943)

Visions of Aleta haunt Val's every movement, and he journeys to his boyhood home, the fens, to find out if this part of Horrit's prophecy is true. Deep in the swamps Val asks the old witch for a spell to help him forget the bewitching young queen, but all he gets is the same old prophecy of adventure, wealth, turmoil and discontent. Heartsick, he seeks the advice of Merlin Ambroseus. The wise old man makes Val realize that he really already has anything a young man could want: adventure, a noble cause to fight for, good friends and splendid enemies, travel, and a maiden to love. There is no such thing as complete contentment, Merlin explains. Confused, Val returns to Camelot.

23: THE LONG VOYAGE TO THULE
Pages 318 (14 March 1943) – 350 (24 October 1943)

Homesick, Val asks King Arthur for a leave of absence, says goodbye to his friends, and begins the long trip to visit his father, the King of Thule. A variety of brief adventures ensues. One evening, a crafty hermit offers hospitality to Prince Valiant and Beric, his squire, but tries to murder Val for his money. Val promptly hangs the miscreant and soon after deals with his outlaw companions. When the two stop to fix Beric's saddle girth, Val makes use of the time by befriending a young crippled boy, giving him a three-legged

dog and encouragement to manufacture arrows for the King. At London, Val books passage on a large ship heading towards Scandia (Sweden) and then rescues Lady Olga and her daughter Katwein from a band of kidnappers. The two women are also bound for Sweden, and Val sneaks them aboard his ship. When the "Poseidon" takes off, Val and Katwein become aware of an unwelcome additional passenger: Skurl, Thane of Hedmark, the over-zealous admirer of fair Katwein who had been responsible for the kidnapping attempt. As the ship slowly wallows north towards Northland (Norway), it is beset by floods, fires, and broken timbers and just barely reaches the shore. When it seems like Skurl has been killed in the turmoil and wreckage, Katwein sadly admits that she really loved him. The blackguard turns up alive, and he is happy to wake up to her smiling face. The two lovers and some other passengers continue on by land, while Val, Beric, and a few others salvage a small boat and sail on towards Trondheim. An undersea earthquake and tidal wave and a terrifying encounter with a ghastly sea monster follow. Finally, after months of hardship and danger, Val and Beric sail up Trondheimfjord to Trondheim. They find that Aguar is holding a great tournament to celebrate the signing of a treaty with Valgrind, King of the Inner Lands. Suspicious, Val disguises himself as a troubadour, joins Valgrind's band, and discovers that there is a plot against Aguar's throne. Val comes home after three years of adventuring across the world (since Story 13, actually four years earlier). Just as Valgrind prepares his warriors to capture Aguar's stronghold, Val kidnaps the plotter and threateningly forces the warriors to give up their plans and return home to the Inner Lands. The formal reunion of Val and his father is happy and tearful. Valgrind is, not surprisingly, beheaded and buried with simple dignity.

COMMENT: *Page 329 is the last one with "stamps," and the new logo (used until 1980) began with page 330. The presence of so-called troubadours, who really existed only in France in the 10th to 13th centuries, is a noticeable anachronism in this and many other* Prince Valiant *tales.*

24: THE SEDUCTRESS
Pages 351 (31 October 1943) – 354 (21 November 1943)

Eric, a tall, powerful Saxon who had accompanied Val in the previous adventure, tries to impress all the girls at the palace. Just as he begins to get along with the ladies, an impudent girl named Ingrid puts him in a rage. She reveals her love for him when he "accidentally" gets injured twice. Gradually, the two fall in love, but Eric is ashamed he is only a penniless soldier of fortune. In order to change that, Ingrid reminds King Aguar of Eric's help in the defense of the castle and has him appointed Jarl of Haldervkik. She leads Eric away to become her slave for life.

25: THE CALL OF THE SEA
Pages 355 (28 November 1943) – 358 (19 December 1943)

Since Thule had been saved only by luck and Val's quick thinking, Aguar and his son try to find out how such treachery could have been possible. Aguar feels he has ruled firmly but justly, yet there is revolt along the prosperous coast. Val calls the Vikings together in council to listen to their grievances. He is surprised to find the men to be frustrated inveterate sea-rovers, furious at Aguar's well-meaning attempts to rid Thule of what he calls piracy. Aguar's beautiful dream of a peaceful, civilized kingdom modeled on Camelot crumbles. He calls in the Vikings and announces that they may return to the seas, urging them to concentrate on exploration and trade and forbidding them to make war on Britain.

26: THE JEALOUS CRIPPLE
Pages 358 (19 December 1943) – 363 (23 January 1944)

Calm settles once again over Thule, and after one day of it Val gets bored and goes hunting. Because of carelessness, he is soon pushed over a cliff by a wounded stag. A young huntress named Sigrid finds the dazed lad and shelters him in her cabin. The girl has a bitter, crippled friend named Gundar Harl, who is talented at carving model ships. Gundar had earlier lost his right leg in a shipwreck in the icy north (he is introduced in page 360 and is to become a recurring character in later years). The three go searching for Val's horse, which was lost in the accident. Gundar, despairing of ever winning Sigrid and jealous of Val, tries to send them all over a waterfall but fails. Gundar is happy when he finds that Sigrid does love him, and Val is happy when he finds his horse. Before leaving, Val tries to cheer up Gundar and informs him that Thule has need of good ship-builders.

27: A QUICK, BLOODY BATTLE
Pages 363 (23 January 1944) – 368 (27 February 1944)

Prince Valiant returns home from his hunting trip to find that the Finnis raids on the borders of Thule have become serious and that the King's army has been cut to pieces by guerilla tactics. Aguar sends his son and some reinforcements. Val joins the tired, bewildered army and leads it in sullen retreat, but the Finnis come in hot pursuit. Val and his men hide on a glacier as the Finnis pass and slaughter the raiders as they wander back to their camp. After the battle, Val disregards some wise advice and enters the tunnel of the glacier's stream in pursuit of a deer to eat. A great fall of ice blocks the entrance. Trapped in a weirdly beautiful cavern, Val and the deer wait in suspense as the cavern fills with icy water. The pressure of the pent-up water hurls the icy barrier aside, and the river gushes forth, carrying a lot of debris, some of which is Prince Valiant. Beric warms and revives his ailing master, who soon leads his victorious army home.

28: THE REWARDS OF TREACHERY
Pages 368 (27 February 1944) – 378 (7 May 1944)

Seeking revenge for their recent embarrassment (Story 22), the men of the Inner Lands ride from the South into Thule, disguised as hunters. They treacherously kidnap Val, who is on his way home from the flood (Story 27). The Prince is tortured and put up for ransom but luckily escapes after giving Einar the torturer a taste of his own cruel treatments. Meanwhile, Beric has followed his master's trail and sends for Aguar's army. Einar is soon shocked to find his secret stronghold surrounded. The army builds a dam to flood the lands and starve the torturers out of the castle. The King and Prince ride home, leaving their warriors to clean up.

COMMENT: *With page 376, Prince Valiant begins a 1½ year period of two-thirds page episodes. Foster devoted the bottom of the pages during 1944 and 1945 to a charming extra feature called* The Medieval Castle, *the "new, exciting story" of two young boys growing up during the time of the First Crusade (ca. AD 1096-1099). The illustrations were typically excellent, and the story was unexciting but pleasingly entertaining.*

29: "THE WINNING OF ALETA"
Pages 379 (14 May 1944) – 468 (27 January 1946)

Obsessed by thoughts of Aleta, Val sets out to find her and force her to release him from the spell he thinks she must have cast on him (see stories 18, 19, 22). Journeying southward, Val reaches the court of King Arthur and is greeted by his old friend Sir Gawain. ("Tristram and Isolde," #381-384: Thinking of their gay adventures of a few years ago [stories 16 & 17], Val and Gawain look for their friend Tristram, hoping he will accompany them to the Misty Isles. They are too late, for Tristram has a rendezvous with destiny: the jealous King Mark of Cornwall finds Tristram visiting with his wife, the fair Isolde, and kills the famous knight. Val and Gawain flee the terrible scene of tragedy and bring the sad news back to Camelot.

COMMENT: *this interesting interlude, based on an incident in Mallory's* Morte d'Arthur *and dramatized in Wagner's* Tristan und Isolde, *does not really do justice to the famous complex, tragic tale, and the subsequent death of the grieving Isolde is not even mentioned.*

After causing some mischief and havoc in Camelot, Val and Gawain begin their quest. The land journey ends at Marseilles, where Beric and Val contract a ride to Crete on a ragged ship. Bad weather causes the ship to crash on the Italian coast. Gawain is briefly "rescued" and held for ransom by Beneti Benoit and rides home after he escapes. Meanwhile, Beric leads his injured master across Italy. Gradually Val recovers his health, and they buy a ship and set out across the Aegean Sea. When Val and Beric land at the Misty Isles, a shore patrol immediately attacks and kills Beric. Mad with hate and anguish and without his full strength and memory due to his recent illness, Val vows to make the horrid Queen pay. Meanwhile, seventeen-year-old Aleta is about to fulfill her duty to her country by choosing a husband from among a glittering array of suitors. She had secretly hoped Val would return to her, but it seems too late. Suddenly a scarred, ragged madman bursts into the banquet and drags the Queen out. Amid the roar and confusion of a great storm, Val escapes with his prisoner and sails to North Africa. Because she is a cruel sorceress, Val plans to punish Aleta by dragging her in chains through all the kingdoms of the world. They ride aimlessly across the endless, burning deserts of Libya. Val soon finds himself protecting the "cruel sorceress," rather than humiliating her as he had planned. Finally, after many bouts of delirium, Val's head clears. Aleta explains the events of the past months to the confused lad, and Val leads her off again, honor bound to carry out his vow. They head for the coast and are soon out of the desert. One day, Aleta finally gets angry and hotly explains to Val that the shores of the Misty Isles are well protected against pirates, but there had been no cruelty involved when Val's men were attacked. Years earlier, when Ilene drowned at sea (Story 9), Val was sure he would never love again, and thus he had believed Aleta's attractiveness was the result of cruel sorcery. Finally, Aleta makes Val realize that the only sorcery she uses is the kind that all women can use, and she gets herself "thoroughly kissed" in the process. Val's surrender to this slim girl's magic is complete and forever.

Donardo, robber Emperor of Saramand, comes upon a pretty scene: a ragged hero and pretty maid falling in love. He decides that the lovely little lady before him should be a bright jewel in his harem. The tyrant's men throw Val over a nearby cliff, allowing Donardo to ride away with his beautiful prize to the gleaming white-walled city of Saramand. Stunned but unhurt, Val climbs back and sets out to rescue his newfound love. Heartsick, Val meets Ramud of Tunis, whose sweetheart was also stolen by Donardo, and the two vow to gather an army and start war on Saramand. They gather support from nearby kingdoms, and the siege of Saramand begins. Val vows to regain Aleta and destroy Saramand if necessary. Aleta disguises herself as a pageboy and escapes from the harem, but goes back after meeting Ramud and hearing of Val's whereabouts and plans. One dark night soon thereafter, Val and a small troop sneak into the city from the water, storm the gates from behind, let in the rest of the army, and sack the city. After a long battle, Val kills Donardo, and the young lovers are reunited after months of anguish and peril. Thus a great city falls and the course of history is altered just so a certain high-spirited lad can sit once more at the feet of a pretty maid. It is not long before Val, the new emperor of Saramand, is forced to get back to the business of reorganizing the city, and he puts it in the keeping of his captains.

COMMENT: *The last two-thirds page Prince Valiant page with* Medieval Castle *was #459; full pages resumed with #460 and continued until the 1970s.*

30: MATRIMONY
Pages 465 (6 January 1946) – 484 (19 May 1946)

After a lot of arguing, Val convinces Queen Aleta, for whom he had journeyed around the world, to marry him. They plan to go to Rome and, because they are of royal blood, be married in state. However, Val learns that Genseric, mighty King of the Vandals, is also planning to sail for Rome. (Historical note: Genseric was actually invited to destroy the city by the Roman Empress

Eudoxia, who wanted revenge for the murder of her husband, Emperor Valentinian II [see Story 17]. Invasions and weddings don't mix, so Val rides to Tunis to meet with Genseric. The Vandal King allows Val and Aleta to sail with him and promises that their wedding will be celebrated before Rome is sacked. After the Vandal hordes land on the banks of the Tiber and march toward Rome, Pope Leo the Great (reigned 440-461 AD) gains a promise from them that the people of Rome will be spared. Emperor Maximus is stoned to death by his people, and the most terrible sacking of all time begins. The Pope flees to Ravenna. Val and Aleta follow him, but they are disappointed to find that he is too busy to marry them. Ex-Empress Eudoxia, seeing that Val and Aleta want a Christian wedding, takes them to a kindly old man, once a great Cardinal, who performs the ceremony. And so, these two who had wanted a royal wedding performed by the Pope are contentedly joined forever by an old hermit.

COMMENT: *There is a charming epilogue to the marriage scene of page 470. Foster says: "Now here, according to approved writers of romance, the saga of Prince Valiant should end. But the winning of Aleta is one thing, costing Val no more than his heart, but living with her is another story...and we think the story is worth telling." How true. Obviously, this story is a major turning point in the saga of Prince Valiant, and the strip will henceforth contain more "reality" than fantasy, and as much warmth and characterization as adventure. Aleta becomes a leading force in Val's life and in the strip.*

The historical background of this story is mostly accurate. Genseric and the Vandals plundered Rome in AD 455 after promising Pope Leo (d. 461; later canonized) not to do too much harm. The incidents involving General Flavius Aetius and Emperor Valentinian [see Stories 16-17] actually happened earlier the same year (AD 455), not several years before as Foster indicates. Emperor Petronius Maximus actually reigned for two more years from the new capitol at Ravenna. Based on the assumption that this story is indeed meant to take place in AD 455, an overall chronology of Val's life can be worked out using this as a reference point.

Prince Valiant and his bride return to the burning city of Rome with Eudoxia and then sails away across the Mediterranean and up the Rhone River to the city of Lyon. There, Aleta goes shopping for new clothes and new servants. They proceed up the Rhone and Soane as far as they can go and then continue overland toward the Seine. Aleta is concerned when she notices that her handmaiden, Cidi, seems to be in love with Val. When Val and Aleta reach the Seine and head for Paris, they release all the servants. Cidi, heartbroken, poisons herself, and Val's servant Amerath, who had come to love the girl, becomes infuriated and plans to get revenge on his "heartless" ex-master. Amerath catches up to Val in Paris but gets killed in an effort to get Val in trouble. On their way out of Paris, Val and Aleta meet a tall, splendid red haired woman, Katwin, who is hired as Aleta's new servant. (Katwin, who is to become Aleta's handmaiden and friend for the next 23 years and eventually Boltar's wife, is introduced in page 480.) Katwin helps Val find a ship, and the three sail down the Seine and across the English Channel to Britain. After wandering at adventure over half the world, Prince Valiant returns proudly to Camelot with the fairest prize a knight ever won. Aleta quickly and happily adjusts to the luxurious, exciting court life at Camelot.

31: War in the Forest
Pages 484 (19 May 1946) – 504 (6 October 1946)

The Saxons have gained so firm a foothold on the East coast of Britain that they have named it "East Saxony" (now called Essex). They encroach still further inland, and war is imminent. Sir Valiant, who spent his boyhood in that region, is sent to gather information for the war council. Aleta disguises herself as a small knight, follows along, and is dubbed "Sir Puny" by her husband, who secretly recognizes her. She is an added anxiety and an amusing nuisance, but she inadvertently finds a band of Saxons and saves the scouting party from a fatal ambush.

While King Arthur and his council prepare for the march against the Saxons, a stag hunt is held in the Royal Forest. As Val, Aleta, and Sir Gawain slowly ride home afterwards, they are suddenly surrounded by a band of outlaws. Hugh-the-Fox, the leader, announces that he is holding them for ransom. Hugh soon finds that these three are the most upsetting people he has ever kidnapped and is even more aggravated when it turns out that King Arthur and all the knights have marched away to war and there is no one left in Camelot to pay the ransom. Val convinces the outlaws to become scouts in Arthur's army in return for a pardon. Aleta is sent back to the safety of Camelot, and Val, Gawain and Hugh's men join the King's army. After blocking the Saxons' supply lines, the scouts lead Arthur's forces secretly and quietly through the forest. The Saxons are thrown into confusion and in no time are sent running in wild defeat. Sinister Sir Mordred (first introduced in page 500) tries to have Hugh and his band of cut-throats arrested, but Val comes to his friends' defense and convinces the King to allow them to become official scouts for Arthur's army.

32: Self-Sacrifice
Pages 504 (6 October 1946) – 507 (20 October 1946)

Sir Mordred, half-brother of the King, is shrewd, ambitious, and ruthless. He is the leader among those nobles who secretly plot to seize the throne.

Mordred oversees a clandestine rendezvous between Sir Launcelot du Lac and Queen Guinevere, who have secretly loved each other for years (this is one of the few times that Foster mentions the famous romance of Launcelot and Guinevere, one of the cornerstones of standard Arthurian mythology). Aleta is also a witness to this tableau and knows that sinister Mordred would try to use knowledge of the incident to create enmity between the King and his right-hand man.

Aleta knows her husband's heart would break if disaster came to the kingdom, and thus, when Mordred dramatically accuses Launcelot of inappropriate familiarity with the Queen, Aleta saves the kingdom by claiming that she, not Guinevere, was in Sir Launcelot's embrace. Guinevere and Launcelot remain silent. Angrily, King Arthur orders Mordred to make peace with the Queen and to go away to aid in some ongoing fighting. Aleta doesn't try to explain anything to her horrified husband. When Val gets home, Katwin berates him for his distrust and explains what really happened. Meanwhile, Aleta has snuck away from Camelot in shame. Val rides furiously through the night to catch up with her and apologize for his mistrust.

33: AGUAR'S DAUGHTER-IN-LAW
Pages 507 (27 October 1946) – 519 (19 January 1947)

Val and Aleta cannot return to Camelot, so Katwin suggests that the King of Thule should meet his new daughter-in-law. They pack all their belongings, journey to the coast, and set out on the long voyage across wintry seas. After five weeks, they reach the coast of Thule and land at Trondheimfjord. Val finds some work to do: the powerful Earl Gunguir of Overgaard is revolting against the King. Aleta is sent on ahead to the palace. ("Trial by Arms," #509-513:

When Val arrives at Gunguir's stronghold, the Thane of Overgaard and his sneering son, Ulfrun [the mighty sea raider who will soon become Val's worst enemy], make angry threats and refuse to calmly discuss their grievances. Val is tricked into calling for a "trial by arms," and a huge brutal champion is called forth to be his opponent. Val is severely wounded but wins the long, exhausting battle. The Prince lies recovering in the rebel fortress for three more days, announces that Gunguir will be tried before the Spring meeting of the Council of Chieftains, and then starts homeward.) Meanwhile, Aleta has arrived at her new home. She tries to keep her identity a surprise by posing as a handmaiden, but her beauty, royal bearing and behavior are dead giveaways. The impudent girl helps Aguar in a political struggle by inviting lonely, rebellious old Earl Jon, Aguar's old comrade-in-arms, for a pleasant dinner party. Val finally arrives home and greets his father after another two-year absence [i.e. since Story 29-A]. Earl Jon invites the newlyweds to be guests for a bear hunt at his fief.

34: THE NEW WORLD
Pages 520 (26 January 1947) – 594 (18 April 1948)

Spring (ca. 456) comes once again to Thule, and it is time for the Council of Chiefs. Val meets an old friend, Gundar Harl, the crippled ship builder (see Story 26), who shows him his latest nautical masterpiece. Gunguir arrives with Ulfrun, who sees lovely Aleta and becomes filled with desire. While Val inspects Gundar's new ship, Ulfrun impulsively kidnaps Aleta and carries her to Gunguir's great dragonship. When the news is brought to Val, he becomes enraged and orders Gundar to prepare his ship for a long voyage. Katwin, her arm broken by Ulfrun's cruel oarsmen, climbs aboard and insists on coming along, showing Val some tiny things that Aleta had been sewing and explaining that her mistress will need a woman's care when she is found! Filled with emotion, Val swears to follow Ulfrun unto death. Ulfrun, realizing he may have been unwise, orders his ship to head out to sea. He is followed relentlessly by Val's red-sailed vessel. The grim chase goes on for weeks, and the ships head westward away from any known land. They pass some large landmasses later to be known as Iceland and Greenland, but the two men are only interested in one small gray-eyed girl, and the discovery is considered unimportant. At the coast of Newfoundland, Ulfrun turns south and proceeds up the St. Lawrence River. The sea-king's men gradually become hungry and desperate and lose all loyalty to their cruel master. Gundar Harl follows mercilessly to Lake Ontario and up the Niagara River. The dragonship is finally found. Ulfrun's crew deserts him. Val runs after Ulfrun and confronts him on the edge of the Niagara whirlpool. The long chase comes to an abrupt end, for Ulfrun is exhausted and afraid and is no longer a formidable opponent. Numb and drained, Val turns back to find his wife, whose captors are now protecting her in return for a pardon. Aleta tenderly soothes her great warrior, and Katwin soothes her long-suffering mistress.

Prince Valiant decides to spend the winter in this new land and sail for home in the spring. The Indians, partly in fear of the Vikings' terrible metal weapons, agree to help the strangers. Since they had never before seen a beautiful blonde, the Native Americans (probably intended to represent the Algonquin tribe) proclaim Aleta to be a woodland goddess. As a cold, eventful winter passes, Aleta learns to love the people and the beautiful, primitive woods except for the porcupines, skunks, and snow (COMMENT: *Foster spent some of his youth in the Canadian woods and was thus able to imbue this tale with particular verisimilitude*). The admiring Great Tribal Council presents Aleta with many gifts, including a middle-aged squaw named Tillicum (Aleta's nurse for many years to come, introduced in page 549). In the middle of winter, Aleta gives birth to a tiny, noisy, unfinished-looking baby. The excited, proud father spends the next few days raving endlessly about his wonderful son, heir to the throne of Thule, who will certainly be a great warrior one day. ("My Life Story," #555: This is an amusing, charming episode in which the baby gives his point of view on life, based on four long weeks of experience.) Gradually, winter's icy grip on the forest is broken, and Gundar Harl begins to prepare for the return journey. Aleta's admiration for the Singing Sword inspires her to decide that the baby will be named Prince Arn, after Val's old friend, the sword's original owner (see Story 9). The proud parents are anxious to return to Camelot for a royal christening and speed preparations. There are dangerous delays because of hostility between some of the tribes. When the day finally comes that the Northmen have to leave their good friends and their happy winter home, Aleta prophesizes that perhaps her son will some day return to the land of his birth and lead the Indians to greatness. (Historical note: Aleta's prophecy, we are told, is the origin of the ancient Indian legend of Quetzalcoatl, the "fair god who would someday return from across the sea." This legend helped Hernando Cortes conquer the Aztecs of Mexico in 1519-1521; apparently, it was all Aleta's fault!) Tillicum decides to come along to remain Arn's nurse. The ship sails swiftly eastward but hits a reef and sinks on the coast of Newfoundland. After weeks of repairs, the voyage is resumed. The long journey across the desolate Atlantic is long and frightening, but Gundar Harl's ship lands safely on Ireland. ("The Charms of Ireland," #584-589: Aleta almost falls into the brutal hands of Roary Dhu, an Irish King. A small war ensues between the Vikings and Irishmen.) After escaping from Ireland, Val and his band reach Britain in a few days. Following a farewell banquet, Gundar sails for Thule, and Val, Aleta, and their small retinue paddle on to Camelot, Indian style.

35: THE MAD KING
Pages 595 (4 July 1948) – 615 (21 November 1948)

Shortly after Val's return, King Arthur finds work for him to do. King Tourien of Cornwall has been killing Arthur's tax gatherers and knights and sending insulting messages. Aleta realizes for the first time how difficult marriage will be, for her man will frequently be leaving on dangerous missions. Val rides to Cornwall and boldly enters the impregnable cliffside fortress. Thinking Val a traitor who wants to join them, pompous Tourien, a fat little madman, and his three brutal sons unfold their plans of conquest. Val plays on their mad ambitions in order to get them outside their castle walls, sends for a secret army from Camelot, and tricks Tourien into captivity. The evil son, Cedric, is killed by his own men. After freeing all the prisoners in the dungeon and turning over power to a representative of King Arthur, Val rides home.

36: AS ARN TELLS IT
Page 616 (28 November 1948)

Another cute baby's-eye view of Aleta and Val.

37: THE CHRISTENING
Pages 617 (5 December 1948) – 624 (23 January 1949)

It is time for the christening of Val and Aleta's son, and they decide that the original Prince Arn, Val's boyhood friend, should be the godfather. Val rides to Ord and meets his old friend along the way. There is much reminiscing. Despite their dual promises never to love again after the death of Ilene (see Story 9), Arn, too, has a wife, Linet, and a son, named Prince Valiant! Linet and Aleta become fast friends and convince the Archbishop and King Arthur to hold a gala double christening at Camelot. Prince Arn becomes godfather to Prince Arn, and Prince Valiant becomes godfather to Prince Valiant.

COMMENT: *Page 623 contains a large, beautiful, marvelously detailed panel showing the christening—one of Foster's finest drawings. It is said that Foster originally wanted to use an authentic Viking name like Arn for his main hero, but the syndicate disapproved. Subsequently, Foster seems to have enjoyed a measure of revenge by using the name for these several other characters.*

38: BLACK MAGIC IN WALES
Pages 624 (23 Jan 1949) – 643 (5 June 1949)

Oom Fooyat, a visiting magician, wreaks havoc in Merlin's workshop and becomes a nuisance in Camelot. Likewise, Sirs Valiant and Gawain fall out of favor and are sent away by King Arthur to investigate reports of black magic in Wales. Merlin prepares Val by teaching him how magic is but scientific trickery. As Val and Gawain ride to the haunted castle of Illwynde, they are joined by a frightened knight, Sir Cador, who tells terrifying stories, which convince Val that the fief is ruled by scare tactics. Resolving to fight fear with fear, Val frightens the inhabitants of the castle by swinging a witch-like clay figure into the castle. Ordered to yield or submit to a trial by arms, the castle's inhabitants send out a champion, the Demon Knight of Illwynde, who is unhorsed by Sir Cador and discovered to be a woman. The leader, elderly Lady Wildwyn, yields possession of the castle to Val's forces and explains that she made her ladies dress as witches only to protect the castle. ("The Romance of Oom Fooyat," #638-639: At Illwynde Oom blunderingly tries to impress Winnie the Witch Woman, who falls in love with him anyway. Queen Wildwyn performs the marriage ceremony. Oom reappears 26 years later, in Story 130.) Val and Gawain recruit a garrison to protect the castle. Sir Cador is ordered back to Camelot, but he has fallen in love with Lady Gwynn and refuses to go. Val's squire, Osk, also falls in love at Illwynde and desires to stay. Gawain also gets romantically involved but is frightened into leaving when Val mentions the prospect of marriage and settling down.

39: THE AMBITIOUS BOY
Page 644 (12 June 1949) – 647 (3 July 1949)

Returning to Camelot, the knights meet and unhorse a 14-year-old boy who foolishly challenges them to a joust. They tell the lad, Geoffrey, that they will take him to Camelot for training. Val rejoins his family and sees his baby son, Arn, beginning to develop a personality. Geoffrey falls in love with Aleta and tells her how impatient he is to be a knight and do great deeds in her honor. Geoff begins his training by becoming a squire. (Introduced in page 644, Geoffrey is later to become the official historian of Prince Valiant and a regular character).

40: Into Scotland
Pages 647 (3 July 1949) – 675 (15 January 1950)

Peacetime makes the knights restless, so Arthur sends Prince Valiant to Hadrian's Wall (see Story 21) to see if it is in good repair and to drive back any Picts who might have settled there. The knights find that the Picts have indeed broken through and have assembled a full-scale invasion force. Val leads his troops into the Scottish side, where they take over the milecastle in which the Picts have been. Now, as the Pictish rovers come to the wall, they are forced through into the British side without arms or food. When the raiders try to fight their way back into Scotland, they are decimated by Val's troops. Val sets up ladders to allow the surviving raiders to return, arranges a truce with two of the clan leaders, and insures a feud between the clans by giving unequal bribes. Geoffrey, who had left Camelot to join the battle, is sent back with a report on the action for Arthur and in his haste steals one of the King's steeds. Meanwhile, Val has been wounded in the fighting, and Aleta comes to nurse him. She single-handedly ends the invasion by talking with the Picts and promising food and safe passage home.

Aleta takes her injured husband to Newcastle near the sea so that he can be transported back to Camelot by ship. She sends Geoffrey to fetch Katwin and Arn, but when the boy reaches Camelot, he is arrested as a horse thief. Geoff escapes long enough to deliver his message to Katwin but is recaptured and banished from Camelot by King Arthur for a year and a day. Katwin, Geoff and Arn sail back to Newcastle, where they encounter Boltar. (#671: Prince Arn narrates the story of his own first tooth, which places him at about 6-9 months of age.) Since Geoffrey's feet cannot touch British soil, Boltar ties his feet into a sack of Caledonian soil and carries him ashore to the place where Val waits. There, a man named Torlay recognizes Geoffrey as a missing runaway lad named Arf, who had fled a wicked stepmother. Torlay reports that she is now gone and it would be safe for Arf to return home. "Geoff" decides to continue his quest for knighthood with Val.

41: Home Again
675 (15 January 1950) – 683 (12 March 1950)

Boltar decides to take Geoff and Val's family to Thule on his ship but goes on a quick raid first. The passengers are endangered by a second raid on a coastal city, and Tillicum, Arn's nurse, berates Boltar for his carelessness. Avoiding further conflicts, the ship passes quietly by Orkney Island and stops at Shetland Island before arriving at Thule. Boltar gives Tillicum a gift of a gold chain and promises to see her again. When the group arrives at Vikingsholm, King Arthur sees his grandchild Arn for the first time.

42: My Sword
Page 684 (19 March 1950)

Arn narrates how he crawled out of his crib to grasp Val's Singing Sword.

43: The Challenge
Pages 685 (26 March 1950) – 691 (7 May 1950)

Winter (ca. 457) comes to Thule with hunting and feasting. Prince Egil is smitten by Aleta and makes unwelcome advances. Arf sees this and challenges Egil to a duel. Val enters the conflict and himself challenges Jarl Egil to a duel. Val enters the duel without his Singing Sword and is quickly put on

foot when his horse is killed. Val manages to unhorse Egil and the two are prevented from uselessly hurting each other only when Arf climbs to a nearby roof and dumps snow on the combatants. Val and Egil give up and part on friendly terms.

44: The Missionaries
Pages 691 (7 May 1950) – 758 (19 August 1951)

King Aguar is petitioned by some Jarls who complain about Christians trying to overthrow their old religion. Aguar questions the evangelists and finds them lacking in knowledge. Since he sees value in Christianity turning his people away from their violent ways, Aguar asks Val, Jarl Egil, Arf, and Rufus Regan to go to Rome to bring back some competent teachers. ("The Cost of Peace," #694-707: Hap-Atla, King of the Inner Lands, is informed that with Val away, Thule is left unprotected. He had promised his father to invade and conquer Thule and now sees his chance. When the invasion begins, Aleta's clever strategies lead the Inner Lands armies into a trap. Aleta then arranges a peace conference and invites Hap-Atla's queen and child. The two women become friends, and Queen Jan forces her husband Hap to give up his dangerous dreams of conquest.) Val and his companions pass through Rouen and decide to go the rest of the way to Rome by the overland route. At the small kingdom of Boisanie, they are held up by border guards posing as robbers. After resisting the ambush, Val and his men dethrone Boisanie's King Dumdrible (!) and prepare to try him for the actions of his men. The King stalls by bringing his marriageable daughters to a feast, hoping one of the knights will be attracted to them. The king is thrown into a dungeon anyway, but Val finds husbands for the King's daughters to rule the Kingdom. Val and his friends next meet Sieur du Lac, a democratic ruler who has given his men the land so he can devote himself to alchemy. One of Du Lac's tricks explodes and burns the knights' hair. Next, the knights encounter a troubadour who asks them to rescue a red-haired, blue-eyed girl who is held captive by an evil man. The knights separate to search, and Arf, Val and Egil each bring back a different red-haired girl, none of whom is the right one. Rufus finds the right girl, and when he tries to "help" her, she wraps a musical instrument around his head. Fleeing from the girl's pursuers, Val's group chances upon the castle of Ruy Foulke, where they aid in repelling an attack force led by Black Robert. When the battle dies down, Val helps arrange peace by having the combatants will the disputed lands to Robert's son and Ruy's daughter, who are in love and plan to wed. As Val and his friends travel on, they begin to see signs of the decay and impending collapse of the Roman Empire (it is now about 458 AD). They encounter an army of barbarians and escape via a secret pass through the Alps. ("The Hunter," #732-738: While hunting for chamois fur with which to make coats for the cold trip through the Alps, Val kills an armed stranger, is hunted by the man's companion, and escapes only after a long chase through the snowy mountains.) Arf's feet freeze during the icy passage through the Alps. Val leaves Arf in critical condition at a hospital in Torino, while he and his men continue their mission. Finally, Val, Egil, and Rufus arrive at Rome (Val's third time; see stories 16 and 30A), where they intend to fulfill their goal of requesting missionaries for Thule. When Val is informed the Pope has moved to Ravenna, he sets forth to that city in a chariot. Val is unable to get to see the Pope, but a committee agrees to send missionaries to Thule.

Val learns that Arf's life is in danger and speeds back to Torino. Arf's frozen foot had to be amputated, and the poor lad has lost his will to live. Val tries to make Arf feel better by telling him encouraging stories about Gundar Harl (the one-legged ship builder; see Story 26) and another one-legged lad who makes arrows for King Arthur (see Story 22). Arf finally regains his spirits and becomes enthusiastic when Val gives him the task of being secretary and making a full report of the mission. While Egil and Regan stay to accompany the missionaries, Val goes homeward by sea with Arf. When the sea journey begins, Arf again becomes depressed about his future. Val reassures him that he was a thinking man anyway and never would have been a good warrior.

When the ship stops at Portugal, a young girl, Adele, comes aboard. Arf immediately falls in love with her and begins to write songs and poetry. With Adele's encouragement, Arf takes to writing and begins his biography of Prince Valiant. (Foster mentions in page 754 how "the author of these pages is very grateful for the time yellowed parchments" of Arf/Geoffrey, later referred to as "The Chronicles," as the source of the Prince Valiant tales.) After a brief battle with some pirates, the ship finally arrives at Britain. The sailors give Arf a wooden leg as a present, and the lad returns to his father's home, accompanied by Adele. The two pledge eternal devotion, and Arf resumes his studies.

45: "?"
Pages 758 (19 August 1951) – 767 (21 October 1951)

Val returns to Camelot and rejoins his friend Gawain. The two enjoy some pranks, the infuriated object of which challenges the two knights to individual jousts. Both end up in the infirmary. Then a message from King Aguar arrives summoning Prince Valiant home. Arf and Gawain join him for a trip to Thule. After the usual duels with strange knights, the travellers rest at Hadrian's wall. At Gawain's home in the Orkney Islands off Scotland, Lothian castle, Gawain's brothers plot against Val because of his northern racial extraction. Angry Gawain forces a trade agreement to be signed between Orkney and Thule. After a storm, Val sails home and rides to his father's castle. An air of mystery hangs upon the castle (an amusing blurb reads: "Next week: ?"), and Val fears Aleta is ill. He races to her chambers and finds out she has given birth to twin baby girls (first seen in page 767) who are now four months old!

46: THE PRINCE ARN STORY
Pages 767 (21 October 1951) – 769 (4 November 1951)

Little Prince Arn is jealous at the attention given to his baby sisters. He narrates the story of his father's homecoming (note an amusing touch: pages 768 and 769 have "Arn" scrawled over the Prince Valiant logo). Val gives Arn a sword and shield as presents, and Arn leaves the castle to adventure in the outside world. Val rescues the boy from a wolf, and Aleta frets that Arn will soon go out into the world. For now, however, he is hers.

47: The King's Justice
Pages 770 (1 November 1951) – 782 (3 February 1952)

The treaty with Orkney is signed. Arf arrives at Vikingsholm. Boltar is arrested for plundering the merchant ship of Adele's father and brought before King Aguar. Tillicum springs Boltar from captivity, and he abducts her. Aboard his ship, Tillicum lunges at the pirate with a knife and then sets fire to his cabin and escapes. As Boltar sails away, Aleta learns that Tillicum is in love with him! Boltar, meanwhile, learns of a Danish invasion descending upon Thule and sends a message to warn Aguar. After hesitating, Boltar's forces help Aguar repel the invaders. Aguar decides to free the outlaw/hero on the condition that someone stands responsible for Boltar's conduct. Tillicum comes forth and says she will be responsible, and she and Boltar decide to marry (the unlikely pair—a fat Viking pirate and slim Indian princess—tie the knot in page 782).

48: A LITTLE HUNTING
Pages 782 (3 February 1952) – 790 (30 March 1952)

Val gets restless after a while at home and goes away on a hunting trip with Arf. Soon after the trip begins they are swept away in the current of a swollen river. The two frustrated hunters build a canoe and try to get home via the river and the sea. The journey is fraught with danger, but eventually they make it to the shore, and, after fixing up the damaged canoe, to Vikingsholm. There is much celebration when Val and Arf, missing and feared dead, return home.

49: THE WAGER, OR VAL EATS CROW
Pages 791 (6 April 1952) – 794 (27 April 1952)

Val sees Aleta training a hunting hawk and makes a bet he can train a better one. He captures a young gyrfalcon. Aguar joins the bet, and they all agree to eat what their birds kill. In the hunt, Val's bird downs a crow, but at the feast Aleta substitutes partridge meat for the crow.

50: ANOTHER CHRISTENING
Pages 794 (27 April 1952) – 796 (11 May 1952)

Rufus Regan returns with the Roman missionaries (see Story 44A), and Aleta plans to have her twins christened. A church is built. Aleta chooses names and the baby girls are christened Valeta and Karen.

51: THE STOLEN RIVER
Pages 797 (18 May 1952) – 799 (1 June 52)

Val and Rufus investigate border trouble. A Thule river has been diverted by settlers across the border of Scandia. In order to prevent a battle, Val dams the river and gets the two sides to share it.

52: SIGURD'S DOOM
Pages 799 (1 June 52) – 810 (17 August 1952)

Riding home, Val is suddenly struck by an arrow in the throat and is luckily saved from injury by his necklace. Rufus and Val capture the would-be assassin, Os, who explains he thought Val was Sigurd Holem, arrogant ruler of a nearby fief. Val decides to meet this tyrant. Os leads them to Holem. After the meeting with the tyrant, Val's departure is interrupted by news that Os has been killed in a suspicious "tavern brawl." The knights are escorted away by a new guide, Jarl Oder, but once beyond the castle walls Val ties up Jarl and disguises himself as the guide. In disguise Val reenters the castle and learns the daughters of the peasants in Holem's fief are slaves and then leaves the castle again, climbing down the clay cliff face. Aguar then leaves the castle again, climbing down the clay cliff face. Aguar sends Rufus back with troops. Val has the men, aided by local serfs, tunnel under the cliff face until an underground stream emerges and begins to wash the clay away. The castle crumbles. Holem meets Val in combat and falls into a chasm to his death.

53: THE STORY TELLER
Pages 811 (24 August 1952) – 816 (28 September 1952)

Arf asks Val to relate the story of the regaining of Thule. Val tells how they returned to his homeland from the Fens and how Sligon gave up his throne (Story 11). Val then relates how he participated in the fall of Andelkrag the Unconquerable (Story 14). Arf records the stories for posterity.

COMMENT: *This episode consists mostly of beautiful reprinted drawings from the great 1939 stories, with a few new framing panels. Foster presumably did this to get ahead on his work so he could take a vacation. Interestingly, this "flashback" device has rarely been used in newspaper comics except for the occasional reused gags in long-running humor strips.*

54: THE HUNTSMAN
Page 817 (5 October 1952)

Prince Arn shoots a rabbit and Tillicum gives him the unpleasant task of cleaning it himself.

55: KIDNAPPED
Pages 818 (12 October 1952) – 825 (30 November 1952)

Boltar returns home and Tillicum invites Arn to visit their home. When Arn strays out of Boltar's house he is nabbed by some of Boltar's enemies. Tillicum finds traces of the deed and starts in pursuit, using her Indian wood lore. Boltar in turn follows Tillicum's trail. Tillicum finds Arn and frees him, leaving a trail through the mud that the kidnappers can easily follow. Boltar comes across the villains and, together with Tillicum, kills them. The group returns home. Val and Boltar sail to Caerlon, which they learn is the home base of the kidnappers, and make the ones responsible pay for their evil deeds.

56: VALHALLA
Pages 826 (7 December 1952) – 836 (15 February 1953)

King Aguar complains to his son that the Vikings are resisting attempts at Christianization. Val takes two men, Helgi and Tor, to the villages to investigate why. They learn the Vikings drove out the missionaries who scorned the old Norse Gods. The three are welcomed by a Druid who drugs Val with a potion.

Val looks into the rays of the setting sun and beholds the ancient gods (this scene in page 828 is one of Foster's most colorful and beautiful panels), but thanks to Merlin's training he is not fooled by the illusion. The three men spend a night in a village where there is rivalry between believers in the old gods and the "new god." Val exposes the Druid's trickery in the temple of Woden and tells the people to go the Christian chapel to learn the true faith. The chapel is destroyed in a suspicious fire, but the villagers offer to rebuild it. During the hard trip home, Helgi is accidentally killed in a forest fire he starts. Val and Tor are saved by rain. Back home, a sulky Val is cheered up by Aleta, but not until after a quarrel.

57: THE EXPLORER
Pages 837 (22 February 1953) – 840 (15 March 1953)

Deciding to have an adventure by himself, Arn goes outside the castle with his faithful dog, Sir Gawain. The real Sir Gawain happens to be nearby, finds Arn, and brings the boy back to his worried, angry parents.

58: THE VANISHING ARMY
Pages 841 (22 March 1953) – 851 (31 May 1953)

While Aleta is called back to the Misty Isles and Tillicum gives birth to a baby boy (page 842; Boltar's son is later named Hatha; see Story 123), Gawain summons Val to see King Arthur regarding an important mission. Arthur fears the five kings of Cornwall are allied with the invading Saxons. Val plans to turn the Saxons and the kings against each other. First, he disguises himself as a troubadour and travels to Restormal Castle. There, he sings Viking songs understood only by the Saxon guests, suggesting that treachery is being brewed by the King. The Saxons in response attack Restormal. Next, Val rides to Launceston castle with news of Restormal's sacking, causing the Saxon visitors at Launceston to be killed. Val returns to Camelot for a fleet which attacks the Saxons. The Saxon invasion of Tintagel is foiled by the navy's fireballs, and the Saxons are starved and forced to temporarily give up their violent ambitions.

Comment: *Foster indicates that one panel in page 844 was based on sketches he made while traveling in Cornwall in January 1953. This must have been the vacation for which he worked ahead and used reprint segments (see comments on Story 52).*

59: THE RULE OF IRISH KINGS
Pages 852 (7 June 53) – 869 (4 October 1953)

Arthur sends Val and some knights to Ireland to seek peace. As they land, a large Irishman, Brien O'Curry, challenges Val to battle. By throwing the Irishman into the water, Val wins the fight and a friend. At Brien's stronghold, Val explains his mission of peace. Brien tells Val he will take him to see Rory McColm, the ruling King. Brien's group encounters a rival clan. A battle begins but is halted by a man named Parrick, who tells Val about his religious work and the nature of the Irish. The two part and Val is taken to Cashel, where he waits two weeks for an audience with the arrogant King. Rory refuses Val's peace overtures and suggestions for a common defense against invaders.

During the banquet that follows, Val jokes about Rory's table manners and is challenged to a duel by the hotheaded king. The battle starts on a narrow platform. Val is at first overwhelmed by Rory's weight, height, and armor, but manages to stick his sword between Rory's eyes, blinding him and cutting off his little finger. Then Patrick appears and tells the angry crowd that Rory can no longer be King, since Irish custom requires Kings to be without blemish. Val slips away but is pursued by Rory. Racing towards the coast, Val sees an Elk Hound, a Viking breed of dog, which leads the knights to the ship of Val's friend, Gundar Harl of Thule. Val quickly gets aboard, leaving behind the raging Rory. Brien says farewell, telling Val that Rory will no longer be king and Patrick (later Saint) will advocate Arthur's call for peace and alliance.

60: MERLIN'S MESSAGE
Pages 870 (11 October 1953) – 879 (13 December 1953)

Val hears that King Arthur is hard pressed by the Saxon cavalry and rides toward Camelot. At Dozmary Pool he meets Merlin, who begins to tell Val that "...Arthur will live if stirrups...." The message is interrupted when a girl named Nimue appears and lures Merlin away. As Val rides back to Camelot; his way is blocked by a troop of Saxon horsemen. Fighting through, Val suddenly understands the incomplete message. Val tells Arthur to have his knights be more lightly armed so they can beat the Saxons—with stirrups. Val goes out to the forest to enlist the aid of Hugh-the-Fox and his men (see Story 31) but is captured by Horsa the Saxon chief. Horsa tortures Val, who deceptively says that Arthur's knights can be decoyed out of Camelot. The attack starts with Val, dressed in Saxon costume, pushed into the front line. Val calls out his own name and is recognized by Sir Gawain. The lightly armed knights demolish the charging Saxons, and Val is a hero.

COMMENT: *Legend has it that Merlin was entranced by Nimue the Water Maiden and never heard from again. He will appear once more, in Story 77, to fulfill this prophesy.*

61: UNDER THE FRIVOLOUS CURLS
Pages 879 (13 December 1953) – 897 (18 April 1954)

Val decides to rejoin Aleta and travels southward through France toward the Aegean. ("The Flirt," #880-883: Gawain comes along and falls for a girl and decides to stay in France. The girl however had flirted with Gawain only to make her husband jealous. Frightened by Gawain's boldness, the girl calls her servant, Pierre, to defend her. Just then the husband enters and at first threatens Gawain but ends up helping him spank the girl for her "naughtiness." Pierre becomes Gawain's slave and squire. Gawain tries unsuccessfully to get rid of the bumbling servant.) Val, Gawain, and Pierre continue their journey. Meanwhile, rumors of disaster to her kingdom in the Misty Isles had brought Queen Aleta home from Thule after several years of absence (the Isles had not been seen or mentioned since Story 29A, 1945). Aleta finds that her throne and her person are in great peril. The nobles scheme to turn the lovely, peaceful Misty Isles into a warlike power.

At the palace Aleta is greeted by her sister, Helene, who has been regent during these past few years, and her ruthless husband Dionseus, who has apparently been the real ruler of the Kingdom in Aleta's absence. Aleta does not immediately assume the throne, spending time instead observing the recent changes in her homeland. Many new laws have been enacted in her absence, including large tax increases and vast expenditures to create an army and navy. The Misty Isles would become wealthy, powerful and feared if the changes would continue, and only the small, seemingly lighthearted Queen stands in the way. She finally assumes her throne but finds that laws have been passed to render her helpless. No one takes her seriously, but this gives her an advantage and enables her to learn much dangerous information. An attempt by the nobles and the army to poison Aleta and her children fails when the royal food taster dies. Aleta orders a great ship made ready for use, commands a review of the troops and hires a company of comedians. Then she orders all foreign soldiers to leave the Isles on the waiting ship, in accordance with a new law against hiring foreign soldiers or mercenaries (which had been intended to eliminate Aleta's Viking guards). Dionseus, furious, is also sent away as commander of the army. The hired comedians make Dionseus an object of ridicule. Sick with rage and hungry for power and vengeance, Dionseus sails away, vowing to return. Aleta tries to console her broken-hearted sister. Dionseus sails his ship into the port of Candia in Crete to re-arm his mercenaries for an attack on the Misty Isles. Simultaneously,

Val and Gawain finally arrive. Aleta calls together the leaders of the kingdom and threatens them with punishment for further treachery, ordering them to change back the laws. Gawain's squire Pierre, seeking adventure in the taverns, stumbles upon a discussion of Dionseus' plot to return and attack the Misty Isles. The noblemen plan not to defend the kingdom. Pierre returns home and informs his master, who calls a council of war. On the day of the invasion, Aleta orders her small army to ignore the invaders. The warlike nobles, who had planned to try adding to the confusion and opening the gates, are sent away, their plans foiled. They join Dionseus' army. Then Val takes the palace guard and quickly vanquishes the confused enemy army. The nobles flee and sail away, rather than face Queen Aleta's gallows, and the leaderless mercenaries lay down their arms. Aleta's kingdom is saved. Although he deserves hanging, Dionseus is banished to Samos and humiliated Helene chooses to join him (the two appear only once more, years later, in Story 131). The other nobles are pardoned on the condition that they pledge their allegiance and provide outstanding service to the kingdom. The navy is converted to a trading fleet.

62: PRINCE ARN AND THE SORCERESS
Page 898 (24 April 1954)

Little Arn marvels at the "spell" Aleta has over her husband.

63: THE PILGRIMAGE
Pages 899 (2 May 1954) – 917 (5 September 1954)

The goal of every Christian knight is a pilgrimage to the holy city of Jerusalem, so now that Aleta's kingdom has been tidied up, Gawain and Val take ship to Jaffa. They purchase mounts from Arab horse dealers and make the long, harsh ride over the coastal plain and across the broken hills. At Jerusalem, Val and Gawain are interrupted in their search for the Church of the Holy Sepulchre by the cries of a strange old man imprisoned behind a barred window. After finding the holiest spot in all Christendom and rededicating their swords to the service of justice and right, the two decide to find out who the prisoner was and why he has been so harshly punished. Pierre finds out from gossiping servants that the prisoner is Sir Basil of Highwood, who has for ten years been the prisoner of Sherif Ben El Rasch. The Sheik has used Sir Basil as a decoy, attracting rescue attempts by Christian knights who are captured and held for ransom. To rescue Sir Basil, Val and Gawain kidnap the Arab Sheik and offer him freedom only if he will release the knight from the dungeon. Ben El Rasch refuses, assuming that his tribe will find him and avenge him. Learning of the kidnapping, friends and enemies of El Rasch gather in Jerusalem, and the Roman guard is doubled. A sly Syrian enemy of the Sheik's finds the kidnappers and threatens to reveal their secret crime if they don't sell their prisoner to him. Pretending to agree, Val arranges to release his prisoner outside the city walls. Pierre spreads their "secret" plan and when the Syrians, Roman guards, and desert tribe all leave the city to find the fugitive, Val and Gawain free Sir Basil and leave the city. Vowing to continue their pilgrimage, the three knights head north to Nazareth. As they follow the road down which Mary and Joseph once trod to Bethlehem, a large band of Arabs search the land for the pilgrims, seeking to avenge their chieftain. Ten scouts find them an launch and attack but are demolished by the great swords and longbows of the Christians. Past the ruins of Jericho, more Arabs close in. Ben El Rasch rides from Jerusalem, hoping to witness the slow death of his British enemies, and hard on his heels comes the Syrian and his followers, eager to satisfy a lifelong hatred for El Rasch. The Syrians capture their enemy. Gawain pauses a moment to rescue a maiden in distress who turns out to be the Sheik's daughter. As the Arabs and Syrians clash, the knights escape and deliver the girl back to Jerusalem. The next day, the knights come safely to Bethlehem and rest, their hazardous pilgrimage completed. Now that they have visited all the sacred places in the Holy Land, they are known as "palmers" and are entitled to wear the sign of the crossed palms. As they leave for the coast to return homeward, they observe the Roman cohort marching by on its way home to aid in a last feeble attempt to save the

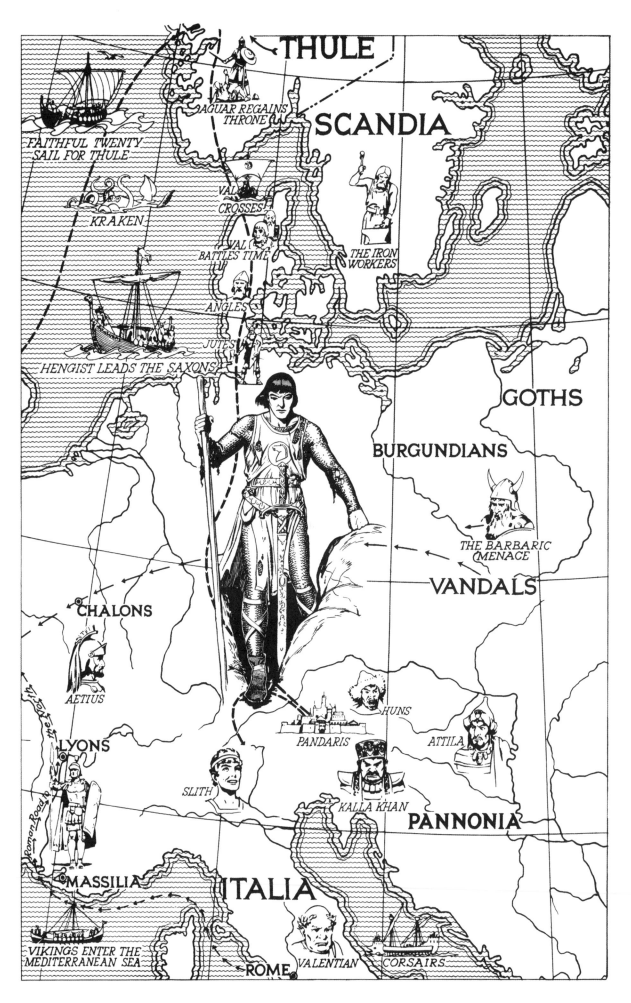

THULE

SCANDIA

GOTHS

BURGUNDIANS

VANDALS

PANNONIA

ITALIA

FAITHFUL TWENTY
SAIL FOR THULE

AGUAR REGAINS
THRONE

KRAKEN

VAL
CROSSES

VAL
BATTLES TIME

THE IRON
WORKERS

ANGLES

JUTES

HENGIST LEADS THE SAXONS

THE BARBARIC
MENACE

CHALONS

AETIUS

LYONS

HUNS

ATTILA

PANDARIS

SLITH

KALLA KHAN

MASSILIA

VIKINGS ENTER THE
MEDITERRANEAN SEA

ROME

VALENTIAN

CORSAIRS

Empire (it is now roughly AD 461, and by 476 the Western Roman Empire will be totally dissolved, its Eastern regions to be taken over by the Byzantine and Ottoman empires). The Dark Age, which has already consumed Europe, begins to cast its shadow over the Middle East.

64: BACK IN THE MISTY ISLES
Pages 918 (12 September 1954) – 931 (12 December 1954)

Putting her kingdom back together (Story 61) has taken so much of Aleta's time that her son feels neglected. Prince Arn and his companion, Paul, are restless for adventure and are helped to "escape" from the palace by a homely young peasant girl named Diane. The little girl leads the boys on an exciting trip to the beach, but Arn and Paul, unable to swim, become trapped on a wave-swept offshore rock. The Queen is upset to realize that her son was in danger mainly because she had neglected to teach him how to swim; the boys, she realizes, are palace bred and need outside experience. Diane, the one who can teach them most, has been excluded from their play because she is a girl, so Aleta issues a royal proclamation decreeing Diane a boy for a year and a day (!). Aleta and Katwin give the children swimming lessons. When Val comes sailing home from the pilgrimage to the Holy Land (Story 63), he spots Aleta swimming and joyfully leaps into the sea to greet her. Back at the palace, Val and Gawain tell of their adventures in the Middle East.

Despite her official change of sex, Diane falls violently in love with handsome, heroic Sir Gawain and begins to drive him crazy. Meanwhile, young Tyrus of Naxos woos Aleta, hoping that Prince Valiant's reckless love of adventure would soon leave the beautiful Queen a widow. Hoping to hasten that event, Tyrus summons out of Naxos a great champion, Bodex the Goth Warrior and Killer of Men, and he also hires an African pirate to attack the Misty Isles. The pirate demands huge tribute or trial by arms with his champion, hoping to lure and kill Prince Valiant. Gawain demands the quest (mainly to flee from the pesty Diane) and sails away for the distant island where the battle is to take place. When the contest begins, Diane, who has stowed away on the boat, watches closely and finds that the dueling ground has been prepared to give the mighty Bodex an advantage. The skinny little girl ends up helping the Iron Knight survive the long, terrible battle by warning him whenever Bodex tries to maneuver him into one of the prepared pitfalls. The duel is called at dusk because of darkness. Val, finally discovering the plot, races away to help his friend. The next morning, an injured Bodex is unable to resume the duel and admits defeat. Val's men round up the pirates and allow them to depart in peace after they have been stripped of their weapons and clothing. Tyrus makes a last feeble attempt to murder Val but is stopped by Gawain and sent away with the pirates. The knights return with the heroic little girl to the Misty Isles. Now that Gawain recognizes her existence and even praises her, Diane loses interest in him and returns to Arn and Paul and a more normal life of eating, fighting, and getting into mischief, danger, and everyone's hair.

65: THE STRANGE ROUTE
Pages 932 (19 December 1954) – 988 (15 January 1956)

Now that her kingdom is once more at peace, Queen Aleta turns to other matters. Prince Valiant must return to the boisterous North, Prince Arn must be trained for kingship, and Sir Gawain is creating havoc among the ladies-in-waiting. The Queen tidies up the political affairs of the Misty Isles and puts aside her crown to become once again a dutiful wife and mother. The great Spring Festival (ca. 462) makes fitting end to their stay in the Misty Isles. They cannot return to the Northlands across Europe because of the savage tribes from beyond the Rhine and Danube over-running the land, and the sea route is ruled out because of the fierce Corsairs dominating the Strait of Gibraltar. Katwin suggests a route she once took from Constantinople to Scandia over a river route through what is now Eastern Russia. The two great ships are manned and filled with trade goods. The ships sail across the Aegean and into the Bosporous to mighty Constantinople, new capital of the Roman Empire. The Vikings trade one of Aleta's sailing vessels for a Viking longship. Katwin flirtatiously talks some Vikings into joining the Northern voyage to replace Aleta's crew, who would probably become homesick over the long voyage. They sail across the Black Sea to Sevastopol in Crimea. There they stay two weeks trading for supplies and recruiting guides and interpreters. At the mouth of the Dnieper River, another light ship is obtained when Katwin works out a trade with a Viking captain going in the opposite direction. On their way up the river, Prince Valiant's ships are opposed at the first rapids by the wild Patzinaks. Val's men distract a band of the men with an onshore battle while the ships are safely guided over the rapids. At the Great Falls where the ships must be dragged overland, the plundering Patzinaks wait in full force. The Vikings win a terrible battle and then force their prisoners of war help move one of the ships.

("The Khan's Bride," #945-955: While Val and his men move all the gear to the ship above the falls, the wild Patzinaks plunder the other ship and kidnap Aleta. When the Northmen return and learn what happened, they swear to find Aleta or die. Guided by a prisoner, Val and his men march toward the city of the Khan, behind whose walls Aleta is prisoner. Aleta, whom the great Dragda Khan plans to make his chief wife, warns that her husband will come for her and lay waste the city. Harem slaves assist Aleta to array herself for the wedding feast, and although she knows Val will arrive, she brings her dagger, ready to kill herself if Val does not come in time. Fighting for time, Aleta talks the Khan into dancing wildly for her after he has stuffed himself with food and drink. At the very moment that the fat Khan declares Aleta his Queen, he falls dead [presumably of a heart attack]. Declaring herself Queen of the Patzinaks, Aleta tries to destroy their unity and stall until Val and the Northmen hew their way into the city, bringing flame and panic. Val and Gawain find the hysterical Aleta after two long days, loot the city and destroy it. They return to their ships.)

The journey northward up the Dnieper continues. Peace finally comes when the Northmen leave the land of the Patzinaks and enter the country of the Polotjans. Aleta insists on a stop at Kiev so she can get a bath, have her hair done, and buy a new dress. The Vikings are forced to leave when Val's warriors get bored and begin to disturb the peace. After a few more days of sailing, the Patzinak captives are released and allowed to return home, so that the Northmen can man the oars during the difficult journey ahead. The food supply runs low, and Val goes ashore to search for food. The hunt is a success, but Val returns on a stretcher, his legs injured by the charge of a great bull auroch. A great deal of meat is stored for the remainder of the trip. At last the ships are brought safely up the Dnieper to the "Great Portage," a terrible road over which the boats must be hauled to the Dvina River (COMMENT: A map explaining the route of the trip and thus clarifying the story appears in page 938). Some native Polotjans are hired to help with the work and supply oxen and wagons. Still too lame from his accident to take part in the labor, Val watchers anxiously as the overland traverse begins. Aleta eases the burden when she discovers that the ships can easily be glided through the muddy swamps. Hedji, the new chief of the Polotjans, tries to blackmail Val by insisting that the fee for their help be doubled or else the Northmen will be left stranded, but all he earns is distrust and a stern Viking guard. When the greedy chieftain is killed by his men, the Vikings help them finish the work of bringing the second ship safely over the Portage. Now the worst of the journey is over. The voyage down the Dvina to the Baltic Sea begins. The stream is turbulent and often the ships have to be hauled around falls, but the warriors feel the call of home and work with a will. Val, charting the river ahead of his ships, meets a hostile group of Swedes seeking trade and plunder. Still weak from his hunting accident, Val is beaten to his knees in the fight that follows and is saved by Gawain and his men. The wounded Val is brought back to his ship to recuperate.

("The Story Teller," #972-980: Prince Arn is furious that his sire was hurt by the Gotlanders and arms himself to seek revenge. Gawain catches him and suggests he learn and practice more before he can be a knight. The boy consults his father. To while away the long days of his recovery, Val tells his children the story of his boyhood—the tales of his first horse, his first meeting with Gawain, his first visit to Camelot and the quest to free the Maid Ilene's parents from captivity [stories 3,4,5,7; the flashback sequence is illustrated mostly with panels from the original 1937-1938 stories].)

When Val finally recovers he begins exercising himself and training Arn for the future. Finally, the two treasure-laden ships reach the sea. Before crossing the Baltic, the Vikings hold a great feast and carve a rune stone to commemorate their Prince's accomplishments during this adventurous voyage. Val's two ships are joined by three others belonging to Irish raiders, forming so powerful a fleet that they are able to sail the channel between Denmark and Scandia unmolested. Gawain says he must return to Camelot and leaves with the Scottish raiders. On the ship to Britain, Pierre discovers Jex, an old friend, now a galley slave. He nobly buys his friend from the sailing master. Gawain is now stuck with two bumbling servants but hasn't the heart to let them go. They land safely at Britain. Val and his family sail north up Trondheimfjord (COMMENT: Foster made a trip to Norway in 1955 and utilized sketches he made there in the scenes of the Thule coast in page 987). Lonely Aguar happily greets his family, and the old castle Vikingsholm soon takes on a more cheerful air.

66: INTO THE WILDERNESS
Pages 988(15 January 1956) – 995(4 March 1956)

The threat of hunger hovers over Thule. There is not enough farmland on the coast to feed the population, and the Vikings are loath to leave the sea and their boats to go inland. Prince Valiant sets out to explore the hills and valleys of the interior in search of farmlands to colonize. Val discovers enough farmland and grazing meadows to make Thule a land of plenty. ("The Mountaineer," #990-994: Arn, who seems to have left childhood and entered boyhood with a bang, decides to climb a tall mountain deep in the heart of Thule. Garm the hunter leads the excited boy up to the dark, icy peak. There they see a still greater mountain, which makes Arn realize that no matter what one does there is always something greater. Darkness falls, and Arn and Garm are forced to spend a dangerous night atop the freezing mountain. Worried Val is proud when his weary son returns, speaking confidently but also humbly.) Finally, Prince Valiant leads his party homeward to report his discoveries. He has found many fertile valleys, but roads must be built if they are to be farmed. Val returns to Aleta bemoaning the inescapable realization that children must grow up.

COMMENT: More sketches from Foster's Norway vacation were used in this story. Foster's family scenes and humble philosophy are consistently charming and amusing.

67: THE WOLF AT THE DOOR
Pages 996 (11 March 1956) – 1006 (20 May 1956)

Earl Jon (see also Story 33), planning a great hunt, invites Val and Aleta to visit his fief. Gundar Harl takes the royal family on the short boat ride to the next fjord. On the second day of the hunt, as the men ride away, old Gunnar Freyssom leads a burly group of raiders across the mountains to steal winter provisions from Earl Jon's nearby fiefdom. Aleta, expecting a quiet, lazy afternoon, is surprised when an ugly raider barges in on her bath. Hoping that the hunting party will see and return, Aleta sets fire to the house. Gunnar, realizing he has committed a crime against royalty, completes the raid, kills all the witnesses, locks Aleta and Katwin in the burning house, and departs with his loot. Frantic at the sight of smoke, Val and the other men return to find fire and death everywhere in the house, except in the watery trough where Val finds Aleta and Katwin. The other men are not so fortunate. After putting out the fire, the angry men thirst for revenge, but they don't know who the raiders were. Gundar Harl, who saw the raid from his ship, helps Earl Jon identify the culprits. The warriors sail to Gunnar's stronghold to await the raiders who are returning by land. The tired miscreants submit without violence, except for

the cruel leader, whom Val is forced to kill. Val makes the prisoners return all the plunder and help rebuild Earl Jon's home. After rewarding Gundar Harl with Gunnar's fief, Val comes home to join Aleta, who had earlier left the chaos at Earl Jon's.

68: SURVIVAL
Pages 1006 (20 May 1956) – 1022 (9 September 1956)

King Aguar, Val and Aleta reluctantly let Arn and Garm go to look for a road through the mountains to the rich farmlands in the interior (see Story 66). At first, the two surveyors meet with little success, for every valley they explore ends in a wild chaos of cliffs and tumbled stone. Climbing to the top of a large hill, Arn has a good view of the countryside and finds a seeming gap in the mountains. Garm leads him there, but they find only a chasm and roaring waterfall. Following the stream, Arn finally stumbles upon a pass through which a road can be built. Happily, Garm records the information. Suddenly, a huge storm develops, and the life of a future King of Thule is in Garm's hands. The hunter frantically looks for shelter, since it could be fatal to get trapped by snow on this side of the mountains. Wrapping the small prince beside the warm body of a slain deer, Barm finds a sheltered nook and builds a makeshift shelter in which to spend the night. Returning for Arn, Garm finds the Prince threatened by a wolf pack, but the kind old hunter scares them off and carries the freezing boy back to the hut, which soon becomes completely buried by the snow. The two imprisoned travelers spend days preparing for the return trip. When the storm ends, they dig out and start plowing through the snow. It takes a day to cross the mountains and find a forest where another night shelter can be built. The next morning the two set off on ski-like snowshoes. Arn slips and falls under the snow but is dug out by his trusty helper. Finally after one more night, Garm and Arn reach their boat, which they had previously left at a lake, and row back to Vikingsholm. Val and Aleta have been very worried, and they are happy and relieved when their little boy nonchalantly comes home to them. (COMMENT: Page 1017, which shows Arn's parents anxiously waiting his return, is one of the most human, touching scenes ever to be portrayed in comics; Val, the worried father, poignantly realizes the grief he must have caused his own father over the years.) Garm reports his findings to the King.

69: TOURNAMENT DAYS
Pages 1023 (16 September 1956) – 1029 (28 October 1956)

Winter (ca. 462-3 AD) settles over the northlands, and Aleta watches Val's growing restlessness. Then Pentecost draws near, and at Camelot King Arthur will hold the great Spring tournament soon. Val sails off. Camelot is a gay place as the Knights of the Round Table begin to arrive. Gawain lustily greets his old squire. When the day of the Grand Melee arrives, two lines of eager young warriors, one led by Sir Launcelot and one by Mordred, face each other. Sir William Vernon of Lydney, a mysterious white knight, receives the winner's chaplet from the fair Guinevere and soon challenges Sir Valiant to a joust. The opponents shatter three lances, but the white knight gets a splinter stuck in his neck and falls. The match is called a draw. His shield arm hurt, Val is soon eliminated from the tournament. The feast of Pentecost ends the festivities.

70: TROUBLE IN CORNWALL
Pages 1029 (28 October 1956) – 1062 (16 June 1957)

King Arthur summons Prince Valiant for a special quest. He is told to go to Cornwall secretly to find out if some rumors of treachery are true (COMMENT: Val performed a similar mission in Cornwall a few years earlier (Story 58); the place seems a virtual hotbed of revolution!). It seems that three kings there have suspiciously closed their borders to Arthur's knights. William Vernon invites Val to ride home with him to Lydney and take a ship for the rest of the way. Val becomes friends with Alfred, a merry steward who is devoted to William.

("The Sacrifice," #1030-1038: When William arrives home, he finds his father has died, and the young knight is now Lord of Vernon Castle. William asks his neighbor Sir Berkeley for the hand of his daughter Gwendolyn in marriage. Unfortunately, William's title to Vernon Castle is clouded. He has a missing half-brother who, if he turns up before William turns twenty, gets both the title and Gwendolyn. Meanwhile, Alfred is summoned by his mother, an old witchwoman, who reveals to Alfred and Val that she was the first wife of Lord Vernon, and thus Alfred is the missing half-brother of William and heir to Vernon's estates. Just before dying, she gives Alfred a yellowed parchment to prove her story and his heritage. Alfred is confused and upset, not knowing whether or not it would be right to claim the castle and the the the girl. When Val and Alfred return to the castle, a storm is brewing, and the boat bringing Lord Berkeley and Gwendolyn for the funeral is endangered. Only the two harbor beacons can bring the boat safely into the proper spot on the jagged reef, but there is nothing dry to light the beacons with. To save Gwendolyn's life, Alfred is forced to set his priceless parchment on fire to light the beacons. Sir Berkeley and his daughter land safely, but at a great price to Alfred. Only Val knows the tragic, gallant sacrifice Alfred has made. After the funeral, Alfred disappears. Val says his farewells and sails away, but is surprised to find Alfred, a stowaway, who agrees to begin a new life as Val's squire.)

Finally, Val sails to Cornwall to fulfill his quest. At Alfred's suggestion Val cuts his hair and disguises himself as a middle-aged palmer from the Holy Lands, one who would be assured a welcome anywhere. Val rides brazenly to Launceston Castle and dines with the suspicious King Durwin. While Val enthralls his hosts with true tales of the Holy Land, Alfred finds out from the other servants that the King is a traitor because of his fear of a mysterious threat from the West. After defeating an overbearing leader of a band of plunderers, Val reaches Restormel, the castle of the second Cornish king and spends the night there. While there is little evidence of treachery at Restormel, Alfred hears more tales of a madman ruling in the West. Finally, Val and Alfred ride to the third kingdom, that of Och Synwyn, who turns out to be the root of the vast treachery. This monster plans to move toward Camelot by land and sea after recruiting sufficient strength. King Och forces Val to pledge loyalty to his evil cause or else be tortured. Calling himself Sir Quintus, Val ruefully sacrifices his honor by swearing fealty to the tyrant, whom he secretly plans to destroy. Slowly, Val develops a scheme. First, he convinces Och to tax the loot of his raiders and to prevent the armies from scrounging the fertile countryside. The many groups of raiders soon turn against each other and Och because of Val's differential taxation and the stories he spreads. The plunderers attack their one-time master's castle. In the confusion Val frees all of Och's prisoners and torture victims, who gleefully kill the King they hate. After burning the prison and letting the armies run wild in the castle, Val destroys them and restores the castle to the good people of Cornwall. His mission is fulfilled, but Val is joyless because he feels he has practiced deceit and lost his knightly honor. Val and Alfred sail to Bristol, buy horses, and ride slowly back towards Camelot.

71: THE RED STALLION
Pages 1062 (16 June 1957) – 1074 (8 September 1957)

Riding home near Stonehenge, Val and Alfred see a splendid stallion and, thought it is apparently a man killer, Val decides to tame it. After trying futilely all day to catch the horse, Val returns apprehensively to Camelot. ("An Affair of Honor," #1064-1066: Val informs King Arthur and the other knights of his recent adventure in Cornwall and announces he must retire from the Fellowship of the Round Table because of his loss of honor. Despite Arthur's contention that Val actually increased his honor by completing the mission, the stubborn young knight refuses to take his seat at the Round Table. Annoyed, the King settles the matter by having all the other knights pledge a fraction of their honor to their adamant compatriot. Touched, Val takes his place and joins his friends in a lusty nightlong siege.) Returning to Stonehenge, Val learns from a Druid priestess how the wild horse became a

man killer because of a brutal master. For an entire day and night, Val and Alfred chase the stallion until it tires, and they are able to tie it down to remove the painful bridle that reminds the horse of its cruel past. Its wounds healed, the stallion finally becomes tame and Val rides it. Returning to Camelot with his splendid new mount, Val meets the son of the evil previous master of the stallion who tries to kill the horse that killed his father. Val is forced to joust against this man, Sador, who becomes mad with rage and is easily vanquished. Val proudly takes full possession of his huge red stallion and names it Arvak after the fiery horse that drew the sun's chariot across the sky in Viking legend. (COMMENT: Arvak is to be Val's warhorse for the next 22 years.)

72: THREE MEN AND A HORSE
Pages 1075 (15 September 1957) – 1083 (10 November 1957)

Not knowing that Alfred had taught it to do amusing tricks, Val tries to unload a stupid old extra horse by selling it to an unsuspecting barbarian. Halgar the Thunderer, the arrogant chieftain of the East Saxons, takes Mayblossom and is surprised by the horse's antics and lack of cooperation. When they realize what they have done, Val and Alfred are amused but horrified, hoping they have not provoked a war with East Saxony. Afraid of punishment, the two quickly leave Camelot, ride to London, and take passage on a ship bound for Thule. They are surprised to find the angry Halgar on board. Luckily, Val is cleverly able to ease the dumb Saxon's anger and eliminate the possibility of war. After a short shopping spree in London, Val sails home to Thule and an ecstatic family, for he has been away from home for about a year.

COMMENT: In page 1013 we see that the twin baby girls are already developing their own distinctive personalities. Karen is a bold, demanding tomboy and Valeta is a sweet coquettish charmer.

73: The Exchange
Pages 1084 (17 November 1957) – 1090 (29 December 1957)

Long ago Val and King Hap-Atla of the Inner Lands had agreed to temporarily exchange sons for training in accordance with old Viking custom. Sadly, Arn says goodbye to his family and rides off. On the way he meets Hap-Atla's son, Sven, who is on his way to live with Prince Valiant. The two boys become fast friends, warn each other about their respective mischievous sisters, exchange gifts, and ride on to complete their trips. Arn soon arrives at his new home and is greeted by his foster parents. He also meets Frytha, a sweet, beautiful child who looks nothing like the monster she was reported to be. Soon she reveals her devious nature with various pranks, but Arn always gets even. Garm brings the dog Sir Gawain to the Inner Lands, which makes Arn a little less homesick.

COMMENT: Arn is to be away from home for the next three years, and the story will return to him from time to time.

74: The Wanderer
Pages 1091 (1 January 1958) – 1105 (20 April 1958)

Every five years the "Council of Kings" meets at Bergan to adjust boundaries, make alliances or renew hatreds. On the eve of the Council, Aguar falls from his horse and is injured, so the King sends his son instead. Val is happy to see Hap-Atla and Arn. At the meetings Prince Valiant stands alone in his decision to avoid a ruinous war. When Val leaves, Aguar's enemies follow his ship and attack at Sognefjord. Val's small fleet avoids a battle and escapes safely at first, but Val is left behind when his boat is wrecked on a jagged rock. Not realizing that his men have vanquished the enemy, the unarmed Prince runs away and sets off for Vikingsholm on foot. His first obstacle is the great Jostedal Glacier, which proves very difficult to cross. In the uncharted region behond, Val meets an old Roman guarding a crumbling outpost, who does not realize Rome is crumbling. Val does not bother to quell the blissfully ignorant man's spirit by telling him the truth and soon resumes his journey. After three weeks of endless struggle, Val comes to a fishing village and asks for a position

on a boat that will take him home. After a duel with a violent sailor hamed Asgaard the Beserker, Val joins the crew of Sigurd Rolf, the Sea King. Luckily, Sigurd's ship encounters a dragonship of Thule, and Val is able to rejoin his father's army in the battle, which ensues. Val then recovers his Singing Sword, which he had lost in the sea battle at Sogenfjord, and finds that it had been his own men, not enemies, that pursued him across the countryside during the preceding weeks. Finally, Val returns to Aleta.

75: Reckless Youth
Pages 1106 (20 April 1958) – 1133 (26 October 1958)

Val and Aleta are summoned to Camelot for some business and some pleasure. Aleta does not enjoy the trip, for Val neglects her and her cabin is uncomfortable. Needing some new gowns to wear at court, the Queen forces Gundar Harl to stop at London so that she can go on a shopping spree.

("The Monster Learns a Lesson," #1110-1113: Meanwhile, Arn is having troubles of hiw own. Princess Frytha continually plots devilish pranks. One time Frytha's mother, Queen Jan, accidentally becomes the victim of a prank intended for Arn, and the "monster" is suitably punished. The angry girl arranges for Arn, whom she blames for her miseries, to be beaten by two other boys. The beating is more severe than she had planned, and she becomes guilt-ridden. Realizing Frytha has learned her lesson, Arn forgives her, and the two become friends.)

After leaving London, Val and Aleta stay for a night with a Roman couple who ask Val to take their son, Claudius, as his squire. Arriving at Camelot, Aleta becomes the highlight of the social season, while Val gets down to business. King Arthur plans a campaign to secure the Eastern marches of his realm, and Sir Valiant is the only knight available to lead such a venture. Alfred, not an eager warrior, stays behind, so Val takes along Claudius and another young knight-in-training, Edwin. Val's forces scour the countryside in search of hostile Saxons and come across a London-bound raiding party in Kent. Though the knights win the short battle that follows, Val is forced to chastise his young friend Edwin for his recklessness. Next comes a successful but terrible battle with more Saxon warriors, in which Edwin is captured, tortured, and killed. Mad with anger, Val slaughters the remaining Saxons and, sick with horror, he throws his cruel sword into the sea. Cleansing himself off in the cool waters, Val is confronted by some scavengers who try to kill him in order to steal his valuables. In helpless rage, Val dives to avoid their arrows, finds the Singing Sword in the water, and returns to his troops. The warriors then disperse the remaining Saxon invaders and warn them to become peaceful settlers or face slavery or death. After the Eastward march is concluded, the knights swing toward London and save the town from a Danish battle party. At London the knights try to replenish their supplies but are cheated by the merchants, and Val ruthlessly threatens to destroy the city if full reparations are not made. The transactions are settled, and Val marches into Camelot with the returning heroes. Sadly, Val gives the bad news to Edwin's mother and others, and he and Arthur realize how tragic war can be. Aleta is relieved to see her husband among the few men that return from their dirty business.

76: The Jealousy of a Queen
Pages 1133 (26 October 1958) – 1137 (23 November 1958)

Aleta is so popular in Camelot that Queen Guinevere becomes jeaslous. The "Fairest Queen in Christendom" (whom Foster draws amazingly beautifully in this story) feels that Aleta is loved more than she. Hoping to hurt Aleta and quell her popularity, the Queen holds a social gathering to which Aleta is not invited, but she feels guilty afterwards. When the cute twins, Karen and Valeta, mischievously run into her chambers, childless Guinevere is charmed and touched. When Aleta comes looking for her daughters in order to take them for a bath, Guinevere asks to come along and help. The Queen enjoys playing with the children and loses all enmity she felt towards Aleta.

77: The Singer in the Tower
Pages 1137 (23 November 1958) – 1152 (8 March 1959)

Val discovers that Gawain has vanished after leading knights into Wales on a mission. King Arthur gives Val leave to go search for his friend. Val and jolly Ivan Waldoc, who has been with Gawain as a guide, ride into Wales. They ride first to the walled city of Caerwent. The headman there reports that a wounded knight lies in Caerlon. There, at an old Roman fortress, Val and Waldoc are disappointed to find that the knight is not Gawain but Sir Beaton, who reports Gawain's last known whereabouts—the stone cross in the Black Mountains. At the cross they meet Ruy the Jongleur, who suggests that Gawain might have gotten involved with jealous King Oswick and his beautiful daughters. The boy leads them to a place from which they can study the Castle Oswick and form plans to find Gawain if he is there. That night, near an ancient Celtic temple, the wizard Merlin Ambrosius appears, gives Val cryptic advice on how to find and rescue Gawain, and then departs with Nimue, the water maid.

COMMENT: *Merlin, Arthur's advisor [Story 4] and Val's tutor [stories 8, 23, 37] appeared seemingly for the last time in page 1141 (until a surprise recent appearance in page 2444 by Murphy), being led away into limbo, as prophesized, by the nymph.*

Unraveling the message, Val enters the castle as Cid, a wandering entertainer. Oswick summons Cid to test his skills. Val passes the test and explains that he had been a mercenary but had succumbed to alcohol. Pretending to be drunk, he staggers out to search for Gawain. When a distant voice joins in one of Cid's songs, Val realizes that Gawain is held in a heavily guarded tower. Sent to entertain Oswick's daughters, Cid tells them fascinating tales of romantic Gawain. Princess Wynn visits the knight, who makes love to her as per Val's instructions. The strong-willed girl gets the key's impression in some wet clay. Val retrieves the clay, fashions a key, and smuggles it to Gawain. On a dark rainy night, a drunken Cid climbs the arm of a construction crane near the tower and rescues Gawain, lowering him unsteadily into the moat. Oswick conducts a search for his lost prisoner, and Val frightens him with a suggestion that Gawain might have escaped by witchcraft. Val convinces the superstitious king that Gawain is invisible and a danger to Oswick, who decides to "lure" the lurker out of the castle by returning his horse and sword and providing rich gifts. Val is let out by the hoodwinked King to deliver the gifts and merrily leads his friend away.

78: Kerwin's Ordeal
Pages 1153 (15 March 1959) – 1162 (17 May 1959)

At the temple ruins Cid and Gawain join Ruy and Sir Waldoc and Cid puts off his rags and once again becomes Prince Valiant. They ride out of Wales. At Caerlon they find Sir Beaton sufficiently recovered from his wounds to ride. Here the group breaks up. Beaton, Waldoc and Ruy ride to Camelot the easy way, but Gawain and Val take ship across the Briston Channel to go by a more adventurous route. The two knights become bored and decide to enter the Great Tournament at Hamlin Garde. To compete against the common folk, Val and Gawain playfully change their clothes and identities. Coth, a ruthless nobleman, gets into a scrap with Val, who learns that the highlight of the tournament will be a contest between Coth and a gentle lad named Kerwin for the hand of fair Lady Alice. Gawain wins the palm of victory in the preliminary contests. Coth hires an assassin to waylay Val, but the man botches his job. Val tries to teach Kerwin, who resembles him, some battle skills for the coming tournament. In the grand melee, Coth does well, striking fighters whose backs are turned, and Kerwin survives using Val's lessons. Coth asks a ruffian friend to challenge Kerwin to a tilt to wear him down. Kerwin defeats the challenger but is wounded. Gawain challenges Coth to a tilt to even the score and hurls him into the dust. Val takes the injured Kerwin's place in the lists and defeats Coth four times, winning the day for Kerwin. Val switches places back with Kerwin, who is given knighthood and Alice's hand.

79: The Marriage Contract
Pages 1162 (17 May 1959) – 1174 (9 August 1959)

The tournaments at Hamlin Garde being over, Gawain and Val ride off on the vast Salisbury Plain, where they run out of provisions. After living off the land for a few days, they reach the King's road and meet a great lady with her servants. Gawain charms the Lady and gets a dinner invitation to Ruthford Castle. Val meets two young sweethearts, Joan (only child of the Count of Ruthford) and a tall squire. Joan is heartbroken to learn that her father has arranged a political marriage for her to Hume of Amesbridge, whom she has never met. The unhappy couple elopes and exchange marriage vows. Just as they try to depart, the gates swing open to welcome Sir Hume. Joan is furious to learn that her peasant lover is himself Sir Hume, who came in disguise to check out the girl he was forced to marry. To maintain peace, Hume renounces his title and becomes Sir Gawain's squire. Joan agrees gleefully to go with him. Gawain is displeased but agrees to her plan so that an official wedding can be held. After a week of festivities, the party leaves. Joan is disillusioned by the miserable trip, and the company arrives at Camelot. All her life Joan dreamed of seeing Camelot but now all she sees of the fabled city is the stable area. Aleta meets the girl, hears her story, and takes the couple to King Arthur to straighten the mess out.

80: The Earl's Justice
Pages 1175 (16 August 1959) – 1187 (8 November 1959)

After spending a month with his family, Val is sent by King Arthur to Lithway Forest to investigate outlaw trouble there. Val requests that Hugh-the-Fox (see Story 31B) come with him. The outlaws capture the two and take them to their lair, where they are treated with hatred. The crippled chieftain sneers at the King's justice, shows Val men who were maimed by the Earl of Lithway and denies the accusations of theft of the King's tithes. Val and Hugh are released and go to Lithway Garde. They are taken before the Earl, a large, florid man, who insists his monies were stolen by the outlaws. Sir Holsing, the Earl's neighbor, also claims to have been robbed in the forest by the outlaws, although Hugh learns Holsig's men had returned to his castle with the treasure due to the crown, falsely accusing the outlaws who were but free men who fled to the forest to escape the cruelty of their masters. Val and Hugh watch in helpless rage as the Earl dispenses his appalling brand of justice. To search for evidencae, Val arms the outlaws and brings them to the castle. They take over and Val prevents them from killing the cruel Earl. When Holsig rides to Lithway, hoping to take it over, Val and the outlaws invade his castle and find the supposedly stolen strongbox there, too. The Earl of Lithway accompanies the group to Camelot, confident he can talk his way out of trouble. When the Earl appeals his case before the King, claiming he had punished the outlaws justly, Val produces the stolen tithes at the crucial moment.

The King banishes the Earl from the realm (probably the earliest recorded tax-evasion case in history!). Val celebrates with his friends and neglects Aleta, who gives her drunken husband a tongue-lashing.

81: The Grail Quest
Pages 1187 (8 November 1959) – 1217 (5 June 1960)

The Fellowship of the Round Table has brought a measure of peace and justice to Britain, but each year lately sees more and more knights take up the quest for the Holy Grail, and all too few of these brave warriors return. The very existence of the fellowship is thus threatened. King Arthur calls upon Prince Valiant to seek out the facts, if the Grail be fact or myth, for he knows Val will not be swayed by unquestioning faith or superstition. Hurt and angry after his fight with Aleta, Val accepts the mission. When Aleta learns of Val's imminent departure for the new quest, she protests. He kisses her and spanks her before he goes, leaving her in a daze. His heart not in the mission, Val finds

HE FINDS ONE ALREADY HEADING FOR THE OPEN SEA AND COMES ABOARD AS ONLY SIR GAWAIN WOULD!

an old Roman road and rides to the ruined city of Sarum. The historian of the city's archives reports that the Roman records no longer exist and directs Val to Stonehenge, where an ancient people live. There Val meets the priestess who had helped him capture and tame Arvak a few years earlier (Story 71). The girl explains that her people, the Beaker Folk, had raised the temple many years before the Druids took over. An ancient priest tells Val that when the Christians came across the sea to Britain four centuries earlier, led by Christ's disciple Joseph of Arimathea, they had reportedly built their first church on an island called Avalon and placed there a symbolic dish or chalice that they thought holy because of its legendary use by Christ at the Last Supper. That church, if it could be found, might have the records Val sought.

Riding westward over the Mendip Hills, Val is led by Sir Tyndal to Och, an escaped slave who disguises himself as an ogre to avoid recapture by his cruel master, Timmera the Terrible. Och leads Val to Avalon, near which the slave was born. At Gastonbury, a friar shows Val the first Christian church, which is now being enclosed by a great cathedral under the supervision of a Prior from Rome. The Prior refuses to answer Val's questions about the Grail. Pondering his failure at the top of Avalon's mountain, The Tor, Val sees in the distance armed men approaching Glastonbury, arms himself, and joins the townspeople against Timmera the Terrible, who has long wanted to plunder the island. After being beaten, the furious raiders burn the half-built Abbey. Timmera escapes, but Val ruthlessly follows. Made reckless by fear, Timmera accidentally plunges into fog-filled Cheddar Gorge. Och at last has his freedom, and he helps Val conquer the late Timmera's stronghold and take back treasure enough to rebuild the Abbey. Work resumes on the Abbey after the battle, under the supervision of Bishop Patrick, who had saved Val's life when he fought King Rory McColm of Ireland (see Story 59). Father Patrick, Val realizes, is the only man who can give him the true facts of the Grail. They speak alone at the top of the windy Tor and Val is convinced that there is no proof that the chalice ever existed. He realizes, however, that the Grail is a valuable symbol of faith, courage and hope.

The knights who take the Quest do more by their example to spread the faith of Christianity than anyone could do by preaching. Val lingers on in Glastonbury for a few days to help Patrick with the plans for the new Abbey and then leaves Avalon.

("The Tyrant," #1210-1216: Riding home along the lonely King's Highway, Val comes to a great castle that promises warmth and shelter. The portals that should have opened in hospitality instead yield forth a huge armed knight who without a word of warning sets his lance and charges Val. After defeating the champion, Val is welcomed into the castle with loud cheering and learns that the challenger, Hugo Ap Dunfel, was a murderous tyrant who plagued the widow Lady Lowry, who had been forced to flee for help with her daughters. She soon returns from Camelot with a now unnecessary champion—Sir Gawain—who is annoyed that Val had spoiled his chance to perform gallantly before the ladies. A good dinner restores everyone's spirits. When Ap Dunfel recovers from his wounds he is to be taken to Camelot for judgment but is found stabbed.)

With heavy heart, Val goes to the King to report the results of his quest. Arthur is told that there is no evidence of the Grail's existence, but the King decides not to interfere with faith, leaving the future fate of the Fellowship to a higher power.

COMMENT: *This story is the only Prince Valiant tale concerning the Holy Grail, the most famous of the Arthurian myths. Sir Galahad, the most famous knight who took up this quest in legends, is never mentioned. Foster notes in page 1205 that the background material was taken from sketches he made during a 1959 vacation in Britain.*

82: THE MAD WARRIOR
Pages 1217 (5 June 60) – 1225 (31 July 1960)

After months of anticipation, Val returns to Aleta. They nervously face each other in silence, neither able to make a move. Inadvertently hurt again,

Val turns coldly away. Aleta is devastated. Numb with pain, Val thunders eastward to join the army and find relief in warfare. The knights are fighting off Saxon invaders (as usual). Val recklessly leads a raid on the Saxon treasure ships and then launches pursuit of the enemies who escaped. After many successful raids Val tries to storm a fortified position, and he is wounded. Arthur summons Aleta, tells her Val has fallen in battle and lost the will to live, and orders her to go to her husband. The lovers are reunited and misunderstandings are resolved. Aleta takes charge of the care of her husband. Katwin and the twins arrive at the camp, and Val's condition improves rapidly in the homelike atmosphere.

83: THE ABDICATION
Pages 1225 (31 July 1960) – 1249 (15 January 1961)

Aleta had recently been summoned back to the Misty Isles because of affairs of state in her kingdom. Aleta prepares for the journey, asking for Gundar Harl's and Boltar's ships. Garm the forester travels to the Inner Lands to retrieve Prince Arn, who has been training at King Hap Atla's stronghold (since Story 73). Arn and Garm follow the long trail back to Thule, exploring the subtle mysteries of the forests. They weather the first storm of winter (ca. 466) and finally arrive at Vikingsholm. Arn sails to Britain on Gundar's ship and gets seasick. Meanwhile, Val has at last recovered enough to be moved back to Camelot on a horse litter. He and Aleta argue over their son's future— he is heir to thrones of both Thule and the Misty Isles. Arn arrives, and the family has a happy reunion. Val agrees to accompany Aleta back to the Misty Isles, where Arn's destiny will be settled. They leave in Gundar Harl's ship and meet Boltar at Gibraltar. Arn decides to travel with Boltar in order to learn the ways of fighting men.

Off the Algerian coast, the ships succumb to the heat and pull into a harbor for water. Boltar asks the port Governor for permission to fill his casks at the town fountain but is enraged to return to find his ships have been attacked by waterfront gangs. Arrangements and restitution are furiously completed. Restocked, the Vikings sail on, with Arn disturbed by the memory of the battle, in which he thinks his arrows have killed a man.

At last, the ships arrive at the Misty Isles, and the Queen is received by her cheering people. Prince Arn, the heir apparent to the throne, receives even greater attention. Aleta is disturbed to find her rich, peaceful kingdom has become too weak, a potential target for envious neighbors. (Note: Last time [Story 61], the kingdom was becoming too strong and warlike; the woman is never satisfied.) She holds a conference with Val, Boltar and Gundar. Thrasos, a neighbor to the west, is the immediate threat. He is invited to help the Misty Isles build fortifications, and the oily rascal gloats over the opportunity to place his best soldiers in the city as workmen. Thrasos' arriving ships are found to contain arms so the "laborers" are jailed. Thrasos is angry but his spies find a flaw in the defenses. Thrasos arranges an attack on the unfinished harbor wall, but the defenses are ready. When the invaders sail into the harbor, chains are raised behind them and a rolling gate of timbers blocks the hole in the wall. The invaders surrender under the threat of being burned in the trap. Thrasos brings a reserve fleet into a nearby cove, and the Viking warriors are unable to defend the Queen's palace. Thrasos finds his way into Aleta's room, and Val prevents him from stabbing her at the last second. Aleta faints and Val goes after Thrasos. After a grueling chase in a storm, Thrasos tries to hide in a blackened tree stump but dies horribly when lightning strikes the tree.

With Thrasos out of the picture, Val returns to the palace to see how Aleta is. He is first barred from seeing her, and when he finally is let into Aleta's rooms he discovers that she has given birth to a baby boy! (Foster had concealed Aleta's pregnancy with flowing robes.) Arn decides to abdicate his position as heir to the Misty Isles in favor of his new baby brother.

84: KIDNAPPED
Pages 1249 (15 January 1961) – 1259 (26 March 1961)

Arn spends some time with his old friends Paul and Diane (see Story 64) at the seashore. The prisoners of war (from Story 83), working on completing the fortifications of the Misty Isles, revolt. Some escape, steal a boat, and capture Arn, Paul and Diane. Arn is to be held for ransom and the other two will be sold as slaves. Val finds out about the missing boat and prisoners and has Gundar Harl ready a ship. A clue is left when the escapees kill some fishermen for supplies. Arn escapes from the boat when it docks at a Mediterranean city and runs to the governor's palace for help. Paul and Diane are beaten and sold to a buyer from North America. The dishonest governor sees Arn as a good source of profit and sends a ransom message to Val. Furious, Val storms the palace, rescues his son, and captures the abductors. He pursues the slave ship and swaps the other children for the kidnappers.

85: THE NEW ERA
Pages 1260 (2 April 1961) – 1263 (23 April 1961)

Aleta, who has been beset with problems of state, collapses from exhaustion. A peaceful era returns to the Misty Isles. Paul, Arn and Diane mature. A gala christening is held and the new child is named Galan. Val takes over Arn's training.

86: THE BUSINESS TRIP
Pages 1263 (23 April 1961) – 1292 (12 November 1961)

Val and Arn rescue the survivors of a shipwreck near the harbor of the Misty Isles. The leader, Sir Owen of Lothian, says they are pilgrims bound for the Holy Land and requests help. Val and Arn decide to sail along to Jaffa as Aleta's ambassadors to promote trade with the Misty Isles. They land in Jaffa and go to Jerusalem, where the pilgrims begin to alienate people by their fanaticism. Val takes Arn on a tour of the Holy City and the Dead Sea. Near the River Jordan, Val purchases a slave, Ohmed, who proves to be a valuable asset as an interpreter. At Damascus, Val hires Nicilos the Greek as a business manager to help in dealing with the local merchants. Val's caravan travels past Aleppo (Northern Syria).

Meanwhile, a young girl named Taloon has been cast out of her tribe and has joined up with a caravan bound for Persia. Past Aleppo, and near the Euphrates, Arn stops to explore an ancient ruin on a mountainside and oversees mountain men setting up an attack on Taloon's caravan. He warns his father, who comes and battles the men with his sword as Arn picks some off with his bow and arrows. Val's caravan next reaches the city of Baghdad in Babylonia. Ohmed yearns to return to the nearby village where he had grown up and been captured as a slave, so Val sets him free. As Val and Arn sightsee in Babylon, Ohmed goes home and finds his village in ruins. Meanwhile, the girl Taloon had been sexually assaulted by one of the guards of her caravan and so had killed him and joined a different caravan. There she was ridiculed by the Zoroastrians for worshipping water, so she rode westward to Baghdad alone. There, she tries to raise money by selling some of her possessions. Val meets the girl, buys a saddle from her, and they share an evening meal. Taloon falls in love with the kind Prince. Val hires her to care for his baggage animals. Ohmed and Nicilos both are attracted to Taloon but are rebuffed. Filled with jealousy, Nicilos talks Ohmed into stabbing Val while he sleeps. Ohmed does succeed in wounding Val, but Taloon bursts in at the right moment, kills Ohmed, and rides away. Val is taken to the home of a nearby wealthy merchant to recuperate and Nicilos rides off into the desert to find Taloon. He confronts her, reassures her Val is still alive, and tells her he loves her. Low-lying clouds conceal the ending of this interlude (!). When Val feels better, he resumes the journey on camel. He and Arn arrive at Deir El Zor where Val had once been a captive and meet his former owner Belchad Abu [see Story 18]. Abu recognizes and fears Val and offers his hospitality. Arn is amused by the stories of how Val had been Abu's slave and had flirted with daughter Bernice in order to gain freedom (two panels from the 1941 story are reprinted). Poor Bernice throws herself at Val and her heart is again broken by his hasty departure. Arn is given a Damascus sword as an incentive not to tell Aleta about the incident.

One night soon thereafter, Alimann the cruel, who has raided a nearby village, invites Val's caravan to stay over, hoping for protection from counter-attacks. When Val leaves, Alimann escapes too by hiding in the baggage as a stowaway. When Alimann is found, Val sends him home, but Alimann is upset to find that in his absence the desert tribe whose village he had raided has taken over his stronghold. Val returns to Aleppo, where he receives letters from Aleta declaring the trading venture a success and instructing him to come home with Boltar, whose ships wait at Antioch.

87: ROME
Pages 1293 (19 November 1961) – 1302 (21 January 1962)

Returning to the Misty Isles, Val enjoys his family for a while. A ship from Camelot arrives with a request from King Arthur that Val go to Rome to ask the Emperor to help in opening the road through Gaul. Aleta and Arn come along on the trip. They arrive in Rome and find it is in sad shape. (Historical note: It is now roughly 468 AD. Rome had been sacked in 455 AD [Story 30], and the fall of the Empire is now nearly complete. Odoacer, the German chieftain, will overthrow the last Western Roman Emperor, Romulus Augustulus, at Ravenna in 476.) Val sets out to find the emperor and is told it might be helpful to hold a banquet for government officials. Meanwhile, Arn tours the city, watching the barbarians destroy great monuments. Behind a garden wall, Arn meets an ill, partially blind little girl who lives in her own fantasy world. Her father, Marcus Severis, learns of Val's mission and offers help. Arn returns in time for the banquet, which is not successful, and brings his father back to Marcus Severis' villa. Severis advises Val that his hope for aid from Rome is futile, since Rome can no longer even protect its own walls. Arn says farewell to the blind girl, and Val says farewell to Rome for the last time (indeed, this is the last time that the fabled city is even referred to by Foster in the strip).

88: THE OVERLAND TRADE ROUTE
Pages 1303 (28 January 1962) – 1327 (8 July 1962)

Leaving Italy, Val decides to explore an overland route to Britain for trade. He takes Arn with him. They land north of Spain (i.e. in south France) and are told there is a road in the south of Gaul, which would be a good place to start. An ex-soldier named Justin, whose village has been destroyed, joins Val's group and volunteers to lead them across Gaul.

("The Mysterious Ruin," #1305-1312: The path through a seemingly peaceful valley is blocked with giant, monstrous plaster figures designed to scare away intruders. The group stops at a ruined monastery and are greeted by the Abbot, who explains he had intended the monsters to keep barbarians away. But now the Goths have found the path and are coming. The Abbot and Brother John, a sculptor, make preparations for the attack. When the vandals enter, they encounter a [wooden] dragon spewing smoke and flee.)

Stephen, a young lad, leads Val's group away from the hidden valley. At Aqueloen, Stephen stops to see his mother, explaining how his uncle, Sadonick, rules there in the place rightly Stephen's. ("The Duke," #1313-1323: Val and Arn meet this Duke, who is mad with power and with fear of Stephen. Sadonick holds Arn hostage and orders Val to decoy Stephen into an ambush. Luckily Justin has escaped and warns Stephen, who decides to trick Sadonick in return, using the Duke's spy system to get word back that Stephen and his mother are going away to their hunting lodge. Val is forced to go with Sadonick's armed men to the lodge. The Duke bursts in and orders

Val to kill Stephen. Val refuses and Stephen's own hidden men come forth. Val races back to Aqueloen, tosses his reins to a stable boy, and enters the castle in search of Arn. The torturers claim Arn has disappeared. After a search, Val finds that his son was the dirty-faced stable boy. Sadonick is beheaded and Stephen becomes Duke.)

Justin decides to return to the monastery to become Brother John's assistant. Val and Arn continue their travels west to the sea and are forced to conclude that there is no safe overland route through to Britain. They find Aleta swimming in the Bay of Biscay (with a jealous otter who steals one of Aleta's jewels, bites Val, and presents the jewel to the first female otter who comes along ["Mr. Whiskers," #1324-1326].) Boltar escorts the royal family to Camelot, where Val makes his report to King Arthur.

89: ARVAK THE WILD
Pages 1329 (29 July 1962) – 1331 (12 August 1962)

When Val arrives home, he learns his warhorse Arvak has reverted to the wild state and won't let anyone near him. Arvak recalls his happy and unhappy relationships with humans in page 1330, which reprints several 1957 panels [Story 71]. Val lures Arvak with oatcakes, bad memories vanish, and Arvak is re-tamed.

90: THE VOICE
Pages 1328(22 July 1962) – 1342(28 October 1962)

On the way to Camelot from Gaul (Story 88), Boltar's ship had stopped at a monastery to get supplies, and the Abbot had convinced Val and Boltar to transport a powerful-voiced monk named Wojan to Britain to fulfill a religious mission. Wojan begins preaching in Camelot and distracts the workers from their duties. Arthur asks Val to observe this monk, and Val finds him to be honest but naive. Wojan hopes to build a cathedral, and his assistants Sleath and Dustad gather money for themselves from the audiences under this pretense. With Arthur's assistance Wojan leaves Camelot, followed by a throng of zealots, to preach in the country. The followers become hungry and undisciplined and begin to pillage the land, and Sleath and Dustad grow rich profiting on misery and selling protection to villages. Val brings the Abbot out of Brittany to help with the situation and has King Arthur send provisions. The Abbot tells the unsuspecting monk what had been going on and suggests that Wojan take the money his aides had gathered to build his cathedral. The two advisors and their henchmen try to guard their treasure wagon, but Val and Wojan capture the loot. Sleath and Dustad are sent away, with their greedy followers, and the building of the church begins.

("Memories of the Past," #1342-50: Aleta, who has been lonely, joins her husband at the church construction site. As the work continues, Val points out the nearby Fens, where he spent his boyhood, to Arn. Val tells of his early life in the marshes [several drawings from the early 1937 pages are reproduced and noted by the artist]. Arn deacides he'd like to explore the place and becomes lost for two days in the channels. Arn's worried father comes into the swamps and finds the boy just as he is about to be attacked by the lurking Thorg, Val's old friend/enemy [from Story 2].)

The Abbot asks Val to take the treasures with him to Camelot. Val agrees and leaves by a sea route. One of the ship's passengers, Ethwald the businessman, covets the treasure. When the ship stops for water, he offers to take Arn hunting but instead kidnaps the boy and holds him for ransom. Val refuses to hand over the treasure chest. Aleta comes up with a brilliant idea and brews a harmless potion. When Val meets again with Ethwald, Val pours the brew into Ethwald's cup. When Ethwald sees crystals in his goblet, he assumes he has been poisoned. Frantic, he agrees to turn over Arn in return for an "antidote." He is given a useless rancid substance (as a punishment). Ethwald is taken back to Camelot to be tried. Val is hailed there as a hero.

91: WAR CLOUDS
Pages 1357 (10 February 1963) – 1374 (9 June 1963)

Rumors of war are heard from the north, so a war council is held. Cidwic, a new king of North Wales, longs to conquer the city of Carlisle to enlist Picts and Caledonians in order to conquer Britain. Arthur sends Sir Kay to the beleaguered city. Sir Kay builds a wall around Cidwic's stronghold while Cidwic attacks Carlisle. The city resists the siege. Val selects a troop of messengers to ride to the site of the action and keep King Arthur posted. As Cidwic's army at Carlisle deserts, he retreats to his stronghold. Val's troop rides to help at Sir Kay's outpost. Arn, who had been a chosen rider, carries the message of the turnabout back to the King and returns to Kay's base, which is now besieged by Cidwic. Desperate for victory, Cidwic challenges Prince Valiant to a one-on-one duel. Arn, who had been observing Cidwic, tells his exhausted father about some weak points he had noticed in Cidwic's battle technique, and Val now topples the King easily. With Cidwic's death the enemy is driven back. Arthur enters and chides Val about spoiling the fight for his knights. Cuddock, 12-year-old son of Cidwic, is crowned King of Wales and becomes friends with Arn. Ruddah, Cidwic's brother, wants to eliminate his nephew and seize power for himself. Rudday steals Arn's arrows to kill Cuddock and blame the Prince. When the boys go rabbit hunting, Ruddah lies in wait and fires one of Arn's arrows. Arn luckily hears a suspicious sound and kicks Cuddock out of the way of the shot. Arn fires his bow at the retreating assailant and wounds Ruddah. Arn discovers that his own arrow had been fired, and simultaneously at the stronghold Ruddah is found to have stolen arrows in his quiver. When the knights go to summon the suspected Ruddah for a trial, he flees the castle. Arn takes on the task of bringing him to justice. With two warriors he pursues him to the sea where the villain kills a lone fisherman, steals a boat, and is smashed to pieces in the swift currents. Val is proud that his son has single-handedly carried a quest through to completion.

92: THE RUSTIC KNIGHTS
Pages 1375 (16 June 1963) – 1383 (11 August 1963)

It is August (ca. 469 AD) when Val and Arn leave for Camelot. It is the season of Pentecost, when many knights travel the roads from one tournament to another. Arn and his father stop at such a tournament, where young knights such as Boswell Farnway and Chetworth Billingford are gathering, hoping to win fame and fortune. In their first match, Bo and Chet lose their armor to Sir Plumpet, a tricky old knight, and later try to steal it back. In calling for redress, Sir Plumpet is given the two men as servants to work out their misdeed and debts. Plumpet soon loses his armor in the jousts, and Val buys his tent and servants. The three decide to take in one more tournament at King Kadonoc's castle. Val takes part in the grand melee there and is challenged by Irish Knight Rory MacAin. Rory is unhorsed, and Bo and Chet strip him of his armor so that Chet can enter the joust. Angry, Val challenges Chet to cure him of his habit of borrowing other people's things. Chet is of course beaten and thrown into the dungeon, but Val feels sorry for him and arranges his release.

93: SEEDS OF REVOLT
Pages 1384 (18 August 1963) – 1393 (20 October 1963)

Finally arriving back at Camelot, Sir Valiant and his stalwart son pay homage to their King. The dignity of the occasion is disrupted by the gleeful greetings of Val's twin daughters. Aleta leads her family out of the palace to a new home she has bought in the outskirsts of town. Arvak is left at the horse runs where he can become the king and protector of his splendid brood of colts.

A very serious Sir Gawain takes Val to a meeting at which Mordred is trying to convince a group of young knights to rebel against King Arthur and his restrictive laws. Val's simple, honest rebuttals undo all of Mordred's efforts, and after the meeting an angry Mordred plots with his half-brothers—Gawain, Gareth, Geharis, and Agravaine, sons of King Lot—to hurt Arthur though Guinevere, Launcelot, Val and Aleta. Gawain cryptically warns his friends to be alert, torn between his fierce clan-loylty and his oath to King Arthur. After a private dinner party including the King and Queen and Val's family, the King's ambitious, devious son tricks Launcelot and Aleta into locking themselves in Guinevere's private garden. Mordred hopes that they will be discovered alone together, Guinevere will become jealous, and the scandal will destroy the unity of the Fellowship. (*COMMENT: This is one of the few times that Foster alludes to the famous romance between Launcelot and Guinevere, which in legend indeed later led to the downfall of Camelot.*) Luckily, Val and Arn find Aleta and Launcelot and wait with them until the next morning, when Mordred barges in and finds his plot to cause jealousy foiled. Fearing Val's anger, cowardly Mordred rides off to his home in Lothian, there to continue his scheming to gain the crown.

94: SAXONS IN THE VALE
Pages 1393 (20 October 1963) – 1403 (29 December 1963)

Mordred has sent ominous news to Camelot: while riding Northwest toward his home, he saw a Saxon war band encamped near White Horse Vale. Arthur decides to send a scouting party, composed of three young knights who wish to distinguish themselves, to find out what the Saxons are up to now. Arn is chosen to participate because of his fine actions during the North Wales

VAL RIDES ON ... AND ON, NOT KNOWING OR CARING WHERE. THERE IS ONLY ONE PLACE HE WANTS TO GO: ON THAT SHIP BESIDE ALETA. TOO LATE NOW.

NEXT WEEK- *The Wanderer*

campaign (Story 91). The war band has moved, but the three young knights find them, observe from afar, and send a messenger to bring the information back to Camelot. In order to discover whether these be East Saxons or West Saxons, Arn and young Owen sneak up to get a better look. Hotheaded, reckless Owen, eager to win his first taste of personal glory, attacks a sentry and runs off, frightened, with the two horses. Trapped, Arn thinks quickly and boldly enters the camp, pretending to be the son of Boltar, claiming to have escaped from the Britons and to be eager to return to his father's ship. Owen returns to Camelot and tearfully tells Arn's parents what happened, and Val frantically rides from the palace. Owen guides Val to the Saxons. Not knowing of Arn's deception, Val worries that his boy has been tortured or has turned traitor, for Arn is seen to be leading the scouting party westward toward the heartland of Britain! During a hunt, Arn is able to quickly get to his father, explain that he is spying on the Saxons, plan a future escape, and return unnoticed to his captors. Later, Arn leaves the camp with a small scouting group. Val, as arranged, is waiting to kill the group and leave indications that Arn was also killed. The Saxons are fooled. Arn and Val ride quickly back to Camelot to inform King Arthur that the raiders are preparing for one great campaign to conquer all Britain. While Arthur presumably makes the necessary arrangements, Arn impatiently rushes home to his mother.

95: Another Abduction
Pages 1404 (5 January 1964) – 1417 (5 April 1964)

Sir Brecey of Brittany, a distinguished guest at Camelot, lusts after Aleta and arranges for Val to die in the great Spring tournament. Slyly, he befriends the golden Queen, complaining of loneliness. Hugo, Brecey's menacing cousin, tries to cripple Val's great warhorse Arvak in order to remove Val's fighting advantage, but he fails. Near the end of the tournament, Hugo the manslayer challenges the weary Sir Valiant to mortal combat. Count Brecey looks on eagerly, while Aleta and King Arthur watch anxiously. Although Hugo's strength is an advantage, Arvak enables him to avoid Hugo's attacks. Realizing that Hugo is the one who had tried to hurt his warhorse, Val angrily brings the fight to its end after an hour of exhausting battle. Launcelot and Gawain retire from the tournament, and for the first time since he came to

Camelot, Val is crowned Grand Champion. Aleta, relieved and proud, is kidnapped by the frustrated Count Brecey. Wearily and angrily, Val and Arn follow and rescue Aleta. Brecey, Ambassador of King Ban of Brittany, father of Launcelot, demands a trial. Unfortunately for him, the result is that the egotistical, greedy Count is substituted for a useful soldier who was to be executed for his behavior in a tavern brawl.

COMMENT: This is another one of the large numbers of "rescuing Aleta from lustful kidnappers" stories. Foster overused this theme, but it obviously must be nearly impossible to write hundreds of completely original stories, especially in a strip created by someone who was originally and primarily an artist rather than a writer. Of course, the average reading public would not remember similar stories from year to year. Interestingly, Foster has been quoted as saying that he indeed found it difficult to continually come up with worthwhile stories to accompany his invariably excellent pictures.

96: The Battle of Badon Hill
Pages 1417 (5 April 1964) – 1436 (16 August 1964)

Early in summer (ca. 469), waves of invaders start gathering at the shores of Britain in order to aid the new Saxon conquest attempt. Arthur is upset that the remnants of defeated armies, whom he had allowed to remain in peace, hoping they would become useful citizens, are beginning to join the uprising. The king sends his knights to call in all debts and levies. Arn is sent to North Wales to ask his friend, young King Cuddock, to repay Arn's past favors (see Story 91), while Sirs Gawain and Valiant are sent westward to Cornwall to ask its three kings for the troops they had once promised when they swore the oath of fealty (Story 70).

In Cornwall, Val and Gawain find that each of the Kings distrusts the others and keeps a great army for protection, meaning they would not be likely to lend forces to Arthur. King Grudemede of Caerloch at first offers only 20 well-armed men, due to the malevolent advice of his advisor, Givric, a former servant of Merlin and cheap trickster. Val knows better tricks and soon convinces Grudemede to supply 300 men, on the promise that Val take an equal number away from the other Cornish Kings. Next comes a visit with King Alrick the Fat, whose stubbornness annoys Val, who decides that a truce between the Kings of Cornwall must be arranged, at least until the Saxon war is over. Gawain, through eloquent flattery and promises, convinces Alrick's Queen to make her husband give Arthur the troops, while Val rides westward to meet the third King, Harloch, a benevolent old man who cooperates promptly by supplying a small group of excellent soldiers. Val then gathers the three kings together, convinces them to sign a treaty guaranteeing temporary peace in Cornwall, and starts training his ragged bunch of warriors.

Meanwhile, Arn finds his friend Cuddock of Wales fretting over Saxon-encouraged Scotti raids. Time is drawing close, and Arn needs to bring back as many troops as possible, immediately. Cuddock, hesitant to weaken his own defenses, agrees to supply at least a small army and rides with Arn towards the battleground at Badon Hill (recall that Arn had shown the Saxons their route in Story 94 and had informed Arthur of all their plans). Arthur's small but proud army begins the defense of Britain against the savage horde of Saxons. At the peak of the battle, Arthur's forces have great trouble, and only the last minute arrival of Prince Arn with King Cuddock and his army enables the knights to sway the tide of the battle and demolish the Saxons. Hengist, leader of the barbarians, escapes, his power broken, and many years will pass before the Saxons mount another invasion.

COMMENT: *The victory of Mount Badon, probably a real event, was the legendary King Arthur's greatest triumph. It was the last of about 12 Saxon invasions that Arthur prevented and probably took place in about AD 510 or 520 (although here it is placed in about AD 469). In legend, Arthur thereafter reigned in comparative peace for another 30 years, until one of evil Mordred's revolts led to his death.*

97: THE MATCHMAKERS
Pages 1435 (9 August 1964) – 1442 (27 September 1964)

Prince Charles, son of King Harloch of Cornwall, is knighted for his honorable performance in the Battle of Badon Hill, and Prince Valiant brings the proud youth home with him. Aleta decides that Charles would be an excellent catch for her fair young ward, Ailianora, while Queen Gayle, wife of Alrick and visitor to Camelot, hopes to nab Charles for her niece, Grace. The two young girls spend weeks vying for his attention, and the twins imitate what they see by torturing another guest, Cuddock. Charles, becoming conceited, shocks everyone by suddenly falling in love with a homely peasant girl and proceeding to marry her. Grace and Ailianora at first have broken hearts but soon forget their sorrows.

98: GUERILLA WAR IN THULE
Pages 1442 (27 September 1964) – 1455 (27 December 1964)

It will never be known exactly what happened next to Sir Charles, Grace, Ailianora, and the rest, for it seems that one of the ancient scrolls upon which the saga of Prince Valiant is written is crumbled and illegible (!). As far as Mr. Foster can tell, the next known location of Prince Valiant and his family was on Boltar's great dragon ship, heading northbound for Thule. At Bergen, Val learns that hostile armies are approaching Trondheimfjord by land and sea. Boltar takes the royal family onward, while Val and a scout sail inland to investigate. The two are joined by Aguar's huntsman, Garm, former teacher of Prince Arn. Val tries to raise an army of his own to resist the forces of the mad Skogul Oderson and after first encountering resistance, gathers support among refugees of Oderson's raids. Val washes out the raiders with waters from a makeshift dam when he encounters the raiders at a farm. Oderson and his remaining men press on to Vikingsholm, destroying everything as they pass. Val recruits and equips an army with weapons of the drowned raiders. Another small band coming down the river is destroyed by a huge pile of timber released by Val and Garm, who mingle with and destroy yet another band in the forest. As Skogul calls his remaining band together for the final

march on Vikingsholm, Val rushes to warn the King. On the way Val and the scouts contrive signs of the path of a monster and build a huge painted wooden dragon, hoping to frighten the superstitious brutes. By the time Val trots wearily into Vikingsholm, the conquering horde has become a fear-stricken mob. Berserk and drugged, Skogul falls into a river and drowns, and his army scatters. Aguar's armies find no one to battle. Boltar's navy handles the sea borne invading forces, and another short episode of peace comes to war-torn Thule.

99: ARN IN THE NEW WORLD
Pages 1455 (27 December 1964) – 1532 (19 June 66)

About 15 years earlier (strip-time), Aleta had promised the Indians of America that one day her son would return to bring greatness to the Algonquin tribe (see Story 34). Arn decides to return alone to fulfill the promise. Gundar Harl prepares a ship but has difficulty gathering a crew. Tillicum, who wishes to return to her homeland, helps Arn recruit a crew; they convince many men that they will make great profits trading with the Indians. More men join Arn after he miraculously survives a wreck of his small boat enroute to Trondheimfjord.

As Spring (ca. 471) arrives, the recruits gather at Boltarstead and start to make trade goods. After a farewell banquet, Gundar Harl's ship is supplied and launched. Using "Greek Fire," an inflammable oil, Gundar repels a pirate attack. The ship makes stops at the Faroe Islands (to load up with fuel), Iceland (to explore), and Greenland (to get water from the icebergs).

Arriving in the New World, the Vikings land at Newfoundland, stop for a while to celebrate and exchange gifts with the Indians, and then proceed down the St. Lawrence River. They are met by an Indian delegation. A battle ensues when an ambitious chieftain tries to gain status by keeping the "Sun-Woman's" son as a prisoner. The Northmen defeat the Indians and take the leader as a hostage as they continue upriver. A parlay with the hostile tribe is arranged, and hostages are exchanged—Tillicum and her son Hatha go to the Indian village, while the Indian boys go aboard the Viking ship. The meeting is a success: the chieftain is released, gifts are exchanged, Tillicum and Hatha are released. The two Indian boys stay with the Vikings, teach Arn to hunt, and help him barter for a canoe. Another group of Indians help haul the ship over the Lachine rapids.

After a stop to allow Tillicum to see her father, the Vikings arrive at the land of the Algonquins, where Arn was born. Arn plans to bring trade, prosperity, and civilization to the tribe. The Vikings build a huge house. The Algonquins plan for war with a tribe to the south. Arn is attacked by an enemy brave but is saved from an arrow by his chain mail. He then spies on the enemy tribe and returns to help with the war preparations. The enemy attacks. The Algonquins and Vikings repel the invaders but at the cost of a burnt village and many dead braves. Winter approaches, and the Vikings store sufficient food. They obtain additional food by trading with the peaceful Hurons. The Iroquois send raiders to steal some of the wealth of food but are repulsed by the Viking-trained Algonquins. A peace treaty between the Hurons, Iroquois and Algonquins is arranged.

Winter comes. Arn maps the territory and dreams of finding an overland route to the sea. Meanwhile, Hatha becomes friendly with Starlight, an Indian girl, in order to learn Indian ways. When Hatha and the girl exchange gifts, the twelve-year-old boy suddenly finds himself engaged, due to Indian custom! Arn helps his friend get out of the predicament without insulting the girl's parents. Arn celebrates his fifteenth birthday (he was born in page 551 in 1947, strip-time winter 456-457). As Spring nears (ca. 472), the Northmen begin to prepare for their voyage home. Because of Arn's efforts, the tribe has learned cooperation and a union of tribes is proposed. The Algonquin nation is born. The Vikings sail past Lachine, where Tillicum says farewell

OUR STORY: YUAN CHEN'S MESSAGE FROM THE EMPEROR OF THE MIDDLE KINGDOM IS A TONIC FOR THE WARRIORS OF CAMELOT: IT PROMISES ADVENTURE AND EXCITEMENT AND A CHANCE FOR GLORY. KING ARTHUR CONVENES THE ROUND TABLE. "THE LAST OF THE ANCIENT SPICE ROUTES HAS BEEN SEVERED BY THE HUNS AND THEIR ALLIES."

"THE EMPOROR PROPOSES A TREATY: A SHARE OF THE SPICE REVENUES IN RETURN FOR FINDING-- AND PROTECTING-- A NEW SPICE ROUTE."

AND WHO WILL LEAD THE QUEST? KING ARTHUR TURNS AS HE SO OFTEN HAS TO PRINCE VALIANT. "HAND PICK YOUR MEN AND COME BACK TO ME WITH A PLAN. WE MUST START AT ONCE." VAL SPENDS A DAY WITH YUAN CHEN AND HIS MAPS.

IT IS A DAZZLING PROSPECT. AT LAST THE KING WILL HAVE THE MONEY HE NEEDS TO FINISH THE REBUILDING OF HIS KINGDOM, RUINED BY MORDRED'S RULE. HIS OLD FRAME IS STRENGTHENED BY UNEXPECTED HOPE.

SOON A PLAN FORMS IN HIS HEAD. HE SAYS TO YUAN CHEN: "THE OLD SPICE ROUTES CROSSED THE DESERT WHERE CARAVANS WERE VULNERABLE TO BOTH THE HUNS AND THE WEATHER. LET US OPEN A NORTHERN ROUTE. RIVERS WILL CARRY US MOST OF THE WAY."

BY LAND AND SEA COURIERS CARRY A MESSAGE FROM KING ARTHUR TO THE EMPEROR OF THE MIDDLE KINGDOM: "WE ARE WITH YOU."
NEXT WEEK: BON VOYAGE

to her father. Guided by the Mohegans and Mohawks, Arn, Hath and some men go inland to map the overland route from the St. Lawrence to the sea. Gundar Harl sails on and makes plans to meet Arn later at the sea. A fight with the Mohawks interrupts the trip. The group reaches the Hudson River and travels its length.

Finally, after "fourteen" months (actually about 16), Arn's great adventure is completed. The route from the St. Lawrence to the sea has been mapped. Gundar has sailed the long route by sea (discovering the Gulf Stream on the way) and meets Arn at the lush island of Manhattan. The time comes to leave, and the trip across the ocean passes quickly and uneventfully.

("The Tournament," #1529-1531: Meanwhile, as Arn passes Ireland on his last stretch of the voyage home, Val is organizing a Viking tournament to bring some excitement to quiet Vikingsholm. However, when the "games" begin, Val and Aguar watch in horror as the battle-hardened veteran warriors abandon all the rules and turn the sporting event into a violent free-for-all. The trumpeter ends the games, but the enthusiastic Vikings don't stop until a table full of food and drink is set up near them). When the wanderers arrive home at last, there are many unashamed tears, and a happy week of feasting and storytelling follows.

COMMENT: Some panels from the original "New World" story from 1947 (#34) are reprinted in pages 1456, 1457 and 1483.

100: Mordred's Intrigue
Pages 1533 (26 June 1966) – 1551 (30 October 1966)

Rumor has it that the warlike Scottish tribes beyond the Roman Wall are uniting with the Picts for an invasion of Britain. Mordred is thought to be involved. Arn escorts his mother and siblings by sea to Camelot while Val takes the rugged route along the coast of Caledonia, hoping to gather information. Val learns the rumors of the raid on Britain are true and that Mordred is indeed behind the scheme. On foot north of the Wall, Val disguises himself as a soldier of fortune seeking employment and starts to infiltrate the enemy forces, hoping to cultivate the ancient distrust between the Picts and Scots. While Val spies on the camp, Mordred hears of the gadfly spreading discontent. While riding back to report to Arthur, Val is taken prisoner by the Scots. During a skirmish, he escapes and recovers the Singing Sword, which he had earlier lost. Having caused bloodshed and setting in flame the enmity between Pict and Scot, Val gallops southward toward the Wall and safety, hoping he has ruined Mordred's plans. In order to escape from his pursuers, Val hides in a mysterious Druid crypt. When he reaches Hadrian's Wall, Val warns all the guards to build up their defenses.

Mordred finally calls for the start of the invasion and is furious to find that neither the Scots nor Picts will attack first and that they prefer fighting against each other more than against Britain. Arthur's evil son gallops back to Camelot to make excuses, and when Val arrives at court, he is dismayed to find that Mordred has already arrived to claim the honor of preventing a costly war. Tired and frustrated, Val returns home to the comforting arms of his wife.

Meanwhile, evil Mordred realizes that Sir Valiant was the spy who ruined his invasion plans and also realizes that Val is the only one who knows the true cause of the current political situation. Thus he plans with Agravaine and Gaheris, his half brothers, to make Val suffer by harming his family and then kill him.

("First Love," #1546-1548: Meanwhile, the twins have reached the romantic age and proceed to fall in love with Sir Howard, the King's messenger. They become jealous and sad when Howard gives his attention to Freyda, an older woman.)

Arn sees Mordred acting suspiciously and so he warns his father of imminent danger. One day when Val apparently takes his family on a picnic, Mordred pays some peasants to kidnap Galan. The criminals are surprised to find they have only stolen a doll, and Prince Valiant is still there to punish them. Val sternly warns the frightened Mordred to see that no danger ever threatens his family again.

101: The Mermaid
Pages 1552 (6 November 1966) – 1555 (27 November 1966)

To relieve the boredom of a hot, dull day, Aleta takes her family to the seashore. After a swim with the children, the Queen of the Misty Isles finds what she thinks is a private grotto and tries some skinny-dipping. Val is surprised when rumors of water nymphs and mermaids reach Camelot and is amused to eventually find his wife to be the cause of the excitement. Aleta is embarrassed and acts demurely for several days thereafter.

("Back to Romance," #1555: When the seashore holiday is over, the twins resolve to settle their relationship once and for all. Realizing that the boy couldn't marry both of them anyway, Karen and Valeta start arguing and broken-heartedly break off their romancing.)

102: The Missing Heir
Pages 1556 (4 December 1966) – 1567 (19 February 1967)

Bala Burwult, an aged warrior from Dinmore, asks King Arthur's aid in finding Prince Harwick, the missing heir of dying King Bedwin. Sir Valiant is chosen to fulfill this sensitive mission, for a power struggle might result if the King dies without a proper heir. Hearing that the Prince is an avid fisherman, Val searches for him at rivers and soon finds his quarry, who hates court life and is disguised as a troubadour and fisherman named Owen. Clever Owen extracts Val's promise to keep his whereabouts a secret, and Val is torn between his duty to the King and his given word. Meanwhile, King Bedwin dies and his faithful chancellor Bala sends some horsemen on the mission to find the heir before his ambitious uncles usurp the throne. The old chancellor finds Owen/ Harwick and begs him to assume his duties, but the Prince is unmoved; he cares only about the love of a woman named Ruth. The crazed chancellor poisons Ruth and himself, leaving Harwick no choice but to take up his new responsibilities. Angry and hurt, Hatwick returns to his castle and is crowned, his chance for freedom and contentment gone. Val did not have to break either of his promises. Harwick forces his two ambitious uncles to swear fealty to him. Understanding his destiny and accepting his new life, Harwick desires to be a good King. Val helps Harwick establish King Arthur's merciful method of justice and then bids farewell, hoping Dinmore will be in good hands.

103: Enter Sir Reynolde
Pages 1567 (19 February 1967) – 1592 (13 August 1967)

Val leaves for Camelot and soon gains a merry companion—Sir Reynolde, son of Sir Hugo of Dinmore, who seeks his fortune at King Arthur's court. Val and Reynolde join a troupe of actors bound for Caldergarde to entertain at a wedding feast. Reynolde decides to have some fun masquerading as Prince Valiant, who enjoys his role as a minstrel. At castle Glenhaven Reynolde falls in love with golden-haired Lady Ann. However, Reynolde is jealous to learn that Sir Fould, an actor, is also trying to woo Ann. Now Reynolde finds the false role a burden. Fould convinces Ann to elope with the villain. Ann realizes she has been deceived but knows that Reynolde really loves her, so she hints that she will accept him once he has really proven himself. Reynolde vows to return to her after doing great deeds in Camelot. Upon arriving in Camelot, Val reports on his experiences in Dinmore to the King, while Reynolde learns about the arduous path to knighthood. After being assigned to beginner's classes, Reynolde meets Val's family and shows them that he knows little about fighting but much about horses. Geoffrey, the famous scribe and historian who was once an eager knight-in-training, is another guest in the Valiant house. King Arthur learns that Reynolde breeds splendid horses and is not a good warrior. When Reynolde is injured, Arthur has him help care for the King's mounts and also asks him to arrange a purchase of some of Sir Hugo's horses for Britain. Geoffrey accompanies Reynolde back to Dinmore and, by telling the boy his own life story, convinces him that being a warrior is not the only respectable occupation. (COMMENT: *Page 1585 uses redrawn and reprinted panels from the original story of Geoffrey, #43, from 1951.*)

In a turmoil, Reynolde arrives at Glenhaven to ask Ann's parents for her hand in marriage. There, Sir Bala Llanwyn, a rival, challenges Reynolde to a duel. Reynolde then goes home to recuperate, give his father the good news, and prepare for the coming duel. Realizing his young friend has no chance, Geoffrey prevents the fight by telling Bala he is interfering with the King's business and suggests he uses his fighting talents for a good cause at Camelot. Just before Reynolde leaves for Camelot with the horses, Ann's parents decide to give their daughter to him rather than to Bala. Furious, Bala leaves Dinmore and joins the group going to Camelot, where he observes the courteous behavior of the great knights and learns that a man does not have to be a bully. Reynolde is eventually appointed knight-custodian-of-horses by the King and rides happily out of our story to claim the hand of Lady Ann.

104: To Have and to Hold
Pages 1591 (6 August 1967) – 1599 (1 October 1967)

After a brief rest, Val hangs his shield in the Hall of Champions. Arthur has an assignment: he sends Val to Wickwain to straighten out a power struggle. Earl Clive has died, and his widow is disputing his half-brother's claim to the estate. Bala (from Story 103) goes with Val as his new squire and seems chiefly interested in fighting and plunder. Val reprimands the roughneck when he gets into an unnecessary fight with Noel, nephew of the late Earl, who is on his way to seek the King's justice. At Wickwain, Val, Bala, and Noel get a hostile reception from the new King Sligol. Lady Clive says her husband's will holds Wickwain in trust for the son of their daughter, Meg. In order to counter this opposition, Sligol decides to wed Lady Clive and have his son, Fonde, marry Meg. Of course, the ladies disgustedly refuse. The existence of the will is contested, and Val finds shreds of a likely looking document in Sligol's charcoal brazier. Noel rides to a neighbor, Sir Grenwold, who witnessed the will, to check its authenticity. Desperate, Sligol sends two of his armed guards in pursuit, but Prince Valiant stops the pursuers. Bala encounters Fonde assaulting Meg and interferes. Noel, Val and Sir Grenwold ride back to Wickwain to settle the inheritance question and find Meg and Bala holding off an attack by Sligol's men. The three find a secret passage into the castle and aid the two. The cowardly Fonde escapes into the forest. Sligol dies of a stroke. Bala risks his life by holding the castle until Val returns. Wickwain now legally returns to Lady Clive, and proud Bala falls in love with Meg, who indicates he might be an acceptable companion at some future date. Val rides back to Camelot with a changed, happy squire, eager to join in the upcoming hunting season.

105: The Berserker
Pages 1600 (8 October 1967) – 1605 (12 November 1967)

The traditional late autumn hunt and harvest is held at Camelot. King Arthur rides in front, excited and carefree. Aleta suffers an embarrassing incident when a stag charges her and removes her skirt. Prince Arn strays from the hunting party, loses his horse and meets an old hag and her demented, wild-looking son. He stays in her filthy hut overnight. The hag gives Arn a strange potion that will make him a wild berserker who will steal pretty things for her. Worried, Val and Aleta scour the forest in search of their son and find him wandering, dazed and bleeding. Arn is relieved to find he has done no great harm while drugged, and Val later burns the evil hag's hut. The hunt

ends successfully, and Camelot will be well stocked with provisions through the coming winter.

106: Slaves in Dathram
Pages 1606 (19 November 1967) – 1621 (3 March 1968)

After three weeks of relaxation, King Arthur comes home to problems. Sir Mordred reports that Gawain is being held for ransom by Balda Han in the land of Dathram. Meanwhile, when Val gets home, he finds Aleta is needed in the Misty Isles. Arthur gives Val leave to sail with her and instructs him to take care of the business in Dathram on the way. At Dathram's Mediterranean port, Val takes off in a small boat by himself and plans to join his family later in the Misty Isles. Val is allowed to travel with a caravan bringing plunder to Balda Han. In the desert the Governor has Val beaten, robbed and taken into slavery, hoping to get the ransom money without giving back any hostages. Val acts very cooperative but secretly plans to rescue Sir Gawain, recover his valuables and sword, and avenge the pain and humiliation. At Balda Han's walled stronghold, Val finds Gawain a slave. After finding a sword buried in an ancient crypt beneath the desert sands, Val plans action. The slaves are made to realize that they outnumber the guards ten to one. Gawain and Val, the only ones armed, attack some guards and thus arm more slaves, who rise up and rampage through the city. The Governor, one of the few who knows the way back through the desert, is made to give back Val's Singing Sword and taken captive. Balda Han is thrown to the angry mob. For three days the freed slaves loot and burn the city. Val wonders what the ultimate fate of these confused, now greedy, men will be. He sets off across the desert with Gawain, the ex-Governor and the ex-slaves. It takes two days to reach the first oasis, and by then many men have dropped from the heat and thirst. The Governor then leads Val to Dathram only after extracting a promise that he and his family will be spared and arranging for a somewhat non-violent takeover of the city. Back at Dathram the Governor sneakily has all the patrols disarm and gives the weapons to the freed slaves. Some are forced to pay tribute to the men they sold into slavery. Val remakes the laws of Dathram after Camelot's fair way. With pride, Val sets sail for the Misty Isles with Gawain and six dancing girls. Unfortunately, as soon as Val's ship is out of sight, the unscrupulous leaders of Dathram put the city back into its comfortable old decadent state.

107: Trouble in the Isles
Pages 1622 (10 March 1968) – 1635 (9 June 1968)

Aleta had returned to find her kingdom in deep trouble that the people were actually enjoying, and she is very relieved and happy to see Val step ashore. The Misty Isles have become weak because of too much wealth, luxury and laziness (again; see Story 83). The two greatest athletes, for example, have become so fat and lazy that they must be carried in a race by teams of servants. Aleta's laws have been corrupted and her armies have become unfit. Walking about the town, Val finds that only the merchants and nobles are wealthy. Most of the workers are really overtaxed, overworked and underpaid, and there are rumors of revolt. A group of pirates attacks the merchant fleet, and Val is angered to see the navy men ill equipped to defend their countrymen. Val is forced to take a few men and rescue a plundered merchant vessel himself. Some adventurous volunteers help Val eliminate the pirate threat. The seafaring spirit of the people is rekindled, and Val creates a new, more effective navy. Meanwhile, Queen Aleta is working with her legal advisors, trying to untangle a system that seems to have given all power to the rich. She calls in the City Council, chastising them for their selfish greed. The corrupt Lord of the Exchequer is sentenced to stay in prison until he fixes up his records. The remaining nobles are tricked into thinking that the Queen has secret, dangerous information on them and are forced to change their ways or resign. Val and Gawain proceed to train and re-equip the army and navy, hoping to make the Misty Isles not only prosperous but also secure.

108: ORTHO BEY
Pages 1635 (9 June 1968) – 1646 (25 August 1968)

Danger lurks in Lycia, where the ruthless Ortho Bey harries his neighbors by land and sea. It is thought that his greedy eyes might be looking toward the Misty Isles. On the pretext of forming a trade agreement with the Bey, the Queen sends spies, including her son Arn, to investigate. The suspicious Bey hopes that the childish prattle of a young Prince will reveal information, but Arn cleverly speaks of nothing but trade. Using a swim as an excuse to observe the passage of ships in the sea, Arn finds a secret war fleet being built. One day Arn meets a beautiful young girl and becomes infatuated until he realizes that she has been sent to obtain information about the strength of the Misty Isles. He cleverly tells her of the legendary prowess of the island's protectors, his father and Sir Gawain, and the Bey sends for historians to confirm the stories (Page 1643 is highlighted by reprints of some of the milestone scenes from earlier stories). The Bey believes he must be a greater leader and continues his evil plans. Just before the Feast of Zoroaster, the trade commission takes its leave of Lycia but, instead of immediately sailing away, first turns toward the secret shipyard and burns Ortho Bey's fleet. Bey, now bankrupt and powerless, is quickly deposed and killed by former "friends." Hearing of the danger her land might have been exposed to, Queen Aleta vows never to let the defenses of the Misty Isles become weak again.

109: AT HOME WITH THE KIDS
Pages 1646 (25 August 1968) – 1650 (22 September 1968)

The three younger children of Val and Aleta are beginning to grow up. Little Galand develops a strong will, discards some of his toys, and seriously starts pretending to be a warrior. The twins (who are now stated to be twelve years old) decide to stop being tomboys and discover that boys and girls are different. A divine spell of puppy love ensues. Meanwhile, Val and Arn long for their northern home and become restless. Captain Helge Hakkon is chosen to take the royal family to Thule. Queen Aleta spends a few last days tidying up her small kingdom. The twins and their tragic young lovers make great promises and part brokenheartedly. As the ship sails away, Aleta, Karen and Valeta look back sentimentally, while Val, Arn and Gawain gaze eagerly forward, thinking of the exciting adventures that will surely follow.

110: RETURN TO BRITAIN
Pages 1651 (29 September 1968) – 1672 (23 February 1969)

The long voyage to Britain begins unpleasantly, for the Captain and Katwin seem to dislike each other. Gawain becomes bored and asks to be let off at Tunis in order to sail for Marseilles. At the harbor, Val asks an old friend, Genseric, King of the Vandals, to provide transportation for Gawain. Years earlier, Genseric had delayed Val's marriage by sacking Rome (see Story 30) and now makes up for it by honoring Val and Aleta with a belated wedding feast and gifts. Gawain and Val sail their separate ways. Aleta decides to go shopping while the ship gets fresh water in a Barbary Coast port. At the bazaar, she and the twins are abducted by the treacherous El Muluk, who wishes that the golden women would grace his castle. Val and Arn angrily arm and gather their men and march towards the palace of "The Vulture." Entering the panicked palace through a small side passage, Arn rescues both Valeta and Karen as Val's men storm and burn the palace. Captain Hakkon enters El Muluk's harem in order to rescue Katwin, whom he really cares for. In the battle with a giant Nubian, Hakkon wins Katwin's freedom but injures his left arm very badly. Meanwhile, Val has found "The Vulture" in the wreckage and gives him a final taste of justice.

Only when everyone is safely out to sea does Helge permit himself the luxury of fainting. Katwin soon realizes that Captain Hakkon's shattered arm will never mend, and despite Helge's pleas, finds a surgeon to amputate the gangrenous limb. Helge is furious and bitter when he awakens from his coma.

As the ship sails past Gibraltar to the sea, Katwin cares for Helge during his slow recovery. He has lost his will to live. Aleta chastises the self-pitying Captain for ignoring Katwin's patient attention and makes him realize how much the woman cares for him. Helge finally forgets his misfortune and begins to recover. He plots a new course to speed the ship to Britain. Fearing that Helge's stubborn pride will end Katwin's dream of having her own home, Aleta arranges for him to meet Gundar Harl and learn how a serious handicap can be overcome. Helge is inspired by Gundar's prowess in shipbuilding, loses his despair, and enthusiastically plans a new future of shipbuilding.

Arn tires of the sea and decides to finish the journey to Camelot by land. He buys a horse and sets off. On the way, Arn befriends a starving, magnificent hound and becomes its master. The name "Skirnir" is chosen, after the servant of the gods in Norse mythology. Arn returns to Camelot before his parents.

About this time the marriage of Captain Helge Hakkon and Katwin takes place aboard ship. It is a simple ceremony of personal oaths, involving no absurd promises and no religion. Weighed down by the Queen's baggage, the plunder from Balda Han's palace and the tribute from Dathram, and the treasures of Ortho Bey, Val and Aleta slowly make the final short trip to Camelot and resume their respective duties.

COMMENT: *This is the last time we see Katwin, the handsome Amazon, who was Aleta's handmaiden and children's governess since 1946 (about 18 years in strip time).*

111: GAWAIN'S MISADVENTURES
Pages 1672 (23 February 1969) – 1681 (27 April 1969)

As Val reports to King Arthur, Gawain rides raggedly into Camelot astride a mule. He proceeds to spend a rowdy night telling Val, the King, and the other knights about his journey from Tunis and Marseilles. At Marseilles Gawain tried to seduce the Governor's wife, so he had to escape from the prison he was put in as well as the cutthroats hired to ventilate his magnificent body. Lyons, Gawain's next destination, was the site of some losing gambling. Next, Gawain was on foot in a storm and was picked up by a widowed lady who brought him to her castle. Unfortunately, the lady's suitor became jealous and challenged Gawain to a joust. Gawain won, claimed the rival's horse as prize, and escaped from a fate worse than death—marriage! Relieved, Gawain entered a nearby tournament, won and had to fight off some thieves who coveted his prize money. The great knight sailed from Rouen toward Britain with a great sorcerer who, upon landing, stole Gawain's money and horse. This is why Arthur's nephew had returned to Camelot in such a sorry state.

112: ARN, THE POACHER
Pages 1682 (4 May 1969) – 1683 (11 May 1969)

Arn tries to train his dog, Skirnir, as a hunter, but the great hound mistakenly kills a sheep. By law, a sheep-killing dog must die. The shepherd prepares to kill Skirnir, but Arn claims responsibility and pays him double the animal's value. Upset over his law-breaking, Arn returns home.

113: THE SAXON DILEMMA
Pages 1683 (11 May 1969) – 1696 (10 August 1969)

When Arthur defeated the Saxon army at Badon Hill (Story 96) and drove them back into the sea, scattered bands settled in Essex. Now the Saxons are being harried by Vikings from Anglia, raiders who have also become settlers, and they ask for King Arthur's help. Arthur calls his council together and asks for suggestions. It is decided to hold ready a mounted force until the King's representative learns the facts. Naturally, Val is chosen to go as the King's representative, and he rides away on Arvak with the Saxons after saying goodbye to Aleta once again.

PRINCE VALIANT, HERO OF MANY AN ADVENTUROUS JOUST IN THE DAYS OF KING ARTHUR, SENDS HIS YOUNG SON ARN FORTH TO EXPLORE A SNOWY PASS THROUGH THE MOUNTAINS... BUT NOT WITHOUT THE PROTECTION AND GUIDANCE OF A FAITHFUL RETAINER, GARM.

ALETA, PRINCE VAL'S BEAUTIFUL WIFE, FEARFUL FOR HER SON'S SAFE RETURN, HIDES HER TEARS, KNOWING THAT THEIR BOY-CHILD MUST GROW UP TO TAKE HIS RIGHTFUL PLACE AT KING ARTHUR'S ROUND TABLE...

UPON HIS RETURN, ARN, FLUSHED WITH SUCCESS, PREPARES TO SWAGGER HIS WAY BEFORE THE KING TO BRAG OF HIS FIRST HEROIC DEEDS, AS ANY NATURAL BOY WOULD DO... EVEN IN THOSE ROMANTIC FAR-OFF DAYS.

NOW FOLLOW THIS ABSORBING STORY IN TODAY'S COLOR COMICS SECTION.

At Essex, the Saxon settlers complain that Arthur leaves them in peace so long as they do not build forts, but without fortifications they are at the mercy of the Viking raiders. Satisfied that the settlers are obeying the King's laws, Val leads his troops northward into Anglia to confront the outlawed Vikings. Val confronts Thoric, the chieftain, who had once been exiled by King Aguar from Thule, and offers a possible pardon in return for peace in Britain. Contemptuous of the two sanctimonious Christian Kings, a brawny warrior named Thorkell provokes a duel to the death with Val and loses. Thorkell's brother, frenzied, declares a blood feud but is also done in by Sir Valiant's agile swordsmanship. Stubborn Thoric decides that his Vikings will harry Britain's shores until they are paid tribute and expels Val from the camp. Arthur's troops bait the Vikings into coming out of the impregnable fort by catapulting fireballs. On foot, the storming Vikings are surprised and forced to retreat to the sea by the mounted knights hidden in the forest. Blood-stained, weary, and defiant, Thoric makes one last stand, but a mighty blow on the helmet with the flat of Val's sword brings him down. Rather than killing his foe, Val gives him a quest: to go to King Aguar, offer his services, and be judged by the King to whom he was once false.

114: WHO BREAKS THE PEACE?
Pages 1697 (17 August 1969) – 1705 (12 October 1969)

A violent tempest makes the homeward march along the coast long and difficult. Hoping to escape the rain, Val crawls into a dark cave near the beach, where he finds a hidden cache of arms large enough to outfit a thousand men. They are of Saxon make. This presumably means the peace is to be broken and another period of warfare is being planned. Scouts are sent to locate the troublemakers. Sir Halwyn, the King's armorer, leads a company of knights to gather firewood and burn the secret arsenal.

After the scouts find the enemy camp, occupied by men who appear to be warriors from across the sea rather than settlers, Val and a few knights call on the enemy chieftain. Earl Thundros appears to be a formidable leader and plans to settle for nothing less than all of Britain. Realizing such a man could arouse the Saxons to unite once more, Val gives him three days to dismantle the fortress. Sneering, Thundros marches to the beach openly with his men, thinking he can easily take Arthur's knights with the hidden weapons. Horrified, his followers find their cave white hot and empty. The knights easily capture the unarmed raiders, and Val sentences the chief to be judged by King Arthur.

The long march to Camelot begins. The problem of guarding and feeding an army of prisoners is solved by letting most of them escape; those who survive to reach the Saxon settlements will help Britain by informing all of the Saxons of King Arthur's powerful knights and great victories. Aleta cries with happiness when she receives a tender letter reporting Val's imminent return.

("The Unicorn Hunt," #1703-1704: Inspired by his mother's bedtime stories, Galan sets off to capture a unicorn. First he must find a maiden pure of heart, for only such a girl can bridle a unicorn. After finding an appropriate little girl to help, Galan finds a one-horned goat and brings it home. Aleta is not impressed, and she sends the girl home and the goat back to the dump.)

A few days after, Prince Valiant leads his weary knights and Saxon prisoners into Camelot. His business completed, our hero becomes just another married man. King Arthur sees what a dangerous man Thundros could be and sadly beckons to his headsman to resolve the problem.

115: THE ENCHANTRESS
Pages 1705 (12 October 1969) – 1708 (2 November 1969)

Valeta sees the power her mother has over her father, studies her techniques, and sets out to trouble a few hearts. After a careful survey of potential victims, Valeta picks a handsome lad practicing at archery. Ecstatic, Valeta gets the boy so bemused he will do anything she asks. Climbing a tree to pick her an apple, he falls and breaks a leg. Karen, the forthright one, rushes to his side, sets the leg, and has him sent to the infirmary. Jealous, Valeta attacks her sister, and the twins enjoy a short, satisfying burst of pent-up violence.

116: GEOFFREY'S FULFILLMENT
Pages 1708 (2 November 1969) – 1716 (28 December 1969)

King Arthur sends Val to Carlisle to report on the northern fiefs. Prince Arn is to accompany his father as far as Chester and then visit King Cuddock of Wales, to assure him of Britain's assistance against sea raiders. On the Roman-built road, they are interrupted by an encounter with Sieur du Laci and his daughter, Adele, and partner, Yousef. Years ago Sieur du Laci had sailed with Val on his return to Britain from Rome, and Adele had made a childish pact with Geoffrey (Story 44). Adele tells Arn her father has promised her in marriage to Yousef, who frightens her. The next morning they go their separate ways: Du Laci to Camelot and Val and Arn to the north. Val rides on as Arn goes alone to visit Cuddock. A dragonship from Thule lands at the port to buy supplies, and Geoffrey is aboard. Arn tells his friend about Adele and Yousef and sends him to Camelot. After Adele and Geoffrey meet and excitedly rekindle their love, Yousef threatens the poet's life. Geoffrey leaves the choice to Adele, who chooses Yousef only in order to save the life of the man she really loves. Yousef still tries to kill Geoffrey but is captured by the palace guards. Sir Kay informs him that the punishment for attacking a favored storyteller is death, but as a stranger he is merely banished. However, Yousef sneaks back to Camelot, filled with hatred. Sieur du Laci approves the marriage of Geoffrey and Adele. Yousef tries to enter Adele's room by climbing a tree. Just as he crawls in the window, Adele slams the shutters closed, causing the madman to fall to his death. A great wedding feast is then held.

117: ARN'S SERVITUDE
Pages 1717 (4 January 1970) – 1727 (15 March 1970)

Meanwhile, after finishing his mission, Arn had ridden up the Welsh coast to report on the condition of the watchtowers that guard against raiders. Arn tries a shortcut home when his horse plunges into a bog and sinks away! Sadly, the Prince uses his spear to end the horse's agony. Now, without shield, helmet, cloak or food, Arn attempts to cross the rugged lands on foot. By following game trails he finds passes through the mountains. He encounters an armed group going in the same direction and is forced to join a group of captives under guard. They are taken to the grim fortress of Llanwick to be slaves in his tin mine. When Llanwick realizes his new slave is from the wealthy Valiant family, he decides to make the boy his personal servant and try to get a large ransom for him. Arn takes advantage of his position to study the fortress and plan an escape. Since the fortress is impregnable and escape is impossible, it must be destroyed. He soon escapes by setting a huge destructive fire that guts Llanwick's castle. Meanwhile, Prince Valiant has received the ransom note and sets off to rescue his son. As the furious Llanwick pursues Arn with his hounds, Val catches up, saves his son, and leaves Llanwick's fate to be decided by the people he mistreated. Arn and his father report on their respective missions to King Arthur.

118: THE VANISHING DEER
Pages 1728 (22 March 1970) – 1731 (12 April 1970)

While hunting in his private park, Arthur discovers that all his deer are gone. When Val investigates, he finds that his old friend, Hugh-the-Fox (see Story 32), is responsible. The former outlaw explains that his men were facing starvation, and Val convinces Arthur to give Hugh's band freedom of the forest by making them wardens. (*COMMENT: It is said that this is about 15 years after Hugh's pardon [Story 32], but that was in about 455 AD, a few years before Arn was born. Since Arn is now considerably over 15 [he had a 15th birthday in Story 96], this must be closer to AD 474 than 470. Foster's chronology in these later years became very inconsistent, unlike in the earlier years of the strip.*)

119: AH! WOMEN!
Pages 1732 (19 April 1970) – 1759 (25 October 1970)

Chivalry, the age of romance, envelops Camelot like an epidemic. (*COMMENT: As noted in the introduction, this is an anachronism. The age of chivalry (meaning the general code of behavior of knights, not just an attitude towards women) in England really was from about 1100-1300, though this story ostensibly takes place in approximately the early-mid 470s.*)

Dale Makinnie arrives at Camelot to win his golden spurs. Dale yearns to become champion of a beautiful maiden. As he searches Camelot to find a lady fair worthy to be his Lady-In-Domini, he sees Aleta. In the tournament, Dale wins the right to challenge a knight of the Round Table and picks one of the most renowned, Sir Gawain. Gawain plucks the young upstart from his saddle. Dale thus learns that the Knights of the Round Table are not ordinary men and that he has a long way to go before he can earn a place among them.

Prince Arn befriends the dejected young man, and Dale is embarrassed when he meets his friend's mother: Aleta, the ideal lady unobtainable. Dale's infatuation is increased. While Aleta tries to cure Dale's infatuation for her by interesting him in a maid his own age, 12 year old Karen decides to become his lady fair and pursues him like a huntress. (*COMMENT: Foster has been holding Karen and Valeta at this age for several years now!*)

Meanwhile, Lady Marvyn asks King Arthur to help her with her absent son's disrupted inheritance. At Val's suggestion, Dale is sent to help, and he is thrilled when Aleta gives him her handkerchief as a token before he rides

off. Dale soon finds that the Lady is more interested in killing her villainous brother-in-law, Sir Lowary, than in the claim. Dale hears rumors that Lady Marvyn's son is actually dead. Both the Lady Marvyn and Sir Lowary insult and bait Dale, but he holds his temper.

Dale meets Lady Marvyn's stepdaughter, Matilda, Lord Marvyn's daughter by his first wife, and she warns him that Lowary plans to kill him by provoking him to a duel. Lowary is fierce and has never been defeated, but when Sir Lowary blows his nose into Aleta's handkerchief, Dale becomes enraged and kills him.

Dale is now treated as a hero by Lady Marvyn. Slowly Matilda falls in love with him, though he still dreams of Aleta. In order to remain mistress of her fief, Lady Marvyn needs a husband and chooses Dale. She seethes when she finds he prefers Matilda, her despised and neglected stepdaughter. The Lady dies when she mistakenly drinks poisoned wine intended for Matilda. Matilda becomes the temporary mistress of Castle Marvyn until a rightful heir can be found. After a thorough investigation, it is found that the son of the late Lord Marvyn had indeed died as a child, meaning Matilda would retain control. The mission completed, Dale prepares to return to Camelot, and Matilda comes along with him. As he had dreamed of, Dale reports his activities to King Arthur. Gradually, Dale falls in love with the innocent Matilda. At Aleta's urging, King Arthur knights Dale in order to give him authority at Marvyn Castle and, he hopes, to restore Marvyn fief to its former strength and strategic importance.

After the wedding of Dale and Matilda a hunt is organized at Marvyn Castle. Prince Arn gets lost while tracking a wild boar and stumbles upon Chariot Garde, castle of the sorceress Morgan Le Fay. Seeking revenge against her enemy Prince Valiant, Morgan takes Arn hostage. Val enters Merlin's laboratory, which has been locked since Merlin disappeared, in search of magic to use against the evil woman. As Le Fay hoped, Val comes to pit his amateurish magic against her sorcery. By coincidence, just as Val insists on Arn's release, the boy escapes from the dungeon, exactly as Val had done years ago. Father and son return to Marvyn Castle to join the end of the hunt.

COMMENT: This is noted to be eighteen years since the day Val had first fought Le Fay for the release of Sir Gawain (Story 8), which is again inconsistent with our chronology. Note that Le Fay's castle was called "Dolorous Garde" in Story 8. Page 1757, ghosted by Gray Morrow in a very Foster-like style, is the first page not drawn predominantly by Foster himself, although Foster was known to have some assistants over the years.

120: THE END OF ROMANCE
Pages 1759 (25 October 1970) – 1815 (21 November 1971)

Sir Valiant must return to Camelot and agrees to escort the flirtatious and pretty Lady Donat. When her horse is injured, Val chivalrously lets her ride in his lap. Aleta, waiting anxiously for Val to return, sees him ride into Camelot with a strange woman in his arms and furiously banishes her husband from their home. Foolish pride maintains a wall of ice between the two, even when the cause of the rift is forgotten. Val rides off to find solace in adventure, not knowing that Aleta has decided to forget her foolish jealousy and take him back.

Val is invited to spend a night in the stronghold of Sir Astaric, where he ends up helping young Guiveric rescue his lover, a fair blonde maiden imprisoned by Astaric in a grim tower. After this battle, Val wanders off, still dejected over his loss of Aleta, and he roams the countryside. Meanwhile, Aleta sails for the Misty Isles on the ship of Gundar Harl.

Tiring of his nomadic existence, Val ends his wanderings at the town where Merlin was born. There the old philosopher Lionors inspires Val to begin his greatest quest: the second winning of Queen Aleta. Quickly, Val returns to Camelot, where Arn tells his father that Aleta had decided to take him back many weeks earlier. Realizing his foolishness, Val immediately sets off with Arn in search of Aleta. A roundabout route to the Misty Isles is necessary, for all of Europe is aflame with wars. Sir Launcelot helps Val sail across the English Channel to Brittany. Aided by Launcelot's friend, Ben Zirara, Val and Arn ride south towards the Mediterranean Sea. ("The Braggart," #1792-1795: They stop to rest at the castle of Sieur Delauncy and are delayed by a Goth attack, in which Delauncy is killed.) Finally, Val and Arn sail to Algiers en route to the Misty Isles. Zirara leads them along the North African coast and across a great desert. They leave Ben Zirara at his home, Quel Hajed, and set off across the desert alone, guided only by the stars.

Meanwhile, Aleta reaches the Misty Isles and resumes her queenly duties. She meets a mysterious visitor, Ortho of Kos, who suggests that a search party be sent along the African coast to look for Val. Two extra ships are secretly sent along to kill Sir Valiant for Ortho, who secretly wants to marry Aleta and become King of the Misty Isles. The search vessel arrives at the African port of Gabes just as Val and his son arrive there, lost. As the escort vessel prepares to take Val and Arn home, Ortho's men attack. After some vigorous swordplay and a bit of subtle trickery, Prince Valiant gains possession of the enemy ship and discovers Ortho's plot. After a few days, Aleta's family is happily reunited in the Misty Isles. Guards sent to arrest Ortho find that he has been killed by a dirty, crazed beggar who had learned of his treachery.

COMMENT: *Page 1760 is the first one drawn by John Cullen Murphy, who also did numbers 1764-1767, 1769-1772, 1774, 1775, 1777, and 1778. Page 1762 was ghosted by Wallace Wood, while 1765 was a second page done by Gray Morrow. Apparently Wood and Morrow were auditioning for the art job, but Foster preferred Murphy, who completed pages 1777-1787 and 1789-on from Foster's scripts and layouts. Page 1788 (reprinted as a large full-color poster by Manuscript Press) is the last done totally by Foster except for #2000. Murphy's art was at first very similar to Foster's but gradually became somewhat cruder and less detailed, taking away some but by no means all of the strip's rich atmosphere.*

121: THE VANISHING GROOM
Pages 1816 (28 November 1971) – 1821 (2 January 1972)

While wandering near the waterfront, Karen and Valeta meet a young man, Zanedon, who fled from his family to escape an intolerable marriage. The mischievous twins agree to hide him in a stable. Aleta hears of the marital conflict and sends her troubleshooter, Amiens, to investigate. Amiens and the jilted bride, Helen, fall in love and marry, and a feud between the families of Zanedon and Helen is avoided.

122: THE INDOLENT CITY
Pages 1822 (9 January 1972) – 1834 (2 April 1972)

Arn's new friend, Prince Gian of Dondaris, is called home because of the death of his father, the King. Arn goes with Gian for the funeral and new coronation. Despite surface appearances, Arn finds Dondaris to be a weak, indolent, unstable kingdom. News of an uprising led by Silas "The Liberator" confirms Arn's suspicions. With Arn as second-in-command, the new King Gian quenches the rebellion, despite the blunders of his ineffectual army. On Arn's advice, Gian listens to the rebel's complaints and promises to help improve their serf-like living conditions.

123: THEFT OF THE SINGING SWORD
Pages 1835 (9 April 1972) – 1841 (21 May 1972)

Val sails to Dondaris to bring Arn home. While Val sleeps at the palace, Klept the jewel thief steals the Singing Sword and flees the city. Val tracks him down in a nearby mountainous forest and recovers his charmed sword.

124: THE LONELY KING
Pages 1842 (28 May 1972) – 1859 (24 September 1972)

Val wanders off absent-mindedly after recovering his sword and enters the city of Atheldag, where he meets the restless, unhappy King Dashad. ("Val's Story," #1846: Val reminisces about his life, philosophy, and fated "lack of contentment.") Val decides that it is his knightly duty to make a man of the fat little tyrant. The two leave on a hunting and fishing trip, and "Dash" is forced to be self-reliant for the first time. Along the way, Dash learns much about the problems of his kingdom, and he returns a new man with many reforms to institute in Atheldag.

125: THE ROMANCERS
Page 1860 (1 October 1972)

This is a charming, tongue-in-cheek page about the stories troubadours and poets told about Prince Valiant, who apparently was quite a legend even in his own lifetime.

126: THE AMOROUS POET
Pages 1861 (8 October 1972) – 1870 (10 December 1972)

Val returns to the Misty Isles and then journeys with his family to Camelot. Val and Arn land at mid-voyage to exercise their horses and encounter Jacques Augustus, "King of the Troubadours," as he flees from some jealous husbands whose wives he had serenaded. They take him aboard their ship. At another rest stop, Jacques meets Joan, a young juggle girl, in the harbor town. Joan's brothers are killed in a barroom brawl. Val takes the sad girl aboard his ship, where she and Jacques fall in love and decide to marry.

127: BOLTARSON
Pages 1870 (10 December 1972) – 1885 (25 March 1973)

Sailing to Britain, Val and his family are forced by a violent band of Viking raiders to land in Brittany, at Launcelot's castle. The Vikings attack the castle but are defeated and turned back. One injured Viking is left behind when the others flee, and he turns out to be Hatha, son of Val's friend, Boltar the Sea King. Arn decides to visit his Viking homeland, Thule, with Boltarson. Naturally, they encounter much excitement along the way, including a battle with some Picts.

128: ARN'S ADVENTURES
Pages 1885 (25 March 1973) – 1959 (25 August 1974)

Arn arrives at Vikingsholm and is promptly sent by his grandfather, Aguar, to attend the coronation of Prince Heidmar of the little inland kingdom of Holvik. Apparently, Heidmar is not eager to begin the boring, confining life of a king. When a murder attempt fails, Heidmar welcomes the opportunity to pretend it had succeeded and slips away to lead what he hopes will be a carefree, exciting life. As Aguar's emissary, Arn stays to attend the coronation of Heidmar's ambitious cousin, Grimner, who had arranged the "accident" that "killed" Heidmar. Arn then returns to Vikingsholm and reports on his experiences to King Aguar.

While wandering about Aguar's palace, Arn meets a lovely, brown haired maiden who soon mysteriously disappears. This girl is Lydia, daughter of Haakon the Sea Rover, and it seems that she ran away because she thought that Prince Arn would never marry a commoner. Arn discovers her identity and sails to Haakon's homeland, Tosenfjord, which coincidentally is adjacent to the new kingdom of Grimner.

("Grimner's Downfall," #1897-1905: Arn anticipates an attack by Grimner on Haakon's lands and sends for soldiers from Vikingsholm. Haakon's Vikings, aided by Arn's army, easily repulse the disorganized raiders from the Inner

Lands. Arn is injured in the battle, so Aguar sends for Val to replace Arn. Grimner is assassinated by army chiefs who disapprove of his ambitiousness. Frieda, Grimner's widow, commits suicide. Val installs Haakon as new King of Holvik. Lydia thus becomes royalty, and her romance with Arn can continue.)

When Lydia's long-lost brother Thorvold visits, Arn sees the brother and sister embrace. Thinking the girl was greeting a long-lost sweetheart, Arn returns to Vikingsholm, jealous and broken-hearted. Arn soon decides to take to the sea; hoping adventure will ease his sorrow. Simultaneously, Lydia travels to Vikingsholm to explain Arn's mistake, but she arrives too late, for Arn has already departed. Aleta invites the saddened girl to spend the winter at Vikingsholm.

Arn's crew gradually becomes bored and disgruntled by the difficult winter traveling, so the men eventually abandon their master. In Paris, Arn decides to "play to the hilt" his new role as knight errant and purchases a fancy new wardrobe. He also finds a squire, the roguish Peter Paul Mathhew Mark Trywellyn of Wales. The two soon begin their melancholy travels.

One Spring afternoon they come upon the castle of Sieur De Volnay and are invited to stay for a week or so. There is a siege and blockade at the castle, and unsanitary conditions soon cause an epidemic of the dreaded "plague." Just before the siege is completed and the castle is destroyed, Paul and Arn escape with a little girl, whom they name Squirrel.

The southward journey continues, and the three encounter Sir Gawain, who is at the city of Nevers for a tournament. Arn enters the tournament but is inexperienced at jousting and is forced to withdraw. Paul seems to be tired of the responsibility of tending Squirrel and starts to run away, but he changes

his mind and returns to get married and raise the young girl in a proper family setting.

Arn sets off with Gawain across Gaul to participate in more tournaments. Meanwhile, Lydia has sent her brother, Thorvold, to find Arn, and the search ends at Valence. Arn finally is made to realize his stupid mistake and eagerly begins a return trip to Thule. Haste causes Arn and Gawain to become lost in ("The Forgotten Land," #1938-1945: The two knights stumble upon a beautiful lost land located in a lush valley from which no one can easily escape. In order to continue their trip, they must tangle with the Mad Duke, Cyril the Tenth, who is madly in love with a woman he doesn't realize is long dead.)

Riding on, Arn and Gawain are forced by a storm to stop again, this time at the chateau of Lady Millicent, who forces them to escort her to Paris, where her husband is gallivanting. Sir Gawain then sails back to Britain, while Arn rides along the windy coast seeking a ship to take him to Thule. Countless delays, the uncertainty of his reception at home, and the pain of an arm broken in a brawl adds to Arn's misery. Finally, Arn sails to Thule and is happily reunited with his family and with Lydia.

COMMENT: *It is noted that the story takes place during the so-called Dark Ages, in the early days of the feudal system, which is roughly correct historically. Page 1926 (1-6-74) was mislabeled as #1974.*

129: KARAK THE TERRIBLE
Pages 1960 (1 September 1974) – 1972 (24 November 1974)

Hap Atla, King of the Inner Lands, seeks Aguar's help in saving his kingdom from the giant Karak, whose power strikes terror in the hearts of all who oppose him. Val is sent with an army. Val enters Karak's camp posing as a wandering troubadour. Eventually, Karak decides to kill the intruder, but Val tricks the simple giant into drowning in a shallow river. Hap Atla's army makes quick work of the rest of Karak's band.

130: The Improbable Journey
Pages 1972 (24 November 1974) – 1975 (15 December 1974)

Val gives young Galan a hobbyhorse for his birthday, and Galan has fantasies about riding it through exotic lands and rescuing fair maidens in distress.

131: The Lady of Quality
Pages 1975 (115 December 1974) – 1980 (19 January 1975)

Kept inactive by a sprained ankle, Val amuses his family and gives information to Court Historian Geoffrey by telling the story of how the beautiful Lady Allison once saved the lives of Sir Gawain and his young squire, Prince Valiant.

132: The Pirate Raid
Pages 1981 (26 January 1975) – 1999 (1 June 1975)

The evil, ambitious Bella Grossi attempts to assemble an empire by laying waste to the Northern lands. Val sets sail for Thessalriga, trade center of the Baltic, to seek the aid of King Leofric in the coming conflict. Val helps to secure the city, but the traitorous Lord Dupuy undermines Thessalriga's defenses. Bella Grossi's raiders easily enter the harbor. As a winter storm numbs the invaders, the hardy Northmen fight back and repulse the pirates. Thessalriga is saved, and Bella Grossi freezes to death when he tries to escape in a small, uncovered boat. Val returns to Camelot, his messy work completed.

COMMENT: The last panoramic drawing of the story, simply captioned "Bella Grossi Returns to Thessalriga," is one of the most subtle, grimly clever, and atmospheric panels ever done in the comic art medium. It is an exemplary use of "visual-verbal blend," a term used by analysts of comic art to describe the interdependence of words and pictures, which is one of the defining hallmarks of good comic art and was too seldom exhibited in Prince Valiant.

133: Milestones in the Story of Prince Valiant
Page 2000 (8 June 1975)

A lighthearted review of Val's long, exciting career, illustrated with reprinted and/or redrawn panels by Hal Foster.

COMMENT: KFS issued a large, full color poster/print of this wonderful anniversary page, which was the last ever to be signed by Foster and graced with his solo illustrations. Foster was said to have continued doing the scripts and coloring, however, for several more years.

134: Another Eventful Journey
Pages 2001 (15 June 1975) – 2032 (18 January 1976)

Aleta must return to the Misty Isles, as royal decree requires her to do every so often. Simultaneously, Val is bored in peaceful Camelot and misses his family. Val impatiently leaves the city but is forced to stop at a smelly little villa when the wintry weather gets too severe. There he meets an old friend, the inept wizard (now "physician") Oom-Fayat (Val's memory flashback to the first time he met Oom [Story 38] is illustrated by an old Foster drawing). Val continues his journey across Britain with Oom tagging along. At Londinium Val finds a ship and begins his journey to Thule. By chance his ship overtakes that of Gundar Harl, which is taking Aleta to the Misty Isles, and the entire family is together once more, except for Arn, who remained in Thule.

("The Wild People," #2009-2014: Meanwhile, Arn grows restless at Thule and decides to visit Lydia. While looking for a river crossing, he gets lost in a maze of mountains and valleys. He meets the twin princes, Hantz and Falla. When the aggressive Falla kills his brother [and rival for the throne] in an angry skirmish, he is banished from his homeland. Arn gladly leaves these brutal people.)

Val's ship lands at mid-journey for supplies. An evil wizard, Hashida, falls in love with the beautiful Aleta. While the Queen of the Misty Isles is shopping, Hashida hypnotizes and kidnaps her. Val tracks them to Hashida's mountain retreat and rescues his beloved wife. Val and his family continue their trip to the Misty Isles, and they are asked to drop young Hector off at Spain. Hector becomes a victim of the romantic mischief of the twins. At a Spanish port, the scheming Duke Julian tries to reopen a profitable trade agreement with the Misty Isles by befriending Aleta. When a ravaging fire breaks out in the town, the serfs become enraged and storm Julian's palace. Prince Valiant leads his family out of the pillaged mansion, not without some difficulty. Hector is finally left at Cadiz, where he is to continue his education.

After another stop to shop at Tangiers, the voyage is continued. Aleta buys a young slave, Zilla, to be her secretary. Finally, the journey is over, and the Queen of the Misty Isles resumes her throne. She finds her kingdom peaceful.

COMMENT: This adventure is said to be taking place "18 years" after Val first met Aleta, which "actually" happened in page 208, 34 years earlier in real time (see Story 18). According to a letter in our possession from Foster to fan Kurt Gore dated Jan. 1976, "...Prince Valiant is approximately 38 at this time; Aleta-35; Arn, 16; Twins, 14, and Galan, 5 years old." However, internal evidence from the stories (e.g. time said to have elapsed between events and other references to the passage of time and seasons, etc.) can lead to several differing estimates of the characters' ages and birth dates. Again, Foster seemingly became less concerned about a realistic and consistent passage of time in these later stories.

135: Treasure of the Bats
Pages 2032 (18 January 1976) – 2050 (23 May 1976)

Zilla, who now has little work to do, falls in love with Tamia, the little handmaiden Aleta had also purchased in Tangiers. In order to buy the girl

WHILE VAL WANDERS IN THE GREAT MAGICIAN'S ENCHANTED GARDEN.

from Aleta, Zilla leads Sir Valiant on a treasure hunt at a ruined palace. The search almost ends in disaster when Val nearly drowns in a pool of quicksand. After much careful investigation, Val stumbles upon the treasure by falling into a stinking bat roost. Satisfied with whatever wealth he could carry away, Zilla returns with Val to the Misty Isles in order to regain his beloved Tamia.

136: THE QUEST FOR HELENE
Pages 2050 (23 May 1976) – 2076 (21 November 1976)

Helene, Aleta's younger sister, is very unhappy. When her husband, Dionseus, was banished for treachery and cowardice years earlier (Story 61), pride and love made her share his fate. Now, desperate for money, Dionseus writes to Aleta asking for aid and threatening the safety of Helene. Val gathers together a hardy crew and sets sail for Samos and another confrontation with his brother-in-law. Meanwhile, however, Dionseus has lost all his possessions, including Helene, in a gambling game and is killed for cheating by the notorious Corsair, Ajaxos. Helene is taken to Ajaxos' ship with the rest of his plunder and they leave Samos just as Val arrives. After a long search, Val finds Ajaxos' ship at Thessalonica. There, Val gets involved in some violent political struggles, and there is much fighting before Helene is finally rescued. Aleta's lovely dark-haired sister decides to remain in Thessalonica and marry the new king, Telamon. Val eagerly gets ready to return home. As usual, there is a delay —a violent barroom brawl with a bully named "Ivosh the Terrible"—but finally the long quest is completed without incident.

COMMENT: *This story uses elements suggested by Bill Crouch.*

137: KING OF THE MINSTRELS
Pages 2077 (28 November 1976) – 2093 (29 March 1977)

Arn, a future candidate for the throne of Thule, travels to Camelot to study statecraft for a year or two. Sir Dinadan, the Court Jester, is assigned by Arthur to be Arn's teacher. Arn and Dinadan eventually take a leave of absence to attend a convention of troubadours in France. Every three years, it seems, the entertainers gather at Poitiers to elect their "King of Minstrels," and the present King, Lazare, is an evil man who sends spies to every castle to gather saleable information. Arn helps install Bertram, a benevolent and deserving man, as the new King of the Minstrels. Arn and Dinadan return to Camelot, disappointed that their trip brought little excitement.

138: QUEST FOR THE RELICS
Pages 2093 (20 March 1977) – 2110 (17 July 1977)

Back at the Misty Isles, Val and Aleta take in Sir Gunther of Germany, a heroic shipwreck victim. Gunther was traveling in search of valuable holy relics that had been stolen from his family. Val accompanies Gunther to Alexandria and Jerusalem in order to track the thieves. At Jerusalem Val and Gunther stay as guests in the safety of Sheik Abdul El Mohammed's palace. Gunther falls in love with the Sheik's daughter, Zara, who nurses him back to health after he is injured in a tavern brawl. With Val's aid Gunther tracks down and kills the thieves and recovers the treasure. Gunther then asks the Sheik for Zara's hand in marriage but is refused. Luckily, he soon finds another girl to court, while Val departs.

139: PETROPOLIS
Pages 2111 (24 July 1977) – 2128 (20 November 1977)

Khazan II, Warlord of the Persians, is hungry for power and is marching his army to Beirut. Aleta has traveled to Beirut on business but leaves for the Mediterranean coast when she hears of the impending trouble. Khazan's scouts follow and set upon Aleta's outnumbered bodyguards, but she and her children escape to the hidden, beautiful, ancient city of Petropolis. Val

searches the deserts of the Middle East for his family and finds them by a lucky coincidence. Khazan dies by drowning when he and his men try to invade the well-protected city of Petropolis.

Val and his family make the long journey back to the coast. ("The Young Amazon, #2119-2128: Karen, who has always been tomboyish and strong-willed, admired the feisty Queen Hypatia of Petropolis, and starts pretending to be an Amazon warrior. Her enthusiasm goes too far, and the girl cuts her hair short and buys a suit of armor. The twins are then kidnapped by the mischievous Assur, son of a Sheik from beyond the Jordan. Val and two men pursue the troublemakers and rescue the twins, with the aid of Valeta's long, golden hair.) The five ride back to Beirut.

COMMENT: *This story uses elements suggested by Bill Crouch.*

140: HERE COME THE AMAZONS
Pages 2129 (27 November 1977) – 2138 (29 January 1977)

There is pirate trouble in the Misty Isles, and Aleta hurriedly returns home with her family. The Royal Family takes in young Hector, a supposed shipwreck victim who is actually a pirate spy. The traitor soon escapes with much secret information. The main force of pirates attacks and is defeated without much difficulty, but another group secretly waits for an opening. Karen and the women are forced to defend the palace until Val's army can return and finish of the remaining pirates.

141: RETURN TO CAMELOT
Pages 2138 (29 January 1978) – 2156 (4 June 1978)

Inspired by a letter from Arn, Val sails with his family to Camelot by way of Marseilles. ("The Tournament," #2140-2143: At Marseilles, the greedy Governor decides to sponsor a tournament starring the famous Sir Valiant. One crazed knight takes the games too seriously and tries to fight Val to the death. Naturally, Val does not lose.)

The next day Val and his family board a barge and journey north up the Rhone River and across Gaul towards Britain. On the way they pick up an interesting storyteller and have an unpleasant stop at Lyons, where the haughty Afghan Caliph tries to buy Aleta ("No Sale," #2146-2150). Then, they meet up with Val's old friend Sir Launcelot and are involved in a short battle with King Claudas, Launcelot's hereditary enemy ("Galan to the Rescue," #2151-2154). Finally they sail with Launcelot across the English Channel and, after a messy horse ride, arrive safely at Camelot.

142: CONFLICT AT CAMELOT
Pages 2157 (11 June 1978) – 2164 (30 July 1978)

Arn is reunited with his family at Camelot. Arthur announces a great tournament, which Val naturally wins. Arn gets into an argument with Orland, a big youth who mistreats Valeta, but their conflict is soon forgotten when the two young knights join forces to rescue Orland's family from outlaws.

143: THE SINISTER STRONGHOLD
Pages 2165 (6 August 1978) – 2173 (1 October 1978)

Tillicum, Arn's beloved nurse, comes to Camelot to seek Val's aid in rescuing her kidnapped husband, Boltar. The Mad Earl of Lolland demands an impossible ransom. Val and Arn sail to Daneland to destroy the Mad Earl's grim castle and to rescue their friend from the horrible prison. Val brings the sick Boltar back to Camelot for medical attention. When Boltar recovers, young Prince Galan, who has never seen Thule, decides to sail with him. Arn goes along to study statecraft at Aguar's court.

144: The Snowslide
Pages 2173 (1 October 1978) – 2180 (19 November 1978)

At Boltar's northern home, Arn is happily reunited with Lydia and with his old friend Hatha. Arn, Galan and Lydia travel on to Vikingsholm. The two young lovers enjoy the winter together until the young girl is killed in a horrible accident.

COMMENT: *Arn's reaction to Lydia's death is so understated that it loses most of its tragedy and effectiveness—an uncharacteristic lapse in Foster's storytelling power.*

145: The Neglected Bride-to-Be
Pages 2180 (19 November 1978) – 2197 (18 March 1979)

At the first sign of Spring, Arn is off to find forgetfulness in adventure. He meets Earl Chute's daughter, Grace, who is contracted to marry the old King Hrothgar, and vows to free the young girl. With some trickery, Arn forces Hrothgar to see his mistake and free Lady Grace from the forced contract. Aguar is forced to banish the scheming old man from Thule. Arn has gradually fallen in love with Grace and asks her to marry him. She refuses, and Arn, dejected at losing two sweethearts in one year, returns to Camelot, where he is reunited with his family after a long absence.

COMMENT: *This story and the next two overlap considerably. Arn, whose characterization in the 1978-1979 pages was a bit shallow and inconsistent, is portrayed very differently from his father. Years earlier Val had been grief-stricken for a long period of time after the death of the maid Ilene and was unable to love another woman until he met Aleta several years thereafter (1938-1941). For further discussion of the many interesting personality differences between Val and Arn, see Carl Horak's article in the fanzine Strip Scene #2, 1977.*

146: A Family Affair
Pages 2193 (18 February 1979) – 2202 (22 April 1979)

On the way back to Camelot, Arn picked up a bumbling companion, Sir Edwin Fitzthrumpet. Edwin's father, Sir Mortrik, decides to enter a tournament at Camelot in Edwin's place. Mortrik eventually realizes that he is too old and out of shape and decides to devote himself to training his son in the ways of knighthood.

147: The Towering Giant
Pages 2200 (8 April 1979) – 2206 (20 May 1979)

Sir Gawain and his squire Prince Arn leave on a new quest, the capture of some bandits occupying the castle of Lord Condon of Wales. With the help of a strange dwarf, the two knights quickly complete their task and return home.

148: Arvak's Daughter
Pages 2207 (27 May 1979) – 2209 (10 June 1979)

Arvak, Val's faithful red stallion, dies of old age. Galan brings his father a beautiful new white mare, which turns out to be Arvak's daughter. Val proudly accepts his son's gift, and his sorrow is somewhat alleviated.

149: Galan Enters A New World
Pages 2209 (10 June 1979) – 2225 (30 September 1979)

Val and Aleta take King Arthur's advice and decide to have Galan trained as a palace page boy. This is the first step on the hard road to knighthood. Galan rides away with gallant Sir Vanoc and his wife, Lady Enid. One stormy night at a country inn, when all the men are out on a mission, Galan single-handedly saves Lady Enid from two miscreant knights. Lady Enid soon becomes a surrogate mother to the boy, who becomes pleased with his new home. One

exciting winter day, Galan bravely protects Enid from vicious wolves and from death by exposure in the winter forest. Lord Vanoc then takes Galan to Camelot for the great tournament, and Galan is happy to see his family again.

150: Trouble in the Irish Sea
Pages 2226 (7 October 1979) – 2246 (24 February 1980)

At the great tournament at Camelot, Val meets a large, loud, red-faced knight named Karran, who has just come from the turbulent Isle of Man to seek aid from Arthur in getting back his lands from marauding Vikings. King Arthur calls a council of war. Prince Arn and two other men are sent to find out if these Vikings pose a threat to Britain. Arn finds that the fierce Northmen intend to remain and form a base from which to raid both Ireland and Britain.

Arn infiltrates the Viking band but is held in suspicion by Thoralf the Chieftain and also meets a strange group of little Irish people who are also threatened by the Northmen. Stuck with the suspicious marauders, Arn is unable to report his findings to King Arthur, but he finally sneaks away and returns to Camelot. Gawain and Arn then return to the Isle of Man with an army and vanquish the invaders without any help from the irresponsible Karran. The knights bring the little people back to their home in Ireland and then travel back to Camelot.

COMMENT: *This is the last story utilizing the talents of Hal Foster, who retired at the end of 1979 at the age of 87(!). The last page credited to him was #2241(20 January 1980). The following week, John Cullen Murphy's signature appeared for the first time, and the subtitle "Created by Hal Foster" was added to the Prince Valiant logo. The change in art is really not noticeable, for Murphy's style had gradually taken over during the previous nine years. The credits for the scriptwriting since Foster's retirement have not been publicized, but we are informed that Murphy's son, Cullen, was responsible for most of the Murphy stories. Cullen Murphy is also a well-known professional historian and editor of the Smithsonian journal Wilson Quarterly.*

151: Corsairs and Salt Mines
Pages 2246 (24 January 1980) – 2259 (25 May 1980)

King Arthur banishes Karran to Scotland. Count Gaston of Bordeaux invites Val and Arn to go hunting boar on a preserve near Royan. A Corsair raiding party attacks looking for slaves and captures Val. The ship heads for Corsica where Val is sold to an Arab for 100 Dinars. Arn follows and seeks the help of Salam Fulda who is living in "a lonely fortress in Brittany." Salam Fulda is no friend of Prince Valiant. He is lucky to be alive. He survived the shipwreck from their last encounter, but drifted at sea for a week before being washed ashore in Brittany. Salam Fulda rebuffs Arn's request for help until he realizes that the unicorn fleet that abducted Val are poachers. Arn accompanies Salam Fulda as he tracks down the poachers and attacks them. Aboard the poachers' ship an older man, Fulk of St. Gall, tells Arn that Val was sold in Corsica. Arn finds the auctioneer in Corsica and convinces him by sword point to tell him what happened to his father. He tells Arn that Val was sold to Maghreb who bought him to work the Berber salt mines at the edge of the Sahara. Arn tracks down Sheik Ahmed Al-Gebr and asks for his help. The salt mine is run by a cruel Sharif who had killed Ahmed Al-Gebr's four "beardless" sons. Arn sees that a Wadi, a type of bulwark against sandstorms, provides the weakest link in freeing Val. Arn and Ahmed Al-Gebr secretly loosen the mortar of the columns. When a sandstorm comes, Arn uses ropes woven from camel hair to pull the columns down. The Wadi falls, and Al-Gebr's army of five hundred men attack the Sharif salt mine. Val is rescued.

152: The Stricken King
Pages 2260 (1 June 1980) – 2270 (10 August 1980)

News of Val's release reaches Camelot and King Arthur decrees a week of tournaments. Unexpectedly, the King falls ill and is taken to his chambers.

As Arthur lies on his deathbed, Mordred plots to "carve up the kingdom." Mordred has poisoned Arthur and has blackmailed the old nurse into gradually poisoning him every evening by spiking his nightly tonic. When Lord Trueheart questions murdering the king, Mordred thrusts a dagger between his ribs, killing him instantly. Galan, who is Page to Lord Vanoc and a student of the historian Geoffrey, rushes away from Geoffrey's wrath for drawing in the King's library books. He bumps into the old nurse who spills the tonic. A dog laps up the tonic and quickly dies. Mordred grabs Galan and locks him away. Galan writes a message using his shirt for paper and charcoal from a long unused fireplace. He stuffs the message in his boot and throws it through a window. The boot is retrieved by Gawain's hound, Ulric who takes it to his master. After reading the message, Gawain runs to Arthur's bedchamber where he confronts the nurse. The nurse explains that she assisted Mordred only to save her son Odo. Arthur wakens from his stupor, but his condition is kept a secret. Mordred has a plan in place to kill Gawain and other knights as soon as word is sent that Arthur is dead. As everyone awaits news of the king's condition, Arthur enters and offers Mordred the poisoned tonic. Mordred, fearing for his life, begs for mercy. Arthur gathers the people of Camelot and publicly disowns Mordred by cutting himself with his own sword, Excalibur, and spilling his blood. Then Arthur turns Mordred's lands over to the poor and banishes him from the realm.

153: MURDER IN CORNWALL
Pages 2271 (17 August 1980) – 2281 (26 October 1980)

Val returns home and is reunited with his family. He finds out that The Singing Sword was recovered by Salam Fulda, who ransomed it back to Arthur. Val is introduced to Lady Gwynn of Cornwall. Val and Aleta travel by royal barge on a "social visit" to castle Cornwall while Gwynn travels overland. By the time Val arrives to see Duke Cuthbert the duke is dead, killed in a hunting accident. Val meets the Duke's sons Brian and Lambert, who are too cheerful at their father's death. Chester the Duke's "bookish" third son "introduces" Aleta to Gwynn. While Aleta gathers information from the castle's women, Val seeks out the gamekeeper. Val sees that the kingdom is in disarray. The knights are all drunkards and the serfs are gaunt and sickly. The rakish Lambert abducts a young maiden, "Lady" Joan, whom he takes to his chambers. When Val follows to challenge him, he finds Lambert already dead. Brian discovers Val with his dead brother and wrongly accuses him of murder. Aleta disguises herself as a man and breaks into the Seneschal's office to look over the ledger books. The accounts are written in Greek, which Aleta easily translates. When an assassin tries to stop Aleta she cuts him on the face and flees. During Val's trial Chester is revealed to be Aleta's "assassin." Aleta quickly throws Val his sword, and he uses its hilt to crack Brian in the throat. When Chester challenges Val, the Seneschal strikes down Chester from behind with his sword. Brian and the Seneschal are thrown in prison and with Gwynn's help Val selects qualified knights to watch over the castle.

154: THE WILD BOY
Pages 2282 (2 November 1980) – 2293 (18 January 1981)

Val and Aleta return to Camelot by way of the stormy English Channel when the tiller breaks. At the mercy of the sea, the ship crashes into "The Needles," huge granite pillars off the Isle of Wight. The survivors brace for an attack by sea raiders when Val realizes the Corsair ship is captained by Boltar. After a small feast, Boltar and Tillicum introduce Val and Aleta to a teenage wild boy they found. The boy's feet are unshackled and he leaps overboard onto one of "The Needles." As he climbs the rocky column he is attacked by a falcon that lacerates his face and puts out an eye. Val, wearing a helmet, climbs to his rescue, killing the falcon. Val, Aleta, and Tillicum return to Camelot and take the boy with them. While hunting with Galan, the wild boy comes across a crying young maiden. It is Sir Breandan's daughter Freyja. Unknown to the wild boy, Freyja is betrothed to Prince Oswald of Saxony. The wild boy brings her a freshly killed rabbit, and the two go off on a sleigh ride together. The

wild boy is made to understand that he and Freyja cannot be together. After Oswald's arrival, the wild boy attacks him for no apparent reason. However, the crest on Oswald's tunic is identical to the tattoo above the wild boy's left ear. After Oswald reveals that his older brother had died and his young son was lost at sea Val realizes who the wild boy really is. Val tricks Oswald into revealing that the wild boy is his nephew. In the ensuing sword fight, Val is disarmed. Oswald accidentally knocks over a flaming brazier and burns himself. Just as Oswald is about to kill Val, the wild boy leaps at him. Oswald turns and kills his nephew but also dies at Val's hand. At the wild boy's funeral "The Wanderer" enters and curses both Val and Arthur for their pride.

155: THE QUEST FOR HUMILITY
2294 (25 January 1981) – 2300 (8 March 1981)

Through messengers Arthur finds out that the North Fleet has been destroyed at sea. A great famine has struck the Goths, and there is a plague in Londinium. "The Wanderer" tells Val he must travel high into the Alps to find a hermit who will teach him humility. When he arrives in Geneva, an innkeeper tells him the hermit can only be located if he wants to be found. As Val tries to cross a fissure using a rope, monstrous imps commanded by "Inish" grab the line and lower him into the abyss. At the bottom of the chasm, a tall old man of "inhuman strength" greets Val. Deep within the bowels of the earth "lie all of man's follies and sorrows." The old hermit gives Val a small casket, which contains enough humility for all of Britain, and instructs him not to open it until the finds "The Wanderer." Val returns and gives the casket to "The Wanderer." She reveals that the casket contains her beauty, which a wizard had trapped there because she savagely mocked a lad who loved her. "The Wanderer" drops the casket into the frozen river, throwing away her beauty. "That is humility, Sir Valiant. Learn it," she instructs. Val watches from the shore as "The Wanderer" floats downstream on an ice floe.

156: THE SIEGE OF CAMELOT
Pages 2301 (15 March 1981) – 2320 (26 July 1981)

Val returns to Thule. He docks at Trondheim and rides two days up the fjord to Vikingsholm. Val learns that Dalgrind, son of Valgrind has been stirring up the mountain tribes with promises of a kingdom. Dalgrind returns the head of an emissary who was sent requesting peace terms. Leaving Vikingsholm, Val scouts out Thule and realizes that Dalgrind's henchmen rule the land at night. Soon Val finds Dalgrind's camp and notices the banners of Finnis and Rus. Val's party is attacked, and he leaps to safety from a cliff to the river below. Unconscious, Val is pulled from the river and taken to Egil Tor where he meets Arn. Arn explains that he has been using the tomb of a King Egil, Val's great grandfather, as a base of operations because the superstitious rebels will not go near it. Arn reveals that Mordred is the true power behind Dalgrind. As the rebels advance, Val and Arn ride to Vikingholm and convince King Aguar to preserve his life by fleeing once more to Britain. Mordred overtakes Vikingsholm and Dalgrind becomes his puppet king. King Aguar lands in the same Fens in Britain where he arrived thirty years earlier. Mordred has planned well, for all the knights of Camelot are away overseeing spring planting. Soon, Mordred sails to Caledonia and enlists the Picts to help him attack Camelot. Mordred's army advances on Camelot, sacking York, Lincoln, Colchester, and Londinium. Val destroys bridges and burns fields in Mordred's path, while Arn secretly moves the small stone cairn's that mark safe pathways through Mucken Mire. Arn then watches from safety as some of the rebels are sucked down into the marsh. Camelot prepares for a siege. The refugees are sent to Cornwall, Val and Sir Gawain bury the royal treasure in the bog, and the twins and Galan are sent with the children to Hibernia for safety. The twins and Galan go to live with Rory Mor, High King of Ireland at the royal citadel of Tara. One day, while exploring the citadel, Galan comes upon a man jailed below the floor. Before the man can tell Arn anything, Rory Mor grabs him and pulls him away. During a hunt, an arrow fells Galan's mount in an effort to scare the boy into silence. Galan goes to the Brehons, the all-powerful

Our Story:
THE CASTLE BRISTOLS WITH ACTIVITY, MEN AND WOMEN ARE SCURRING IN ALL DIRECTIONS TO THE IMPENDING BATTLE FAR ON THE HORIZON...
...A SOMBER MOMENT FOR VAL.

VAL CONTEMPLATES ARNS SUDDEN OUTBURST OF ANGER THE LAST FEW WEEKS AGO. "OH LORD, IF YOU ONLY KNEW MY TRUE QUEST IN LIFE". THE IMAGE OF THAT PHRASE WILL HAUNT VAL SOME TIME.

JUST THEN, A COURT GUARD HAS BROUGHT GRIM NEWS TO VAL ON THE WHEREABOUTS OF ARN. APPARENTLY, HE IS FALLEN CAPTIVE TO THE LEADER OF A FAR NORTHERN BARBARIC TRIBE. STUNNED, VAL KNOWS ALL TOO WELL WHO HOLDS HIS COMRADE HOSTAGE.

judges of Hibernia, and tells them his story. The Brehons tell Galan that the prisoner is a great criminal. Galan is relieved until he sees Rory Mor and the prisoner talking in a moonlit glen. Galan convinces his sisters that they must leave and the three children book passage on a merchant "hafskip" bound for Iceland. At the Shetlands, Rory Mor's warships overtake the merchant vessel and the king retrieves the runaway children. Upon their return, Galan uncovers that Rory Mor and the prisoner are actually twins. Under Brehon law they were to fight to the death with the victor to be crowned as king. Since neither brother could kill the other, they decided to share the throne on alternate months. Galan agrees to keep Rory Mor's secret only if he comes to the aid of Camelot. Galan sends word to Aguar, while Rory sends word to the Corsair chief, Salam Fulda, whose pirates use Hibernia as a refuge. Rory requests a fleet of one hundred ships meet him at Clontarf. The fleets converge at Cornwall and quickly dispatch the Pictish garrison stationed there. Galan, who knows the terrain around Camelot, lays out a plan of attack, and the three rulers follow his lead. The armies attack on three sides, the Thules through Mucken Mire, the Corsairs up the river Test, and the Irish "Carls" from across the western plain. Into this melée ride the knights of Camelot led by Prince Valiant. Mordred flees the battle and attempts to sail to Greenland. Arn, who has hidden upon the small boat, attacks Mordred, but a whale interrupts the fight and destroys the boat. Mordred is lost at sea while Arn drifts helplessly on the waves.

158: MAEVE
Pages 2321 (2 August 1981) – 2322 (16 August 1981)

In Thule, Dalgrind has been killed in a revolt led by the people, and in Camelot life returns to normal with one exception—Aleta is pregnant. After a week adrift, Arn's raft comes to an unknown shore. There he finds Maeve, a huntress maiden who not only is skilled with a bow, but also commands a troop of hounds. Arn attempts to talk to Maeve, but is attacked by her hounds. Arn is led to a small town where he is put on trial. To win his freedom he must battle Sawtooth, a huge mastiff. Arn wins the fight and is placed on a boat and towed out to sea. Maeve watches sadly from the cliffs as Arn departs.

159: THE INLAND JOURNEY
Pages 2324 (23 August 1981) – 2326 (6 September 1981)

Arn sails back to England, but marks his route by the stars, determined to return one day. Arn's return to Camelot is a welcome one because everyone had thought him dead. Soon preparations are made to sail to the Misty Isles ,where Aleta wishes to have her child. The family sails down the Rhine, taking the inland passage to avoid the Corsairs. Along the way there are many toll stations. At the last station Val and Aleta are invited to dinner by two brothers, Gunther and Grendl. Everything in the brother's castle is divided including the dining table and the sleeping arrangements. When Val witnesses Gunther shove Grendl's prize sapphire down the throat of a calf he offers to buy the animal for thirteen solidi. Gunther cannot say anything least he reveal what he has done. Unknowingly, Grendl agrees to the sale and in return Val has earned enough to pay his tolls.

160: RETURN TO THE MISTY ISLES
Pages 2327 (13 September 1981) – 2333 (25 October 1981)

Val and his family travel overland to the Danube and sail on to Constantinople by way of the Black Sea. Upon their arrival the Emperor Justinian greets them. Justinian warns Val that a civil war is brewing between two parties—the Greens and the Blues, and the riots extend even to the Misty Iisles. Justinian, who is without a male heir and is secretly plotting to steal Aleta's child, should she have a boy, promises to send the court physician to attend to her needs. Upon returning to the Misty Isles, Val seeks out Hippolytus who teaches the prince chariot racing. Val enters the contest disguised as a Green. On the last lap he pulls off his tunic to reveal the white and gold of Queen Aleta. Val wins the race, and silences the Green and Blue factions who were ready to revolt.

161: ARN'S QUEST
Page 2334 (1 November 1981)

Arn leaves the Misty Isles and sets off for Maeve's island. After the couple is reunited, Maeve tells Arn that she bears a terrible secret that he must uncover. Only if he can learn her secret, and win his spurs as a knight of the Round Table, may he then return to her island.

162: NIMROD
Pages 2335 (8 November 1981) – 2340 (13 December 1981)

Val saves the midwife Theta from rogues along the coast. Theta explains that she and her niece Diana were swept ashore Nimrod's Island, from which they just escaped. Val travels to see the alchemist Nimrod, a distant cousin of Aleta's, and becomes suspicious that he is hiding something. Val returns to the island at night and sees that Nimrod has enslaved children to do his labor. He also sees Nimrod plotting with Justinian's man Thanatops. Val is hit over the head by a servant, shackled near crates of explosive powder, and left to die. Nimrod and Thanatops take Diana and leave for Constantinople. Aleta's men free Val, who sends word to Justinian, who executes Nimrod and returns Diana to her aunt Theta.

163: THE STORY
Pages 2341 (20 December 1981) – 2342 (3 January 1982)

To pass the time, Val tells his family a story from when he was a squire to Sir Gawain—before he met Aleta. While fishing one day, the pair came upon a superstitious man named Tancred. Gawain, wishing to prove Tancred wrong, did everything opposite of what Tancred believed. Tancred, wanting Gawain to believe him, shared the secret of a love potion with the knight. The potion worked too well and Gawain had to flee the wrath of a jealous husband. Val reveals that the potion did not work, but that he had actually played a trick on Gawain. Filled with remorse, Gawain tries every superstitious remedy possible to restore order. As the family laughs Gawain appears from the shadows. Word has reached Camelot that something is amiss with Justinian.

164: JUSTINIAN'S MAD SCHEME
Pages 2344 (10 January 1982) – 2357 (11 April 1982)

Val and Gawain leave the Misty Isles and head for Egypt. They pass through Karnak and Luxor, but upon approaching Thebes they find the outpost deserted. Belisarius, Justinian's great general, has attacked and defeated all of the outposts in the region. Fearing the army's advance, Val and Gawain race to Jawa: Lost City of the Black Desert. The knights arrive at Jawa and empty the great cistern, depriving Belisarius' army of water. Belisarius decides to turn to Damascus, thus revealing his presence in the region. His plans ruined, Belisarius makes for Constantinople when he runs into Val. The two men fight until neither can stand. Gawain interrupts the fighting and Belisarius reveals Justinian has been plotting to usurp the throne from his uncle Justin. Belisarius tells them that he is marching to the Emperor's aid. Belisarius also reveals that above all else, Justinian hates Val's family. Justinian's personal physician, Priam, arrives at the Misty Isles to take care of Aleta, just as news of Emperor Justin's death arrives. The coronation of Justinian is held in the Basilica of Hagia Sophia, and Val and Gawain are present. At the coronation, Val sees "The Wanderer." The two knights follow her to a house in the slums of the Persian District. Inside the house flows a river that reflects Val's past. As he approaches the present "The Wanderer" warns Val that Justinian covets two things of his, and she tells him a riddle: "What all men want but cannot stand, can love but cannot bear; and a faraway kingdom no man rules whose ruler is always fair."

With the help of the Viking, Sven Fork-Beard, Val and Gawain escape back to the Misty Isles. Sven's warship, a roman trireme, is attacked at sea by three vessels, but it successfully defeats all three. As the time for Aleta to give birth nears, Priam and the midwife Theta busy themselves among the Misty Isle's poor. On the day Aleta gives birth, Priam steals the young boy away, while Theta replaces it with the stillborn child purchased from a poor woman. Priam leaves the Misty Isle before Val arrives, but once he gets to Constantinople, Justinian tells him his wife has give him a son, and to dispose of Val's and Aleta's child. Unable to kill the infant, Priam gives it to a Jewish peasant woman in the bazaars. Val arrives at the Misty Isles only to find Aleta in shock. The midwife Theta confesses her part in the deception to her niece Diana then hangs herself.

165: The Quest for Nathan Begins
Pages 2358 (18 April 1982) – 2365 (6 June 1982)

Justinian begins rebuilding his navy and plans to invade The Misty Isles. With Nimrod's explosive powder Justinian seems invincible, so Val calls for a council of war. Val, Arn, and Galan revisit Nimrod's Island and bring back a powerful crystal magnifying glass. When Justinian's navy commanded by Belisarius attacks, Val uses the crystal to magnify the rays of the sun and set the ship carrying Nimrod's powder aflame. The resulting explosion scuttles several ships, and the small boats of the Misty Isles, led by Sven Fork-Beard, defeat the rest. Val defeats Belisarius in a duel, but releases him in exchange for information about his kidnapped son. Gawain, knowing that Val cannot leave Aleta's side, gives Arn a royal quest to find his brother.

166: Yuan Chen and the Sacred Ring of India
Pages 2366 (13 June 1982) – 2384 (17 October 1982)

In the meantime, Valeta, Karen, and Galan go fishing, where they meet Yuan Chen, "a poor scholar half a world from home" (Cathay). Galan, who is twelve, becomes Yuan Chen's student and the boy finds that he has a passion for learning. Val agrees to place Galan in Yuan Chen's care, and the two scholars set off for the great city of Ujjain, Pearl of India. Once inside Ujjain, Galan and Yuan Chen find an empty jeweled box that was dropped by thieves. The two are falsely accused of the theft, and taken into custody. The sacred ring is missing, so Galan and Yuan Chen are taken before the Emperor Harsha and his twelve-year-old daughter, the Princess Mayana. Galan and Yuan Chen are interrogated and beaten badly, but each night Mayana visits them in secret, and rubs healing salves into their broken bodies. The ring is revealed to be a symbol of power, and now it, and its twin, are both in the hands of Harsha's evil brother, the tyrant Timur. Galan is freed to find the missing ring, but if he does not return with it, Yuan Chen's life is forfeit. In a tavern in Timur's desolate kingdom, Jagat, the leader of a troupe of actors, befriends Galan. Jagat's actors perform for Timur, and distract him while Galan finds the sacred ring. Galan and the troupe escape and return to Ujjain in time to save Yuan Chen from being beheaded. Mayana becomes empress, and Timur dies an untimely death, his kingdom passes to Mayana.

167: The Rescue of Nathan
Pages 2385 (24 October 1982) – 2397 (16 January 1983)

With Belisarius to help guide him, Arn finds the physician Priam, who tells Arn that he gave his brother to "a peasant from the frontier." Arn travels eastward and is taken in by a Cappadocian abbot named Basil, who hides him from Justinian's soldiers. Arn leaves "The Caves of the Gods," and follows the goat tracks across the wilderness. He finds a traveling companion, Ezeliel, who is both a goldsmith and a Rabbi. Arn tells Ezekiel about his brother, and the two travel from village to village looking for the infant. Justinian, angered at his defeat, sends his general Thanatops to the frontier with orders to kill all the infants under one year old. Arn finds his lost brother Nathan just before Thanatops and his soldiers arrive. In their flight to safety, Ezekiel is mortally wounded and entrusts Arn with his book—his portion of the Talmud. Just as Thanatops is about to attack, an army of Persians led by the great Khosru

swarm Justinian's soldiers, killing them all. Arn stays with the Jewish couple Matthias and Judith, who have raised his brother Nathan. Arn tells the couple that Nathan is his brother, and invites them back to the Misty Isles. As he awaits their decision, Arn travels down the Tigris and delivers Ezekiel's book to the rabbis in Ctesiphon. Arn, along with Matthias, Judith, and Nathan travel to the Misty Isles, and return Nathan to Aleta and Val.

168: The Dalmatian Twins
Pages 2398 (23 January 1983) – 2418 (12 June 1983)

For fulfilling his quest Arn is summoned to Camelot, and happily departs. Aleta becomes upset that Nathan does not recognize her as his mother, and takes out her frustrations on all around her. With the court in chaos, Val decides to join Alp Arslan, and make a tactical retreat, by attending King Zog's tournament in the Dalmatian port of Salonae for two weeks. Aboard ship Val discovers that Karen and Valeta have made a tactical retreat as well, and stowed away. Val and Alp Arslan enter the tournament in which the winner is rewarded with the hand of King Zog's daughter Grendl. Val soon finds that their only competition is an older man and a young boy wearing masks. One day, after the tournament, Alp walks through the streets of Salonae and accidentally knocks over Ulf, a nobleman who looks like his identical twin. Both Karen and Valeta vie for Alp's affections, each posing as the other. Karen, not wishing to be outdone by her sister, tries to sabotage the possessions of the masked strangers so Alp can win the hand of Grendl. As she steals into their room, Karen discovers that the masked strangers are Galan and Yuan Chen. Val and Alp are taken before King Zog, who reveals that Alp and Ulf are indeed twins. Unfortunately, Dalmatian law specifically states that one of the twins must die. King Zog orders a chess match to be held using live people as the pieces. Val plays for Alp, and the masked boy is chosen to play for Ulf. Unfortunately the masked boy is no longer Galan, but Adam, a former suitor of Grendl's who is desperate to win her hand by winning the game. In order to save both Alp's and Ulf's lives, Val orchestrates a stalemate. Since both Val and Yuan Chen are married, and Alp is her brother, Grendl can only wed Adam, much to King Zog's annoyance. Alp turns down any claim to the throne. Valeta has a strange encounter with "The Wanderer" who teaches her a lesson about despair and hope. Val, the twins, and Galan sail back to the Misty Isles and find the Isle of Sloth along the way. The isle's high priest, Torpor tells Val "the longer one stays here the lazier one becomes." It takes all of Val's resolve to leave the isle, but marks its coordinates for future use.

169: Arn, Parker of Orr
Pages 2419 (19 June 1983) – 2434 (2 October 1983)

Val and Aleta's reunion is a heated one. He had abandoned her in her hour of need (although it was to save his own neck). It is mutually decided that the family should return to Camelot. Arn, who had left for Camelot weeks before, arrives in the City of Marvels. Arthur makes Arn a "Parker," or keeper of the king's parks, and sends him off to East Anglia to rid the land of marauding Saxons. Upon arriving in the city of Orr, Arn is attacked by three Saxons, and kills them all. A boy takes him to Orr Abby where he finds the townspeople hiding. They tell Arn that every night the Saxon chieftain comes and fights a brave young soldier for their freedom. Through trickery Arn defeats the chieftain. Osbern, the mayor of Orr complains about the fight, so Arn concludes that he is either a fool or a traitor, and locks him in a cellar. Arn makes a lad named Ninian his Bailiff, and the two set out to explore the vast domain of Orr. Ninian tells Arn that Orr Castle has been taken over by the Saxons. They are ambushed by thieves, who turn out to be natives of East Anglia, and had been forced from their homes by the Saxons. Ninian recognizes Mungo, one of the group's leaders, and he and Arn are freed. Arn offers Mungo and his men a pardon if they will aid him against the Saxons. Arn begins devising a plan. After a second Saxon army lands, and he receives word from Arthur that he cannot send troops, Arn frees Osbern and tricks him by telling him a false story. Osbern goes to the Saxons, relays the information, and is hanged. Arn's men dam up the river that flows by Castle Orr, which reveals an underwater aqueduct. Unaware of the aqueduct passageway, the Saxons believe that Arn's men have magically walked through the castle walls, and are defeated by their own superstitious nature. Arn allows the remaining Saxons to escape to the second castle, for he knows their tales of magic will lead to a bloodless siege. As Arn's army approaches, the Saxons try to leave, but their boats are beached on the dry riverbed. Arn offers them a swift death, or a life in service of Arthur and the people of East Anglia. Just as the last man swears allegiance, Arn raises his hands and the undammed river washes away the Saxon boats.

170: A HISTORY LESSON
Pages 2435 (9 October 1983) – 2438 (30 October 1983)

Arn is summoned by Arthur to explain why he has allowed Saxons to live in Briton. Since most of the able-bodied men in East Anglia had been killed, Arn explains that it was his only choice if the lands were to prosper. That night Arthur takes Arn into a locked room high in a castle tower. There the artifacts and history of Briton's past are stored. Arthur explains that his father, Uther Pendragon, once told him, "We are all mongrels," and that Arn's decision to allow the Saxons to remain and live in peace was just. Val, Aleta and the rest of the family arrive, and a banquet is held in their honor. However the gaiety of the feast is shattered when Arthur finds out about Arn's interest in Maeve. "'Tis treason to see her again." Arthur shouts, and then sends him on his way.

171: THE RING OF MERLIN
Pages 2439 (6 November 1983) – 2448 (8 January 1984)

Before the crops are harvested and winter sets in, Val and Gawain set off with a hunting party in order to help restock Camelot's larders. "Impelled by memories of Merlin Ambrosius, Val wanders deep into the forest." Lionors, Merlin's oldest living pupil, leads Val into the bowels of the earth where the great sorcerer now lives. The blind and ancient Merlin leads Val to a large pool, and in the waters appears the image of Maeve. "The secret of Maeve's birth can destroy two families and two kingdoms," warns Merlin. Then he gives Val a ring to pass on to Arn. The ring "has but one use and can be used only once," and if Arn can determine what that is then all will be well. Val travels to Orr to spend Christmas with his family. He gives the ring to Arn and tells him of Merlin's message.

172: THE VALLEY OF DEATH
Pages 2449 (15 January 1984) – 2465 (6 May 1984)

All the knights of Camelot leave for Gaul to aid the Frankish King Chlotar defend his lands against the Visigoths—all save Val. Since Val has promised Aleta he would stay with his family for one year he cannot go, and so he comes under much ridicule from the other knights. With time on his hands Val decides to spend it with Nathan. Val takes Nathan into the wilderness where the boy is befriended by a hibernating female bear. Val helps Nathan escape. They run into a mountain man by the name of Waldo who tells Val of a man-beast that haunts the land and slaughters cattle and sheep. Val returns Nathan to Camelot and joins Waldo in search of the man-beast. Dunstan, the chief scribe of Camelot, tells Val that there is a spy in Camelot, and that all the letters sent from Waldo to Arthur concerning the man-beast are missing. Val and Waldo search the valley at night, and survey a raiding party hiding weapons in a cave. The two scouts are set upon by the man-beast, but Val manages to wound it. They track it back to Camelot, and tell Arthur what they saw. The weapons are retrieved, and Dunstan is revealed to be the man-beast in disguise. Dunstan runs away and takes Nathan with him. While in pursuit Val is shot in the right arm with an arrow, and falls unconscious. In The Valley of Death the scribe makes a last stand, but is killed by Nathan's bear. Waldo dresses the wounds of the soldiers, rescues Nathan from the bear,

and calls for help from the Dawn People. The Dawn People live under the earth. They have called this land their home since before the time of the Druids. When Val asks how he may repay their kindness, Cynan asks if his son and Nathan could be exchanged for a short while after the boys have come of age? As Val and the others return to Camelot, it is revealed that it is Maeve's father, Mordred, who is behind the plan to overthrow Arthur.

173: THE TOURNAMENT AT PENTECOST
Pages 2466 (13 May 1984) – 2472 (24 June 1984)

As the Tournament of Pentecost approaches, Karen is in love with Gawain's squire, Marcus, grandson of Manlius, last governor of Roman Britain. Marcus is brash, cocky, and vain, but also a natural born leader. Valeta laments that she has no admirers, so Val has a new suit of armor made, enters the competition as Sir Trueheart, and asks Valeta if he may honor her name by carrying her colors into combat. After Val's horse stumbles Marcus is declared the champion of the melee. Since he had not defeated "Sir Trueheart," Marcus challenges him to combat; however, Val had broken his right arm when he fell. Just as Val is about to be found out, Alp Arslan takes his place as Sir Trueheart and defeats Marcus. Alp gives the champion's laurels to Valeta and the two become quick friends.

174: THE VENGEANCE OF MORDRED
Pages 2473 (1 July 1984) – 2491 (4 November 1984)

Mordred, who was believed to be dead, returns to northern Britain and begins a well-planned advance on Camelot. It is he who had been hiding weapons in Arthur's kingdom, and it is he who is Maeve's father. Mordred's hatred of Arthur is fueled by past failures, and the loss of his right leg to the sea after his last skirmish. As retribution he kills all the mayors of the towns he conquers, and sends their right leg to Camelot. Mordred has planned well, for all the able-bodied knights are still in Gaul, and Camelot is defenseless. Val, Arn, and Marcus disguise themselves and join Mordred's army as spies. Arn sees Maeve among the roguish army, and finds out her dark secret. Under the cover of night, Maeve meets Arn and tells him she disapproves of what Mordred is doing. She reveals Mordred's battle plans to Arn, in order to help thwart her father's schemes. Her covert actions are found out, and Mordred uncovers that Val and Arn are spies in his ranks. Mordred feeds Maeve false information, so he can make a surprise attack on Camelot. Val and the others retreat through Mucken Mire, but Galan has left a parting gift—a cask of Nimrod's powder. The resulting explosion sends many rogues to their deaths. It is Galan's first "kill" and he does not take it well. Maeve, realizing she has been found out, disguises herself and slips away with Marcus. They swim out to Val's ship, which has just set sail. The crew throws the swimmers ropes. They haul in Marcus, but upon seeing Maeve, Arn cuts the line. Too late does Arn learn that she had not betrayed them. Mordred is reunited with his daughter, and calls for the sacking of Camelot.

175: THE WAR IN LAPPLAND
Pages 2492 (11 November 1984) – 2523 (16 June 1985)

Arthur spends some time in Gaul, where he gathers his knights. They are men without a country, so Aleta makes the decision to head to Thule and winter in Vikingsholm. All are welcomed and pass the time telling tall tales. Aleta discovers that King Aguar is in love with the young widow, Lady Fenia. Everyone in the castle knows of their love, but he cannot bring himself to tell Val. Aleta immediately decides to help Aguar, and suggests they need to make Val believe his father's courtship was his idea. Aleta arranges that Val meet Fenia at a banquet during The Festival of Vali. Aleta's plan works too well, and Val becomes enamored of Fenia. Mikkel, an envoy from Lappland far to the north, disrupts the festival. King Aslak lies dying and his twin sons Nils and Niilas are fighting for the throne. Unknown to all, Aslak's illness is a plot of Mordred's, who wishes to cause a civil war in Lappland, and a general war in the northern territories. Val and Arn, led by Mikkel, travel to Lappland. While passing through the Inner Lands, Arn is reunited with Sven, son of King Hap Atla, whom he had lived with for some time as a youth. Sven allows Arn to pass through his lands. He gives Arn a carved reindeer bone, and tells him to send it back should he ever need help. Val and Arn arrive at the royal winter camp as King Aslak dies. Aslak is put on a boat and ferried to the sacred isle of Ukonsaari to join his forefathers. Hetta, a powerful woman who nursed Aslak during his final days, takes control of the camp. Soon the camp comes under attack by the forces of the rival twins, for at its center is the Sky Pillar, and, according to law, the twin that scales it first will become king. The siege is a long one, but both northmen and knights defend the camp well. Mikkel steals the reindeer bone, given to Arn by Sven, and travels to the castle of Hap Alta to ask for help. In the meantime, Val sends word to each of the brothers that they have the support of Thule. When Nils and Niilas attack the camp they find that everyone has fled. The armies begin fighting as the brothers climb the Sky Pillar. Sven arrives with reinforcements, and helps Val and Arn send a stampeding herd of reindeer into the camp. In the confusion, Hetta tells Mikkel to climb to the top of the Sky Pillar. Mikkel reaches the summit before either of the brothers. A Shaman steps forth, and announces that Aslak had married Hetta in secret, and that Mikkel is their son. Since he is of royal blood, and scaled the Sky Pillar first, Mikkel is now King of the Lapps. Nils and Niilas are abandoned on a small island to live out the rest of their lives. Upon his return, Val tells his father that he should woo Lady Fenia. With a knowing twinkle in his eye, Aguar happily complies.

176: IN THE VALLEY OF THE NORNS
Pages 2524 (23 June 1985) – 2526 (7 July 1985)

Arn tells Sven about Maeve, so Sven takes his friend to the Valley of the Norns to see a hermit there. The way is treacherous only when Arn's mind strays from thinking about Maeve. Among the hundreds of earthenware jars that fill his home, the jolly old hermit instructs Arn to lift the one that has his name on it. The jar is heavy, too heavy for one man to lift. The hermit tells him to think of Maeve and suddenly the jar becomes light enough for Arn to carry it by himself. However, when his mind strays from Maeve, his burden turns heavy again. It is the glimmer of hope Arn had asked for, but it comes at the cost of knowing that the future holds more than his share of pain and loss. As he leaves the hermit's home there is a partial message in Latin above the door. The full text reads "Tu ne quaesieris, (scire nefas) quem mihi, quem tibi" or "Do not ask (it is forbidden to know) what final fate the gods have for thee" (Horace, Ode I.11). As he leaves the valley, Arn etches on the cliff face "Omnia vincit amor" or "Love conquers all."

177: "TO CAMELOT OR TO DEATH"
Pages 2527 (14 July 1985) – 2591 (5 October 1986)

King Arthur and King Aguar have devised a plan for winning back Camelot. The kings of Europe, fearing Mordred may attack them, pledge ships and knights to Arthur. Val and Aleta are secretly sent as envoys on a mission to the Saxons, for Arthur still needs an army of foot soldiers. They go to Cerdicopolis and meet with the Saxon Chief, Cerdic. Before Cerdic will talk to Val, he must complete "The Three Challenges." The first is to bring the outlaw Rollo to justice, the second is to defeat a troll named Orlog and bring back his head and hoard of gold, and the third is to find the missing treasure of the great Saxon warriors Hengist and Horsa. Val rides off and is befriended by the merchant Brian who knows the land well. They first go to the Castle Orlog and find that the townspeople in the surrounding village live in fear of the creature. Every night they put food before his statue, and in the morning, it is gone. With the superstitious townspeople ready to kill them, Val and Brian topple the statue to uncover a nest of rats that had been eating the tribute. The townspeople realize they have been duped, and storm the castle. Captured by Val, Orlog tells everyone

that he had once been married to the daughter of the Saxon King Hengist. One day, while fighting off the Alemanni, he was betrayed by Cerdic who coveted Orlog's wife. Orlog suffered at the hands of the Alemanni, who broke his body. After escaping, Orlog fled to the valley and took on the guise of a troll. The townspeople, who have never been harmed by Orlog, have sympathy for him and make him their king. Val, Brian, and Orlog pledge to find out what Cerdic is planning. In the town of Dundarn, the home of the bandit Rollo, Brian tells how Cerdic had taken into custody all of the women and children until tribute could be paid. He explains that it was this act that drove Rollo and his men to become thieves. Val's party is attacked by Saxons, who are easily defeated, and Brian is revealed to be Rollo. Back in Cerdicopolis, Aleta takes interest in Cerdic's son Cyrnic, whose hobby is chickens. For some unknown reason Cyrnic's chickens lay eggs year-round, as if it were summer. Aleta guesses the reason, follows Cyrnic to the henhouse one night, and sees him digging up the Hoard of Hengist. Cyrnic takes Aleta to where he has stashed the hoard and tells her that he knows he is not Cerdic's son. Aleta sends word of her discovery to Val, who returns to Cerdicopolis on the eve of the Yule festival. He brings with him Orlog and Rollo, both bound in breakaway ropes. In front of the Saxons, Val tells of Cerdic's misdeeds. Cyrnic pulls off his tunic revealing a birthmark and announces that he is not Cerdic's son. To everyone's surprise, Orlog rips open his own tunic, displaying an identical birthmark—Cyrnic is his son. The Saxons immediately make Cyrnic, grandson of Hengist, their new king. King Cyrnic agrees to come to the aid of Arthur, but Saxons who fight must be given land in Britain. Val agrees and a treaty is made.

Upon his return to Thule, Val's ships takes refuge from a storm on the Isle of Covetousness. It takes all he can do to save himself and the landing party from the pull of the isle, but they make it off. With the battle plans set, three mighty fleets of Boltar's warships set sail for Britain. One fleet carries the knights of Camelot, the second King Aguar and his men, and the third will carry the Saxon army. The three armies land at three different locations in Britain, and all converge at High Cross. They make final preparations and advance on Camelot. The first wave does not go as planned. Val's forces are outflanked. Gawain's knights cross the tournament grounds only to become stuck knee deep in mud, compliments of Mordred. When Arthur tells Arn to sound the advance, the young prince instead sounds the retreat. Infuriated, Arthur beats Arn until Aguar intercedes. Val and Arn scout the forests and lands around Camelot at night, and map out all the traps. Arn finds the old woodsman's cottage and travels back though the underground tunnel that leads into Camelot's great cistern. There, in the dungeons under Camelot, he finds Maeve in prison. Pledging to come back for her, he returns to Val and devises an attack plan. Preparations are made, and Arn's plan is put into effect. First Arn takes a small contingent of men through the cistern, frees Maeve, and then attacks the blockhouse over Merlin's Gate. Arn raises the gate while his archers rain down barbed death from the battlements. Arthur's troopes advance through the safe areas around Camelot, leaving the booby-trapped places for Mordred's soldiers. As Mordred's forces collapse as they are caught in their own traps and defeated. Mordred leaves through the underground cistern, but The Dawn People thwart his escape. Their leader, Cynan the bard, has been watching from the shadows all the while. The Dawn People defeat the soldiers, rescue Maeve, and easily capture Mordred. King Arthur returns to Camelot. Maeve and Arn are finally reunited, and Arthur, who owes the restoration of his kingdom to the Parker of Orr, makes Sir Arn a knight of the Round Table. In exchange for their help, Cynan asks Val to exchange Nathan for his son, Aelfred, for one year. Val and Aleta comply, but only if Judith and Mathias/Matthew accompany Nathan. No trace can be found of Mordred, and when Arthur questions Cynan, the bard lies. The Dawn People pass judgment on Mordred themselves, and place him in a deep pit at the center of the Earth until he dies.

COMMENT: *Mathias is renamed Matthew beginning on page 2589.*

178: The Wedding of Prince Arn
Pages 2592 (12 October 1986) – 2611 (22 February 1987)

Arn's first order of business is to find a pack of hounds for Maeve. Arn takes Maeve into the woods and introduces her to her new "friends." Afterwards Arn proposes and Maeve accepts. Upon hearing of the betrothal, Arthur, in front of his knights, proclaims that since Maeve is blood of his blood, the first child of their union shall inherit the throne of Camelot. "And after my death," Arthur tells Arn, "until such time as this child may be fit to govern, you shall be Regent in the child's name."

Cynan of the Dawn People arrives, and his son, Aelfred, is exchanged for Nathan. Being so small, Aelfred has a hard time acclimating to Camelot. Because of his greater size among the Dawn People, Nathan becomes cocky and takes what he wants. Cynan teaches the brash young prince a lesson by taking him fishing. Nathan quickly learns that many hands working in unison can accomplish more than size and strength alone.

The meeting of minds between Aleta and Maeve is challenging. Aleta wants a large wedding, full of spectacle, while Maeve wishes it to be small. Maeve's engagement ring is a precious heirloom of the house of Thule that has been worn by twenty generations of queens; however, it is too big for her. Rather than lose it, she puts it in a drawer. One day, Maeve opens the drawer to retrieve it, but it is gone. Galan discovers that the cabinet had once been owned by Merlin Ambrosius, and begins taking it apart. There are many hidden traps, but before long he finds not only the ring, but Merlin's book of formulas as well. Galan tries his hand at Merlin's magic, but cannot get the spells to work properly.

With the ring returned, Maeve once more turns her thoughts to her wedding. As a compromise, she asks Aleta for seats for her guests. Aleta generously awards Maeve the choir loft, though she is uncertain who her daughter-in-law-to-be will invite. The Festival of Valentinus, the day of the wedding, arrives. Much to Aleta's chagrin, it is Maeve's pack of hounds that take their place in the choir loft. Arn and Maeve are married, and the future of Camelot is secured. The festivities last late into the night. The happy couple slip out of Camelot, and Sven Fork-Beard ferries them to Gaul to honeymoon in a castle given to them by Salam Fulda.

COMMENT: *Maeve and Arn are married on Valentine's Day, 1987, fifty years to the day after the strip first appeared (Page 2610).*

179: The Northern Spice Route
Pages 2612 (1 March 1987) – 2676 (22 May 1988)

Yuan Chen returns to Camelot on a mission from the Great Kahn. The Huns have severed the spice routes connecting east and west. In return for a portion of the spice revenues, the Emperor, with Arthur's help, wishes to create and protect a new route safe from attack. Realizing that the money can help rebuild Camelot, Arthur quickly agrees. Soon Val, Galan, Gawain, and Yuan Chen sail for Birka, while Aleta, Aelfred, and the twins set off for the Misty Isles.

Gunndar Harl commands Val's ship, which lands at the Island of Unbearable Virtue to take on fresh water. Upon the island everyone is too courteous. To get his men to leave, Val tells them that they need to go back to the ship so they can give away all their possessions. Once off the island, its spell no longer holds them.

Once in the city of Birka, Val finds a guide named Alta who can show him a route eastward. The conversation is overheard by Grubb, an unsavory man, who plans to learn the new route and then kill them all. Val and his party travel to the lands of the fierce Balts, and make landfall. Val and his party are soon captured by the Balts, who take them to Truso, capital of the Baltic

lands. They meet Oleg, leader of the Balts, who sentences them to "The Ring." Amidst a circle of standing stones Val, Gawain, and Yuan Chen are told to point out which stone Polaris, the North Star will appear over. Yuan Chen pours wine into Val's cupped hands, and places in the liquid a lodestone. The compass point settles on North, and their lives are spared. As reward for their achievement, Oleg has a Pathfinder fashioned for Val. The Pathfinder is an instrument created by the legendary Askold that, when placed in a groove on top of special columns, charts the path from Truso to the Pacific Ocean off the coast of Cathay.

Val heads deep into Asia, but is unknowingly being followed by Grubb, the Beast of Birka. Upon reaching the Greek outpost Hippopolis, City of the Sun, Gawain realizes that they are surrounded on both flanks. They are captured by Greek soldiers, who take them before their leader, the Grand Solon. The Solon explains that the city was built by Alexander the Great around one of the Pathfinder columns. After Alexander died it was decided that, in order to maintain their safety, they must remain anonymous, so all travelers are never permitted to leave. Since the town is named after a horse of myth, Val conceives of building a huge wicker Trojan Horse with which to escape. The Solon approves, and the Agora is built. When it is done, it is large enough to hide twenty men in its belly. The huge statue on wheels is set in the marketplace, and that night accidents, or bad omens, begin occurring. The Hippopolites decide that the gods are angry, and they must dispose of the wicker horse by casting it over a cliff. The huge horse rolls down the hill, but before it can go over Val hacks through its hind legs, causing it to fall backwards. The knights of Camelot climb out and push the horse over the cliff to hide their escape. Fleeing the search parties, Val and his knights take refuge with a band of nomads. The nomads exchange their food and warm clothing for the finery of the knights. The exchange is costly for Grubb, for he follows Val's tunic a long way before realizing Val is not wearing it.

On the Misty Isles Aleta tends to affairs of state. Two young cousins whom Aleta knows, Castor and Pollux, lodge a complaint against their uncle, Mephisto for stealing their inheritance. Mephisto, an old suitor of Aleta's, is thought to be a spy for Justinian. Aleta convinces Mephisto she is available,

AETIUS, LAST OF THE GREAT ROMAN GENERALS, HERO OF THE BATTLE OF CHALONS, WHERE THE MAD CAREER OF ATTILA, THE HUN, WAS HALTED. HIS TIRED FACE IS LINED WITH SORROW, FOR HE KNOWS THE EMPIRE IS CRUMBLING, DESPITE HIS HEROIC TRIUMPHS. HE RETURNS NOW TO ROME AND AN UNDESERVED DOOM.

in order to gain his trust. She finds out that he had converted all of Castor's and Pollux's fortunes into gold, and hid it as armor in his villa. Aleta has her blacksmith make duplicates of the armor, and has her men exchange them. She also tells Mephisto in "secret" that the Misty Isles are in desperate need of wheat and wine, and plan to buy as much as they can in Constantinople. Mephisto sends word to Justinian, who buys all the wheat and wine he can in order to sell it at a higher price to Aleta. When the ships from the Misty Isles arrive they are loaded with surplus wheat and wine for sale. Castor's and Pollux's fortunes are returned to them, and Mephisto must spend his remaining days caring for the poor.

Winter sets in as Val's party crosses Siberia. They are trapped on a cliff by a pack of wolves, but Val has his men pour water into the crevasses between the rocks. When the water freezes, the ice expands, causing an avalanche that buries most of the wolves. The guide Alta finds an eastward flowing river, so Val and his men build a Viking longboat. As they press deeper into the Asian heartland they are stopped by a greedy tribe known as the Avarissi demanding a toll. The Avarissi are lead by a bully who calls himself "The Bronk," but the true power lies in his wife, Maria Francesca. She is of royal Roman birth, but bought by "The Bronk" to be his slave and wife. Maria Francesca is impressed with Val's ship and suggests, rather than kill Val and his party, they build the Avarissi a fleet of longboats. The longboats are built with special rivets that will break apart in a storm. Upon completing the ships, Val and his men are released and head east. The ships of the Avarissi encounter a storm and break apart. "The Bronk," clothed in his finest armor, sinks to his death, and Maria Francesca swears vengeance on Val.

Val's party arrives at an arid land north of Cathay. They come upon a strange underground room containing flying monkeys known as the Fleech. They search deeper into the chamber and come upon a huge glacial cistern. Inside the cistern, frozen in ice, is a vast menagerie of strange animals. They encounter an old man with white skin who speaks in an ancient language that no one can understand. He takes them to his underground village where Yuan Chen meets a man who knows many ancient languages. Finally, they find a common tongue, and the old man tells them of how his people secluded themselves away to avoid the Great Flood of Noah. The Cavern People secretly drug Val's

and the knights' wine with a potion of sleep and forgetfulness. All but Galan drink the wine; however, he fakes that he is asleep. The Cavern People call upon the Yeti to carry the men back to the surface, but two of the Yeti escape in the process. The party awakes without memory of their adventure—all except Galan who keeps the secret to himself. Without witnesses, Galan frees two Fleeches that he had secreted away.

Val enters Turfan, an oasis city along the "Silk Road" and gateway to Cathay, announcing that a new trade route has been created. The people are jubilant, for there are many merchants living in the town who have not been able to trade with the west since the Huns severed the main road. Val tells the merchants that they can only travel the route with a knight of Camelot, and that they must tithe ten percent of their revenues to Arthur. The merchants are not happy, but it is a fair deal. At night Grubb breaks into a cabinet containing copies of the trade route, and sells them to the merchants. But Galan has drawn a mistake on each of the copies, and when the merchants try to find their way they reach an impasse. Just as the mob of merchants return to take revenge on Grubb, Val intercedes. Val blames the merchants for their own greed. Then Val takes Grubb's profits and places him and his men each in a "cangue" (a Chinese restraint which makes eating and sleeping impossible).

180: A Case of Mistaken Identity
Pages 2677 (29 May 1988) – 2686 (31 July 1988)

Val, Galan, and Yuan Chen sail on the Yangtze River to Nanking, "the capital of the Southern Kingdom and home of the great and esteemed Emperor Wu Ti." Wherever they go Val is mistaken for Prester John, a silk trader from Venice. Soon Val, Galan, Gawain, and Yuan Chen enter Emperor Wu Ti's throne room—it is more spectacular than that of King Arthur. There is a disturbance, and two Imperial Geomancers, Joo Dee and Tim Wah, say that the laws of nature have changed. Joo Dee tells everyone how she dropped a little cake spread with honey, but it landed honey side up, which never happens. To this Val jokes that perhaps Joo Dee spread the honey on the wrong side of the cake? The remark comes to Wu Ti's notice, and he too mistakes Val for Prester John. Wu Ti calls for Val's beheading, but Yuan Chen intercedes on his behalf. To save them all, Yuan Chen suggests that Wu Ti keep Galan until he, Val, and Gawain can return with the real Prester John. Though a captive in a gilded cage Galan uses his time wisely and learns as much as he can.

181: The Battle of Orr
Pages 2687 (7 August 1988) – 2702 (20 November 1988)

The story shifts for a bit from Val to Arn. The Parker of Orr has returned to govern his lands with his new bride. Maeve is unaccustomed to courtly manners and goes with the men on a hunt. When she, rather than Sir Guy, the Sheriff of Orr, fells a buck, the men of Orr become angry. Maeve's assertiveness spreads to the other women, which upsets "the quiet tenor of life in the villages of Orr." Arn writes a proclamation announcing the harvest tournament; however, he neglects to make it open to men only. The omission is not as popular among the men as it is with Maeve and Mathilde, the wife of Sir Guy. While preparations are being made for the tournament, brigands begin raiding the northern perimeter. Seeing that Orr's defenses are weak, the brigands send for thugs from all around Britain. At the tournament, the women of Orr take many of the prizes. The Victualer's wife wins the knife-throwing contest, and the ring-spearing competition goes to the miller's wife. Out of jealousy, Sir Guy sabotages the horseracing competition by cutting the girth of Maeve's saddle. During the race, the girth snaps and Maeve falls to the ground, thankfully avoiding the stampede of horses that come after her. Believing he is unbeatable, Sir Guy races for the finish line only to be beaten by his wife Mathilde. Arn is out for Guy's blood, but Maeve has another idea. She feigns injury and has to be carried off the field on a litter. She is carried to the archery range where Guy has hit the target dead center. Lying on the litter, leaning on one elbow, Maeve lets fly an arrow that splits Guy's shaft in twain, thus winning that competition. Just then, a townsperson enters to tell everyone that the city is being sacked. Arn sends the knights into the city from the east while he gathers the townspeople on the west side to lay in wait. As the bandits leave the city, Arn and his people ambush them and defeat the bandits. For his misdeeds, Sir Guy pledges to teach every boy and girl over the age of eight horsemanship and self-defense. The women of Orr, in order to keep the peace, hold a banquet where Maeve "realizes for the first time that charm can be as potent a weapon as a drawn sword."

182: "Vanni"
Pages 2703 (27 November 1988) – 2713 (5 February 1989)

Aleta sends word to Arn that Karen has run away, and appears to be heading for Venice. Arn leaves Orr at once to try and intercept his sister. As her boat neared Venice Karen wondered if her leaving was such a good idea. Unfortunately, she had spent all her money on the voyage and had nothing left when her ship docked. Karen, disguised as a boy, is accosted by two slavers wishing to sell her for wine money. A young man named Giovanni (who prefers to be called just "Vanni") comes to Karen's aid and beats up the slavers. Vanni is surprised to find out that Karen is actually a girl, and takes her to the boarding home where he is staying. Vanni, a country bumpkin at heart, is looking for his father, and the only clues he has are a partial map of Venice and the name Farabutto. Farabutto turns out to be an evil man who becomes worried when Vanni comes looking for his father. Farabutto convenes a meeting of several important men in Venice—they all become very concerned over Vanni. After he leaves the men call for an assassin who kills Farabutto. When Vanni and Karen go to see Farabutto in the morning they find that he is dead. They also see where a second part of the map had once hung on the wall. They trace marks that were left on the wall from age and dust onto a new piece of parchment and compare it to Vanni's map. The combined maps make out a trail through Venice. As Karen kisses Vanni, Arn enters. Arn begins to fume at Karen when the good-natured Vanni introduces himself, and asks Arn for his help. Arn, who is completely unprepared for Vanni's kindheartedness, agrees to help him.

183: Prester John
Pages 2714 (12 February 1989) – 2738 (30 July 1989)

A fire-breathing mechanical dragon attacks Val, Gawain, and Yuan Chen. The dragon is a weapon of war designed by Prester John, who finds them and invites them to his home. Over dinner, Prester John tells them of how he not only found treasure, but has also amassed an army of over 400,000 soldiers. Even in Cathay Val is legendary, and Prester John wants him as his general. Gawain and Yuan Chen are placed in chains, and Val is told that all their lives are forfeit if he should decline, or lose the war. With his friends held hostage by Prester John, and Galan held hostage by Wu Ti, Val complies but secretly hopes to engineer a stalemate.

Arn, Karen, and Vanni follow the old spice route, which leads them into Cathay, and to the city of Chang-An. There they learn of a man who set out to the City of the Dead some ten years before. Not knowing if it was Vanni's father, the three travelers leave for the mountainous tombs.

Wu Ti's army has marched across Cathay to vanquish Prester John. The Imperial Army is impressive, and it is Prester John's war machines that keep the battle even. At Chang-An, Val is finally able to halt Wu Ti's advance, and the Emperor must fall back to regroup. At the City of the Dead, the armies of Prester John and Wu Ti converge, but so too does Arn. With Karen and Vanni, Arn discovers the tomb of the great Emperor Ch'in Shih Huang-Ti, which is filled with thousands of full-sized clay people and animals. Within the tomb Vanni finds his father's map. Sitting atop the mountain of the City of the Dead, Prester John finds that he cannot use his thunder lances (cannons) because of avalanches, and Wu Ti realizes that his army will not advance because of their superstitions. The armies are at a stalemate. Prester John goes mad, sings a song of clay men, and sets off the thunder lances. Vanni hears the song and remembers it being sung by his father in his youth, but before he can reach Prester John the mountain collapses. Val and Vanni dig up Prester John, and for a short while father and son are reunited. Prester John dies and the army elevates Vanni as the new Prester John. Karen and Vanni are reunited, and the love they share is noticeable even to Val. "At least he has royal blood," Val says, smiling. Vanni meets with Wu Ti to forge a treaty. For lasting peace Vanni must promise to wed Wu Ti's daughter. Heartbroken, Vanni agrees, for too many lives are at stake should he not comply. Val and his family leave Cathay by way of the southern spice route, traveling back to Camelot. Vanni travels to Nanking and meets his betrothed, but notices that she too is in love with another. All of Nanking gathers for the Imperial wedding—all that is except for Vanni, who has left during the night to follow his heart.

184: Lessons in Kindness
Pages 2739 (6 August 1989) – 2745 (17 September 1989)

It has been over a year, and time for Nathan and Aelfred to rejoin their respective families. Cynan has taught Nathan many things, but the most important one is that "love of your fellow man is the virtue from which all others flow." On a rainy day King Arthur is separated from his hunting party and becomes lost in the woods. His horse stumbles and the king crashes to the ground. Weak, cold, and feverish he slumps unconscious on the ground. Not knowing that it is King Arthur, Nathan and the Dawn People bring him into the mountain. Nathan and the Dawn People nurse Arthur back to health. Arthur is far from an ideal patient, and makes everyone's life miserable. Everyone is relieved when Arthur is well enough to leave. As he is about to go he promises to repay their kindness. Britain has not seen rain like this in a decade, and water soon begins to flood the home of the Dawn People. Arthur comes to the aid of the Dawn People by having his men build a bulwark to divert the waters. Kindness begets kindness, but the floodwaters had a disastrous, unforeseen consequence. Deep within the earth, the pit containing Mordred fills with water, and the evil tyrant floats up and leaves his place of captivity.

185: The Four Horsemen of Gunderit
Pages 2746 (24 September 1989) – 2756 (3 December 1989)

Val's family is reunited in Camelot. Arthur has been receiving profits from the opening of the northern spice route, so in honor of Prince Valiant's achievement, the king declares a tournament be held. Additionally, for his services in Cathay, Arthur presents Galan with the boyhood sword of his father, Uther Pendragon. Many knights and soldiers of fortune descend upon Camelot. An Ostrogoth named Gunderit enters his band of four aging horsemen Alpha, Beta, Gamma, and Delta in the tournament. In addition to managing his men, Gunderit is a bookie and runs his own gambling business. In fact, his tent is even more popular than the taverns. Gunderit's four horsemen are a hapless bunch, and lose at all the individual competitions. After a week it is time for the team competitions. Each team consists of four men, and Val has chosen Arn, Gawain, and Tristram. Gunderit's four horsemen win their competitions easily, but unknown to the crowd, the four aged men have been replaced by four young Ostrogoth warriors who are each as strong as an ox. These men are trained "in the techniques of the great Ostrogothic cavalry masters Alatheus and Saphrax," and with their helmets on, none can tell that they are not old. To everyone's disbelief Gunderit's men defeat Val's team and walk away with the prize. However, Aleta notices that Sir Alpha, who had sliced his leg the day before, walks without a limp and spryly jumps a small stream. Just then Galan arrives to tell Val that he had wagered Uther Pendragon's boyhood sword on his father winning the competition, and now he has lost it. Val quickly goes to Arthur and suggests a plan. Arthur calls for one more competition between Gunderit's men and Val's, with the winner taking all of his estates in Cornwall. The entry purse is more than he has, but Gunderit is greedy. Val agrees to loan Gunderit the money, but only if he puts Uther Pendragon's sword up as collateral. The competition is a simple relay race run in four legs, but on the final leg the rider must first accept a kiss from Queen Aleta. Val's knights fare poorly in the races but when Sir Gamma approaches Aleta he realizes that he cannot take off his helmet and reveal that he is not an old man. Val casually trots up, dismounts, and kisses his wife before galloping to victory. Gunderit is allowed to leave, for he was an amiable rogue, and who knows when Camelot may need him as an ally.

186: The Escape of Mordred
Pages 2757 (10 December 1989) – 2767 (18 February 1990)

After his escape from the pit, Mordred lives from hand to mouth, thieving from kind families. While lost in a forest Mordred meets a small man named Simplex who offers him half of his meal. Mordred knocks Simplex senseless with a rock and takes all his possessions, including a knife. Luckily a forester finds Simplex and takes him to where he is mended and fed. Mordred makes for Orr and arrives there on Christmas Day. Mordred cons Maeve into believing he has reformed his ways. Maeve has pity on him and over the course of several days sneaks food and clothing to him. A night guard tells Arn that he has seen the light of two lanterns meeting at the faerie ring on a nearby hill. Arn suspects Maeve of meeting in secret. One night he sets off on his horse and confronts Maeve and Mordred. Infuriated at Maeve's deception, Arn draws his sword and confronts Mordred, who crumbles to the ground sobbing. Moved to pity, Arn attempts to help Mordred stand up, when suddenly Mordred uncoils and stabs the young prince. Mordred laughs at Arn and Maeve, then mounts Arn's horse and rides away. Maeve calls her hounds and they come to her aid. She creates a sledge out of branches and her cloak, and ties a makeshift harness around the hounds, who then drag Arn to Castle Orr. It is days before Arn's fever breaks, but after it does Maeve sets out to find Mordred. She is stopped along the way by "The Wanderer" who tells her to turn back "if not for your husband then for the sake of your unborn child." Maeve is stunned, and "The Wanderer" tells her that it has been prophesied that she will bring forth monarchs. Maeve is "wonderfully shaken" and return to Castle Orr.

187: The Lost Colony of Thule
Pages 2768 (25 February 1990) – 2789 (22 July 1990)

King Aguar arrives in Camelot with a quest for Val. Many years ago forty families were sent to colonize the newly found lands west of Greenland. But no one has heard from them for generations, and now King Godfred of the Danes wants the lands for himself. On the voyage Val takes Nathan. It is his first adventure and his first taste of being out to sea. With Gundar Harl as the ship's master Val sails westward. They plot their course using a Gnomon to keep their course true, but a spy is aboard ship and sabotages the instrument, causing them to sail north to Greenland. Past the southern tip of Greenland they encounter a party of Skraelings in kayaks and umiaks hunting several narwhals. A wounded narwhal attacks the longship, piercing its hull and knocking Gundar Harl overboard. On its second pass Val cuts off its tusk with his Singing Sword. Once more the beast returns, but this time it grabs Gundar Harl in its jaws. Val leaps on the back of the narwhal, grabs on to one of the harpoons, and shoves his fist deep into the creature's blowhole. The narwhal panics and releases Gundar Harl before diving away to safety.

The Skraelings have seen what has happened and are impressed with Val. In a simple sign language they invite Val and his shipmates to dinner. They eat muktuk, which is the flesh of the narwhal. Val realizes how important whales are to these people and gives them the tusk he had cut from the narwhal. The gift is a high honor to the Skraelings, who now regard Val as a friend. A young boy by the name of Oomoo comes forward, speaking in Val's own language. His people are called the Inugsuk, and when he was small a Danish raiding party, lead by King Godfred, took him as a slave. He was only freed years later when Skraelings attacked the Danish vessel on which he served. Oomoo tells Val of the Beothuk people, but he does not think they are the lost colony he is seeking. Val decides to check them out anyway, and Oomoo goes with him as a translator. They sail west for over a week. When they finally make landfall Val finds evidence of runic symbols—the language of Thule. Val and Oomoo are attacked by a Beothuk warrior. With Oomoo's help Val is able to subdue him, and the man takes them to his village. A Beothuk elder allows Val and his men one week to search for the lost colony as long as they do not come into the village. To make sure Val complies, Nathan remains in the village. Nathan finds out that the villagers are actually white like himself, but every week they stain themselves red. Nathan joins in and stains himself as well. When Val returns after a week, unable to find the colony, he doesn't even recognize his own son. Looking every bit a Beothuk, Nathan tells his father that he can talk with and understand the other boys. Suddenly Val understands what has happened to the colony. Just then a watchman arrives with word that King Godfred's ships have arrived.

Val and his men hide their ships and weapons, and stain themselves to look like the Beothuks. Then Val devises a war plan taken from Hannibal. The Beothuks will lure Godfred and his people into the woods then, with his flank exposed, Val and the rest of the "Beothuk" Thules will attack from behind. The strategy works and Godfred is taken captive. Unbeknownst to Godfred all the warriors, Beothuk and Dane alike, are properly buried. The Beothuks call for a feast, but after everyone has eaten, they fool Godfred and his men into thinking that they had eaten the flesh of the fallen warriors. Godfred leaves the Beothuks, never to return. A Beothuk elder recounts the tale of how they came to be. After settling the land, the Thule colonists made contact with the Beothuk people who had lived here for generations. Soon the peoples mingled and began to live in peace. Because they no longer wished to be part of the violent world across the sea, they decided to break off contact. Only one family of merchants knew of their existence and sent supplies every year. It was a young man from this family who sabotaged the Gnomon. Val complies with their wishes and vows to keep their secret.

188: The Isle of Lost Youth
Pages 2790 (29 July 1990) & 2791 (5 August 1990)

The men of Thule set a course for home, but become lost in a mist. Gundar Harl insists on pulling into a harbor until the mists clear. Val goes ashore to explore and Nathan and Gundar Harl join him. The only inhabitant is an old man who tells them that it is the Isle of Lost Youth, and if they but desire to be young again they will youthen until they are no more. Gundar Harl laughs when suddenly he is younger and his missing leg and hand have returned. Both Val and Gundar Harl begin to grow younger at an alarming rate. The magic has no effect on the six-year-old Nathan who only wants to be older—not younger. Quickly Nathan drags the infant Val and Gundar Harl to the boat and rows to the ship. The farther away they get the weaker the magic becomes, and the men grow up once more.

189: William of Orr
Pages 2792 (12 August 1990) – 2799 (30 September 1990)

Back in Orr Arn finally awakens. He remembers Maeve and Mordred and is deeply hurt, but he soon comes to forgive her. Maeve tells Arn that he will soon be a father. It is important news, for their child will inherit the thrones of both Thule and Camelot. Word is sent to Camelot about Mordred's escape, and Aguar, along with Lady Fenia, travels to Orr to conduct the search. While Arn is healing, Aguar conducts Orr's affairs. Abbot Ethelred approaches Aguar to tell him that a small fortune in Lapis Lazuli had been stolen from the monastery's storeroom. A search is conducted, and the Lapis Lazuli is found in the possession of a mute boy named William. Unable to protest or explain why he had the stones, William is taken away for judgment. At his sentencing, Aguar notices that William has calluses on his fingers from holding a quill. When asked if he can draw, William takes them to his hovel in the forest. Upon entering, Aguar finds some of the most beautifully rendered manuscript pages ever made. William had always wanted to be a monk, but the Abbot would not let him because he could not sing. William had not stolen the Lapis Lazuli for his own gain, but rather to prove his worthiness to be a monk. Aguar suggests that William be allowed to become a monk, and the boy is welcomed into the community. William, the Chronicles say, ends his days in Hibernia illustrating the Book of Kells.

190: On the Forks of a Dilemma
Pages 2800 (7 October 1990) – 2809 (9 December 1990)

In Britain, Aleta goes riding and finds a villa occupied by a woman named Julia, daughter of Claudius. Julia invites Aleta to dinner and shows her a fork. Aleta is excited, and sells some of her "least favorite baubles" to pay for the making of hundreds of forks. At dinner the forks do not go over well with the knights, who use them for mini sword fights. Infuriated, Aleta decides to go among the common folk and sell her forks. Word of a queen and a prince traveling with very few guards makes it to Dio, the leader of the northern brigands. Dio's thoughts turn to ransom. Some townspeople buy Aleta's forks, but not to eat with. Unbeknownst to Aleta some buy them as mementos of her visit, while others use them as combs or other kinds of tools. The party is attacked by the brigands and takes up a defensive position across a small bridge that goes over a shallow muddy river. The brigands get stuck in the mud and cannot cross, and they fall back to regroup. That night the air turns cold and Val can feel a frost coming. Val knows that if the mud freezes the brigands will be able to easily cross the river, and overrun them. Val wakes Aleta and the knights, and, under the cover of darkness, they plant thousands of forks, tine-side up, in the quickly freezing mud. At dawn the brigands attack across the mudflats and impale themselves on the forks. Men and warhorses alike are in a panic, not knowing where to step. Val commands his archers and many of the brigands die in a hail of arrows. The remaining brigands drop their weapons and gingerly step their way across the mudflats. One brigand, in exchange for leniency, tells Val where they have hid all their plunder. Aleta's forks have brought the family a small fortune after all.

191: The Story of Boudicca
Pages 2810 (16 December 1990) – 2823 (17 March 1991)

Galan attempts to find owners for the brigand's stolen items. Among them is the decaying shield of Boudicca. Galan explains to Yuan Chen that Boudicca was the wife of Prasutagus, the leader of the powerful Iceni tribe. On his deathbed, Prasutagus willed his lands be evenly divided between Boudicca and Rome. The move was meant as a bribe, but Rome wanted all of Britain, so they attacked the Iceni and tortured Boudicca. A natural leader, the fiery-haired Boudicca waged war on Rome. Boudicca attacked Colchester, Londinium, and Verulamium, burned them to the ground and slaughtered their inhabitants. A Roman army led by Suetonius defeated the Britons. Boudicca fled into the woods where she killed herself with poison. Boudicca's body was hidden in a secret cave with a vast treasure, its whereabouts forgotten. Galan, convinced the shield is part of that treasure, questions Dio's men. One man confesses that he stole it from an old farmer in the fens whom he killed. Val, Galan, and Yuan Chen find the farmer's widow and question her. She tells them the shield was handed down from father to son for generations along with a poem. The poem leads them Turtle Knoll, where they realize the surface of the shield is a relief map of the area. They find Boudicca's cave, get past the booby traps, and discover her skeleton. Once Val touches Boudicca's skeleton, the cave fills with water. They escape, but only a small dagger Galan had slipped into his belt remains of the treasure. "The Wanderer" arrives, and a magical message appears on the blade of the dagger that warns, "Awaiteth him vile death's cruel pause, who useth me without good cause."

192: Ivarr the Slave Merchant
Pages 2824 (24 March 1991) – 2836 (16 June 1991)

Vanni walks to Britain to be reunited with Karen. He is robbed of his money, and does laborious work just to eat. Eventually, Vanni saves enough to book passage to England. The ship becomes lost in a fog and is destroyed by a huge Merchantman vessel. Vanni clings to flotsam and is washed up on the Northumbrian shore. He is taken to Ivarr, a powerful land-owning Thane (knight), and made a slave. The Thanes are called to Camelot to swear fealty to King Arthur. Ivarr takes his slaves with him to sell. Ivarr reaches Camelot with only a few slaves left—one of them is Vanni. Vanni sees a stablehand bearing the stallion insignia of the house of Thule. Vanni jumps the stablehand, and asks the man to get word to Val. The stablehand sees

Karen and relays Vanni's message. Karen has the stablehand take her to Ivarr's auction where she purchases Vanni. As Karen and Vanni head back to Camelot he asks her to marry him and she accepts. Val is furious with Karen for taking such a foolhardy risk, and Aleta is in shock over the betrothal. Val detains Ivarr and his men, and they are jailed for slavery. Aleta and Val give Karen and Vanni four challenges that will test their resolve. Each of the four challenges will involve one of the four great virtues: wisdom, courage, temperance, and justice." Karen and Vanni accept the decision.

193: The Heir of Two Kingdoms
2836 (16 June 1991) – 2844 (11 August 1991)

Camelot's physician, Morgan Todd, falls ill. Maeve's child is due and there is no doctor to attend her. Hildegarde, an itinerant physician who was trained at the University of Salerno in Sicily, arrives in Camelot. Hildegarde's healing powers are unmatched. Her commanding manner convinces Arthur to clean up Camelot. First go the rats, and the rubbish in the streets. Next, Hildegarde operates on Arthur and removes his cataracts, restoring his vision. A grateful Arthur tells Hildegarde that whatever she asks for he will give her. Her request is that each household be provided with a cast-iron stewing pot. Due to the iron, "food cooked in such a pot makes people stronger and less tired," she explains.

Maeve gives birth to a girl. Hildegarde sees Galan's keen interest in healing and entrust him with a book called *De Usu Partium* (essentially *On the Usefulness of the Parts of the Body*). The book is by Galan, the greatest physician ancient Greece ever knew. The boy Galan becomes thoroughly captivated with learning all he can about healing, and asks Hildegarde to let him study at her side. As the time for the Christening draws near, an aged man is secretly carried into Camelot on a litter. It is Mordred in disguise, and he has come to see his granddaughter. The child is Christened Ingrid, heir to the thrones of Camelot and Thule. Mordred, disguised once more, is carried out of Camelot and leaves without incident. Hildegarde sends word to Val that she is ready to leave Camelot and is willing to take Galan with her. Galan happily accepts.

COMMENT: *The birth of Ingrid is recorded on Page 2839, 7 July, 1991.*

194: The First Challenges
Pages 2845 (18 August 1991) – 2857 (10 November 1991)

Gawain follows a man who has stolen Sir Edmund's shield from the armory. When he enters the room he sees two men, and neither will confess to the crime. Both men are taken before Val, who turns the matter over to Karen and Vanni. As "Justice" is one of the four challenges, they must determine who stole the shield and why. Vanni realizes that it is a left-handed shield, and tricks the thief into catching an apple with his left hand. The man's name is Offa. He tells them he only needed the shield to protect his village of Ashdown from marauders, because Lord Athelstan refuses to help. Val, Gawain, and Offa go to Ashdown. They are attacked on the way, but dispatch the marauders easily. Before one dies, he reveals that they worked for a magician. Val and Gawain find Lord Athelstan to be a weak man whose advisor, Alfred, is an illusionist. The knights are secretly approached by Lea, who tells them that Alfred is manipulating Athelstan. Val notices that all the peasant's clothing is green and deduces that the water runs through a copper mine. Since there is no operating copper mine in Britain, whoever controls the mine would be very rich. Athelstan believes in Alfred's magic so completely that he will not discuss Val's suspicions. Offa shows Val and Gawain a secret passageway. They watch Alfred performing his "magic," and witness a woman being sawn in half. During the performance, Val and Gawain crawl into either end of the sawed box, and surprise Alfred. Alfred confesses. Lea takes over and asks Val if he will help the men of Ashdown take care of the marauders. Alfred is sent to labor in the copper mine.

195: Cormac
Pages 2858 (17 November 1991) – 2875 (15 March 1992)

Val and Gawain head to Northumbria to oversee the razing of Ivarr's castle. King Arthur has decreed that it should be destroyed, as a warning to all that slavery will not be tolerated in Britain. Val notices a sacrificial altar that has been recently used. The two knights change into peasant clothing and search for Druids. On the eve of the winter solstice, the Druids plan to make a human sacrifice. Gawain releases a boar, disrupting the ceremony. Val stops the Druid from killing the man on the altar. However, the man lying on the altar is really Cormac, their high priest. Cormac leaps from the altar, knocking Gawain senseless. Cormac has been expertly trained, and knows both barbarian and Roman fighting tactics. Cormac ensnares Val's leg with a rope and pulls him over. He knocks the Singing Sword out of Val's hand then faints. Before he lay on the altar, Cormac drank from a cup containing a sleeping potion designed to ensure the cooperation of those being sacrificed. With their high priest unconscious, the people disperse. Cormac awakens, tells them he is of royal blood, and recounts how Druids in Brittany raised him to be both a scholar and a warrior. Cormac leads Val and Gawain to a nearby castle, where he is greeted by several hounds. Val is impressed with Cormac's knowledge and fighting skills and makes him an offer. Val will show Cormac all that Britain has to offer, and in a year, if he still wishes to be sacrificed, Val will release him. Cormac agrees.

Cormac is surprised to find out that in the smaller towns people rule themselves. Several of the Northumbrian Thanes meet with Val, who tells them that Ivarr has been declared a "Nithing." The sentence is reserved for the worst criminals. It means that Ivarr is stripped of his freedom, honor, lands, identity, and his very name. The Thanes squabble over who should govern the land, and Val tells them to return in one week. On the way to Ivarr's castle Gawain is surprised by a booby trap, and he falls into a stream. The trap was set by children, who were among Ivarr's slaves, but were not yet old enough to be sold. Since Ivarr left they have prospered in peace by living off the land. In order to save the children from the warring Thanes, Cormac suggests a Tontine, or compact. By Druidic custom all participants swear a solemn oath that whatever is coveted will belong to the last among them to die. The Thanes swear the oath, but as they leave they fall prey to the same pranks that sent Gawain into the river. The children strip the castle of anything of value, and Val torches it.

196: The Second Challenge
Pages 2876 (22 March 1992) – 2877 (29 March 1992)

Cormac is no more than a country bumpkin. With young Nathan he is a friend, but with the shy Valeta he is equally shy. Aleta announces to Val that Karen and Vanni will face their second challenge, which will be prudence. Arthur recounts how his father, Uther Pendragon, once condemned Merlin for predicting the future. Too many of Merlin's predictions of disasters had come true, and to avoid any more catastrophes Uther sentenced Merlin to death. Arthur asks if anyone can guess Merlin's "final" prediction? Vanni whispers to Karen, "Were I in Merlin's shoes, I would predict that the king would die the day after I did." "A prudent reply," Karen laughed, "but were I in your shoes I would not say so out loud and ruin the king's story." Karen's reply was as prudent as Vanni's solution, which turned out to be the right answer. Val turns to Aleta and says, "I think we may consider the second challenge to have been met."

197: Alaric
Pages 2878 (5 April 1992) – 2896 (9 August 1992)

Valeta seeks to cure Cormac's shyness, and gives Nathan careful instructions. While playfully sword fighting with Cormac, Nathan cuts the Druid's leg. Valeta, who is watching close by, hurries in to clean Cormac's wound and bandage it.

The ruse works. Cormac is a "strange mixture of warmth, wisdom, wit, and unhappiness," for he possesses a dark, brooding side that none can fathom.

A badly beaten Gunderit returns to Camelot and calls for Val. He had heard the name of Alaric spoken in hushed conversations. Gunderit reveals that Alaric, who is part Hun, part Briton, part Roman, and part Ostrogoth, is "behind much of the world's lucrative woe." Alaric is so powerful and so evil that even Mordred fears him. To many, Alaric is simply an eccentric collector of rare exotic butterflies, but through blackmail and assassinations he is the unknown puppet master of Europe. Gunderit warns that Alaric seeks to kidnap Pope Joannes. Word reaches Camelot that Pope Joannes, while en route to Ravenna, was abducted. All the great lords are called to an enclave at Augusta Treverorum, and Val and Gunderit accompany Arthur. Alaric's demand is read. If the Pope will anoint Alaric Emperor, and all the rulers do him homage, the Pope will go free. Arthur, realizing the other rulers are being blackmailed, sends Val on a quest to save Pope Joannes. Val, Arn and Gunderit go to the monastery of St. Gall. They ask a monk named Vladimir to teach they all he can about butterflies. Vladimir shows them two of his rarest specimens. "They are called the 'Blue Triangle,' from a land more distant than Cathay." The monk gives Val a precious gift: two pupae of the Blue Triangle butterfly.

Val and his companions find Alaric's castle. It is high in the Alps, accessible only by pulley, rope, and basket. Val tells Alaric his name is "Lepi." Alaric is suspicious until Val identifies a rare butterfly from the Spice Islands. The next day, Val opens his pouch and releases one of the Blue Triangles. To Alaric's horror, it flies out the window. Alaric runs out of the castle alerting all of his guards to find the butterfly. Val, Arn, and Gunderit rescue Pope Joannes, and disguise themselves as guards. Val sends the others to the basket, but stays behind to burn Alaric's library—except for one document. As they descend the cliff, Alaric's manservant Slug sees them. One of Alaric's henchmen tries to cut the rope, but Val and his companions swing the basket so wildly that the man falls to his death. At the bottom, Val cuts the rope to avoid being followed. Since Alaric cannot pursue them, Val and his party pass through the checkpoints unmolested. Unfortunately, Val had torched the room containing information on people already dead, thus leaving Alaric's power intact. Pope Joannes is returned to Rome safely.

198: The Letter
Pages 2896 (9 August 1992) – 2901 (13 September 1992)

In Rome, Val reads the letter he had kept, and realizes it was written by a spy in Camelot. The letter tells of a beautiful woman named Fiona whose father was a relative of Uther Pendragon's. Fiona fell in love with her distant cousin Mordred and, since her father disapproved, they eloped. Fiona eventually learned of Mordred's evil nature, but soon gave birth to girl and boy twins—Maeve and Cormac. Mordred neglects Maeve, but plans to raise Cormac to be like him. Fiona, not wanting Cormac to be evil, wrapped him in a blanket embroidered with his name on it in a Druidic script called Ogham, and left him with nomadic Druids. Furious, Mordred banished Fiona then gave Maeve, wrapped in an identical blanket, with a nurse to raise. Fiona's father took her back, but somehow Alaric found out and blackmailed them. Deprived of her children Fiona eventually died from grief. Val tells Arn everything. They return to Camelot immediately to resolve the matter with Cormac, and find out who the spy is in Camelot.

199: The Island of Second Chances
Pages 2902 (20 September 1992) – 2904 (4 October 1992)

Sailing out of Ostia, Val's ship encounters fog, and they find themselves at the Island of Second Chances. Fortunus, the custodian of the island, greets Val, Arn, and Gunderit. Fortunus offers each of them a chance to go back to a moment in their lives and do something differently. Val and Arn know to remain silent, but Gunderit gives into temptation. "I wish…" Gunderit

begins, but Arn quickly covers his mouth as Val concludes, "that we had sailed south from Ostia, not west." The three men are drawn into a great vortex, and find themselves on their ship, sailing south.

200: The Rabbit War
Pages 2905 (11 October 1992) – 2941 (20 June 1993)

Val's and Arn's return calls for a celebration. Cormac dresses for the occasion with a shirt embroidered with his name on it in Ogham. When Maeve arrives at Camelot, she hands Princess Ingrid to Valeta. Cormac sees that Ingrid's blanket is embroidered with his name in Ogham. Knowing that Maeve is Mordred's daughter, Cormac deduces his lineage. He screams and runs away. Val tries to talk with him, but Cormac draws his sword and beats Val. Cormac rides to the land of the Druids. Arthur's scribe, the hidden spy, sends word to Alaric. Mordred is summoned by Alaric and told about Cormac. Alaric sends Val a gift of a butterfly. Knowing the Druids walk the lands, Valeta leaves a letter for Cormac in a fairy circle. The winter solstice arrives. As Cormac approaches the altar stone to be sacrificed, lightning strikes a nearby oak, and in the flash Cormac sees Mordred. Taking Cormac to a nearby lodge, Mordred cares for him, and tells him lies about Arthur and Val.

Mordred introduces thousands of rabbits to Britain. With no natural predators the rabbits will multiply quickly, eat the crops, and create a famine. Hildegarde and Galan report to Arthur, suggesting they let nature fight nature. Arn and Maeve go to Thule to collect foxes, Hildegarde and Galan to the king of the Franks to collect stoats, and Val goes to Frisia to gather goshawks from a falconer named Jupp. The army of animals is sent to Britain and released. An old Druid takes Valeta's letter to Cormac. The letter gives him courage to stand up to Mordred. Cormac sends a letter to Arthur, and tells him where Mordred plans to strike next. Arn is placed in charge of the fleet of warships. Using a corvus, they board Mordred's Merchantman vessels and easily defeat them. Arn moves his command to the Merchantman ships and raises the butterfly sails of Alaric in order to fool Mordred. Val's land assault becomes mired in mud. Arn's fleet lands, and Mordred realizes Cormac turned against him. Mordred is washed away in a sea of mud, but is captured by the Dawn People, who put him back in the pit. Val sends Alaric's butterfly back to him with a small replica of the Singing Sword through it. Vanni and Karen discover that Alaric's spy is the scribe and subdue him. Since Vanni and Karen showed both courage and temperance in capturing the spy, Val declares that their challenges have been met and that they are now officially betrothed.

201: The Madwomen of Hoggar
Pages 2942 (27 June 1993) – 2966 (12 December 1993)

Seeing the betrothal of Karen and Vanni makes Guinevere and Aleta feel old, so they plan a trip. A storm washes out a bridge and the queens, separated from their entourage, take refuge at an inn. The innkeeper mistakes them for two "madwomen" who have escaped from the Baron, and locks them in the barn. Guinevere embroiders their story into a piece of cloth, and attaches it to the housekeeper's cat. The woman reads the embroidery and releases the women, who then hide in a cave. The two "madwomen" arrive at the cave, and use sign language to talk to Guinevere and Aleta. The queens return to the inn with their bodyguards and confront the innkeeper and the Baron. The women had washed ashore from a shipwreck, but no one could understand them, so they were thought to be mad. A translator reveals that the "madwomen" are Queen Amma of Hoggar in North Africa and her daughter Princess Asha. The queen explains how her husband, the king, was killed by his younger brother Musa, who sold them into slavery.

Arthur sends Val and Gawain to Hoggar to restore Queen Amma to power. They hire Berber, a nomad, to guide them. Musa's passion is camel racing, which he cheats at by using young boys as jockeys instead of men. At a great race Musa's camels win, but Amma removes the disguise from one of the

Art copyright Brian Kane and
Al Williamson, 2000.

Our Story: SIR MAXWELL PRESENTS HIMSELF TO ARTHUR, ANNOUNCING THAT HE HAS COME TO ENTER THE GREAT TOURNAMENT AND WIN HONOR TO HIS NAME.

THEN HE MAKES HIS OBEISANCE TO THE QUEEN. NO MAN CAN LOOK UNMOVED AT THE FACE OF GUINEVERE, BUT MAXWELL'S EYES WANDER TO THE TALL LADY-IN-WAITING.

THE LADY MAUD, A WIDOW WHOSE HUSBAND WAS KILLED IN BATTLE, NOW BEFRIENDED BY THE QUEEN, HAS BECOME A LADY-IN-WAITING.

"I MIGHT AS WELL BE A WIDOW FOR ALL THE ATTENTION YOU PAY ME!" STORMS ALETA.. "YOU SPEND ALL YOUR TIME TRAINING WITH THE OTHER KNIGHTS."

SHE TURNS AWAY ANGRILY AND ALMOST BUMPS INTO GOOD-NATURED SIR MAXWELL. "OH, SIR MAXWELL, WOULD YOU WEAR MY SCARF IN THE TOURNAMENT AND BE MY GALLANT KNIGHT?"

THE LADY MAUD HAD HOPED SIR MAXWELL WOULD CARRY HER GAGE. WELL, TWO CAN PLAY THAT GAME..... SHE SEEKS OUT VAL AND HE, JEALOUS, ACCEPTS HER SCARF. SO ANY BRAVE DEEDS HE ACCOMPLISHES WILL BE IN HER HONOR.
2158

IN THE ARMORY TWO WARRIORS ARE RESTING AFTER PRACTICE: "JUST HOW DOES IT HAPPEN THAT I CARRY YOUR WIFE'S GAGE INTO THE TOURNAMENT TO DO DEEDS IN HER HONOR INSTEAD OF LADY MAUD'S?" "WOMEN!" ANSWERS VAL SAGELY. "THEY ARE HALF ANGEL, HALF IMP.

EITHER SPANK THEM OR KISS THEM." (AND THAT, DEAR READER, IS THE SUM TOTAL OF VAL'S KNOWLEDGE OF WOMEN AFTER TWENTY YEARS OF MARRIAGE)

6-18   NEXT WEEK— A Proud Moment

jockeys and exposes Musa's cheating. Musa flees, but is caught by nomadic tribes led by Berber. All of the boy jockeys kidnapped from the nomads are reunited with their families. Musa's punishment is to clean camels for the rest of his life. Amma is made Queen of Hoggar once more. Before leaving North Africa, Val and Gawain travel to Egypt so Val can be the first Viking to climb to the top of the pyramids. When he reaches the top, however, he finds the name Halfdan etched into one of the stones.

202: The Wedding of Karen and Vanni
Pages 2966 (19 December 1993) – 2972 (23 January 1994)

Hildegarde's niece, Lady Bridget of Bath, arrives in Camelot to help with the wedding arrangements for Karen and Vanni. Bridget is very beautiful, and Galan, her junior by several years, falls in love. Galan, jealous of Gawain's advances towards Bridget, consults one of Merlin's books, and puts itching powder in the knight's bed. Hildegarde figures out Galan's mischief, reprimands him, and then pulls the same prank on Galan. At long last, Karen and Vanni are wed.

COMMENT: *The wedding of Karen and Vanni appears on Page 2972, 23 January 1994.*

203: The Earthen Fort
Pages 2973 (30 January 1994) – 2985 (24 April 1994)

Sven Fork-Beard tells Val the Saxon's need iron, and they plan to attack Arthur's iron ore mine. With Arthur's approval, Val begins construction of an earthen fort to protect the mine. Baldred, commander of the Saxons, attacks the fort but is repulsed. Baldred lays siege to the fort, but after weeks his men begin to starve. Arn and some knights circle around the raiders and burn their ships. The starving Saxons attack again, but Val loads bread and meat on the ballistas, and launches the food into the attack force. The Saxons halt their attack to eat. They surrender without incident. Val notices the high degree of craftsmanship of the Saxons' metalwork and suggests to Arthur that he should trade with the Saxons peacefully.

204: The Shield of Achilles
Pages 2986 (1 May 1994) – 3005 (11 September 1994)

Val, Aleta, and Nathan sail to the Misty Isles, but Alaric knows and sends Corsairs to capture them. Aleta and Nathan are held hostage, while Val is sent in search of the Shield of Achilles, which was lost in a shipwreck fifty years ago. According to legend, anyone who touches the shield must tell the truth. Val goes to the coast of Gaul where the ship had wrecked and is washed into a cave where he finds the survivors. The cave entrance is only accessible for a few days once a year. Val finds the shield, and Claudio, the leader of the survivors permits him to take it if he promises to find new settlers for their village. While Val is away, Nathan escapes up the chimney every night and scouts around the castle. He finds the chamber of blackmail letters and takes some of them back to Aleta. When Val arrives, Alaric takes the shield. Since he cannot lie, he begins insulting his own guards. Eventually, Alaric flees with slug to the basket at the cliff. On their way down Alaric tells Slug what he really thinks of him, so Slug cuts the rope and they fall to their death. Val destroys all the blackmail letters, and then tells Alaric's servants about Claudio's people. In less than a year, they all travel to the coast of Gaul to join Claudio. Val, Aleta, and Nathan set sail for the Misty Isles, and, while at sea, Val drops the lead-covered shield into the water.

205: Necromancy
Pages 3006 (18 September 1994) – 3031 (12 March 1995)

Off the coast of the Misty Isles Val comes across merchant ships destroyed by marauding Corsairs. Aleta returns to find that Ajax, the new steward, has taken over running the palace. Though Ajax's stewardship is impeccable, he is behind the pirate attacks on the merchant ships. Val figures out how Ajax is

signaling the pirate ships, and destroys their fleet with a burning liquid called "Greek fire." Ajax reveals that he is working for Justinian. Ajax is sentenced to death, but Aleta has him imprisoned for life, so he can use his vast knowledge to help the Misty Isles. Val consults Claustro, an itinerant locksmith, on how to secure the palace. When Claustro hears that their enemy is Justinian, he tells Val to contact a locksmith in Constantinople named Clavis. Clautro and Clavis are identical twin brothers and their names mean "lock" and "key." Soon after Val arrives in Constantinople the city is struck by a plague, and Theodora, Justinian's wife, dies. Clavis shows Val secret passageways through the castle, and they discover that Justinian is hiring necromancers in order to talk to Theodora. Val takes some of Theodora's items from her room, and, posing as a necromancer, convinces Justinian he can talk to the dead. During the séance, Clavis whispers to Justinian and persuades him that he is Theodora. Justinian is made to regret his infatuation with Aleta, and is told if he removes the rats that the plague will go away.

206: The Island of Omniscience
Pages 3032 (19 March 1995) – 3033 (26 March 1995)

Heading back to the Misty Isles Val, accompanied by Clavis, comes upon the Island of Omniscience. On the island the guardian can answer all questions, as long as they are not about the future. Fighting breaks out among the crew over some of the answers. Val asks how they can get back to the ship, and the guardian tells them that they need to ask him a question that he cannot answer, so Val asks, "Why?" They immediately appear back on the ship.

207: The Isthmian Games
Pages 3034 (2 April 1995) – 3040 (14 May 1995)

Val heads for Corinth to see the Isthmian Games, and runs into Gunderit, who is sponsoring athletes from Goth. When the Corinthians will not allow the Goths to compete, Val helps Gunderit by hiding the oxen that are needed to haul ships over the isthmus along the Diolkos road. The Corinthians give in and include the Goths in the games. Gunderit fails to make money off the games, since none will bid against the Goths.

208: Princess Regent
Pages 3041 (21 May 1995) – 3056 (3 September 1995)

Since Cormac has gone with Arthur on his annual hunt, which lasts several months, Valeta returns to the Misty Isles. Aleta hires Valeta to be her new steward. When problems arise that she cannot solve, Valeta consults Ajax. Valeta becomes adept at managing affairs of state. Aleta and Val leave to visit friends, and make Valeta Princess Regent in their absence. When an earthquake rocks the Misty Isles, a quick-thinking Valeta commands everyone to take higher ground to avoid a tremendous tidal wave. Val and Aleta's ship is crushed by the wave, and drifts to a nearby island where the inhabitants kill all strangers. Val carves maps of their location, sets them adrift in the sea, then he and Aleta go into hiding. Ajax, his tower prison destroyed by the earthquake, disguises himself and leaves the Misty Isles. Ajax finds one of Val's maps floating on the sea, and returns to the Misty Isles to tell Valeta. Val and Aleta are captured and sentenced to death. Valeta arrives in time to stop the execution. She then pardons Ajax of his crimes and sends him off on a fishing boat.

209: The Cave
Pages 3057 (10 September 1995) – 3060 (1 October 1995)

Nathan, who was left on the Misty Isles, leaves the palace to seek adventure. He falls through a fissure created by the earthquake, and finds a cave with prehistoric paintings in it. "The Wanderer" appears, gives him chalk and charcoal, and tells Nathan he will be an artist. Nathan draws a doorway on one of the walls, and when he goes to enter, it magically yields and leads him out of the cave. Men find him unconscious on the surface, the chalk and charcoal still in his hands.

210: Jaguar Paw
Pages 3061 (8 October 1995) – 3086 (31 March 1996)

In the ruins left over from the earthquake a chest is found. Clavis and Claustro determine that the chest is of Phoenician origin, with many booby traps to it. They open the chest to find a golden figure and papyri. The papyri tell of the Mayan civilization in Central America. Val returns to Camelot, and an expedition is sent to find the Mayans. With Sven Fork-Beard as his admiral, and Arn as his second in command, Val sets sail from Camelot with a fleet of ships. The fleet sails south to the Fortunate Islands (The Canaries), then westward. They slowly pass through the Sargasso Sea, and arrive in Guatemala near the city of Tikal. Val meets Jaguar Paw, the ruler of the Mayans. When Val refuses to become a mercenary for Jaguar Paw, the Mayan leader holds several of Val's men hostage. Val capitulates, but secretly has his men build a trebuchet. Disguising boulders as owls and a dog (messengers of the underworld), Val uses the trebuchet to deliver a message to the Mayan people that Jaguar Paw has offended the gods. Jaguar Paw releases Val's men just as the enraged mob kills him.

211: The Island of Crippling Foresight
Pages 3087 (7 April 1996) – 3088 (14 April 1996)

Leaving Guatemala, Val lands upon the Island of Crippling Foresight. On the island people know all the future consequences of any of their actions. When Val sees the dire consequences of returning to Britain, he pauses, but Arn intervenes by asking him what were the consequences should he not return. Val realizes "it is pointless to second-guess the future," and they are on their way again.

212: The Druid War
Pages 3089 (21 April 1996) – 3102 (21 July 1996)

Due to Cormac's departure as high priest, the Druid tribes of Hibernia and Western Britain become embroiled in civil war. Cormac, wishing to right this wrong, sneaks out of Camelot, and leaves for Hibernia. Infuriated, Valeta, along with Galan, secretly follow. Disguising himself as a traveling bard, Cormac takes refuge in a monastery whose monks follow the man named Patrick. The monks tell him of the rival Druid priests Cathbad and Conchobar. At the feast of Beltain, Cathbad and Conchobar contend against one another in the singing competition. When they are done, the two Druids are deadlocked, so Cormac enters the competition. Partway through his ballad, Cormac's voice falters, but Valeta, who had arrived just moments before, continues the song, enthralling the audience. The judges decree Cormac the winner of the competition, and a crown of mistletoe is placed on his head. Only then does Cormac reveal his name. He is hoist upon the ceremonial shield, which he shares with Valeta, and places the crown of mistletoe on her head. With Hibernia united, Arthur prepares for war. Soon Cormac's armada arrives, and is met by Arthur and the knights of Camelot. However, the ships are empty, for they have come to take the Hibernian refugees back home. Valeta decides to stay in Camelot.

213: Utopia
Pages 3102 (21 July 1996) – 3119 (17 November 1996)

On the open sea, Val meets the Christian monk Brendan. The monk asks for directions to "a mysterious land far from human ken." Val points westward and Brendan sails away. The ships arrive at the island city of Utopia. They are greeted by Adam who tells them that in Utopia there is no money, no want, and everyone takes only what they need. However, a group of Utopians called the "Committee of Six" secretly kills any citizen who disturbs their perfect way of life through a process called "selection." Val uncovers the truth and is

captured. Before he can be executed, pirates attack Utopia led by Zoltan. Val convinces them to let him go free so he and the knights can protect the city. The pirates are defeated and Zoltan dies in a fire he had set himself. Val disbands the Committee of Six, and citizens are chosen at random to rule the city. Continuing home, a fierce storm threatens to dash the ships along the Hibernian shore of Skellig Michael. When the lanterns prove to be too dim, Val has the Tikal scrolls brought out of their secured chest and burned. The beacon guides the fleet out of harm, but destroys the only evidence of that civilization.

214: The Stone of Destiny
Pages 3119 (17 November 1996) – 3571 (10 August 1997)

Aleta, Maeve, and Ingrid are sent by Arthur to visit all the major market towns and knights castles in Britain. "The Stone of Destiny," or "The Stone of Scone," as the Pictish people call it, is stolen by Alaric, and carried south across Hadrian's Wall. Alaric, though crippled and broken, had survived the fall thought to have killed him, and now he plots against Arthur. A swatch with a dragon emblem is left at the scene, and the Picts believe Arthur is to blame. The Picts raid towns south of Hadrian's Wall in search of the stone, but take no lives. Aleta, Maeve, and Ingrid head toward Lord Hussa's castle, but while fording a stream during a storm, they are swept away. The women are saved by Picts, who are especially impressed with Ingrid. It is the winter solstice, and Pictish legend tells how a female child will be borne out of the waters on this sacred day to lead them. Ingrid is treated like royalty, and they are taken to the town of Dunedin. They are taken to see Kennyth, the leader of the Picts. Kennyth, an educated "barbarian," tells Aleta and Maeve that the lands of the Picts were given to them by Constantine the Great. He then tells them about the stolen "Stone of Destiny," and that they have one month before the Picts declare war.

The Picts release the women and they head to Lord Hussa's castle. However, when they arrive, they are thrown in prison. Alaric had one document on him when he fell, and he had used it to blackmail Hussa. With the women in prison, Alaric sends word to Camelot that they are being held by the Picts. Aleta, Maeve, and Ingrid escape from the castle on horseback, pulling the crippled Alaric lying in his specially made bed on wheels. With the armies of Arthur and Kennyth converging, Aleta and Maeve ride between the two armies. They pull back the cover and reveal that Alaric's bed is also a conveyance for the Stone of Destiny. The celebration is short-lived as Anders, King of the Jutes arrives with an invasion force. Alaric had planned for Anders to arrive and easily destroy what was left of both armies. Arn suggests a clever ruse, to trick the Jutes into believing the war had taken place. Both armies lay "bloodied" on the field, and the Jutes march carelessly into the trap. The Jutes are defeated and sent back home in humiliating defeat, and Alaric is sent with them. Hussa escapes with a pouch of Alaric's blackmail papers, but Mordred finds him and kills him for threatening his daughter and granddaughter. Mordred takes the pouch of papers. Everyone goes back to Dunedin to celebrate, but just as The Stone of Destiny is uncovered, "The Wanderer" appears. She touches the stone and makes a dire prediction about a future war between the Picts and Britons, then vanishes. The episode ends with feasting and boasting.

COMMENT: *Dunedin, or Dun Eidin meaning "Fort of Eidin," is misspelled Eidan in the strip. Eventually Dun Eidin was made a burgh, and was renamed Edinburgh. It was made the capital of Scotland in 1325.*

Page 3131 (9 February 1997) is the sixtieth anniversary of the strip, and is a retrospective of events in Val's life.

215: The Man and the Moon
Pages 3157 (10 August 1997) – 3168 (26 October 1997)

Val travels through a village where a second moon appears every night. When Val goes in search of the second moon, he finds that Galan is behind the apparition. Galan takes his father to the house of an eccentric inventor known as "The Tinkerer." Val learns that the second moon was really The Tinkerer's attempts at creating a hot air balloon. The Tinkerer shows Val a boat with four balloons attached. After Val and Galan get in the boat, The Tinkerer cuts the mooring lines, and they are carried aloft. The aircraft heads towards the North Sea, where it is swallowed up by a thunderstorm. The rain cools the hot air, and lightning destroys one of the balloons, causing the vessel to drop. Val and Galan grab the ropes from the deflated balloon, and drop to earth. The Tinkerer manages to keep the other three fires lit, and, lightened by the lack of two passengers, he floats over the sea.

216: "Truth" or "Contentment"
Pages 3169 (2 November 1997) – 3171 (16 November 1997)

Back in the fens, Val goes to Horrit's dwelling only to find it empty. He follows a set of stairs under the dwelling where a man shows him that, like him, there are many who see truth, but have never known contentment. As they go to leave, they have to choose between one of two doors—"truth" or "contentment." They both choose "truth."

217: The Fall of Camelot
Pages 3171 (16 November 1997) – 3212 (30 August 1998)

Gawain has fallen in love with Lady Cordelia, and his former squire, now "Sir" Cecil, has become an important knight. Cecil had fought in the Battle of Watley's Glen and emerged a hero, though he has no memory of it. However, no one ever saw his face because he wore a helmet. Barbarians, who have been driven from their lands, attack Briton. Arthur decides to fight them, but only after a large enough army has amassed, so they can all be dealt with at once. Refugees flock to Camelot by the thousands. Ethelbert takes control of the various barbarian tribes, and molds them into an army. Val finds out that Cordelia is the daughter of the traitor Sir Juvenal whom he had defeated twenty years earlier. Cordelia, who has been a spy all along, escapes and rides to Ethelbert, to whom she is betrothed. Cordelia gives Ethelbert all the information she has gathered, including a map showing safe paths through Mucken Mire. The first day of battle ends with Arthur and the knights of Camelot near defeat. On the second day of fighting, Cecil engages the foe, but is met by his "twin" who confuses the army. Cecil's "twin" is none other than Cordelia in disguise. Cordelia confuses the knights, and the front line collapses. The knights retreat. Arthur secretly meets with Cecil and knights him. During the third day of battle the front line collapses, Arthur leans towards Val and whispers, "We will not prevail this day. Camelot will endure, but only without me. You will understand—but not at once. Good-bye my loyal prince." Soon afterwards, Arthur is gone, and everyone falls back to Camelot. By a bridge at the edge of a wooded cove Arthur meets Cecil. He gives Cecil his tunic and armor, and with Excalibur strapped to his back, slips into the forest. No sooner does Arthur leave when a horde of barbarians approach. They try to cross the bridge, but Cecil, knowing he must protect Arthur, blocks their way. For a while Cecil holds his ground, but is killed by the mob. Camelot is under siege, and Ethelbert's men begin undermining the outer walls. Sven Fork-Beard sails down the River Test to rescue Camelot's survivors. Camelot is abandoned, and Sven Fork-Beard sails his fleet out into open sea through a straight known as "The Jaws." The pursuing barbarian fleet, not knowing about the jagged, underwater rock formations is destroyed. Camelot's refugees head to Tintagel, the childhood home of Arthur. Ethelbert marries Cordelia and crowns them both king and queen.

218: Gudrid
Pages 3213 (6 September 1998) – 3222 (8 November 1998)

The Round Table has been brought to Tintagel, and the refugees begin making it their new home. The last ship to unload gets caught in a storm and Val has

to rescue Gudrid Olafsdottir. Gudrid had come from Iceland seeking help against unseen forces ruining their land. Maeve whispers in Ingrid's ear, and the heir of two kingdoms takes her place on the royal throne. It is decided that the knights will go to Iceland to find the cause of their problems.

219: The Wandering Arthur
Pages 3223 (15 November 1998) – 3238 (28 February 1999)

Wherever Arthur wanders, a black bird follows him. He eventually makes his home in a hilltop village as a common laborer. His wisdom and silent ways ingratiate him to the villagers who simply call him "Grandfather." Ethelbert sends his nephew Stulto to govern Arthur's village, but he is "foolish and stubborn." Stulto is a harsh ruler, but Arthur takes on the quest of teaching him about civilization, and becomes his advisor. Under Arthur's guidance, Stulto's lands are the only ones at peace. Wanting to know why, Ethelbert has Stulto come to Camelot, and Arthur accompanies him. Through Stulto, Arthur begins to advise Ethelbert on ways to restore Camelot. Suspicious of "Grandfather" (Arthur), Cordelia convinces Ethelbert to make him his First Counselor.

220: In The Land of Fire and Ice
Pages 3239 (7 March 1999) – 3267 (19 September 1999)

Once in Iceland, Val and his crew are greeted by Eric Blacktooth. Blacktooth is a rogue, but fear has put him in a position of power. Val is told to go back to Britain, but stays to find out what is causing all of the misfortune in Iceland. The knights are divided into groups to scout out the island. Everywhere they go they are watched, and, if need be, saved by a mysterious figure. Val and Gudrid see the solitary figure and follow him to a cave in the ice. Once inside they find a treasure-trove of artifacts and books from all over the known world, but they leave without seeing the stranger. Val and Gudrid return with Gawain and Arn, and meet the "Nameless One." The "Nameless One" tells them that he is the last descendant of the Neanderthals that roamed Africa and Europe. When no place was left for them to live in peace, they were taken to Iceland by Pliny the Elder (AD 23-79). The "Nameless One" explains that he had started the mischief to scare away the villagers, but it was Blacktooth who made the mischief deadly. Blacktooth's intent is to become king through fear. The Icelanders vote at a communal meeting called the Althing, which ends in a tie. The "Nameless One" appears and votes against Blacktooth, but Blacktooth kills him, and instructs his men to kill those who voted against him. Suddenly, Mount Hekla erupts, which gives Val and half of the town time to retreat. The two groups meet on an ice floe to battle, but the lava from the volcano travels under the ice, and it breaks away. Blacktooth, who is hanging by a rope, threatens to fall into the lava, taking Gudrid with him. Val swings down and grabs Gudrid, while a mortally wounded "Nameless One" jumps onto Blacktooth, sending them both into the lava.

222: Flora Magnesia: The Isle of Anagrams
Pages 3268 (26 September 1999) – 3269 (3 October 1999)

Val's crew lands at Flora Manesia: The Isle of Anagrams. They are greeted by Proteus – the Top User, who tells them that everything anyone says is turned into an anagram. Val has everyone request "toe baths," and at once they are back on "the boats."

COMMENT: *Flora Magnesia is an anagram of "Isle of Anagram" minus the final "s."*

223: A Hibernian Tale
Pages 3270 (10 October 1999) – 3297 (16 April 2000)

Soon after Val returns to Tintagel, Valeta arrives from Hibernia. Valeta explains that, with the encroachment of the barbarian tribes, Hibernia has become a safe haven for art and literature for all of Europe. Many have sent their art treasures and books for safekeeping. However, Corsairs have found out and are attacking the ships, taking the gold and destroying the books. Two abbots, Claro and Fusco, oversee the shipping routes, but both are suspect of giving away information to the Corsairs. Since the next shipment coming from Europe travels through Bordeaux, Val heads there. On the voyage to Hibernia, Val's ship slows to aid a boat in distress, only to find it is a ruse. The gold and silver are taken, and the crew is pressed into servitude. They are taken to the remote Isles of Aran and to the stone fortress called Dun Angus. Salted fish is taken off the island in barrels and traded for peat, which is used for fires to smelt gold and silver. Val hides in one of the fish barrels, and sneaks off the island. The monk Dionysius Exiguus (Dennis the Little) aids Val, and shows him the way to Tara. Val discovers that Fusco is behind the pirating, and that he has been shipping the gold to Tara as gray-painted armor. Fusco has Val, Cormac, Claro, and Dionysius locked in a chamber with crates of books and scientific equipment. Claro finds a container of Aqua Regia, an acid that melts gold. Val tells the guard that Fusco deceived them all, and that the armor really is not gold at all. Then he puts a gold buckle in the Aqua Regia, and the guard watches it melt. Fusco's band of traitors, wearing the soft gold armor are no match for Cormac's men dressed in real armor. When Fusco's men try to ford a river, the heavy gold pulls them down and they drown. Fusco escapes the river but is killed by the prison guard for deceiving them. Fusco was actually a stooge for a vengeful Maria Francesca whose husband, "The Bronk," drowned in episode 179: The Northern Spice Route.

224: The Battle for Camelot
Pages 3298 (23 April 2000) – 3336 (14 January 2001)

Maria Francesca's compatriot is Sal Gelidus, a powerful merchant who not only controls the salt trade, but the ice trade as well. When Sal Gelidus stops purchasing ice from Thule, the country can no longer purchase salt. Without salt, foods taste bland and meats can no longer be preserved. This causes a chain reaction that causes a food and economic crisis in Thule. Next, Sal Gelidus withholds salt from Hibernia, and threatens to do the same to Britain if Ethelbert does not invade Tintagel. Ethelbert relents, but Arthur takes a boy named Alfred, who knows that "Grandfather" is really Arthur, and several boys to the old Roman saltworks, and rebuilds it. An accident burns down Sal Gelidus' warehouses, and he needs to buy sawdust from all over Europe in order to transport ice once more. Arthur's saltworks produce enough high grade salt that he convinces Ethelbert to trade with Thule for ice and thereby circumvent Sal Gelidus' monopoly. Cordelia discovers the "Grandfather" is really Arthur, and poisons the table salt. When the dinner guests become sick, Cordelia accuses "Grandfather" and reveals that he is Arthur. As Ethelbert's men move in to take Arthur, Alfred, having seen Cordelia in Arthur's room, drops Excalibur down to the king. Arthur is defeated, and Ethelbert tries to kill Arthur with Excalibur, but the blade will not go near the king, so he discards it. Alfred picks up the sword and escapes. Arthur is put in chains and thrown in a dungeon. Val finds Alfred and takes him to Tintagel. Knowing that Arthur is alive brings new hope to Val and the Knights of the Round Table. Ethelbert sides with Sal Gelidus and Maria Francesca, and wages war on Tintagel. Ethelbert's army takes up a position on the vast farming plain before Tintagel, but Val has soured the water by pumping it full of brine from the saltworks. When the battle is finally engaged, Ethelbert's army is lured to the river where makeshift bridges have been built atop of pontoon boats. Just as Ethelbert's armies cross the bridges, a wall of ice, which was shipped from Thule, kills many of the soldiers. Cordelia clings to a boat and is swept out to sea. Ethelbert's army is in disarray, while Val, Gawain, and a several of the other knights, ride to Camelot where they free Arthur. Ethelbert is reduced to the status of a savaging brigand, Cordelia's boat lands at a lonely crag whose only occupants are religionus women, and Sal Gelidus dies in an explosion when he accidentally ignites one of his own sawdust warehouses. Only Maria Francesca's survived unscathed.

225: Paradise Found
Pages 3337 (21 January 2001) – 3408 (9 June 2002)

The monk Dionysius Exiguus returns to Camelot to enlist Arthur's aid. Dionysius explains how the ruins of Nero's golden house were found underground. By command of the Pope, Dionysius went into the ruins and found the treasury of the philosopher Seneca. There he was struck from behind and knocked unconscious. When he awoke he found the bodies of several slain emissaries, and an empty box that one held the map to "Paradise"—to the fabled Garden of Eden. At the Pope's request, Arthur sends his bravest knights, Val, Gawain, and Arn, to find the map and bring the murderer to justice.

Yuan Chen arrives in Camelot, captaining a replica of an ancient Greek warship called a Trireme. Aleta and Nathan decide to go along as far as the Misty Isles, and Galan accompanies Yuan Chen. They defeat Coesairs, but the only information they find out is that the pirates were paid in amber and purple dye. In Rome they meet the Pope, who shows them the only clue—a piece of cloth with the Greek letter psi on it. They also meet the Pope's Prefect, Hortus, whom Val does not trust. Testing the Trireme, Yuan Chen encounters a whirlpool the crew calls Charybdis. The whirlpool almost draws them in, but the ship with three tiers of oars sails with the current and pulls out of the vortex. In Rome, Val, Gawain, and Arn meet the merchant Quintus who takes them on the underground sewer, the Cloaca Maxima, to find a boat with a purple sail and fly-in-amber insignia. Gladiators attack them, but when the knights begin winning, the gladiators jump into the Cloaca Maxima and are eaten by crocodiles. Quintus tells Val that the Rus tribal leader Ivan, who controls the amber trade, has formed an alliance with Justinian, who controls the purple dye trade. Val arrives in Constantinople, but one of the gladiators had survived and sent a warning to Justinian. Before the guards can capture Val and his entourage, Digitus, a friend of Quintus, hides them. The blind Digitus leads Val to an opening that looks out onto the Praetorium. There he sees that Justinian is readying for a campaign to find the Garden of Eden.

Val, Gawain, Arn, and Galan join Justinian's campaign by finding work as baggage porters. Because of his skills with medicine, Justinian makes Galan a physician. In order to get closer to Justinian, Gawain finds work in the stables grooming horses, and Arn becomes a blacksmith. The expedition passes Mount Ararat, and deep into the eastern mountains. The expedition is being watched, and one of the followers is captured. He dies before he can say anything, but Val keeps the psi necklace he wore. When Justinian's advisors cannot find a safe route, Val, disguised as a common laborer, suggests following the sheep routes. The Rus celebrate the solstice by erecting a totem of birch. Val takes an axe of imperial design, destroys the totem, and leaves the axe in the rubble. Ivan finds the axe, and a fight breaks out between the Rus and Justinian's men. The Rus leave in the night.

Justinian's map has a blank space on it and four sets of three holes, but the exact location of the Garden of Eden remains a mystery. Val deduces the secret of the map by using one of the psi necklaces, and knows where the garden lay. Gawain sneaks off to the Garden of Eden, and Val, Arn, and Galan follow. Within the garden everything is tranquil, until Gawain tries to drink from the river. Suddenly, the river freezes, a storm builds up, and the animals turn feral once more. Val and his companions flee the garden, but once outside they run into Justinian who finally recognizes Val. As Justinian approaches with a small contingent of men, Hortus arrives with an army of local tribesmen. The two armies battle and Hortus drives Justinian back. Hortus explains to Val that he and his tribe have watched over the Garden of Eden for millennia. They watch as Justinian's army comes under attack by the Rus, thanks to Hortus. Justinian flees. For their help, the Rus want directions to the Lost City of Alexander. Hortus shows them the way.

226: ICTHYOPOLIS——CITY OF THE FISHES
Pages 3409 (June 2002) – 3450 (23 March 2003)

Val takes some of the legionaries Justinian abandoned, and beats Justinian back to Constantinople. The legionaries tell everyone of Justinian's cowardice. Val, with the help of Yuan Chen, sails from Constantinople before Justinian gets there. Justinian sends his fleet after Val, but most of it is lost as Yuan Chen draws the ships into the whirlpool known as Charybdis. Val orders the ship to the Misty Isles to save Aleta and Nathan. As the remaining ships in Justinian's fleet bear down on the Misty Isles, Aleta takes Nathan and leaves in a small fishing boat. The royal warship, acting as a decoy, sets out for open sea. Justinian overtakes the ship. Not finding Aleta, he torches the vessel with all aboard. A sudden storm capsizes Aleta's boat, killing the lone fisherman sailing it. Aleta's boat washes up to a small island containing sheep and orchards. Nathan swims under water and finds an ancient city. When he does not surface for air Aleta dives in after him, and they are both caught. They are taken to Icthyopolis, or the City of the Fishes, in a diving bell, and are greeted by Pericles who tells them that they can never leave. Pericles tells Aleta how, after a volcanic eruption, their city partially sank into the sea, while the rest of it was covered with ash. Philomena, one of the city elders, convinced the people to stay and rebuild under the ash. The city is ruled by a democracy, and Pericles' rival is Faustus, another "recruit" who wants off the island. Justinian's fleet finds the island, and Faustus tells Justinian about a land entrance to the city. Aleta convinces Pericles that they need to

follow the water route out of the city. The city-dwellers commandeer the unmanned ships sitting in the harbor, just as the volcano begins to erupt. Justinian and his men are trapped underground, but Faustus shows Justinian the diving bell. As the city-dwellers leave, they are followed by the rest of the fleet, which is attacked by Val in Yuan Chen's Trireme. Justinian kills Faustus, and washes ashore on an unnamed island. He is picked up and set to work rowing as a galley slave, but eventually the captain decides to ransom him. The city-dwellers settle on one of the smaller, secluded Misty Isles. Hortus is made Pope.

227: THE ISLAND OF INDECISION
Pages 3451 (30 March 2003) – 3453 (13 April 2003)

On the Island no one can make a decision except for Gawain. When Val cannot decide to leave, Gawain tells him that he will now have Aleta all to himself. Val follows.

228: GALAN'S GRAIL QUEST BEGINS
Pages 3454 (20 April 2003) – 3470 (10 August 2003)

The plague begun in Constantinople has reached Camelot. Hildegarde convinces Arthur to disperse the healthy people throughout all of England, so they do not contract the sickness. Val and his family go to a castle on the border of the Druid lands to see Arthur. There they tell stories to pass the time. Galan finds a crypt under the castle containing the sarcophagi of the ancient rulers of Britain. They find a chalice that Arthur believes could be the Holy Grail, and the reason for the plague. Galan rebuffs Arthur who in turn tells him, "Your eyes are open to reason—but blind to mystery!" Then Arthur gives Galan a quest: to return the cup to Jerusalem in order to find humility. Galan accepts. The guardian of the crypt tells Galan three things. "First, bring the needle to its home; second, climb to the place where ten were given to one, and third, follow Hezekiah backward from where he went for water." In Rome, Galan finds an Egyptian engineer named Tut and his daughter Nefertari. Tut has purchased an ancient Egyptian obelisk called "The Needle" that he plans to take back to Egypt. Galan joins Tut's expedition.

229: Horridus
Pages 3471 (17 August 2003) – 3513 (6 June 2004)

A band of barbarians attacks a group from Arthur's castle, and all but Aleta and Maeve are murdered. They are taken high into the western mountains, where they meet Horridus. Horridus rules by spreading fear and preying on the weak. Using a dog whistle, the women create a diversion and escape. Horridus begins his campaign of terror, attacking small, defenseless towns, including trading villages that have never seen war. He attacks Vikingsholm in Thule on the Yule, and burns King Aguar's castle to the ground. Horridus calls for ambassadors from all the monarchs of Europe, except for Camelot. His terms for peace are simply to exclude Camelot from all trade. The ambassadors comply. Arthur gives Val six months to find a solution, but young Sir Draco fights Val continually. Val finds out that Horridus is hidden on the small island of Ouessant off the coast of Brittany. Draco betrays Arthur and sides with Horridus. When Draco convinces Horridus to attack Londinium, Val goes to Ouessant and erects three false lighthouses to misdirect Horridus' returning fleet. The ships are dashed on the rocks, but Horridus escapes. Horridus goes to Draco in secret and blackmails him into caring for him. Arthur retires and installs Val and Aleta as Regency Council until Ingrid comes of age.

COMMENT: *Page 3501 (14 March 2004) is the last page illustrated by John Cullen Murphy. The following week, Page 3502 (21 March 2004) begins Gary Gianni's tenure as artist.*

King Arthur's "retirement" on Page 3513 (6 June 2004) is a thinly veiled reference to John Cullen Murphy's retirement from the strip. Mr. Murphy passed away less than one month later, on 2 July 2004.

230: Galan's Quest Continues
Pages 3514 (13 June 2004) – 3536 (14 November 2004)

The "Needle" is returned to Egypt, and Galan finds out that his next destination is the Sinai Peninsula. Tut introduces Galan to a turquoise merchant named Malachite who can guide him through the desert. Galan and Nefertari make it to Jebel Musa, the Mountain of Moses. Galan realizes that Mount Sinai is his second destination, and that the clue, "where ten were given to one," refers to Moses receiving the Ten Commandments. Galan and Nefertari ascend to the summit of Mount Sinai, where they meet an old hermit who tells them about the last clue. Galan and Nefertari go to Jerusalem, where they are arrested by Imperial soldiers and taken before the Procurator. The Procurator, who is interested in the Grail, tells them he is concerned for their safety. Malachite finds the Gihon Spring. Galan and Nefertari swim down into the waters and come to a cave containing hundreds of "Grails." The guardian tells them that it was never the cup that was important, but always the quest.

231: The Lake Dragons
Pages 3537 (21 November 2004) – 3586 (30 October 2005)

Val becomes bored as Camelot's Regent so Aleta sends him off to go adventuring with Nathan as his squire. In the wild moors above the Cotswold Hills, Val and Nathan come upon a trio of witches—the sisters of Horrit. The trio restates Horrit's prophesy that Val will never find contentment then vanish. Val befriends Borgut, a Pict of the Raven Clan who convinces the knight-errant to save his village from dragons. Once in Caledonia, Val sees the lake dragons and attempts to capture one. Nathan argues with Val over harming the creatures then goes off to hunt for food, but is captured by Bel, Borgut's daughter. Val eventually captures a lake dragon (a Loch Ness Monster), but his virtuous act is tarnished as Borgut is revealed to be a madman. Borgut falls off the cliff, and is eaten by the dragon. Val releases the dragon, and Nathan falls in love with Bel.

COMMENT: *This storyline begins Mark Schultz's tenure as writer of the strip. With his take-over, references to a specific timeline become blurred, and the characters become noticeably younger.*

232: The Haunted Watchtower
Pages 3585 (23 October 2005) – 3622 (9 July 2006)

Val and Nathan board a merchant vessel and head south for Camelot. The merchant ship is attacked by Norse Raiders led by Skyrmir. Val and Nathan are held for ransom, but Nathan swims to safety. Val cripples Skyrmir by cutting his hamstring. Thorwolf replaces the wounded Skyrmir as captain. The ship lands on a desolate isle off the Iberian Peninsula to restock. They meet Zamestra Dagon, the watchtower guardian. The guardian tells them about the lost treasure of King Solomon, and all but Val and Skyrmir search the building for gold. The crew is driven mad, or killed by Thorwolf, who is crazed by greed. Zamestra Dagon releases Val and Skyrmir, and Thorwolf becomes the new guardian of the gold.

233: King Solomon's Gold
3623 (16 July 2006) – 3725 (29 June 2008)

Val pledges to return King Solomon's gold to its rightful owner. He rescues Makeda, Princess of Ab'Saba from a band of Visigoths. Nathan returns to Camelot and tells Aleta about Val's abduction. Aleta, along with several knights, ventures southward on a rescue mission. Makeda is a descendant of Makeda the Beautiful, beloved of King Solomon. She tells Val that the golden treasure resided in the kingdom of Ab'Saba until it was stolen by Carthaginians and taken to the watchtower. The trio goes to the watchtower where Makeda defeats the Djinn guarding the treasure. Neshem, Makeda's father, arrives with a small garrison of Ab'Saban soldiers and secures the gold. They sail to Africa. At an African village bat-winged harpies attack the party. A jealous Ab'Saban warrior named Bukota trips Skyrmir, and the Norseman is taken by two harpies. Skyrmir escapes the harpies and is eventually rescued by Aleta, who has been tracking Val.

Once in Ab'Saba, Nesham realizes that the warlord Twedorek has orchestrated a coup in his absence. The gold is rushed to safety in a mountainous redoubt. Makeda searches for the three jewels that can open a special vault. Skyrmir arrives dressed as Solomon in an attempt to distract Twedorek and his army. During the fight, it is discovered that a ruby from the pommel of Val's Singing Sword is the final key to unlocking Solomon's vault. Makeda dons the crown of Solomon and the insurrection ends. Val and Aleta are reunited. Bukota admits his part in trying to harm Skyrmir, who pardons him. The ruby from the pommel of the Singing Sword is revealed to be "The Blood of Solomon." In its place Val is given its sister jewel, "The Blood of Ab'Saba." Skyrmir stays behind to live out his life as a pampered nobleman. Bukota's punishment is to be Ab'Saba's first ambassador to Camelot.

COMMENT: *The idea for the jewel in the pommel of Val's sword, Flamberge came from Brian M. Kane. In the original pitch the name of the jewel was "The Song of Solomon." The mythical history posited that "The Song of Solomon" was the source of the weapon's nickname "the Singing Sword."*

234: The Sargasso Adventure
Pages 3726 (6 July 2008) – 3756 (1 February 2009)

Along the west coast of Africa, Val's ship, caught in the pull of a young hurricane, is carried far into the Atlantic. The ship is trapped in Sargasso weed and is attacked by a giant crab, which is swiftly killed and eaten. While foraging for water, Val is attacked by a monstrous octopus. Gawain and Bukota unsuccessfully try to free Val when suddenly, poisoned arrows pierce the tentacles and drive the creature away. Their rescuers are three Neanderthals. The party is captured and taken to the tribal leader, Gru-Zor, who speaks an archaic form of Pictish. They escape when a large creature disrupts their stoning. Val and the others, along with three of the Neanderthals, return to the ship and fight off Gru-Zor's raiders. During the fight, a large turtle becomes caught in the ship's moorings and pulls the vessel out to sea.

235: The Great Beast
Pages 3757 (8 February 2009) – 3783 (9 August 2009)

The Neanderthals' names are Nudder, Bup, and Ig, and Aleta attempts to gentrify them. It does not go well. After the three Neanderthals each kidnap a fair maiden, Bukota intercedes and secures their freedom. Before the negotiations can be concluded, a great beast from the Sargasso Sea invades Camelot. The Antediluvian lizard breeches Camelot's walls in search of its egg, which Gawain had taken. Val grabs the egg, takes it to the coast, and throws it into the sea. The beast jumps off the cliff, retrieves its egg and swims off.

To Be Continued...

Transition of Artists

Page(s)	Artist
I - 1756:	Hal Foster
1757:	Gray Morrow
1758 - 1759:	Hal Foster
1760:	John Cullen Murphy
1761:	Hal Foster
1762:	Wallace Wood
1763:	Hal Foster
1764:	John Cullen Murphy
1765:	Gray Morrow*
1766:	John Cullen Murphy
1767:	Gray Morrow*
1768:	Hal Foster
1769:	John Cullen Murphy
1770:	Gray Morrow*
1771 - 1772:	John Cullen Murphy
1773:	Hal Foster
1774 - 1775:	John Cullen Murphy
1776:	Hal Foster
1777 - 1787:	John Cullen Murphy
1788:	Hal Foster
1789 - 3502:	John Cullen Murphy+
3503 - 3755:	Gary Gianni
3756:	Mark Schultz
3757- Present	Gary Gianni

* These three entries were previously listed as "Unknown." Gray Morrow's widow, Pocho, confirmed that Gray illustrated these pages.

+ Gary Gianni assisted John Cullen Murphy on the following pages: 3354, 3362, 3366, 3371, 3377, 3385, 3394, 3398, 3401, 3407, 3414, 3419, 3432, 3442, 3448, 3472, 3486, 3491, 3499, 3501, 3502.

Summary and Overview of the Life of Prince Valiant of Thule

Todd Goldberg and Carl Horak

Prince Valiant has been one of the few comic strips to portray a reasonably realistic progression of time in the lives of its characters. Among the "classic" strips, *Gasoline Alley* is the only other obvious example that comes to mind. It has been said that at one time Foster had plotted out Val's entire life from cradle to grave. Arn was eventually to become the bearer of the Singing Sword. These plans, which would be absolutely fascinating to see, were eventually dropped, probably when Foster realized his creation could run indefinitely.

The passage of time is a thorny problem for continuity strips. Even an otherwise realistic comic strip cannot be totally accurate and literal in time, since real adult characters would have to grow old and die over the long run of a successful strip. Therefore, perhaps in order to avoid portraying a doddering middle-aged ex-knight by the 1970s (which perhaps could have yielded some interesting stories...!), Foster and Murphy appear to have slowed down time to a variable extent in the strip, so that approximately 25 years of fictional time are supposed to have passed during the 44 years of Foster's tenure on *Prince Valiant*. Val started as a teenager and is now in his 40s, with children who are themselves now up to their teens and twenties in some cases. The time progression was more realistic and consistent in the earlier years of the strip than in the later years.

Prince Valiant
BY HAL FOSTER

Our Story: KING AGUAR OF THULE LANDS IN BRITAIN WITH HIS QUEEN AND FIVE-YEAR-OLD SON, PRINCE VALIANT.

THE YOUNG PRINCE SPENDS HIS BOYHOOD IN THE WILD FENS LEARNING THE HUNTER'S SKILL AND THE ART OF SURVIVAL.

HE MEETS SIR GAWAIN AND A LIFELONG FRIENDSHIP BEGINS.

IN KING ARTHUR HE FINDS A LEADER WORTH SERVING TO THE VERY END. BUT IT IS GUINEVERE'S SMILE THAT INSPIRES HIM TO MASTER THE ARTS OF CHIVALRY.

THEY RIDE TO CAMELOT AND THERE HE WILL SPEND MONTHS AND YEARS IN HARD TRAINING.

THE 'SINGING SWORD' FLASHED LIKE LIGHTNING, AS HE HELD THE BRIDGE AT DUNDORN GLEN AGAINST A SAXON RAIDING PARTY UNTIL HELP ARRIVED.

AFTER THE GREAT BATTLE OF THE FENS, KING ARTHUR CALLED FOR ONE PARTICULAR HERO. DRAWING EXCALIBUR, HE TOUCHED EACH SHOULDER: *"RISE, SIR VALIANT, KNIGHT OF THE ROUND TABLE."*

THE NEW-MADE KNIGHT SO HARASSED ATTILA THE HUN, THAT HIS CROSSING OF THE ALPS WAS DELAYED, GIVING TIME FOR ATEUS TO CONTRIVE HIS DEFEAT AT CHALONS.

SHIPWRECKED IN THE AEGEAN SEA HE BEHELD ALETA, GREY-EYED QUEEN OF THE MISTY ISLES. THROUGH SORCERY, SHE CAST A SPELL UPON HIM THAT TROUBLED HIM, BUT PLEASANTLY, FOR THE REST OF HIS LIFE.

BOLTAR, THAT HONEST MERCHANT AND PIRATE, CAME ROARING INTO HIS LIFE AND REMAINED FOREVER HIS FRIEND.

HAL FOSTER

ONCE HE STOOD ALONE BEFORE THE WALLS OF SARAMAND AND VOWED TO DESTROY IT.... AND DID.

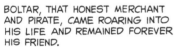

BEFORE THE HOLY SEPULCHER IN JERUSALEM HE DEDICATED THE 'SINGING SWORD' TO THE CAUSE OF JUSTICE.

AGAIN HE MEETS ALETA, THE SMALL GOLDEN ONE, AND IS QUITE CONTENT TO LIVE UNDER HER SPELL FOREVER.

"BOSH!" EXCLAIMS WISE MERLIN, *"WITH SUCH BEAUTY AS HERS, NO SORCERY IS NECESSARY."*

PRINCE VALIANT WANDERS THE WIDE TURBULENT WORLD IN SEARCH OF ADVENTURE BUT EVER HE RETURNS TO SEE IF HER SPELL STILL HOLDS, AND IS GLAD IT DOES.

PAGE **2000** 6-8   NEXT WEEK- *Page Two Thousand and One*

Although we have made an attempt to outline a consistent timeline of the life of Prince Valiant, it must be acknowledged that Foster himself apparently either did not keep careful enough track of the timing of events in his own stories or else intentionally avoided trying to keep a consistent chronology for various reasons. During our work on this publication, we noticed several times that while Foster frequently referred to previous stories and events, the passages of times cited were inconsistent and obviously incorrect. For example, Hatha (Boltarson) is noted to be 12 in 1966, yet the Twins, who were born a year before Hatha, are noted to be 12 in 1968 and again in 1970. Some other examples are mentioned at various points in the index. Therefore, any attempt to impose a rigid chronology on the later years of the strip is partly arbitrary. Nevertheless, this time-line is still roughly accurate, gives a nice overview and perspective on Val's career, and serves as a useful index for quickly locating major events and stories.

NOTE: The time-line presented below is based on the timing of historical events mentioned in the strip and on mentions of the passage of time and seasons in the stories. The Sack of Rome in AD 455, depicted in story #30, is used as the base reference point. Several other historical incidents referred to in the strip could also have been used, which would merely have shifted the hypothetical time-line by a few years.

ca. AD 433: Prince Valiant is born to King Aguar of Thule and a nameless mother.

ca. 436: Birth of Aleta, future Queen of the Misty Isles.

ca. 439: (Strip begins). Aguar deposed by Sligon, exiled to Fens of Britain.

ca. 446: Horrit prophesizes life of adventure and discontent for young Val. Val's mother dies.

ca. 447-8: Val leaves home in search of adventure, meets Gawain and Launcelot, visits Camelot for first time, becomes Gawain's squire, meets Ilene, studies with Merlin.

ca. 449: Death of Ilene. Val given Singing Sword by Prince Arn of Ord. Tenth Saxon Saxon invasion of England defeated, Val knighted. Aguar regains throne of Thule from Sligon.

ca. 450-451: Attila conquers Italy and Andelkrag (which actually occurred in AD 452-455). Val fights Huns, visits Rome.

ca. 451-453: Val regains Singing Sword from Angor Wrack, meets Aleta, makes first pilgrimage to Holy Land, visits Greece and Africa with Boltar, returns to Camelot, scouts Roman wall, returns home to Thule in disguise. Gundar Harl introduced, becomes shipbuilder of Thule.

ca. 454: Val kidnaps Aleta, drags her across Africa.

ca. 455: Val becomes Emperor of Saramand, marries Aleta during sack of Rome, honeymoons in France; couple returns to Camelot with Katwin. War in royal forest. Mordred plots against throne. Aleta meets Aguar in Thule.

ca. 456-457: Aleta kidnapped by Ulfrun, Val and Vikings rescue her across the ocean, discover America; Prince Arn born in America; Indian Princess Tilllicum becomes his nursemaid. Return to Camelot; Arn christened along with Prince Valiant, son of Prince Arn of Ord.

ca. 457-459: Picts driven back into Scotland by King Arthur's forces. Val returns to Thule then goes on missionary voyage to Rome. Geoffrey (Arf) becomes official historian of Thule and begins to compile "The Chronicles," putative source of the Prince Valiant stories. Twins Karen and Valeta born in Thule during Val's absence. Boltar and Tillicum fall in love and marry.

ca. 460-463: Arn kidnapped. Val spreads Christianity in Thule. Saxon raiders again defeated. Val meets Saint Patrick. Aleta returns to Misty Isles and reestablishes her authority. Val and Gawain go on 2nd pilgrimage to Holy Land. Overland trip back to Thule; Aleta kidnapped by Dragda Khan.

ca. 463-465: Val returns to Camelot, crushes rebellion in Cornwall. Arvak becomes Val's warhorse. Visit to London; return to Thule. Arn goes away to Inner Lands for training. Council of Kings held in Thule. Val and Aleta return to Camelot, stay in London. Val cleans out Saxon camps. Merlin led into limbo by Nimue the water maiden. Val rescues Gawain in Wales.

ca 465-470: Quest for the Holy Grail; St. Patrick (actually d. 461) settles issue negatively. Arn returns to his family. Return to Misty Isles; Galan born there; Arn gives up inheritance to throne of Isles to Galan. Val takes Arn on trade mission to Holy Land, Syria, Babylon. Missions in Rome (where Empire crumbling) and Gaul. Misadventures with Monk Wojun in Camelot. Siege of Carlisle. Launcelot and Guinevere's romance causes conflict in Camelot. Battle of Badon Hill (final Saxon invasion). Guerilla war in Thule.

ca. 470-475: (Timeline no longer consistent) Arn in America. Mordred's invasion. Holiday at seashore. Adventures in Camelot. Val and Gawain held as slaves in Dathram, lead revolt. Misty Isles navy rearmed against invaders. Return to Camelot; during trip, near Barbary Coast, Aleta and twins kidnapped by El Muluk. Katwin marries Helge Hakkon. Peace with Saxons maintained with difficulty. Diplomatic mission in Wales. Geoffrey marries Adele. Arn held for ransom in Wales. Age of chivalry envelops Camelot (anachronism). Val rescues Arn from Morgan Le Fay. Aleta and Val separate over jealously and misunderstanding; Aleta returns to Misty Isles while Val wanders about Britain; couple reunited after Val's roundabout trip across Africa. (John Cullen Murphy art begins.) Adventures in Aegean area, then return to Camelot. Arn visits Thule with Boltar's son Hatha, falls in love with Lydia Haakon, and wanders about Europe when she mistakenly rejects him. Couple finally reunited in Thule. Siege of Thessalriga. Aleta's sister Helene's husband killed; Helene marries King Telamon of Thessalonica. Arn studies statecraft at Camelot. Tomboy Karen emulates Amazon. Misty Isles defended against pirates. Val returns to Camelot via France, rescues Boltar from kidnappers, takes Galan and Arn to Thule. Arn's girlfriend Lydia killed in snowslide; dejected Arn meets and rejected by another girl, Grace, then returns to Camelot. Arvak dies of old age. Galan brought to Britain to be trained as palace pageboy. War in Irish Sea.

NOTE (BMK): When Cullen Murphy takes over as writer, the seasons correspond to the publication date, therefore a year in the strip becomes equal to a year in real life (ex: 475 = 1980, 476 = 1981, etc.). When Mark Schultz begins as writer, there is no longer a set timeline.

Below: Prince Valiant artist John Cullen Murphy with his daughter/colorist, Meg Nash, and son/scribe Cullen Murphy.

Above: Color engraver Jack Adler invented the four-color separation process used by comic strip and comic book colorists during most of the twentieth century. In this 1937 photo, Adler is working on *Prince Valiant* page 36 (see opposite), adding hues previously unattainable using the old methods. The process was so revolutionary that publishing tycoon William Randolph Hearst visited Adler for a demonstration. In addition to *Prince Valiant*, Adler was also the colorist of *Action Comics* #1, featuring the first appearance of Superman.

Above left: During my last visit with the Fosters on November 6th, 1967, Hal told me about his plans of ending the strip. "I will have King Aguar fall from his horse, either in battle or in a tournament. He'll not survive and I'll end the story with a magnificent great big panel showing the coronation of Valiant. As there will no longer be a Prince Valiant that will be the end of it. If somebody wants to tell the adventures of Prince Arn, I'll have no objections." While I was there a new visitor came in and Hal introduced him as "Hugh Donnel, my color man." Hugh brought page 1613, split in three parts, each attached to a thick board. Hal immediately said that he was not satisfied with the shade of red on the vultures' necks. A humorous discussion followed until Hal said: "It will be my way—after all, the vultures are mine!"

In a letter dated January 9th, 1970, Hal wrote: "I am sorry to say that Mr. Donnel, my color man, passed away last September. I have been doing the color work myself with the help of my background assistant. I tried out several but they just couldn't do the class of work I insisted on. My background man is named Wayne Boring."

Sven H. G. Lagerström
Borås, Sweden, 2008

The sixteen-page color section contains eight Hal Foster pages from the Syracuse University collection. The collection contains first-strike engraver's color proofs printed on white boards of nearly every page of Foster's thirty-four year run on the strip. These digitally restored color pages represent, for the first time anywhere, the *Prince Valiant* strip as Foster originally envisioned it. The John Cullen Murphy pages were selected by the Murphy family, and color checked by Murphy's daughter and colorist Meg Nash. The Gary Gianni pages were selected by the artist, digitally colored by Brian Kane, and color checked by Gianni.

Prince Valiant

Registered U. S. Patent Office

SYNOPSIS:
THE BARON BALDON AND SIR OSMOND ARE MAD WITH RAGE AND FEAR AS SIR GAWAIN ESCAPES FROM THEIR STRONG CASTLE AND SPEEDS TO KING ARTHUR WITH NEWS OF THEIR VILLAINY. EVERY EFFORT IS BEING MADE TO RE-CAPTURE HIM. VAL, WHO EFFECTED HIS ESCAPE, HAS PLUNGED INTO THE MOAT AND THEY WATCH FOR HIM TO RE-APPEAR IN VAIN.

FOR HOURS SOLDIERS WATCH THE MURKY WATERS BUT SEE NO SIGN OF VAL'S BODY.

THOUGH PARTLY STUNNED BY THE GREAT PLUNGE, VAL KEEPS HIS PLAN IN MIND AND SWIMS UNDER WATER —

TO THE FRINGE OF REEDS BENEATH THE CASTLE WALL, STIRRING THE MUD TO RENDER HIS MOVEMENTS INVISIBLE. THERE HE CUTS A HOLLOW REED.

LYING IN THE MUDDY SHALLOWS AND BREATHING THROUGH THE REED, HE WAITS FOR THE SEARCHERS TO GROW WEARY.

36 10-16-37

WITH INFINITE PAINS HE ARRANGES A SCREEN OF RUSHES AND SLOWLY LIFTS HIS HEAD—AT LAST HE CAN BREATHE WITH EASE AND WATCH THE SOLDIERS AT THEIR SEARCHING.

AT LAST THE WEARY DAY ENDS AND IN THE DARKNESS A DRIPPING FIGURE EMERGES FROM THE WATER TO GO IN SEARCH OF THE WAITING GAWAIN.

HAL FOSTER

NEXT WEEK— *GAWAIN WOUNDED*

73.

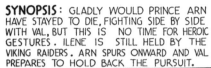
IN THE DAYS OF
KING ARTHUR
BY
HAROLD R FOSTER

SYNOPSIS: GLADLY WOULD PRINCE ARN HAVE STAYED TO DIE, FIGHTING SIDE BY SIDE WITH VAL, BUT THIS IS NO TIME FOR HEROIC GESTURES. ILENE IS STILL HELD BY THE VIKING RAIDERS. ARN SPURS ONWARD AND VAL PREPARES TO HOLD BACK THE PURSUIT.

"I WISH THE GODS HAD MADE YONDER BRAVE FOOL MY FRIEND INSTEAD OF MY SWORN ENEMY."

THE JEWELLED HILT OF THE "SINGING SWORD" FITS SNUGLY IN HIS HAND, AS VAL MARCHES RESOLUTELY TO HIS FATE.

THE NORTHMEN ARE BEWILDERED AT SUCH FOOLHARDY COURAGE, SUSPECTING A TRICK— BUT ONE HUGE VIKING—

A CAPTAIN, STEPS FORWARD SAYING, "MY TWO-EDGED AXE WILL SOLVE THIS RIDDLE"— VAL'S BLADE SWISHES SOFTLY, WAITING—

BUT ERE THE AXE CAN FALL, THE "SING-ING SWORD" SHRIEKS EXULTANTLY, AS THE KEEN EDGE BITES THROUGH SHIELD AND HELMET AND A WARRIOR'S SOUL GOES WINGING TO VALHALLA.

"COME CLOSER," TAUNTS VAL, "MY BEAUTIFUL SWORD IS THIRSTY," AND HALF A HUNDRED HARDY VIKINGS CROWD FORWARD.

AGAIN AND AGAIN THE TERRIBLE SWORD RISES AND FALLS, GLEAM-ING WET IN THE SUNLIGHT, AND ABOVE THE ROAR OF THE WATERS AND THE CLASHING OF ARMS CAN BE HEARD VAL'S RING-ING BATTLE-CRY, "FOR ILENE."

= NEXT WEEK =
THE EXECUTIONER

HAL FOSTER

71 6-19-38

Prince Valiant

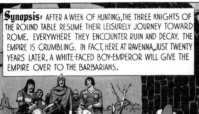

Synopsis: AFTER A WEEK OF HUNTING, THE THREE KNIGHTS OF THE ROUND TABLE RESUME THEIR LEISURELY JOURNEY TOWARD ROME. EVERYWHERE THEY ENCOUNTER RUIN AND DECAY. THE EMPIRE IS CRUMBLING. IN FACT, HERE AT RAVENNA, JUST TWENTY YEARS LATER, A WHITE-FACED BOY-EMPEROR WILL GIVE THE EMPIRE OVER TO THE BARBARIANS.

AS THEY ENTER THE CITY'S GATES, A STOOPED FIGURE IN ORIENTAL GARB APPRAISES THEM WITH KEEN EYES.

RAVENNA, THE BEAUTIFUL, GLEAMING WHITE IN THE SUNLIGHT! NEVER HAVE THESE NORTHERN KNIGHTS SEEN SUCH BUILDINGS, EVEN CAMELOT, THAT CITY OF MARVELS, CANNOT MATCH THE SPLENDOR OF ITS CARVED MARBLE AND SINGING FOUNTAINS!

FOR A WEEK THEY LINGER AMONG THE MANY WONDERS. THE WEALTH OF ITS LIBRARIES FASCINATES VAL.

AT NIGHT THEY REVEL IN THE LUXURY OF ROMAN ENTERTAINMENT

LIGHT-HEARTEDLY SIR GAWAIN SETS OUT TO LEARN THE LOCAL CUSTOMS AND DOES RIGHT WELL, DESPITE HIS LIMITED KNOWLEDGE OF LATIN.

TRISTRAM FINDS LIGHT EXERCISE IN A DUEL OR TWO. IT IS ALL GOOD CLEAN FUN AND NO ONE IS INJURED TOO SERIOUSLY.
183 8-11-40

AS THEY PREPARE TO LEAVE, THE ORIENTAL APPEARS.– "NOBLE SIRS, YE BE KNIGHTS OF TABLE ROUND, BOUND BY OATH TO PUNISH WRONG AND BRING JUSTICE TO THE WEAK... I AM A JEWEL MERCHANT ROBBED OF HALF MY WEALTH BY THE GUARDS I HIRED TO PROTECT ME. EVEN NOW THEY LIE IN WAIT FOR ME ALONG THE ROAD, PLANNING FURTHER ROBBERY. MAY I BEG YOUR PROTECTION UNTIL THAT DANGER IS PAST?"

NEXT WEEK–
Let the Punishment Fit the Crime!

Copr. 1940, King Features Syndicate, Inc. World rights reserved.

HAL FOSTER

75.

Prince Valiant

ANGOR WRACK

Synopsis: WHEN ANGOR WRACK COMES TO WED THE PRINCESS MELODY, VAL SEEKS TO SETTLE OLD SCORES. FIRST, HE CONTRIVES THE ELOPEMENT OF MELODY AND YOUNG HECTOR; THEN WITH YOUTHFUL OVER-CONFIDENCE, TRIES TO REGAIN THE "SINGING SWORD" BY FORCE.

BURNING WITH ANGER AND HUMILIATION, THE SEA KING ATTACKS WITH SUCH FEROCITY THAT HIS NIMBLE OPPONENT IS DRIVEN BACK, BACK........!

①

VAL STRIKES THE FLOOR BELOW WITH STUNNING FORCE AND IS EASILY DISARMED BY TWO SERVANTS.

②

KING LAMORACK IS ANGRY. "YOU HAVE BETRAYED MY HOSPITALITY, INSULTED MY HOUSE, ASSAULTED MY GUEST; FOR THAT YOU WILL DIE TERRIBLY!"

③

④ WHILE A HUGE STONE COVER IS BEING LIFTED, VAL'S CHAINS ARE REMOVED AND A KNIFE HANDED TO HIM.

A ROPE IS PASSED THROUGH HIS LEATHER BELT AND, WITH A SUDDEN JERK, HE IS TOPPLED FROM THE EDGE AND HELD SUSPENDED OVER A DEEP CISTERN.

⑤

⑥ FAR BELOW, THE GREEN SEA FLOWS IN AND OUT A BARRED WINDOW. SLOWLY HIS EYES BECOME ACCUSTOMED TO THE DIM LIGHT. THEN HE SEES A SHOCKING SIGHT; STARING UP AT HIM WITH UNBLINKING SMALL EYES IS A MONSTER MORE HIDEOUS THAN A SICK MAN'S DREAMS!

HAL FOSTER

NEXT WEEK— **The King.**

Prince Valiant

IN THE DAYS OF KING ARTHUR

BY HAROLD R FOSTER Registered U S Patent Office

Synopsis: PRINCE VALIANT FINISHES THE GRAVE AND PLACES BERIC'S SWORD AT ITS HEAD. THEN HE LOOKS TOWARD THE DISTANT CITY WHEREIN RULES ALETA, QUEEN OF THE MISTY ISLES.

LIGHTNING FLASHES AND THUNDER ROARS, OMIN-OUSLY, BUT MORE THREATENING STILL IS THE GLEAM OF MADNESS IN HIS EYES, THE THROBBING IN HIS BRAIN AND THE SICK HATRED IN HIS HEART.

GREY-EYED ALETA, QUEEN OF THE MISTY ISLES, IS ABOUT TO CHOOSE A HUSBAND FROM AMONG THE GLITTERING ARRAY OF SUITORS, WHEN THE CURTAINS ARE FLUNG ASIDE BY A HANDSOME YOUTH. ON HIS RAGGED CLOAK IS THE DUST OF LONG, FAR ROADS, HIS ARMOR IS SCARRED WITH MANY BATTLES......
THEN THEY ALL DRAW BACK IN HORROR.....IN HIS EYES THERE IS THE LIGHT OF MADNESS AND IN HIS HAND A GLEAMING SWORD!

NEXT WEEK — **The Abduction of Aleta.**

409 12-10-44 COPR. 1944, KING FEATURES SYNDICATE, Inc. WORLD RIGHTS RESERVED

The Mediæval Castle   BY HAL FOSTER

34

CHRISTMAS IS AT HAND AND TIME FOR THE GREAT HUNT. ALREADY THE SERGEANT-AT-ARMS IS BUSY IN THE ARMORY, PUTTING A RAZOR EDGE ON THE BOAR SPEARS.

EACH DAY ARN AND GUY MOUNT THEIR HORSES AND TAKE THE DOGS FOR A LONG RUN TO HARDEN THEM FOR THE COMING CHASE.

COPR. 1944, KING FEATURES SYNDICATE, Inc. WORLD RIGHTS RESERVED   12-10-44

THE GUESTS ARRIVE. THE DUKE IS GUEST OF HONOR AND SIR MORVYN, THE KING'S HUNTSMAN, WILL LEAD THE CHASE (AND SEE THAT THE KING RECEIVES HIS SHARE OF THE MEAT!)   *TO BE CONTINUED*

Prince Valiant

IN THE DAYS OF KING ARTHUR

BY Harold R Foster

HAL FOSTER

Synopsis: *TWINS!* FOR A FULL MINUTE PRINCE VALIANT GAZES, WITH WILDLY BEATING HEART, UPON THE LOVELINESS OF HIS WIFE, ALETA. DURING THE LONG YEAR OF HIS WANDERING HE HAS DREAMED LONGINGLY OF HER BEAUTY AND NOW, HERE SHE LIES, LOVELIER THAN HIS DREAMS.

IT IS THEN HE NOTICES THAT THE TWO SQUIRMING LUMPS BESIDE HER HAVE A MEANING; A DEFINITE, IMPORTANT MEANING. HE KNEELS BESIDE HER COUCH. HE HAS TO, HIS KNEES ARE WEAK.

"YES, DEAR HUSBAND, THEY ARE REAL AND YOU ARE THE FATHER OF TWIN GIRLS, FOUR MONTHS OLD," LAUGHS ALETA. "NOW PULL YOUR EYES BACK, CLOSE YOUR MOUTH AND COME KISS ME!"

767   10-21-51

IN THE SILENCE THAT FOLLOWS A LONELY FIGURE APPEARS IN THE DOORWAY. THE FORGOTTEN MAN, THE LOST GENERATION. IT IS PRINCE ARN, SUFFERING FROM AN ALMOST FATAL CASE OF 'HAVING HIS NOSE OUT OF JOINT!'

NEXT WEEK:— The Prince Arn Story

Prince ARN
IN THE DAYS OF KING ARTHUR
FOSTER

Synopsis: "MY LIFE OF ADVENTURE BE-GAN WHEN MY SIRE, PRINCE VALIANT, RETURNED FROM HIS LONG QUEST AND DISCOVERED THAT I HAD BECOME A MAN—ALMOST. I DECIDED TO BE HIS TRUSTED COMPANION AND WE WOULD GO QUEST-ING TOGETHER."

"WHILE HE WAS INSPECTING THE HORSES I TRIED TO PICK ONE OUT FOR MYSELF, BUT THEY WERE ALL SO TERRIBLY BIG!"

"NEXT WE HAD TO GO TO THE RIVER TO SEE IF THE SALMON WERE RUNNING YET. THIS WAS THE FIRST TIME I HAD BEEN OUTSIDE THE CASTLE GROUNDS."

"I STOPPED TO BATTLE A HORDE OF DANES WITH GOLDEN HELMETS, AND SLEW HUNDREDS"

"WHEN I REACHED THE RIVER MY SHIELD SLIPPED OFF MY ARM AND I HAD TO CLIMB DOWN THE CLIFF TO GET IT. MY FATHER WAS NOWHERE IN SIGHT."

"BUT SOME PEOPLE ACROSS THE RIVER WERE AWFULLY EXCITED. I COULD NOT HEAR WHAT THEY WERE SHOUTING, FOR THE RIVER ROARS ANGRY HERE."

"I STARTED HOME, BUT THE WAY WAS VERY LONG AND STRANGE. THE CASTLE WAS NOT WHERE I LEFT IT, BUT I COULD HEAR PEOPLE CALLING MY NAME IN THE DISTANCE."

"I WAS HUNGRY AND MET A BEAST THAT LOOKED HUNGRY TOO! CLOSE AT HAND I COULD HEAR MY SIRE SHOUTING AND THE THUNDER OF HOOFS."

769 11-4-51

"THEN A SPEAR HURTLED BY AND THE BEAST FELL. MY SIRE, THE PRINCE, HELD ME VERY TIGHT AS WE GALLOPED HOME"

HAL FOSTER

"SOON I WAS SAFE IN MOMMIE'S ARMS WHERE NO HARM CAN EVER TOUCH ME. IN A STRANGE, TIGHT LITTLE VOICE SHE SAID TO MY FATHER: 'SOON ENOUGH HE WILL HAVE THE LOOK OF EAGLES AND THEN YOU WILL TAKE HIM OUT INTO THE WORLD AND TEACH HIM MAN'S WAYS. UNTIL THEN HE IS MINE!'"

NEXT WEEK:— **The Treaty.**

Prince Valiant

IN THE DAYS OF KING ARTHUR

BY HAROLD R. FOSTER

Synopsis: TWO SCORE LEAGUES FROM HOME PRINCE VALIANT AND ARF LOSE THEIR HORSES AND MOST OF THEIR GEAR WHILE CROSSING A SWOLLEN RIVER. IT IS IMPOSSIBLE FOR ARF TO CROSS THE RUGGED MOUNTAINS WITH BUT ONE LEG, SO THEY CONSTRUCT A CANOE AND ATTEMPT TO FOLLOW THE UNKNOWN RIVER TO THE SEA.

AND AT TIMES THE RIVER IS FRIEND-LY, GLIDING SMOOTHLY THROUGH MILES OF DUSKY FOREST......

...... WHILE AT OTHER TIMES IT RUSHES THEM AT DIZZY SPEED DOWN FOAMING RAPIDS.

BUT MOST OFTEN THEY HAVE TO CUT A PATH THROUGH THE FOREST AND PORTAGE THEIR CANOE AROUND THUNDERING CATARACTS.

THEY LIVE ON FISH AND BERRIES. ONCE A BLUE-BERRY PATCH IS DISPUTED AND THEY STAND FOR A LONG, BREATHLESS MOMENT WHILE AN ANGRY MOTHER TRIES TO MAKE UP HER MIND AS TO WHETHER HER CHILDREN ARE BEING ENDANGERED.

LATE ONE DAY THE RIVER CARRIES THEM INTO A NARROW CANYON. TOO LATE THEY HEAR THE OMINOUS ROAR OF TUMBLING WATERS.

NO CANOE COULD STAY AFLOAT IN SUCH A MAELSTROM, BUT VAL AND ARF CLING DESPERATELY TO IT, FOR THE BLADDERS AT EACH END KEEP IT FROM SINKING.

WHEN AT LAST THEY DRAG THEM-SELVES ASHORE NIGHT HAS FALLEN. IN THE MORNING THEY WILL BE ABLE TO TELL WHETHER OR NOT THEIR FRAIL BOAT IS DAMAGED BEYOND REPAIR.

NEXT WEEK:- The Deer Hunter.

HAL FOSTER

Prince Valiant
IN THE DAYS OF KING ARTHUR
by Hal Foster

Our Story: YOUNG PRINCE GALAN HAS HEARD SO MUCH OF THULE THAT HE LONGS TO SEE IT FOR HIMSELF. FIRST HE ASKS TILLICUM, AND THAT STRANGE, SILENT WOMAN BOLTAR HAS BROUGHT FROM ACROSS FAR SEAS SAYS HE CAN SAIL WITH THEM IF HIS MOTHER APPROVES.

QUEEN ALETA, OF COURSE, SAYS NO; THE SEA VOYAGE IS TOO DANGEROUS. BUT THEN, WHY NOT? BOLTAR IS THE BEST OF THE SEA ROVERS AND WILL PROTECT HIM.

BOLTAR, AS USUAL, FIRST ROARS, "NO! MY SHIP IS NOT A NURSERY!" THEN HE GRUMBLES, "OH, WELL, COME ALONG BUT KEEP OUT OF THE WAY."

IT IS A GAY PARTY THAT MAKES ITS WAY TO BRISTOL, FOR SUMMER IS ENDING IN A BLAZE OF AUTUMN COLORS AND HIGH ABOVE, THE WILD GEESE ARE CALLING.

THEIR SHIP IS FLOATED DOWN THE AVON RIVER TO WHERE THE TIDE OF BRISTOL BAY RISES AND FALLS. HERE AT LOW TIDE THE HULL IS CAULKED AND PAINTED IN READINESS FOR THE LONG SEA JOURNEY.

VAL IS BEGINNING TO MISS THE ROLLICKING GALAN WHEN ARN BURSTS IN: "FATHER, I WISH TO SAIL WITH BOLTAR...

"...FOR I AM IN LINE FOR THE THRONE OF THULE AND WHERE ELSE CAN I LEARN TO RULE SUCCESSFULLY BUT FROM AGUAR, ITS GREATEST RULER?"

2170

VAL AGREES, KNOWING A YOUNG EAGLE MUST TRY ITS WINGS. HOW LONESOME IT WILL BE EVEN IN CAMELOT WITH HIS TWO SONS AWAY.

NEXT WEEK — The Voyage   9-10

Prince Valiant IN THE DAYS OF KING ARTHUR
by HAL FOSTER

Our Story: HIS ORDEAL AT THE HANDS OF THE MAD EARL OF LOLLAND HAS LEFT BOLTAR WEAK, AND HE IS CONTENT TO SIT ON DECK AS HIS SHIP SAILS WESTWARD DOWN THE BRISTOL CHANNEL.

BUT ERE THEY REACH THE SEAS HE IS BELLOWING ORDERS LIKE A SEA LION AND HIS CREW SMILES, FOR THIS IS MORE LIKE THE CAPTAIN THEY ARE USED TO.

PRINCE GALAN HAD OFTEN TRAVELED BY SEA BUT NEVER BEFORE IN AN OPEN BOAT WHERE ONE ATE AND SLEPT IN THE RAIN AND WIND. BUT HE SOON BECOMES ACCUSTOMED TO THE HARDSHIPS. HE DOES NOT COMPLAIN FOR BROTHER ARN IS WATCHING HIM.

AND ONCE, BEFORE SUNRISE, HE IS AWAKENED BY THE ROAR OF WINGS AND ARISES TO SEE THE GREAT AUTUMN MIGRATION OF WATERFOWL FROM THE NORTH.

A PLAYFUL POD OF WHALES PLAY AROUND THE SHIP MOST OF THE NEXT DAY. GALAN IS SPEECHLESS WITH WONDER.

AND NOW BOLTAR AND TILLICUM SPEND THE DAYLIGHT HOURS IN THE BOW, LOOKING AHEAD FOR THE FIRST SIGHT OF HOME.

2171

THEN, JUST BEFORE ANY LANDMARKS APPEAR TO SHOW THEM THE ENTRANCE TO TRONDHEIMFJORD, THE FOG ROLLS IN AND OBSCURES THE COAST. BOLTAR DECIDES TO STAND OFF UNTIL TOMORROW.

NEXT WEEK— *Home* 9-17

Our Story: WITH THE DAWN, THE FOG SLOWLY MELTS AWAY AND BOLTAR SAILS HIS SHIP TOWARD THE AWESOME COAST. *"WHERE ARE YOU TAKING US, BOLTAR?"* QUERIES ARN. *"THIS IS NOT THE ENTRANCE TO TRONDHEIMFJORD."*

"NO," ANSWERS BOLTAR, *"BUT I HAVE A SON TOO. ONE I HAVE NOT SEEN FOR ABOVE A YEAR. HIS MOTHER AND I ARE ANXIOUS TO SEE HOW HE FARED DURING OUR LONG ABSENCE.... SO WE GO TO OUR HOME FIRST."*

THE FJORD THEY ENTER IS A FITTING ABODE FOR ALL THE NORSE GODS, AND HERE BOLTAR HAD BUILT A HOME FOR TILLICUM, THE MYSTERIOUS QUIET WOMAN HE HAD BROUGHT FROM OVERSEAS, AND HATHA, THE SON SHE BORE HIM.

NEXT WEEK— Sweethearts United 9-24

2172

Hal Foster's **Prince Valiant** IN THE DAYS OF KING ARTHUR
BY JOHN CULLEN MURPHY

Our Story: A LARGE PORTION OF VAL'S PARTY WILL REMAIN AT TURFAN TO SERVE AS GUIDES AND DIRECT THE FLOW OF TRADE. BUT PRINCE VALIANT HEADS EAST WITH YUAN CHEN AND GALAN AND SIR GAWAIN. THEIR OBJECT: NANKING...

....THE CAPITAL OF THE SOUTHERN KINGDOM AND HOME OF THE GREAT AND ESTEEMED EMPEROR WU TI.

"IT IS A MOST DIFFICULT TIME FOR MY PEOPLE," YUAN CHEN EXPLAINS. "OUR LAND IS DIVIDED BETWEEN NORTH AND SOUTH.

"THE MEN WHO RULE THE NORTH ARE THE SONS OF BARBARIANS, AND THERE IS MUCH FIGHTING AMONG THEM. EVERY YEAR, IT SEEMS, BRINGS A NEW EMPEROR. THUS IT WAS IN THE SOUTH, TOO, UNTIL WU TI MOUNTED THE THRONE."

ONCE IN A PROVINCE THAT YUAN CHEN CALLS KANSU, PRINCE VALIANT LOOKS UP IN WONDER AT A MOUNTAINSIDE THAT HAS BEEN CARVED INTO WHAT LOOKS LIKE A TEMPLE. *"THAT IS THE GALLERY OF A THOUSAND BUDDHAS,"* SAYS YUAN CHEN. *"THE FOLLOWERS OF THE BUDDHA HAVE BECOME MANY IN MY LAND IN RECENT YEARS. YOU WILL SEE — THE EMPEROR IS ONE OF THEM."*

HAL FOSTER'S   GIANNI AND SCHULTZ

Prince Valiant®

Our Story: ALETA HAS RESCUED THE STRANDED SKYRMIR, AND HAS BEEN REPAID WITH INFURIATING TALES OF HER WANDERING HUSBAND'S GLORIOUS EXPLOITS.

HER ESTIMATION OF VAL COULD NOT GET MUCH LOWER. BUT, ON THE FAR SIDE OF AFRICA, VAL IS FEELING RATHER SMALL HIMSELF...

...IN THE FACE OF THE GRANDEST CITY HE HAS EVER SEEN. HE HAS COME AT LAST TO AB'SABA—AND BESIDE THIS PLACE JERUSALEM, AND EVEN ROME, SEEM LIKE BACKWOODS VILLAGES.

NEXT:

Uneasy Arrival

3692

Our Story:

TWEDOREK'S REBEL ARMY IS THROUGH THE REDOUBT'S SHATTERED GATES! VAL AND MAKEDA'S LOYAL WARRIORS MEET THEM ON THE NARROW INCLINE OF THE GRAND STAIRCASE, GRIMLY BUYING TIME FOR THEIR QUEEN'S ESCAPE.

HAL FOSTER'S Prince Valiant
BY GIANNI AND SCHULTZ

BUT THE WAVE OF INVADERS IS OVERWHELMING, AND EVEN THE BRAVE PRINCE OF THULE FEELS THE HAND OF FATE CLOSING DOWN ...

...WHEN, FROM OUTSIDE, COMES THE WAILING OF A THUNDEROUS HORN. ALL FREEZE BEFORE THE TERRIBLE SOUND!

NEXT:
Out of the Past

86.

STILL, THERE ARE CASUALTIES BEFORE VAL AND BUKOTA FIND VULNERABLE FLESH.

Our Story:

AB'SABAN SPEARS ARE ALL THAT KEEP A MAMMOTH DENIZEN OF THIS WEIRD, WEED-CHOKED SEA FROM WREAKING TOTAL HAVOC ON VAL'S CREW.

WITH A COMBINED EFFORT, THE CREW MANAGES TO HEAVE THE MORTALLY WOUNDED CREATURE OVERBOARD.

IT THRASHES SPASMODICALLY AMIDST THE WEED FOR LONG MINUTES, THEN IS STILL. *"IT MAY BE BIG, BUT STILL A CRAB. THAT MEANS GOOD EATING IN THE MISTY ISLES "* ALETA VENTURES.

AND SO, UNDER HER SUPERVISION, NORSEMEN BECOME BUTCHERS, AND THE MEN OF CAMELOT ARE MADE SEA COOKS.

3733

NATHAN SAMPLES ALETA'S CRAB STEW. HE SMACKS HIS LIPS. *"DELICIOUS, BUT SALTY. A REMINDER THAT WE NEED... "*

NEXT: Fresh water

Hal Foster's Prince Valiant BY GIANNI AND SCHULTZ

Our Story: WANDERING KNIGHTS TELL MANY TALES OF DRAGONS VANQUISHED BY THEIR PROWESS. WHO CAN SAY IF THESE STORIES ARE TRUE, BRAVADO, OR RESUME-PADDING?

REGARDLESS, THE DRAGON THAT NOW CRAWLS TOWARD CAMELOT SEEMS IN LITTLE DANGER OF BEING VANQUISHED.

STILL, AN ENERGETIC DEFENSE IS MOUNTED. AS VAL RUSHES IN, SOMETHING ABOUT THIS SHAMBLING FORM PRODS HIS MEMORY.

"THIS MONSTROUS BRUTE—IS IT NOT THE SAME CREATURE WE SAW ROUT THE BEASTMEN ON THEIR WEEDY ISLAND?"

NEXT: The battle for Camelot

OF MEAD, WHISKEY, AND BRANDYWINE:
THE ARTISTIC BLOODLINE OF PRINCE VALIANT

by Brian M. Kane (2009)

When I began my serendipitous trek through illustration researching artists who influenced Harold Rudolf Foster, I first combed through his interviews looking for names. Several times Foster mentioned his usual suspects: J.C. Leyendecker, Edwin Austin Abbey, Howard Pyle, and N.C. Wyeth. Yet these are names we would have expected to hear an accomplished artist of Foster's stature reveal as his influences. They give *Prince Valiant* a certain unquestioned artistic pedigree. However, were he to have said, "My earliest influences were a bunch of British cartoonists, some unknown advertising artist, and the freelancers that hung around the *Popular Mechanics* office," many of us would scratch our heads simply thinking that he was having a good joke on us. In the case of Hal Foster, I believe his style was more heavily influenced by the popular visual culture of his time then he ever admitted. Influences are an interesting conundrum. Sometimes they creep in unawares at the periphery of our perceptions and become part of our style. I believe that Foster's style was a synthesis of the artists of the Golden Age of Illustration, advertising, and the graphic journalistic tradition of the European illustrated press.

Two artists often believed to have influenced Foster, but who did not, were J. Allen St. John (1875–1957) and Harry Cornell Greening (1878-1930). In Foster's own words, he never studied the illustrations of St. John before drawing *Tarzan*, nor did he ever see Greening's *Prince Errant* comic strip before beginning *Prince Valiant*.[1] *Prince Errant* is easy to substantiate, since the strip was developed for the Los Angeles *Illustrated Daily News*, and Foster did not move to Chicago until 1921. Foster's denial of St. John's influence, however, leaves many scholars frustrated, and the apocryphal tale of how Joseph Neebe found Foster slaving away at a drafting table in St. John's studio still persists. One only needs to compare the physiognomy of either artist's protagonist to understand that no anatomical influence can be found. What is important to remember with both of these presumptions is that, no matter how obvious an influence may appear, without Foster's corroboration, all anyone can do is to make

plausible recommendations based on the facts available at the time. Such is the case with the majority of the artists referenced in this investigation.

Of those artists he mentioned outright, Foster's greatest influence was J.C. Leyendecker. As a clothing catalogue artist for the Hudson Bay Company, and throughout Foster's entire life, Leyendecker was one of his favorite artists. Not surprisingly, Foster owned a Leyendecker original, as evidenced in Arn Saba's interview (see page 110). Much has already been written regarding the importance of Howard Pyle's impact on Foster's development of *Prince Valiant*.[2] From reading Foster's interviews, and by comparing illustrations (Figures 1 & 2) we can observe that Pyle's influence lay primarily in the storytelling and not the art. N.C. Wyeth's contribution to Foster, however, has been largely underexamined. Foster was a Romanticist, and was drawn to the heroic fantasies in Wyeth's beautifully illustrated volumes, *The Black Arrow* (1916), *Robin Hood* (1917), *The Boy's King Arthur* (1917), *The Scottish Chiefs* (1921), and *The White Company* (1922). In actuality, Val shares more in common with Robin Hood and Dick "The Lawless" than he does with any of Arthur's knights. It was also Wyeth's sense of grandeur that Foster adapted into his illustrations, presenting them as if they were leaves in a book rather than sequential panels. One Wyeth piece that bears mentioning, and was probably seen by Foster, is "The King's Henchmen" (Figure 3). It is a 1927 Steinway and Sons advertisement showcasing a Val-like figure ten years before *Prince Valiant* appeared in print. I have said it before, but it bears repeating, that, artistically, Foster was a stepson to Howard Pyle and a half-brother to the sons and daughters of the Brandywine Tradition.

The Palenske-Young Studio

Other known artists that directly influenced Foster were his fellow workers at Palenske-Young Studio. As part of his job at Palenske-Young, Foster supplied covers and interior art to the Chicago-based publication, *Popular*

Figure 1, Above: "The Lady of the Lake Sits by the Fountain in Arroy," from The Story of King Arthur and His Knights *(1903). Text and illustration by Howard Pyle (1853-1911).*

Figure 2, Below: "Prince Valiant meets Aleta, Queen of the Misty Isles for the second time" from Prince Valiant, *page 251, 30 November 1941. Illustration by Harold Rudolf Foster.*

Mechanics, during the 1920s and 1930s. The chiaroscuro technique Foster employed illustrating *Tarzan,* while relatively new to comic strips, was comparable in style to the black & white spot illustrations utilized in magazines. The high-contrast method was chosen because it reproduced better on pulp paper than fine-line pen work. In an unpublished 1972 interview conducted by *film noir* scholar Bob Porfirio, Foster recalled, "When I first did *Tarzan,* it came to me in book form to illustrate the book. So I was an illustrator. But it had to be done sketchy, because I was going to use it later on as a daily comic strip, and that's why it was done in that form. So I used my professional technique that I used in advertising illustration and I never got out of it. I don't think I could have done anything else."[3] Regarding his thoughts on why he was chosen, Foster commented: "It wasn't at all that I was the best, but I was a good second-rater. And there were hundreds of others. There were two boys in the studio that were better than I, but somehow doing the cartoon pleased me. I liked to do it."[4]

The "two boys in the studio" Foster was referring to were more than likely the studio's co-owner, Reinhold H. Palenske (1884-1954) and Paul Proehl (1887-1965). Palenske studied at the Art Institute of Chicago under Wellington Jarard Reynolds (1865-1949), and began his professional career with Scroll Publishing Company in Chicago as a binding designer. Palenske contributed to the *Chicago Daily News,* and, for many years, was under exclusive contract with Brown and Bigelow to produce a number of his original etchings for the advertising specialty market. An avid sportsman and hunter, Palenske co-founded the "Trail Riders of the Canadian Rockies" with J. M. Gibbon and Carl Rungius. Palenske's horse paintings hang in the Library of Congress, the New York Public Library, and the Royal Gallery of London, England. Considering Foster's past in Canada, he would have quickly gravitated to the outdoorsman in Palenske. Paul Proehl, whose black & white technique was similar to Foster's, probably contributed to the *Tarzan* strip, possibly as a background inker. Proehl is best remembered for his travel advertisements, including vintage posters of Chicago that are still found in many print shops today.

M.D. Charleson

Another Chicago illustrator, Malcolm Daniel (M.D.) Charleson (1888-1943), was a complete unknown to me when I began researching Foster's influences. Charleson's cover for *From the Tower Window of My Bookhouse* (1921, Figure 4), printed by the Chicago-based The Book House for Children publishing company, displays the closest image of Prince Valiant ever painted by any artist outside of Foster, yet the book was printed sixteen years before the strip premiered. Coincidentally, Charleson was born in Canada (Brandon, Manitoba), moved to Winnipeg, was married less than a year after Foster married Helen, then, like Foster, moved to Chicago where he established himself as an illustrator. Considering the ages of Foster's sons Edward and Arthur, and his own penchant for fantasy, it is highly likely that the Bookhouse books made their way into the Foster household, either as gifts for his children, or while doing research for the strip. However, as close as the image is to a mature Val of the late 1940s, it bears only a cursory resemblance to the young Val pictured in the early years of the strip.

Matt Clark and Frank Godwin

Stylistically, Matt Clark (1903-1972) and Frank Godwin (1889-1959) appear to have had a marked influence on Foster's spotting of blacks within his art. Clark produced illustrations for several magazines including *The Saturday Evening Post,* which Foster read. Clark's black & white dry brush depictions of horses and cowboys had a loose, spontaneous feel to it that is similar to Foster's. Foster would have known of Clark's command of the brush and gleaned from it for his own use. It should also be mentioned that many comic strip historians and aficionados consider Clark to be a major influence on Alex Raymond during his "painterly" period on *Flash Gordon* in the mid-1930s.

Godwin illustrated several children's books in the tradition of N.C. Wyeth and Maxfield Parrish (1870-1966). Godwin produced illustrations for *The Blue Fairy Book* (1921), *Robin Hood* (1923), *The Black Arrow* (1923), *Treasure Island* (1924), *Tales from Shakespeare* (1924), *Kidnapped* (1925), *Robinson Crusoe* (1925), and *King Arthur and His Knights* (1927). Though a student of James Montgomery Flagg (1877-1960), Godwin had a more refined sense of casual physicality and a richer command of tone than his teacher. By evaluating how Godwin created the textures of elements within his illustrations (Figure 5),

such as the stones and fabrics, we can see similarities between his and Foster's approaches. Today, Godwin is best remembered for his newspaper strips *Connie* (1927-1944) and *Rusty Riley* (1948-1959).

The Press Art School

In 1925, Percy Venner Bradshaw (1877-1965) published *Art in Advertising: A Study of British and American Pictorial Publicity*. Bradshaw founded The Press Art School in 1905, and, from 1916-1920, authored sixteen portfolio volumes in *The Art of the Illustrator* series, featuring such artists as Frank Reynolds, W. Heath Robinson, F.H. Townsend, Harry Rountree, Fortunino Matania, W. Russell Flint, and Lawson Wood.[5] *Art in Advertising* was a profusely illustrated, in-depth look at the business of advertising, and included an extensive look at the career of Frank Brangwyn (1867-1956), one of Europe's most compelling turn of the century illustrators and muralists.[6] Informative chapters examined topics such as "Pictorial Composition, Design and Layout," "The Art of the Printer," "The Advertising Agent and His Work," "Commercial Studios and Their Work," and "Notable Advertising Campaigns." While this would not have been a book that Foster may have owned, copies would have been available at the Art Institute or in the Palenske-Young Studio. Certain aspects of commercial design discussed in *Art in Advertising* are evident in Foster's advertising art. Whether that influence came directly from Foster reading the book, or one of his instructors who was teaching from it, remains uncertain. Several artists spotlighted in *Art in Advertising* have styles comparable to Foster's early dry brush technique. Those artists include Henry Coller, Septimus E. Scott, W. Smithson Broadhead, Frank Newbould, Leo Cheney, and a man with the curious name of Harold Forster (note the additional "r" in the last name).[7] Forster produced illustrations for Black Magic chocolates and Barclay's "Lager," and painted the famous wartime *Keep Mum, She's Not So Dumb* poster. The United Kingdom's National Archives owns a color

Figure 3, Above: "The King's Henchmen" (1927). *Published as an advertisement for Steinway and Sons. Illustration by Newell Convers Wyeth (1882-1945). Used with permission by The Kelly Collection of American Illustration.*
Figure 4, Below: *The cover to* From the Tower Window of My Bookhouse *(1921). Illustration by Malcolm Daniel (M.D.) Charleson (1888-1943).*

Figure 5, *Above:* "The Ladies and the Knights Gave the Tiny Boy into the Stranger's Arms" *from* King Arthur and His Knights (1927) *by Elizabeth Lodor Merchant. Illustration by Francis "Frank" Godwin (1889-1959).*

Figure 6, *Above Right:* "Prince Valiant, Gawain, and Sir Basil before Jerusalem." *Vignette of a panel from* Prince Valiant, *page 917, 5 September 1954. Illustration by Harold Rudolf Foster.*

Figure 7, *Opposite:* "The Four Leaders of the First Crusade—Godfrey, Raymond, Bœmund, Tancred" *from* Cyclopædia of Universal History *by John Clark Ridpath, LL.D., V. 2. Illustration by Alphonse-Marie-Adolphe de Neuville (1835-1885).*

gouache on board illustration by Forster titled *Pharmacist.* What is unusual about this dual light sourced, chiaroscuro-styled portrait is that it looks eerily like Hal Foster from the1950s, yet the Archives dates the painting between 1939-1945.[8]

The Crusades

Foster worked on his designs and concepts for *Prince Valiant* for two years prior to its publication, which coincides with the release of Cecil B. DeMille's adventure film *The Crusades* (Paramount, 1935). Originally, Foster wanted to focus his stories on the Crusades, but abandoned the idea because "[I] couldn't very well leave the Holy Land or Asia, I thought it would get a little bit monotonous. So I kept going back and back until finally I struck the days of King Arthur."[9] However, several elements from the film made their way into the strip. Though King Arthur's era was six centuries before the Crusades, much of the clothing, armaments,

and décor are consistent with those pictured in DeMille's film. The scene of the slave market of the Saracens, where women are sold for pleasure, appears to have been the impetus for Val's capture and enslavement of Aleta. The subsequent abduction of Aleta by Donardo, and the fall of Saramand, also draw parallels to the capture of Berehgaria (Loretta Young) by Saladin (Ian Keith) and the fall of Acre.[10] It should also be pointed out that Val's handsome companion, Gawain, bears a striking resemblance to Saladin, Sultan of Islam.

Ridpath

Since Foster initially intended the strip to focus on the Crusades, it was necessary to review what research material was available to him at the time. At the top of the list are the lavishly illustrated historical reference books by John Clark Ridpath (1840-1900). These are the *Cyclopædia of Universal History* (3 volumes, 1880-1884), *Ridpath's History of the World* (8 volumes, 1894), and *Ridpath's Universal History* (16 volumes, 1895). The majority of the illustrations from these volumes are wood engravings that were originally produced for European history texts. Some of the more notable artists included de Neuville, Doré, Lix, Bayard, and Vierge.[11] As with Pyle, Foster appears to have found inspiration from the stories these illustrations depicted, rather than the art itself. By comparing some of the Ridpath illustrations with panels from *Prince Valiant*, conclusions may be drawn as to which stories resonated most within the strip. For example, Figure 7, depicting four kings riding off on the first Crusade, is of significance when we compare the face of Prince Bœmund of Tarent (third from the left) with that of Crusader Sir Basil in Figure 6 (also third from the left). The memorable *Prince Valiant* storyline dealing with *The Storming of Andelkrag*, as seen in Figure 9, is equivalent to Doré's *The Storming of Antioch* in Figure 8. Finally, the comparison between Figures 10 and 11 needs no explanation. There has been speculation among scholars and artists as to whether or not Foster's source for "Kalla Khan Receives the Head of Karnak, the Ferocious" was Robert E. Howard's short story "Shadow of the Vulture," which appeared in a 1934 issue of *Oriental Stories*. While it has already been established that Foster's fellow Palenske-Young artist and fishing buddy, Charles F. Armstrong, introduced him to the fantasy writings of James Branch Cabell and Lord Dunsany, the "leap" to Howard from these two masters is not much more than a "shuffle." One possible answer is that the Ridpath image influenced both creators.

The Influence of The Illustrated Press

Foster lived in Winnipeg during World War I, and would have received most of his information about the war from the pages of newspapers such as *The Illustrated London News, The Graphic*, and *The Sphere*.[12] These illustrated newspapers, along with their counterparts in Paris and Germany, unintentionally became the first art primers for the growing middle class in mid-to-late nineteenth century Europe.[13] Delacroix, Vernet, Manet, Monet, Renoir, and many other prominent artists contributed to illustrated newspapers. The influence of these Graphic Journalists was extensive. For example, 1) The Van Gogh Museum alone maintains a collection of over 1,500 pages, which were amassed from various illustrated newspapers by Vincent and his brother Theo; 2) Some of the world's first comic strips, illustrated by Swiss schoolmaster Rodolphe Töpffer (1799-1846), were first published in *L'Illustration* in the 1840s; and 3) *The Illustrated London News'* Yokohama-based news correspondent, illustrator, and humorist Charles Wirgman (1832-1891) laid the groundwork for Japanese Manga in 1862 with his self-published *The Japan Punch*. Even in America, Robert Henri (1865-1929) introduced his *Philadelphia*

Four peers to the caricatures of Honoré Daumier (1808-1879) and the cartoonists of *Punch* upon his return from Paris, thus foreshadowing the illustrated press's influence on the emerging Ashcan School/Urban Realist movement. Considering their global impact, it is of little surprise that Foster's own pre-1920 "bigfoot" cartoons, such as the one on page 119, owe much to *Punch* cartoonists "Phil" May (Figure 13), Reginald Cleaver, A.S. Boyd, E. Hopkins, G.D. Armour, and Charles Keene.[14]

The Great War witnessed the last vestiges of graphic journalism fighting its own battle against the encroachment of photojournalism in the weekly pages of the illustrated press. Incredible images by artists such as Woodville, Forestier, de Haenen, Begg, Koekkoek, and Matania depicted scenes of battle unmatched by today's politically-restricted, high-tech news reporters.[15] Since war reportage for photojournalists was still in its

infancy, it became incumbent upon the graphic journalists to chronicle the conflagrations. These artists took readers into the conflict by creating huge battle scenes, often measuring 11" x 19" (Figure 12), which appear more real than the photographs with which they competed. These extraordinarily designed illustrations with their "cast of thousands" had their roots in nineteenth century French Academic military paintings by such artists as Ernest Meissonier and (the aptly named) Édouard Detaille.[16] Foster's ability to capture the energy and emotion of a mêlée in his battle scenes is a direct outgrowth of that artistic lineage.

Finally, one newspaper-advertising artist who appears to have played a significant role in Foster's depiction of people was Leo Cheney. Though he was not a graphic journalist, Cheney's advertising art appeared in many of the illustrated newspapers mentioned above. Cheney was the first

pupil to enroll in Percy Bradshaw's cartoon correspondence course through The Press Art School. Following in the tradition of the great British caricaturist "Phil" May (Figure 13), Cheney combined acute draftsmanship with his own brand of stylized realism. Cheney created the famous "Striding Man" version of the character Johnnie Walker for John Walker and Sons Scotch Whiskey. At the time, the "Striding Man" was the most popular personality in advertising, and Cheney's full-page advertisements appeared regularly in the illustrated press between 1915 and 1919. There can be no doubting that Foster saw Cheney's art, and one need only compare the facial features of the Australian infantryman in Figure 14 with the Yankee infantryman in Figure 15 to see the resemblance. Perhaps not so coincidentally, Foster enjoyed his whiskey, and Johnnie Walker was one of his whiskeys of choice.

Conclusion

No artist can be the product of only one influence and claim to have a unique voice. Style is developed from a synthesis of a multitude of influences. Sometimes what creeps in at the periphery of our perceptions can be just as important as those things we embrace with open arms. Sometimes they are merely the catalysts that allow all of the other ingredients to ferment into something fresh and innovative. Style is like a good mead, whiskey, or Brandywine that needs time to mature. Foster's artistic vision is both a profoundly personal synthesis of the visual culture of his times, and the stories of the writers he tried to emulate. That vision, that artist's voice is what made *Prince Valiant* unique.

Figure 8: *Above:* "The Storming of Antioch" *from* Cyclopædia of Universal History *by John Clark Ridpath, LL.D., V. 2. Illustration by Paul Gustave Doré (1832-1883).*
Figure 9, *Opposite, top:* "The Storming of Andelkrag" *from* Prince Valiant, *page 122, 11 November 1939. Illustration by Harold Rudolf Foster.*
Figure 10, *Opposite, below left:* "The Cardinal of Lorraine Receiving the Head of Coligny" *from* Cyclopædia of Universal History *by John Clark Ridpath, LL.D., V. 2. Artist unknown.*
Figure 11, *Opposite, below right:* "Kalla Khan Receives the Head of Karnak, the Ferocious" *from* Prince Valiant, *page 160, 3 March 1940. Illustration by Harold Rudolf Foster.*

The author wishes to thank Mark Schultz and Bob Porfirio for their input while preparing this essay.

Endnotes

[1] For J. Allen St. John see Fred Schreiber's 1969 interview in *NEMO: The Classic Comics Library* #9, October 1984, p 12, and for *Prince Errant* see Bill Crouch's interview in *Cartoonist PROfiles*, No. 22, June 1974, p 45.

[2] See *Hal Foster: Prince of Illustrators* by Brian M. Kane, and "Howard Pyle and the Roots of the Artistry of Hal Foster" by Giulio C. Cuccolini in *Hogan's Alley*, No. 5, pp 56-62, 1998.

[3] Unpublished Bob Porfirio interview from the collection of the author.

[4] Ibid.

[5] Frank Reynolds (1876-1953), William Heath Robinson (1872-1944), Frederick Henry Linton Jehne Townsend (1868-1920), Harry Rountree (1878-1950), Fortunino Matania (1881-1963), Sir William Russell Flint (1880-1969), and Lawson Wood (1878-1957).

Figure 12, "'Like a Human Avalanche': A Furious Charge of Irish Troops at the Taking of Guillemont" *from* The Illustrated London News #4042, 7 October 1916. Illustration by Amédée Forestier (1854-1930). *Detail from a two-page illustration measuring 19.5" x 11". Reprinted at original size.*

[6] From 1927-1930, Dean Cornwell (1892-1960), one of America's most prolific illustrators, lived in England and studied mural painting under Brangwyn.

[7] Henry Coller (circa 1886-1950), Septimus E. Scott (1879-1962), W. Smithson Broadhead (1888-1960), Frank Newbould (1887-1951), Leo Cheney (1878-1928).

[8] The portrait can be viewed at http://www.nationalarchives.gov.uk/theartofwar/prop/production_salvage/INF3_1746.htm

[9] Porfirio interview.

[10] Page 410, 17 December 1944–Page 465, 6 January 1946.

[11] Alphonse-Marie-Adolphe de Neuville (1835-1885), Paul Gustave Doré (1832-1883), Frédéric Théodore Lix (1830-1897), Émile-Antoine Bayard (1837-1891), and Daniel Urrabieta Vierge (1851-1904). De Neuville studied under François-Edward Picot and Eugène Delacroix. Bayard is best know for his illustration of Cosette that was used as the logo for the musical adaptation of *Les Misérables*, while Vierge is considered "The Father of Modern Illustration."

[12] *The Illustrated London News* (1842-2000), *The Graphic* (1869-1932), and *Punch* (1841-1992).

[13] *L'Illustration* (1843-1944), *Le Monde Illustré* (1857-1938), and *Le Charivari* (1832-1937) were some of the Paris-based newspapers that helped inspire young artists. *Le Charivari*, or "Hullabaloo" in English, was the precursor to *Punch*. Originally, *Punch* was subtitled *The London Charivari*.

[14] The Van Gogh Museum website. http://www3.vangoghmuseum.nl/vgm/index.jsp?page=13365&lang=en ; Zurier, Rebecca. Metropolitan Lives: *The Ashcan Artists and Their New York*. New York: National Museum of American Art, 1995 ; Philip William "Phil" May, R.I. (1864-1903), Reginald Thomas Cleaver (1870-1954), Alexander Stuart Boyd (1854-1930), Everard Hopkins (1860-1928), George Denholm Armour (1864-1949), and Charles Samuel Keene (1823-1891). Some of these artists' work was collected in a series of six volumes titled *Pictures From Punch*, and published in the early 1900s.

[15] Richard Canton Woodville (1856-1927), Amédée Forestier (1854-1930), Samuel Begg (1853-1919), Frederic de Haenen (1853-1928), Hermanus Willem Koekkoek (1862–1929), and Fortunino Matania (1881-1963).

[16] Jean-Louis-Ernest Meissonier (1815-1891). Jean Baptiste Édouard Detaille (1848-1912) was a student of Meissonier, and his book, *L'Armée Française*, is considered the definitive guide on war painting.

Figure 13, Above: *A cartoon by Philip William May (1832-1903) from* Punch.
Figure 14, Below left: Johnnie Walker Scotch Whisky *advertisement. Leo Cheney (1878-1928). The Illustrated London News #3992, 23 October 1915.*
Figure 15, Below right: *A 1943, World War II cartoon by Harold Rudolf Foster.*

HIGH COMPLIMENTS ON THE TUNISIAN FRONT

SOON THE HUGE CREATURE
GOES STRIDING BY!

THE MAN WHO DRAWS PRINCE VALIANT

by Virginia Irwin (1949)

Harold R. Foster, creator of the exquisitely drawn adventure strip *Prince Valiant in the Days of King Arthur*, which appears in the *Sunday Post-Dispatch*, was fired from the first regular job he ever held for taking off on a busy day to go duck hunting. Reporting for work after his day's hunting trip, he was summoned by his boss, handed the pink slip, and made to listen to a somewhat lengthy lecture.

"You seem," concluded the boss, "to think that duck hunting is more important than business."

"Isn't it?" asked Foster, in genuine amazement that any living being could hold a different opinion.

All that was many years ago, but Hal Foster, now in his fifties, still thinks that work is something you do in between times when the ducks aren't calling or the fish aren't biting.

"My working schedule is really harsh," says Foster, who recently acquired an old Connecticut farmhouse and several hilly acres some half-hour's drive from this little village of Georgetown. "If I look out of my studio window and see a limb fall off a tree, I've got to investigate. Usually it's hours before I can make myself return to my drawing board. But at nights and on bad days I catch up on the hours I spend out of doors."

Actually hours of labor go into the production of each of Foster's Sunday pages. And because in *Prince Valiant* he carefully recreates the authentic flavor of the days of King Arthur, Foster spends endless hours in research.

"I made a few historical boners at first," he grins. "Such things as having dinosaurs showing up in the medieval times. But every time my hand was called, it made me more careful. Some of the fan mail I get on *Prince Valiant* is amazing. Students write in with all sorts of fascinating information they've unearthed in their studies of that period of history. Many of *Prince Valiant's* greatest fans are not children, but professors I picture as spending their lives in great libraries studying the literature on medieval times."

Foster, himself, has had almost as adventurous a life as Prince Valiant. Gold prospector, north woods guide, Canadian fur-trapper, and boxer, his life has been filled to the brim with drama, color, adventure, and excitement. Born in Halifax, Nova Scotia, of English/Prussian/Irish ancestry, he comes from a family of seafaring men and ship owners.

"We were of the shabby gentility," he smiles. "Old highbinders on both my parents' sides of the family founded a considerable fortune and their descendants spent it. By the time the family got down to me there wasn't anything left but a lot of odds and ends in the attic which the old boys had accumulated in their travels, things like an old swordfish saw, a Jamaican hat, some dueling pistols and stacks of old log books."

At the age of 10, Foster was sailing a 30-foot boat alone in the dangerous waters off Halifax; at 14, while prospecting for gold, he was earning a living as a trapper in the Nova Scotian wilds. When Foster moved to Winnipeg with his family, he found that his English accent and mild face and manner were interpreted by the other boys as indications of a slight sissiness. After taking several beatings at the hands of the school bullies, he decided to take up boxing. He fought a few professional bouts and then lost interest. Fishing, he decided, was much more fun than fighting.

In school, Foster liked only one subject—art. He remembers that the highest praise he ever drew from a teacher was a remark one of them made to his mother, "He's not exactly stupid, but…"

So Foster quit school and got his first job as an office boy in mercantile business and promptly got fired for going duck hunting.

"Then I got my first job as an artist," he recalls. "It was as an illustrator for a Hudson's Bay company catalogue. I remember my first chore was to illustrate a page of women's drawers. That was around 1910 when they were wearing drop-seat suits with lace around the legs.

"From ladies' drawers, I graduated to princess slips and corset covers. The day I got to men's herringbone tweeds, which were considered the tops because of the fine lines you had to draw, I knew I'd gone as far as I could go. So I quit."

In the meantime, Foster had met and married his wife, Helen, an American girl from Topeka, Kansas. He had also saved up enough money to consider some serious study in the field of art. So bundling his wife off to her grandmother in Topeka, Foster set off on a 1000-mile bicycle trip to Chicago to study at the Chicago Art Institute.

He joined a firm of young advertising artists and soon had his family, which by now numbered a wife and two sons, ensconced in a Chicago basement apartment.

Above: Foster and his wife Helen take time out for lunch.

"I was doing all right, but then came the Depression and every advertising artist was on an enforced diet," Foster grimaces. "Five people committed suicide within the sight of my studio window. There wasn't much for us artists in the firm to do, so we set up a ping-pong table and a dart game and had a little fun while we were slowly starving to death."

Times were tough, but Foster, his wife and two children, managed. Swimming in the lake was free and that's where the Foster family spent most of its time. Then came 1931 and Foster was approached to draw an adventure strip, *Tarzan of the Apes.*

In spite of the fact that he had been earning very little money, he was fairly happy in the achievement of a certain artistic success. His pictures had been hung in various places and he had taken his share of prizes. He did not exactly relish the idea of becoming a comic artist.

"But I sold my soul to the funny papers and it paid," he says. "I had a certain obligation to the guys with whom I was in business and for six months the money I earned from *Tarzan* was the only dough that came into the firm."

Soon Foster had made a name for himself in the field of comic art.

"The appearance of Harold Foster's work," wrote one critic, "started a new period and almost finished it; the man was so good at his particular job that there remained little for subsequent workers to improve on, and very few have had the ability to come anywhere near him.

"For the first time, Foster brought to the strips a complete mastery of figure drawing. Foster possesses also the true illustrator's passion for periods and authentic detail. He is a remarkable figure among comic artists, and his place in strip history is unique."

Above: Prince Valiant...A mighty knight of King Arthur's court.

In 1936, Foster turned *Tarzan* over to another artist and went to work for King Features Syndicate, under contract to produce *Prince Valiant*. The strip, with its exciting blend of legend and history, not only caught the immediate fancy of the young fry among comic page readers but was soon being praised by educators for its educational treatment of that fascinating period in history. A great admirer of the strip is the Duke of Windsor and he is rated as *Prince Valiant's* number one fan.

"God in His wisdom endowed me with certain imperfections but I have made Prince Valiant as I wish God had made me," says Foster. "Also I like to think of my wife as Mrs. Prince Valiant. You know when the Prince gets a little bumptious, Princess Aleta, his wife and the mother of his baby son, Prince Arn, quite often slaps his ears down. That's the way Mrs. Foster does me."

In spite of his snow white hair Foster has a young face and a lithe body that comes off hours tramping through the woods building bridges, cutting down trees and generally working around his wooded acres.

He is perhaps as contented a man as exists in the world. He says he hates "important people who are just important people and nothing else." He prefers to pick his own friends rather than be bothered by folks it is considered smart to know. He has one superstition, born when he was a boy hunting and fishing in the Canadian woods.

"Never," he says, "fail to face north and take a drink to the Red Gods before casting a rod or loading a gun." And he adds, "never shoot a sitting bird; never take more fish than will fit in a frying pan; never take more liquor than you can hold like a gentleman. I often think of what my first boss said about business being more important than duck hunting," he smiles. "It isn't, you know. For instance I could make more money than I do by working harder, but then I'd have no time to enjoy spending the money."

Foster is no gatherer of possessions. He's satisfied with his simple life in the Connecticut hills. His house is comfortable, his wife is happy; his two sons are well on the way to success of their own.

"The piling up of possessions is regarded with much approval," says Foster. "Many people strive to do that all their lives. Monkeys and bluejays also collect bright objects. So few people take time off to enjoy what they already have that trout streams and hedgerows are left for the peaceable enjoyment of such leisurely financial incompetents as I."

Actually Foster is far from the financial incompetent he pictures himself. *Prince Valiant* appears in more than 100 Sunday papers throughout the United States and before the war upset conditions abroad, was carried in dozens of foreign papers and translated in some 10 different languages, including Spanish, Dutch, Danish, Italian, Swedish, Finnish, Norwegian and Portuguese. But more than of the success of *Prince Valiant*, Foster enjoys talking of the joys of his "estate."

"It has," he says contentedly, "everything. There are deer in the woods and that trout stream outside my kitchen door talks to me in the night."

Above Right: Prince Arn...The baby son of Prince Valiant.
Right: Foster with his hunting dogs.

NOW MY DAY STARTS. MOMMIE DOESN'T TALK VERY PLAINLY, BUT SHE MAKES NOISES THAT TICKLE ALL OVER..

HAL FOSTER: DRAWING UPON HISTORY

by Arn Saba (1985)

Harold Foster was sitting in the enclosed porch behind his modest home in a small Florida town. He was 87 years old. He sat straight in his chair, a tall handsome man, still trim and healthy looking. But his cane never left his hands, and a walker was close by. The chattering of birds on the lawn attracted his attention; he craned his neck to see.

"Doves," he said. "Sometimes we get quail, up here at the bird feeder. Of course, I can't shoot them any more. I gave away all my guns when I became lame." A fan labored against the heat, and wind chimes occasionally stirred in the breeze.

It was October 6, 1979. I was a young, longhaired cartoonist who had turned to journalism for money. I had talked a major Canadian magazine into sending me down to talk to one of my heroes. I sat next to him, setting up my tape recorder, trying to make small talk with a legend. I was not exactly nervous, but all my senses were on full alert. I knew this would be a once-in-a-lifetime meeting, and I didn't want to forget a detail.

I had come upon Foster at a dramatic moment. A few weeks earlier, he had sent his last sketch of a *Prince Valiant* page to John Cullen Murphy, who would do the completed drawing. That page would be published on February 10, 1980. After 43 years, Hal Foster was finished with *Prince Valiant*.

Foster was old. I realized it more and more throughout the three-hour visit. He seemed like a man on the way down, on the way out. I began to wonder how he had managed to write the strip as long as he had. Though he had a certain *pro forma* humor and conviction, he seemed to be speaking from far away. His gaze concentrated on a point in the air

Left: Aleta and Prince Arn from Prince Valiant, *page 555, 28 September 1947. Courtesy of the Ohio State University Cartoon Research Library. Panel reprinted at original size.*

over in the corner of the room. He was most alive and animated when he spoke angrily about people who had wronged him. He seemed only half interested in talking to me, and less than half aware of who I was. I began to realize that his conversation had a certain rote quality to it. He had told it all before. Perhaps he was tired of telling stories.

Helen Foster was, on the other hand, a prodigy. At age 83 she was tireless, sharp, and full of inspiring good humor. They had been married 64 years. Foster has said that he used himself as the model for Prince Valiant. "I deleted what I disliked, and he's sort of my body with muscles. He's all the things I would have loved to have been." It was also obvious immediately upon meeting her that Mrs. Foster is the model for Val's wife, Queen Aleta of the Misty Isles. I noticed especially the same wide mouth, forever ready to break into a smile.

Helen Foster and I made an immediate connection when I told her that my great-aunt Zoe (my maternal grandmother's sister) was their old friend Zoe Collins, whom they had known 65 years earlier in Winnipeg. My aunt had told me of social evenings spent around the piano, singing. This slight thread between my life and theirs pleased me inordinately, but Mrs. Foster seemed genuinely excited as well. Zoe, it turned out, had given their son the nickname Teddy, which had become his name for life. Zoe had also said that she had been engaged to one of Hal Foster's best friends, Eric Bergman, who was to become a well-known Winnipeg artist; Foster, however, told me that Bergman got engaged to every girl he went out with. I didn't report that back to my aunt.

Cautioning her husband to speak up for the tape recorder, Mrs. Foster retired discreetly to the next room, never quite out of earshot. Clearly, she was intimately involved with the daily fortunes of the comic-page prince, but she never forgot just who was the creator of what the Duke of Windsor once called "the greatest contribution to English literature in the past 100 years."

Above: Hal Foster, age 4.

In 1915, he met a pretty Kansas girl, Helen Wells, at a dance. They were married the same year. Their honeymoon was spent in a canoe on unmapped lakes that no white woman had ever seen before. Soon, there were two small boys to feed. "By 1921, I'd reached my peak in Winnipeg as an illustrator. So I talked another fellow into bicycling the 1,000 miles to Chicago. The worst thing on the whole trip was the vicious dogs. We got so we could kick the teeth out of farm dog in one stroke." They were robbed within an hour of reaching Chicago and Helen received a telegram on their wedding anniversary reading, "Help—send emergency fund."

Foster got a job with Palenske-Young, a prestigious Chicago studio, turning out ads and magazine covers. He took evening classes at The Art Institute and The Chicago Academy of Fine Arts. "I became a very good second-rate illustrator." Then came the Depression, and the market for advertising art dried up. Suddenly, things looked bleak.

Tarzan came to the rescue. In early 1929, Foster had illustrated a brief newspaper adaptation of Edgar Rice Burroughs' famous novel. It had been so well received that in 1931 Foster was chosen, by Burroughs himself, to do a regular *Tarzan* color comics page. He admitted that at first he was just scratching out the pictures. Then the fan mail started to arrive. "When you do a funny-paper page and you know that you're entertaining people, it's a big lift. It was my own ignorance really. I didn't appreciate the comics until I started to be a cartoonist." Foster was never again to do less than his best for the funny-pages.

Foster's work is, of course, not really cartooning, as we usually understand the term. Instead, he brought academic technique to the comics. His figures have a tangible solidity; shadows are placed loosely yet accurately, so that every setting seems three-dimensional. His lines are supple, yet spare, and every line is in place. He can draw anything.

Nor was his work ever a comic strip. He illustrates a text, rather than using dialogue balloons. Nevertheless, his effect on the comic-strip business was electric. There was a sudden demand for cartoonists who were not funny, and among those who rushed to fill the breach were several other artists who would influence the course of comics history: Chester Gould, Milton Caniff, and Alex Raymond. It was a watershed period for the comic strip.

Hal began to be restive about the story he was being asked to illustrate. "I despised it," is what he said to me. "It was so far from natural." Though he had never before thought of himself as a writer, his innate sense of craftsmanship rose to the occasion. "I started to edit the story. It was tiresome, but inspired me, because I kept criticizing the writer. I'd say, 'I can do better than that.'"

In 1935, press baron (and comics fan) William Randolph Hearst took a liking to Foster's work, and King Features, Hearst's newspaper syndicate, offered to create a strip for him. But Foster had been thinking up a story of his own. He chose King Arthur's day, nominally the 5th century. He wrote up six months' worth of plot, and sat down to draw. Again, his craftsmanship intervened. Foster stalled King Features for 18 months while he did research into the costumes of the period, the weapons, the architecture, the customs, the horses' bridles, even the kitchen utensils. Then, finally, he drew.

The first *Prince Valiant* page appeared on February 13, 1937. No one could have guessed what was to come. The first few months seem not unlike *Tarzan*—slightly cramped artwork, and an action-filled if somewhat

The Duke may have over-estimated a trifle, but Foster's work is already assured a place as a landmark of popular culture. For there is more to *Prince Valiant* than a simplistic tale of blood and thunder. In writing a fantasy of medieval England, Foster created the quintessentially American interpretation of the King Arthur legends complete with nuclear family, the democratic ideal and the man-child hero whose boyish high jinks often lead to high adventure.

Prince Valiant may be an American but Foster was a Canadian. Harold Rudolf Foster was born, in the east coast seaport city of Halifax, Nova Scotia, on August 16, 1892. His father died when Hal was four. He did not care much for school, preferring to spend his time wandering the docks or adventuring in Halifax harbor on his raft. It was from his stepfather Cox that Harold got his taste for hunting and fly-fishing; Cox far preferred such activities to those of the business world. As a result, he went broke, and the family moved to the prospering prairie city of Winnipeg in 1906, in search of better times.

Harold left school at 14 to help support the family. Showing the penchant for hard work and self-improvement that would serve him so well all his life, he continued his education on his own, using books from the library. He also practiced his artwork, sketching himself in the nude in front of a mirror until he turned blue from the cold. His ambition right from the start was to be an artist. He eventually found a job drawing merchandise for the Hudson's Bay Company catalogue. He was inspired by the great advertising artists of the day: Maxfield Parrish, J.C. Leyendecker, N.C. Wyeth, James Montgomery Flagg. He studied their work, improving his skills.

Above: Helen Wells, soon to be Foster.

Arn, born in the Niagara Falls area during a pre-Columbian Viking sojourn to the New World. With the addition of family life, a warm glow settled over the strip, and an even fuller sense of the range of human drama. As Val aged and the children (four in all) grew, youthful high spirits came to be focused in this next generation.

Val and the strong-willed Aleta have the quarrels and love scenes that are part of any volatile marriage. Foster manages to depict all of life's little moments, often in the midst of more dramatic ones, and to extract the lessons which we try to learn. One touching story from 1956 is of Prince Arn, age 8, who determines to climb a mountain. He returns to report: "Yes, sire, I looked down in triumph on the world below. But beyond was still a higher mountain. I guess no matter what one does, there is still something better to do." It could be Foster's own perfectionist motto. Val feels "mingled pride and sorrow. Never more would he feel a grimy little hand take his for protection."

"I think many people have missed the family humor in *Prince Valiant*," Foster told me. "They read it and forget it in favor of the violence." There certainly was no cessation of Val's bone-cracking adventures. Foster has no compunction about showing tragedy, bloodshed, and death. There is often a positive relish of the gigantic battle—portrayed, of course, with absolutely authentic military tactics. Yet Foster's sincere sense of honor is always present, plus an ironic awareness of the ambiguities of right and wrong, and an old-fashioned morality—one that does not preclude killing, but that condemns needless cruelty. There is a fascination with kings and nobles, but there is a markedly democratic leaning in Foster's depiction of King Arthur's realm as a land of peace and freedom for all. Foster's version of the Middle Ages is a blend of obsessive authenticity and selective idealism.

He found his finest expression in the everyday lives of his invented characters. Even his adventure stories move with the earth-bound pace of real life. He was, in many ways, a decidedly ordinary man, in both art and

simplistic story. By the sixth month, Foster had begun to us a more stately page design and larger, more detailed pictures. Publishing in the large 14" x 20" page size that was standard for Sunday pages before the war, he made each panel an individual composition. They can be massed with figures, bursting with action, or serene in evocation of Foster's beloved outdoors. The coloring is sensitive and subtle.

The entire strip is alive with the sense of vigorous outdoor life. The diverse settings are meticulously real. "Every country or area has its own type of geography, trees, and buildings. A tree is individual. You have to draw *a* tree. The same with architecture."

But the story is what brings it all to life. He started the strip as a knights-and-dragons epic, but his love of authenticity began to take him over. "The characters just became too real for me to do much fantasy." There is seldom a cliché in Foster's writing. Even the most minor characters are distinct. The central figures are, by any standard, three-dimensional and fully realized, and it is they who lift the story beyond pulp adventure and into the realm of literature. There are no completely good or completely bad characters. Foster is not afraid to show the foolish side of his heroes, nor their lighter moments.

The young Prince Val is constantly falling in love, roistering with friends, and striving to become a knight. He is not immune to pratfalls. The early years of the story rejoice with the exuberance and earnest nobility of youth.

Val ventures on many a quest and exhibits his rash temperament in several brushes with real history—a skirmish with Attila the Hun, battle with Horsa, the Saxon chieftain and presence at the assassination of Emperor Valentinian of Rome. His greatest quest, however, is for the hand of Aleta. Foster exercised all the impulses of his romantic nature as Val searches the world for the Queen whom he believes has put an evil spell on him. It is, in fact, the same old spell. At last he finds her again, and after much delay, they marry in a sylvan glen. The fateful page appeared on October 2, 1946, and the strip achieved its definitive style.

Suddenly, the gay, romantic prince was a married man. Cynics have often wondered what happens in the "happily ever after" of a fairy tale. Foster, innocent of cynicism, proceeded to tell. The first event was a child, Prince

MY EARLY INTERESTS WERE GOLD PROSPECTING (ACCOMPANIED BY MOSQUITOS!) IN MANITOBA, FUR TRAPPING NEAR MY HOME IN NOVA SCOTIA, BOATING OFF HALIFAX AND EXPLORING NORTHERN RIVERS.

life. His greatness lies in the clarity and craftsmanship that enables us to feel the decency, the enthusiasm, and the tenderness that imbue his vision of the world.

In 1944, the Fosters moved to a six-acre lot in Redding, Connecticut. Here Foster could indulge his passion for hunting right on his own property. Stories have it that he kept a gun by his drawing table, and would sometimes shoot at pheasants out his studio window without ever getting out of his chair. "I only shoot birds," he said to me. "I wouldn't shoot a deer. They're such a part of all our canoe trips." He once gave his credo as: "Never shoot a sitting bird, never take more fish than would fit in a frying pan, never take more liquor than you can hold like a gentleman."

Foster worked a 53-hour week up to the age of 78, but in 1971 did the unexpected: he quit drawing, and turned the art chores over to John Cullen Murphy. Relocating in Florida, he arranged to send Murphy the weekly script and roughly sketched layouts for the pictures. The master illustrator had completed his transformation into a writer.

For my article, I also visited "Jack" Murphy. He was, in 1979, a boyish and exuberant 60 years old. Following Foster on *Prince Valiant* was, he said, "awesome." But he added with a grin, "I've got a great ego." When he started on the strip in 1971, everyone was braced for a drop in circulation, but it didn't budge. The strip's size, however, was reduced by King Features to a half-page or third-page format, from the full page which it had kept throughout Foster's tenure. It had been the last strip, by some 30 years, to be published in that size.

Working with Foster was a learning experience, Murphy said. "His layouts are in a much more traditional style than my own. He always says I can change anything I want, but I rarely do. It's pretty hard to improve on Foster."

During my interview with Foster, he grumbled that Murphy's art had deteriorated, although Murphy mentioned that Foster had not given him any criticism for a long time. I suspect that Foster's complaints were more imaginary than real, engendered by frustration at not being able to do it himself.

Below: John Cullen Murphy and Hal Foster. Photo courtesy of Bob Binding.

Now Murphy was preparing to take over the art completely, with a writer not yet decided when I spoke to him (in recent years, the strip had been written by Washington commentator Cullen Murphy, son of Jack). Without Foster's layouts, the last of his relaxed dignity passed from the strip. Murphy's drawing style is more angular and somewhat busier than Foster's, reflecting his own kinetic personality. Foster at one time had Val's life planned from cradle to grave, but those plans had long been scrapped. "Hal once told me," said Murphy, "that how he planned to have a big battle, and have all the knights get killed. That's how he planned to end the strip. I don't know if he was serious or not." Instead, Foster left no guide as to Val's direction.

I could see that quitting had not been an easy decision for Foster, although he put a brave front, with the mixture of pride and bitterness that is often the province of the elderly. "I quit in time," he said. "Somehow I don't have the confidence now, to write such stories as I did before. I know that I've been good, and I couldn't stand to see amateurish work." His hands, when I met him, were afflicted by arthritis. His last three layouts for Murphy were, he said, "lousy." Helen Foster had to urge him to sign the last one. She also had been encouraging him to do some watercolor painting, but he had little interest.

He politely acknowledged compliments, but resisted the suggestion that his work is in any way important. "A number of people over the years have told me I am great. But I know myself better than anybody else does. I have to look at myself in the mirror when I shave, and I ask myself, is this fellow really so great?"

He said that he did not give much thought to what he was leaving behind. "When I'm gone, I won't know about it. And I'm not doing the kind of work that will last for future generations. Mine is a comic, during this century. What people like in this century might not be popular in the next one. Besides, paper doesn't wear well."

At one time it appeared that posterity was going to have a tough time getting to see Foster's work. Newsprint self-destructs in less than a century, and for most of his career, funny-paper art was considered so worthless that originals were given away or thrown out by the syndicates. Foster told me the usual horror stories of originals being burnt, and of stock-room boys stealing them to sell for five dollars. A Foster original today [1985] sells for a minimum of $5,000, and is going up. When I visited him, Foster himself had only two of his own pages.

The publisher seeking to collect *Prince Valiant* in book form is often stuck for a good copy to reproduce. King Features has the early pages only in blurry microfilm. Consequently, some truly horrible reprints have been unleashed onto the market, most notably the criminally mutilated Nostalgia Press editions of the mid-'70s. More recently, however, the Pacific Comics Club has published seven volumes of relatively good-looking reproductions, and now Fantagraphics Books has started a series, with color that is yet again slightly better. Real honors, however, go to Manuscript Press, who is reconstructing the pages, using diverse sources. They are restoring Foster's original printed size of 14" x 20". So far they have released the first two years of the strip, in two volumes. Each sells for $100, and is the definitive *Prince Valiant* (Readers interested in a very articulate appreciation of Foster's work should see Dale Luciano's review of these volumes in *The Comics Journal* #95).

Harold Foster was growing tired, so I packed my things and said my goodbyes. As Helen Foster showed me out the door of the bungalow,

I looked back one last time to the proud figure sitting with his hand on the cane. He was lost in thought, staring off into the corner. I drove away in the Florida sunshine and steered aimlessly for an hour along the winding two-lane coast road, lined with tacky restaurants and jerrybuilt cottages. But I was thinking about Camelot, the noble land of Foster's imagination.

Meeting Foster had been an experience suffused with sadness. To this day I cannot be sure how much I projected onto the experience, but when I hear the tape of his voice with its slow, almost sing-song recitation, I can see again his mournful air, and the rather hurt expression on his face. It seemed to be a look of affronted innocence. I felt I understood. He had been a man of action, who loved the outdoors and loved his work. Now he had neither to enjoy. Old age had affronted him, had robbed him of the ability to act, leaving him with no means to deal with this final challenge.

I did not get the impression that he had ever been a person of any introspection. He did not speak of God or any spiritual underpinning to his life; indeed, *Prince Valiant* is strangely devoid of any such references. Nor did he speak of any particularly personal tie with his work, although such ties are obvious. I would guess that much of what he did was intuitive; that he simply reacted to his own experiences and created stories that pleased him.

That these unselfconscious creations reflected what he felt and thought would have been unimportant to him if he ever considered it. I have found this attitude in many of the greatest cartoonists of the older generation; they do not have that belief in "personal expression" that is taken for granted by those of us who are now becoming professional. The older cartoonists took themselves much less seriously.

If he had been an introspective person, perhaps he would have been able to deal more easily with retirement and infirmity—he could have had some perspective on it, and could also have taken pride in his accomplishments. But it seemed to make little difference to him that he had produced highly acclaimed and well loved work. In fact, he went out of his way to deny its importance. It mattered to him only that he could produce it no longer. My praise and reassurance fell on deaf ears. Hal Foster died on July 25, 1982, just three weeks short of his 90th birthday. When I heard he had died, I wrote to Helen Foster to offer my sympathy and tell her that I knew her husband would be remembered for a brig time. I received back a very nice short note. And that is the extent of my contact with the Fosters.

It may be that mine was the last interview Foster ever gave. I have heard of no others being published since mine. (Does anyone know?)

I wonder if I am dramatizing Foster's discontent toward the end. I remember him sitting in his enclosed porch in Florida gazing into the air, with his words saying one thing and his manner another. "I feel very well satisfied," he said. It was as if he felt he ought to say that but I hope his words were true. I hope I am wrong about his malaise. I would like to believe that he could appreciate the love and admiration directed his way by so many that he could realize he was leaving a legacy of uncommon beauty.

He did say it. Maybe I am wrong. "What I've done is what I had to do, and what I enjoyed most. I can give up quietly. I feel repaid."

—Arn Saba

Above: This Prince Valiant and the Tarzan image on page 112 are from the collection of Jack Gilbert, and appear with his permission.

AS: I don't think that in Canada, most people realize that you are Canadian. Do you still think of yourself as Canadian?
HF: No, I've been down here too long—since, oh, 1920, just after the First World War. I came down here and, oh, it was another 15 years I guess before anybody except my landlord knew that I was down here and a Canadian.

AS: You don't keep track of Canadian events any more, I suppose?
HF: They interest me, yes, but they're not too important.

AS: No, no. Did you become an American citizen?
HF: Yes, but I've been back quite a lot. I was prospecting up in Canada for a while, one summer and Helen and I used to go back every second year or so for a canoe trip. I knew the country pretty well and all the picturesque places so we'd load our stuff into a canoe and take off on some river or other and spend a month or so.

AS: Well, you've always had a great love for the outdoors, haven't you?
HF: Yes, but I'm not as athletic as I used to be, as you've probably noticed. So I have to take tourist trips, more or less.

AS: Not as much fun, I guess.
HF: No, it isn't. Of course, it's interesting, but the last couple of tours I missed a lot by being too lame to keep up with the crowd.

AS: Frustrates you, I guess.

HF: Yes, I wanted to see the Aztec ruins, and I got there, had to go on a tour, and they took about 30 or 40 people in a plane and took us over to Nicaragua, and I got off the plane, walked a bit, and the whole crowd, all the guys, they went ahead, and I came limping along, about halfway, and that's when I knew I was going to be lame. I gave up, so I never did see the ruins.

AS: That is a shame. But you have traveled a great deal, not only in the outdoors, but also around the world, I believe, haven't you?

HF: Yes, every year we'd take a trip someplace.

AS: I find it fascinating that you are so conversant with architectural styles. You obviously know a lot about the different styles, not only of different countries, but different eras as well.

HF: Yes, I had to study that because, well, I've seen people make illustrations for books, and illustrations, somehow, unless it's modern, never seems to do anything for the story you're reading because the story might be of London, but the architecture in the street scene is New York or Brooklyn.

AS: Uh-huh, it's very wrong, yes.

HF: So I've always made a point of studying, not only the architecture,

and costumes, but the trees. You can tell a picture, you can tell it's Italian or Roman by the square buildings, and the columns, and the trees. These pine trees run up straight and have an umbrella top on them, and the oak trees like you see out here—

AS: Oh, the—what are those called, those tall ones?

HF: Well, I call them cedars. They have a name, but I don't know what they are.

AS: I was looking at an illustration of yours last night. I had one of those Hastings House books, which had a place in North Africa, and it had those tall, thin trees I can't think of the name of . . . but I was just admiring the way you always get the feel for the place, whatever place it is.

HF: That's because I'm interested in that. I've always been interested in the whole country, not just the people or the architecture, and things like that, but everything that has to do with it.

AS: Your illustrations have a very great feeling of realism to them. All the characters have a lot of weight and solidity, and you can just sense that they're right for the place that you've put them in. They sit and stand with such authenticity.

HF: Of course, I have to fake a lot, because it's pretty hard to tell what . . . in the era of King Arthur, you've got nothing to refer to. [laughter]

AS: That's true.

HF: There's very few illustrations from that day, and if there are, they're generally illustrations of people during the Crusades, and all the armor is Crusader. Not only Crusader, but 13th, 14th century. They're all these things that knights . . .

AS: With their great big heavy suits of armor.

HF: Yes, they didn't have those in King Arthur's day.

AS: I see. So did you have to make up a lot of what you've used?

HF: Yes, oh, yes. But consider what materials they have. You know, every little bit of information comes together at last. So you know that from reading the Crusaders and before that, you can make up a composite. They have a lot of remnants, artifacts, from the days of Richard the Lion-Heart, right down to Henry the Eighth, can see the difference, and you can modify the weapons, and armor, and things.

AS: I see. So it's detective work in a sense, isn't it?

HF: Yes.

AS: To go back a bit, we were talking about the landscape and the trees and that sort of business. Were you interested in that sort of thing before you started *Prince Valiant*, or has it always been an interest of yours, or did you become interested when you had to?

HF: Oh, I became interested quite early, because I spend an awful lot of time in the woods and on ships, and when I see illustrations where you knew it was faked, and the artist, in the illustration, just put trees, a couple of stickups like this, that just makes me mad. You know, why couldn't they draw a tree? They're drawing trees, why can't they draw *a* tree?

AS: A real tree, yes.

HF: Yes.

AS: So when you were doing your work—say, the advertisement work you did in Winnipeg in the '20s, and the oil paintings, and so on—at that time you were researching them carefully as well, I presume.

A Prince Valiant panel from page 935, dated 9 January 1955.

HF: Oh, yes, yes. Everything seemed to be interesting. I'd have a better education if all these things weren't so interesting, but, while all my friends in school were studying, I was down on the docks. [laughter]

AS: Well, that's an education, too, isn't it?
HF: Out on the harbor, yes.

AS: This would be in Halifax now, what you're referring to, I guess.
HF: Yes.

AS: When you were a young man—say in your teens—was it your ambition to be an illustrator? Had you always wanted to be an illustrator?
HF: Yes. Even as a kid, I could draw things in proportion. It didn't interest me to draw a ship, like this, two masts, a couple V's for sails.

AS: You wanted to draw the real thing.
HF: Yes. That, to me, wasn't a ship.

AS: Right. So you didn't start out in one direction to do some other career and end up in illustration by accident.
HF: No, I was pitchforked into a business career, but my artistic talents hadn't been developed enough to be of any use, and my school education wasn't of much use either, because I hadn't gone far enough, so I became an office boy. Finally took up shorthand and typewriting, became a . . . well, an office slave. Oh, that used to gripe me. Everything was so cold, dusty, and all figures, and all you could hear was business, business, business, as if there was nothing else in the world but that particular business, and I never envied those that had a good job in business, because it seemed so curtailed there, they couldn't think of anything else, they didn't know any of the useless things that I used to enjoy. The last job I had, in an office, I was a stenographer, and in the duck-hunting season, I'd always go duck hunting. Nothing was said about vacation, I'd hinted it once or twice. A friend of mine said, "The bull marshes are just covered with ducks, they're coming in by the millions." So I took off, put the stuff in the canoe,

decoys and everything, paddled down the Red River to the bull marshes. I had a wonderful time; I came back with enough ducks to put them in the freezer so that the folks could have duck dinners for a month. So I came back, went back to work, and the boss came up to me with his eyebrows down here, just frothing, he said, "Where have you been?" And I was so full of the pleasure of hunting I said I had been duck hunting, and he scowled even more, and told me, "Wasting your time on such frivolous things as duck hunting!" He said, "You seem to think that duck hunting is more important than business." And I honestly said, "Yes. Why do you think I wasted all this time duck hunting if it wasn't more . . ."

AS: If it wasn't more important . . .
HF: So that was the end of my business career.

AS: That was it?
HF: Yes.

AS: How old would you have been at that time?
HF: Oh, 17 or 18, I guess.

AS: And then you went into artwork after that?
HF: Yes, I had a lot of drawings, scribbles, most left over from school, you know, and that was one of the subjects that you took—drawing. I always took prizes at it, but I never thought of it as a future career. So I gathered up all my sketches, my scribbles, and the drawings I'd made. I went down to an engraving house that was doing the Hudson's Bay mail order catalogue. And of course, they were starved for artists; in Canada, there's no career in art. So I applied for a job, and they gave it to me, and then I had to learn the catalogue business all over again.

AS: Did that ever become useful later?
HF: Well, I learned a lot with other artists down there, not good ones, but illustrators that could illustrate men's clothing, women underwear, and shoes, and miscellaneous.

Above: Hal Foster attending a life-drawing class in Winnipeg.

AS: At that time in your career, it would have been useful, I suppose.

HF: Oh, yes, it was. Because there's always the inspiration of artists better at this. Now there are artists—this fellow, Leyendecker, is a fashion artist. He used—

AS: Is that an original Leyendecker you have over there?

HF: Yes.

AS: Wow.

HF: That's a rough sketch for a painting.

AS: Isn't it a beauty?

HF: So there was quite a number of good artists, and they did all the high-class clothing, the new stuff that had come out. So it wasn't as stuffy as you might think.

AS: You would see the top people, of course, Leyendecker and Parrish and I suppose some of the later—Rockwell—and you'd be inspired by those people.

HF: Yes, oh yes.

AS: Flagg, I guess, would be another. Who are your favorites?

HF: Oh, Leyendecker, Parrish all those that you mentioned are . . . I can't remember anything now. I've not only lost my legs, but I've lost my memory.

AS: Your memory seems pretty good to me.

HF: I can't remember names.

AS: Well, anyway, that school of illustrators, the top illustrators of that time would have obviously been a significant inspiration.

HF: Yes, they were very easy to learn from because they were so direct. You know, you look at this, you see everything that he's done. For instance, the relation of one color to another. They all blend in: the blue, for instance, would be deadly if it wasn't for that orange-red. Each one has a place.

AS: Yes, that's something that you have learned very well, the way the colors work with each other. 'Cause some work against each other, as well. Did you ever consider branching out of illustration and going into what we call fine arts—you know, gallery art?

HF: Yes, I've had a fling at it, I got a few pictures in there.

AS: Are those your work there, on the wall?

HF: That's the last big illustration I made for *Prince Valiant.*

AS: I thought I recognized this. I have the newspaper page of that.

HF: Well that's . . . I quit then. That was my last fling.

AS: That's a beautiful one. Later on I'd like to go over and look at that. You know at the time that you were just finishing doing the illustrating for *Prince Valiant*, I was collecting very avidly, I had the great big pages every week, and I watched with great perplexity as you would do a page, and then somebody else would do a page, and then you would come back and do a page. I couldn't figure out what was going on, and then I realized that somebody else was taking over for you, and I remember that panel coming out, that one with your signature on it, and I waited for another one, and I waited for a long time, and I realized that there wasn't going to be any more. And so I have often remembered that one as being . . .

HF: Yes, that's the time when [John Cullen] Murphy started to take over.

AS: You had a couple of other people doing pages, did you not?

HF: Yes, two other artists that I had draw a page. I was testing, I was looking for an assistant at that time. And so I tried out a couple, and they made a page, and they were acceptable—but somehow not enough. I guess I was too conceited to think that anybody could do the same as I did, but I find fault with, oh, some little thing that I would have done different, so I thought, "That little error spoiled the page." Except that it didn't, it just spoiled it for me.

AS: I can understand that, though. You have been a perfectionist, and you have wanted to do things really right, and wanted to see your creation carried on. How did you settle on Jack Murphy?

HF: Oh, I gave him several pages, and he really can draw, he's really a good illustrator. But, unfortunately, I think he took on too much work. And I paid him very well. I thought that would satisfy him, he'd work only on *Prince Valiant*, but apparently he did a lot of other work. I saw his work just deteriorate over the years. When he first started out, I couldn't tell his work from mine. He had the same qualities that I had. He's a very good illustrator, and he can make hands talk. Now, if you'll notice any other illustrator, any other illustration that you see, they'll paint the face, and probably feet, and they'll paint the hands, but the hands are useless, they're not doing anything. They're turned over too much, or they droop too much. Every expression on the face has to be confirmed by the hands.

AS: That's a very good point.

HF: Yes. If a man is startled—

AS: —his hands will react.

HF: Yes, he'll show it in his hands.

AS: I think that even right now, you and I are using our hands to talk. I think it always happens. Do you feel that Jack Murphy's work is still at a low point? Or do you feel that it's going up again?

HF: I think it'll go up. You see, now he's not an assistant artist, he is *the* artist on *Prince Valiant* now.

AS: Starting very soon.

HF: Yes, and his pride will make him better, unless he's greedy. I don't think he is, he might be, because he has such a big family, but now most of them are married or working, but if he starts to feel pride in this, that this is his, well, I think he'll go back to the style he had.

AS: You still feel that the work he's done over the last year or two is not as good as it was?

HF: No, not as good as the first year.

AS: It's interesting that you feel that because—I should go back and compare, but I actually felt that he got better. For the first year, I felt that his work was too stiff, and he did some things that you would never do. I remember one page where he had a vase, I think, was being thrown down from a window, and there were action lines of a very crude kind, and I thought, "That's too much like a cartoon, Foster would never do it that way."

HF: Unless it's something that has humor to it.

AS: Yes, but not in the serious moments.

HF: No.

AS: Yeah, I don't know now, I'll have to go back and check, but I would have thought that you would say that his work had gotten better, because I felt it was much too angular at first. I can always tell the difference right away, you have the nice smooth flowing line— your lines are very precise, but they have a nice smoothness to them, where he often would have a sharpness, and too much sketchiness. I think there's a lot of times, when his lines in the backgrounds, where he's shading . . . it's just there's a whole lot of scribbly lines, which I don't care for, which you've never done [laughter]. Well, I'll definitely go back and compare. I suppose, anybody you chose, it would have been difficult for you to be happy with.

HF: Oh, yes.

AS: Your shoes are very difficult to fill. Nobody's work is like yours. In fact, that brings up one of my questions. I know you worked all the time in the tradition of the illustrators that we were discussing before, Leyendecker and Parrish and so on, and I know that Murphy feels that he works in that tradition as well. Do you feel that that's a tradition, which is still going on? Do you see other young illustrators coming up, working along those lines?

HF: Yes. But, oh, apparently I'm not as critical as I used to be. I used to try to learn from every illustration that I liked. I tried to say,

Right: Story illustration for Popular Mechanics, *November 1934, page 657.*

"Now, how does he arrive at things that I'm trying to arrive at?" But since I got bigheaded and a bit conceited, why, I say, "Ha! Who are they?" You learn, every bit of work that you see that's good, you learn something.

AS: Well, I would honestly say that your work has been so excellent over the years that there'd be very little for you to learn, really, after a certain point. I think that after you'd been doing *Prince Valiant* for four or five years, you really reached a point where it just couldn't be any better. You just went on and just kept being great after that.

HF: Quite a lot I've criticized my own work, and I see where I could improve. Pretty nearly on every page I do, I see something that doesn't satisfy me. And I wonder why I didn't see it when I was doing it.

AS: Crush of the deadline, maybe, or something like that.

HF: No, that never bothered me. You see, I had only one page a week, whereas in *Tarzan*, I had, let's see, six illustrations on the daily, six to eight, and seven days a week, that was an awful lot of drawing. But on *Prince Valiant*, I only had one page with eight panels on it, once a week.

AS: So you didn't feel that was too much to do, then?

HF: No, but it was all I could handle, if I had to do it good. I did have to do a lot of studying, on the terrain and architecture, street scenes, and ships.

AS: And there's the writing as well, which, I think, a lot of people would tend to not think about, how much time you must have spent on the writing, because it's excellent writing, it's not just a throw-away story. It's definitely a very solid story, I would say. Did you ever think of yourself as a writer before you started *Prince Valiant*?

HF: No, I thought of myself as a writer when I was doing *Tarzan*.

AS: Did you write the stories for *Tarzan*?

HF: Let's say I edited it. The first book was, of course, all Burroughs. And the story was so far from natural that I despised it.

AS: Really?

HF: Yes, even though it was highly praised.

AS: A best seller.

HF: It was highly praised because it was the first of story illustration. And it was from a writer that was well known, Burroughs, and of course, that helped it. But, later when I'd finished that one book, *Tarzan of the Apes*, there was no more Burroughs writing in *Tarzan* at all after that. They sold the idea to the syndicate, to United Syndicate, and they had a staff writer write the story, and oh, it was so ridiculous. A lion and an elephant in the same jungle, tigers swimming across the river—of course, things like that are possible, but, it was like, oh, somebody who could build apartment buildings trying to build a palace. There's no reality to it.

AS: I understand exactly what you mean. Very slapdash kind of work, I guess.

HF: So when I handled it, I tried to make the jungle a jungle, and the animals realistic, though I still had to make every monkey a gorilla, because the stories said they were "The Great Apes."

AS: So after a while you got sick of that sort of thing, I guess, didn't you?

HF: It was tiresome, yes, but that inspired me, because I kept criticizing the writer and the descriptions of the scenes and things, and I began to say, "Well, I could do better than that. Why didn't he use those phrases? Why did he try to make it like wording in a dictionary? Why didn't he put more spirit in it?" So, I got sick of it, and in my spare time, I started to dream up a story. By that time Hearst had seen my work on *Tarzan*, and he said "Get Foster." You see, Hearst owns King Features: "Get Foster." And when Hearst said anything, it was like an edict from Heaven. Everybody scurried around. That's why he was always right. All he had to do was say something, and there were so many people trying to make it come out right in the end. So I was dickering around on this *Prince Valiant* story, I hadn't a name for it, and I hadn't a date. I thought of a young man in the Crusades, I thought that was one, and then it suddenly occurred to me, after the Crusades were over, what? Then I'd have to change the whole character of the story, put him in some other, not in a different environment, but a different part of history. So when I got the word that Hearst was [trying to get] ahold of me, well, I got to work. I had a lot of stories that I'd thrown away, get another one, and finally it was *Prince Valiant*. He was an earl, or the son of an earl, I didn't want to make him a prince or a king, because I thought that was a little bit ostentatious. So I started to write the story, and make sketches of it, and all this time, King Features were sending me telegrams and phone calls, "When are we going to see the story?"

AS: So, they were putting you under pressure.

HF: And of course, they were under pressure from Hearst. You know, when Hearst snaps his fingers, you jump.

AS: Ha, you didn't jump fast enough, I guess.

HF: No, no, I. . . So finally I had the idea, and I picked up the phone and said, "No, it's not ready yet," put it down, and worked some more.

AS: You were still working on *Tarzan* at that time?

HF: I hadn't quit yet, that was bread-and-butter money. I wrote the *Prince Valiant* story and went over it and corrected it, and I put a bright, blank sheet in front of me, and started to draw the story. So I finished, I think it was about eight pages, colored, had them photostatted, colored the photostats, so the engraver would know just what colors I wanted, and then I had the story written. Helen typed it out, over about five, six months. Then I picked up the phone, told King Features that I was ready, ready to show something.

AS: Finally.

HF: Yes, I had just put the telephone in the cradle, and a King Features man was in the studio. So I didn't have to do any selling.

AS: That was wonderful.

HF: So Brad Kelly—you've heard of Brad Kelly, haven't you?

AS: No, I haven't.

HF: He was the man in charge of comics. Yes, everybody knew him. He liked everybody. He was easy to get along with, but he got the work done, he gave the criticism and everything. So he came out to the studio. I was in Topeka, Kansas then, hotter than hell. And he came out, I remember he had a light flannel, a light linen suit and a sweater, so I brought over a bottle of scotch. I don't know whether it was my work or the bottle of scotch that sold him, but we finished the bottle, and I put him in his rented car and sent him back to Kansas City, where he could get a plane.

AS: With your artwork?

HF: No, not that time. But he went back and he reported to Conway, who was the head of the syndicate, and Conway came out and he saw the pages and colors, the color sketches. Remember, I had a bit of the story. And he seemed to be pleased but he couldn't show any pleasure at all, because he's a big shot. He had no emotion, so he took my finished originals and the story, and these beautiful colored photostats. And what did he do? He lost the colored photostats. So he wrote me a letter, saying that he had an idea: Why didn't I have these pages photostatted and color them?

AS: A very clever idea, yes. God!

HF: I never liked Conway after that. Pompous big shots.

AS: Now, that strip as you conceived it, those six pages or so that you did, did you make any substantial changes in those, or were those the ones that were actually published?

HF: They were the ones that were actually published, but I had to have them all photostatted, and get them back here, and color them. The best page I ever did was Prince Valiant in the Aegean sea, and he'd been cast away in a small boat, and through the mist, he saw this island with a palace on it, stretching up into the sky and it was misty, water, at the beginning this island they're all in the mist, but right in front of him was the beginning of a whirlpool. Do you remember that?

AS: I remember that page, yes. It's one of my favorites.

HF: And this building, this palace went up, oh, I'd spent days on this, all the little towers, and bridges, and Conway sent it back, and scribbled in blue pencil on the corner was, "Not enough action." That's the best page I ever did.

AS: He published it anyway, didn't he?

HF: No, that one was never published.

AS: Really. So you did a revised version of that.

HF: I don't know what they did . . . oh, I colored the page and gave it to my son, and his house caught fire and burned the couple of pages out. But I don't remember exactly what they did.

AS: Oh, isn't that a shame! I know that the story, I know the part of the story where Prince Valiant gets caught in the whirlpool and rows out of it. But obviously you redrew that page in a different fashion.

HF: Yes, I drew two or three pages to cover up, to fill in that hole they made on it.

AS: To revert to an earlier question about the writing, before *Tarzan* you didn't do any writing? You were never writing short stories for your pleasure or anything like that?

HF: No.

AS: So the fact that you became a writer was, I suppose, a bit of a surprise to you?

HF: Yes, I found it easy because I have so many favorite authors who write in the same vein.

AS: Can you name some?

HF: James Branch Cabell. I love Cabell's work. It had everything. All these authors, oh, they struck a familiar note, in a way, the way I would like to say things, and they said it so easily.

AS: Well, you have said a lot of beautiful things in your work. This is one of the things that I was going to discuss with you, the fact that your strip, *Prince Valiant*, is so much, more than just a pulp story that goes on and on. You really expressed your own soul through this work. It seems to me that through reading it, one can get to know you as a person, to some extent. I feel that I really have some sense of your ideas on life, and your sense of morality, and your sense of what the world is all about; you really put yourself into it. It's like a true piece of writing—you're an author, you're not just a hack, cranking it out. Did you feel as you were doing it, that it was work, that you have to do it, or did you always feel inspired?

HF: I would say inspired. Inspired by the beauty of my own work, and the loveliness of the stories that I stole from better authors. I always worked alone.

AS: You say you worked alone, meaning no one else wrote with you?

HF: No, no, when I first started with *Tarzan*, and the beginning of *Prince Valiant*, I worked all week in a studio, advertising studio, and did all kinds of advertising illustrations, and that was interesting too, because I had a good scope there, because I got the best work that came into the studio. Not the best in Chicago, but high-class, so that you had to study, your own pride would keep you going so that you wouldn't do a messy job. So that was interesting. And then I started this, then came the Depression. And a salesman for an advertising firm had a brilliant idea. He said, "Now, all these plays and books, you know, they're written, they're seen, and then forgotten." He says then the comics are written by people who have never written before, now they're just putting words to a cartoon. He says, "Why can't we make a strip from a good play or a good book? Why can't we do that?" And he formed a little company, and before they did anything else, they got me to agree to illustrate for them. And the first book that they put out, they tried, was one that had just come out, and it was quite the rage: *Tarzan of the Apes*.

AS: Now, that wasn't such a high-class book, really, was it?

HF: No, but it was the most popular book on the stands at that time. Everybody was wailing about it, it just hit a hidden desire at that time. People were getting too commercial, so a thing like that, everybody thought how nice it would be to get away from this mess, and just climb a tree,

Below: Hal's sons (l-r), Arthur and Edward.

eat fruit, and it's so easy to live in the wild, you know, if you've never done it before [laughter]. So, he asked me if would do it, I said, "Yes." I'd do it, there was nothing else to do. So for two or three years, Helen and I ate ape.

AS: I see, better than eating crow, eh?
HF: That first book, that was 300 illustrations, *Tarzan of the Apes* came out in book form. It didn't go. But then, they made it into a strip, and then I said, "Yes, I'll handle the strip." We made money off that, in fact, we ate ape for another five or six years. And then, of course, the Depression was on. In the whole studio, I was the only one making money, and I split it up with the other four boys because nobody had anything to eat.

AS: So this is the whole time you were doing *Tarzan*, you were still in a studio.
HF: Yeah, yeah. Then we moved to Topeka, Kansas. It was cheaper.

AS: Where were you at first, was that Chicago?
HF: Chicago, yes. And there I had plenty of time to do *Tarzan*, did the daily strip, and I did the Sunday page, and that got me into the cartoon business. And all this time, I was thinking, "I could do it better than that. I could do better." And to prove it wasn't conceit, to prove I was really confident, I started the *Prince Valiant* story.

AS: Well, it certainly proved it, didn't it? I think you've been quoted before as saying that when you first started the *Tarzan* strip, you felt very much that you were lowering yourself, that the comics weren't a very good medium.
HF: Yes.

AS: You obviously must have changed your mind.
HF: Quickly, yes.

Above: A panel from Hal Foster's Tarzan of the Apes *book adaptation.*

AS: Well, do you feel that comics are, or have been, I suppose it's hard now, with the small size, but have been a worthy vehicle for good illustration? You didn't feel at the end that you were lowering yourself?
HF: Oh, no, not at all. Except that I didn't particularly like Edgar Rice Burroughs' writing. And then, among the comics was a lot of little gag cartoons and things like that, that, oh, were not top-drawer.

AS: Yeah. You were certainly able to do excellent work.
HF: But I, yes, it was my ignorance more than anything else. I didn't appreciate the comics until I started to become a cartoonist and then, of course, I thought they were geniuses.

AS: [Laughter] Immediately. Did you develop a taste for other comic strips, then, at that time?
HF: Yes.

AS: What were some of your favorites?
HF: Milton Caniff. He wrote well, he knew how to be dramatic, and he

had great artistic ability. And . . . there I go again, my mind becomes a blank every time I try to think of a name. And I know all these fellows, met them, talked with them, and everything.

AS: Well, don't worry yourself over it. Let me ask you if you've ever developed a taste for a totally different kind of cartooning, such as, say, the Walt Disney style, or that kind of funny cartooning. Have you ever enjoyed that sort of thing?
HF: Yes. Oh, yes.

AS: It's very different, of course.
HF: I don't know why it is that some fellows can draw a little kid like, what's his name, Charlie Brown, a little kid like that, with just a round head, round nose, and no particular body, and yet give the thing a personality. I still can't understand that, and see where the little things he says and the funny little illustration seem more real than some of the best-drawn strips, the adventure strips.

AS: I can't quite figure it out either. Have you ever tried that? Have you ever tried drawing real cartoony-type drawings just to see if you could do it?
HF: Oh, yes, but they finally get too illustrative.

AS: You immediately get back to your own style?
HF: Yes.

AS: Well, everyone does have his own style, of course.
HF: Yes, in my little journals I'd write on these canoe trips, a lot of comical things go on, like having a tent fall down during a rainstorm at night. And I'd write the journal up, and illustrate it, all I'd try is to illustrate it with cartoons, then I'd look at it, and then I'd look at it a year later and think, "Good god!" They're not funny, they're maybe a bit ridiculous, but somehow I couldn't put the humor into them.

AS: I see. But you put humor into *Prince Valiant*, a very different kind of humor, a much more natural kind of humor.
HF: Oh, yes. That's to conform with the story and the illustrations.

AS: Am I correct in thinking that you started out *Prince Valiant* intending it to be much more of a fantasy, in fact, than it turned into?
HF: Yeah.

AS: You were going to have dragons and all that kind of thing.
HF: Yes, I had the big sea crocodile, and then *Prince Valiant* was in the fens, and of course a big blood turtle emerged, and there was a dragon, a big swamp dragon.

AS: There was a cave of time, too, which was fantastic.
HF: Oh, yes.

AS: I loved that story. But I suppose—tell me if I'm wrong, I'm guessing—but as you started writing it, the characters and the time and place became so real to you, that you couldn't see making it unreal like that.

HF: That's right.

AS: Because the characters have a lot of depth of character to them, they're very real. And that's why it became such a good family sort of strip, you develop that whole domestic side of it. They ran away with you, I guess. You did so much beautiful work and so much of it now is difficult to find. Do you feel that you've sort of thrown your work out into the world and it's lost, disappeared?

HF: Yes, I cast my ink upon the waters. I had all these, my best original pages, were given to Syracuse University, and they put it in drawers, and shut the drawers to keep the dust out. And they kept everybody else out, I think. They just disappeared.

AS: They don't know where they are now?

HF: They're in the university, Syracuse University, in Syracuse.

AS: Are they available for the public to see?

HF: Yes, yes.

AS: But, on the other hand, of course, they're hard to get to, aren't they?

HF: Yes. They're not documented or anything. I also gave them all my original sized proofs.

AS: Color proofs?

HF: Color proofs, newspaper size, I save them all of those, and I paid, oh, about $2,400 for books to put them in. And these volumes had cellophane bags in there, to hold two, one on one side, and one on the other. I gave them, I finished one book, to show them how it should be done, gave them instructions and everything. They ended up in drawer someplace.

AS: So they are all just hidden away?

HF: Yes. I think all those albums I gave, I think they're still in their original wrappings.

AS: They never put them in. Somebody ought to do a much better job than that.

HF: Yes, they're trying to collect all the work of cartoonists, and the cartoonists were willing to give all the original work, for the simple reason that it was a tax dodge. Now, we got soaked awfully hard by the taxman, because we had very little to show, we stand there kind of naked, and usually we're stripped of all our money by the tax people. So, you'd give all your work, you get a price on a page and you give so many pages to a university and that is a donation, you can take that off. So I gave about 400 pages, I think, took the deduction, and oh, boy I could have them, they sell for $2,000 a page.

AS: I know, the few that are available for sale. It's too bad you couldn't have kept some and be selling them now.

HF: Yes.

Above: The Fosters—Doris (née Douglas) Foster, and husband Arthur James Foster, Harold Rudolf Foster, Helen (née Wells) Foster, Errol Edward Foster (on Helen's lap), Margaret (née Lucy) Foster and her husband, Edward Lusher Foster. Photo circa 1942.

AS: You don't have any left of your own, I guess.

HF: No.

AS: No. Somehow a few of them escaped out into the market and those are the ones that are selling. I think they're selling for perhaps more than $2,000 a page. I know it's more than I will ever be able to afford, anyway. Well, so many artists now, if you have been working in oil painting, say, and hanging in galleries, and that sort of thing, your work today undoubtedly would be a lot better known than it is, but the fact that you worked in a medium which people tend to look down on, they think, "Oh, comics," you know, they don't take it seriously, or even illustration they don't take seriously, that means a lot of your work is still waiting to be appreciated by a wider public, waiting to be taken seriously, that is.

HF: It's catching on.

AS: It is. I'd like to predict that before too long, there's going to be a big renaissance of interest in your work, and people will start to appreciate what a fine artist you are. Do you see a difference, in your opinion, between the art of illustration and the gallery arts, do you think that they are very different in fact, or it's just a difference in terms of the way they're published?

HF: Well, the fine art. It takes a lot of studies, awful lot of work to finally achieve it.

AS: The same is true of illustration, though, isn't it?

HF: Illustration, you mean book illustration?

AS: Or your type of illustration. Just simply that illustration that's somehow looked on as lower class than gallery art. I don't think it is, myself.

HF: Well, it is, in a way, because I couldn't afford to draw a page every week, and have it called fine art. It'd take too much study, of architecture and costumes, foliage, fashions. All these things have to, that go into a gallery painting, would have to go into . . .

AS: You say it'll be more work to make a painting. I think that the aims of illustration are different. I think that the fact that you're bringing so much life out through your work, that it's unfair to illustration to compare it to gallery art, because it's a different purpose.

HF: A good painter can put so much feeling, so much atmosphere into his work that an illustrator can't. An illustrator must draw and color for reproduction, and right there, there's a line drawn. You have to use colors that the printer can imitate. They used to be able to, the plate-makers, they used to be artists. I have some proofs that are really masterpieces of their work, but they did every color and every tone and everything, and those are all gone out of business. They're too expensive. Now they have a reproduction system. I've been through a printing place where they print, or make the plates for cartoonists, and a bunch of girls there, with plates in front of them, and one woman, the superintendent, she goes around and marks certain colors, and certain half-colors and certain quarter-colors. Pretty good, but nothing like the old, of course, the old engraver . . .

AS: It really would be nice to see the comics still treated the same way, wouldn't it?

HF: Too expensive.

AS: I guess so.

HF: Everything has to be done cheaper.

AS: Yes, I guess the comics today are not really the place for a good illustrator, are they? They're too small, and not printed well, and so on.

HF: Oh, someone will come up with a cartoon, or even a gag panel, and have something new that'll get the popular fancy.

AS: It may become popular, but I think it would be very difficult for someone like you to do any kind of good work in today's little, tiny sizes that they give you.

HF: No, I couldn't express anything except action.

AS: Very simple action, yeah.

HF: Yes. Now, I put in all degrees of emotion, action . . .

AS: Well, you've been writing *Prince Valiant* right up until the last few months, haven't you? You just finished, I believe. You managed to keep the story very complex and the drawing, I know you were doing layouts for Jack Murphy; you managed to keep the quality right through, even despite the odds.

HF: Yes, I quit in time. I don't, somehow, haven't got the confidence now, I don't think I could go back and write such stories as I did before.

AS: Well, your stories up till now that I've seen have been just as good as ever. It seems to me that you've kept the vigor of the work very strong. I presume you've enjoyed keeping up with it all the time.

HF: Yes, you cannot do good work unless you enjoy it and like it, and I would correct it, and improve every now and then on something. That's what keeps you going, you look at your work, and say, "Oh, I couldn't have done that 10 years ago."

AS: So you've been self-critical all these years, and still try to be.

HF: That's all I've ever had, is self-criticism. Don't know if that's good, or if I'd done better if I'd had a boss over me.

AS: I don't know, seems to me, you did pretty well.

HF: Helen is fairly lenient.

AS: [Laughter] Not quite tough enough, maybe. Well, it seems that one of the secrets of success, which is no secret at all, is hard work, seems you've always been a very hard worker. You've not been easy on yourself. You have a fine sense of craftsmanship, you always seem to think, "Well, there is a better way." And try the better way.

HF: Yeah.

AS: With your great ability to draw the outdoors, so beautifully and so accurately, your work in some ways reminds me of the Group of Seven. Do you know the Canadian artists called the Group of Seven?

HF: No. Oh, wait, yes, I have.

AS: Like Lauren Harris is one, and Tom Thompson and so on. Do you know their work at all, or not?

"VENISON ? JUST THRUST A SPIT THROUGH IT AND HOLD IT OVER A FIRE !"

Left: Mark Twain meets Prince Valiant in a humorous cartoon from A Treasury of Redding Recipes. *The cookbook was made to help raise money for the Mark Twain Library in Redding, Connecticut and contained several recipes by Helen Foster.*

116.

HF: Seems to me, I've had a letter from an old friend of mine, from Winnipeg that painted, with a group, but I can't remember now, but that sounds very familiar.

AS: But it's obviously nothing that you're strongly familiar with.
HF: Weren't they in Ontario?

AS: That's right. And this is back in, say, the '20s. Do you feel that your upbringing in Canada has had any particular influence on the kind of work that you do, or in any way on your life?
HF: Oh, yes, greatly. It gave me all my backgrounds. I didn't do very well in school. Of course, I always won a prize in drawing, but so many kids in school were better than I was at learning, I suppose that's why I went to the outdoors. Halifax harbor was such a romantic place. Gosh, on a summer day, look up the harbor, and the harbor is just covered with white canvas.

AS: Really, of course, yes, it would have been all sailing ships at that time, wouldn't it?
HF: Yeah, square riggers, and schooners, and dirty little coasting ships.

AS: Must have really caught your fancy.
HF: Oh, yes, and then I was always down at the shore, so many interesting things. Life on the shore, the tides, the wind, always meant something. Of course, it meant something to me. I was surprised to find that when I beached my raft, one day when I knew the tide, same time I'd taken it out, I'd beached it there and I thought, "Now, the tide will go out, the boat'll be there and I can get it just at this time tomorrow, when the tide is in." And I discovered that the tides didn't work that way.

AS: A little different, isn't it?
HF: Yes. Made a mistake with the tides, and my raft drifted out. I'd crossed the harbor on that raft, and, the same time Cunard liners were coming up the harbor. I didn't hasten, I don't know if the boat stopped or if we missed each other. Mother and grandmother were on the porch looking out over the harbor, and Mother said, "Look at that little boy out there on that raft. You'd think their parents wouldn't allow that." And grandma, taking out the binoculars, came out, saw little Harold with a wet ass sitting on this little craft. She put the glasses away, never said anything on it to mother.

AS: It seems you had a very great sense of romance, even very young, you always were more interested in the world of nature and life as it was being lived, rather than what was being taught in school.
HF: Yes. I was fairly interested in history, because I lived where history was made—in Canada, Newfoundland, and Nova Scotia. The kind of history that appealed to me.

AS: I enjoyed what you said before about business, and how boring it was, and how the people in the business offices were so obsessed with just this little tiny piece of life. It seems to me that you have a much more, you have a wider sense of what life is about. I really admire your perspective on life, it's not a narrow one, it's very wide and very enjoyable perspective on life.
HF: Yes, I always credited my natural stupidity for putting me in the way of learning and experiencing things.

AS: It's not what I call stupidity, it's what I'd call an adventurous spirit.
HF: I could tell every ship, every schooner, every coaster that came to Halifax. I could tell just where it came from, by the smell.
AS: Really? What kind of smell?

IN '21, I DECIDED TO STICK WITH ART, BICYCLED 1000 MILES TO CHICAGO'S ART INSTITUTE. MY SERIOUS PAINTING RECEIVED THUNDEROUS APPLAUSE FROM ME, MILD APPROBATION FROM THE PUBLIC.

HF: Well, Jamaica would come in with a delicious smell of rum, mixed with bilge water, and other boats would come in, for instance, smell of onions, that came from Bermuda. My step-father, he was the one that imported the first Bermuda onion, and they went over so well, on the East Coast, everybody went in for it, and the old man, of course, wasn't such a good businessman and he lost out on it. It just left him with the smell of the onions.

AS: And tears in his eyes, perhaps, yes.
HF: And, of course, the fishing boats came in. Oh, what beautiful boats those were.

AS: Little fishing boats?
HF: Two-masted schooners, one of them was the Bluenose.

AS: Did you see the Bluenose?
HF: Oh, yes. And I saw her 50 years later, mast cut down, with a box on the back, where you had the controls, the diesel engine, and I stared . . .

AS: Yeah, cut down. But you know there's a replica of the old Bluenose, did you hear about that?
HF: No.

AS: Yes, they've built an exact replica of the old Bluenose, and it's sailing again, around Halifax for tours, I think, but they keep it very pure. I don't even think it has a motor in it. So if you went back again, you'd see it.
HF: I went back to Halifax 50 years after I left it, and, as I told you, the harbor used to be just covered with white sails all kinds of ships going and coming. Fifty years later I went back, and not a ship on the harbor, not a boat, not even a rowboat.

AS: Nothing?
HF: One ship, one ship, a great big freighter. And I looked at this immense thing, and it could carry more goods than all these little ships in the harbor could do in a week.

AS: Isn't that amazing? What a difference.
HF: But all the romance was gone, here was this great big, efficient steamer.

AS: Isn't it shame, really, when the romance is taken out of something. Efficiency carried too far is no fun. There's a great deal to be said for the color and the fun of life, rather than the efficiency of life. I'm not very fond of it, myself. If I may ask a question, this is a little family question, you made mention of your stepfather, is that where you got the name Foster? Were you actually born with another name?

HF: No, no. His name was Cox. I was about 12, I guess, when mother married again.

AS: So you kept the name of Foster. Foster is your natural name. I just thought, for the history books, I better get that straight. It seems to me that the turn that you took, away from schooling and towards experiencing nature and experiencing life, really served you very well in your artwork.

HF: Yo.

AS: And did it, I'd like to know—I don't know how I can put this—I've always felt that art has a very important place in the world, for the artist, it's something that an artist must do. He feels that he must do it, that he's

Below: From l-r, Foster's best friend Eric Bergman, Jack Schaflein, and Hal Foster. The three worked at Brigdens Ltd. and went hunting and prospecting together.

Below right: The lighter area in the rock is a quartz vein containing the gold Foster and his friends found.

expressing something very important to him. Did you feel a sense of great satisfaction all your life, at being able to take the things you saw and put them out again on paper?

HF: Yes, it was the same as taking photographs, you know, something impresses you, and you haven't got any camera, can't afford one, but you can afford pencil and paper, so you draw a ship or a train, a waterfall, anything that's impressed you, and you can do it better every time.

AS: Uh-huh, you get more of the feel, I guess, of what you saw, yeah. So do you feel satisfied in general with all the things you've done?

HF: Yes, very well satisfied.

AS: That's good.

HF: I realize what most of my friends miss, that I have, and it was just because of my inability to be as successful in business as my friends, instead of staying home to make money, why, I'd get in my canoe and go up the English River for a week or two of prospecting, with two friends, that was quite an experience. Through the most god-awful country.

AS: This is in the north of Canada, I guess.

HF: Yes, this was in Ontario, no, Manitoba, we went up Lake Winnipeg and went in the Manigatagan River, where there was a gold strike.

AS: Did you find any gold?

HF: No.

AS: Oh. [Laughter]

HF: Oh yes, we got what they call a showing, you know, you break off a piece of that white stone, quartz, a bit of quartz, wet it and look at it very, very carefully and sometimes you see a little bit of gold there.

One of Hal's cartoons from his days at Brigden's Ltd. (circa 1916).
From l-r: Eric Bergman, Hal Foster, and Jack Schaflein. See Of
Mead, Whiskey, and Brandywine: The Artistic Bloodline
of Prince Valiant *on page 89 for Hal's early artistic influences.*

AS: Didn't make you rich, though, did it?
HF: Oh, we made quite a rich experience.

AS: That's quite important.
HF: And the mosquitoes, muskeg country. That is, rocky ridges, and, of course, between each ridge, there's marsh, muskeg, trees. Little trees grow up all around it, and in through it little hemlocks grow up and die, most depressing country. So you portage over one of these rocky ridges, get down to the muskeg, now you've got to get across, sometimes there's a lake there and you can paddle across, sometimes you have to wade across, and mosquitoes. Rain every noon.

AS: Oh, gosh, sounds horrible.
HF: It was really something, it was. I learned a lot there. I learned how to live among the mosquitoes, and to keep my companions from going crazy. One of them did. It was our last day, we were on our way home, tomorrow would have been safe. And I was awakened at night, here is my friend, behind the tent pole, he'd squeezed in behind the tent pole and the back of the tent, and he had my blanket, and he was pulling me, he says, "We're sinking in the muskeg." And he'd been sinking in the muskeg for two weeks now, and I guess it finally got him, and he's one of those poor fellows that attracts mosquitoes, and in that country, it just drives you crazy. Well, it finally drove him crazy. So, when we got back, a couple of days, just settled, and I was so glad that I wasn't this weak type, you know, that'll go crazy but a lot of those fellows out there did get funny.

AS: Did he recover?
HF: Oh, yes, soon as we got home, he recovered. Soon as he stood on firm ground.

AS: Back on land.

HF: But, one night, a couple of days later, I woke up and tried to get Helen to get up, rushed to the window, and looked out, and she said, "What's the matter?" I said, "Somebody's out there in the muskeg, you have to go out and bring them in." I was looking across a golf course, and there was a light in the window of a house across the way, but I really felt it, I felt it. I got up, got as far as the window, jerking at the covers.

AS: So they got you too.
HF: Yes, I wasn't so proud of myself after that, it can happen to anybody.

AS: I guess it shows it really could. Well, you were saying that you had a lot of wonderful experiences, well, not all of them wonderful, but they've all been good for you.
HF: Oh yes, every experience, no matter how uncomfortable, leaves you with something, just the desire not to do it again.

AS: If only that, right. Well, I'm very glad to hear you say that, that it's all been very satisfactory, and I should think that your artwork has played a great part in that, you hadn't been a very unhappy person probably.
HF: Yes, and a very lousy one, too.

AS: Lousy businessman.
HF: Yes, the idea of exchanging a bit of goods for a bit of money is very uninteresting. Now, if I could raise apple trees and sell apples, now that would be something that . . .

AS: A bit more . . .
HF: Yes, it would be the natural thing. You wouldn't have to go to a bank, or you wouldn't have to get up at a certain time every day, and go to lunch at a certain time, and go home at a certain time.

around, blow the water out of their nose. Well, I've come up so close to a moose that I was able to lay my paddle on his back. If you do it quietly, coming through the rushes towards them.

AS: They didn't run away or charge or anything?
HF: No, see, the sight of me and the canoe never changed. See, I saw them there and I got in position by drifting into position, and as soon as he put his head down underwater, I'd paddle fast, and give a count. I knew that by the time I counted to 12, he'd bring his head up. So when it came to 12, I'd quit paddling. And he'd get a little bit nervous. Any movement, and he would immediately have gone into the woods. But I'm coming right towards him, so he didn't remember it that I was just a little thing, and the next time a big thing, and it finally became too obvious when I got too close. You'd have your camera all set, take the pictures, and he looks up.

AS: Great, must have gotten some nice pictures.
HF: So you have no desire to shoot.

AS: So you never did hunt the big game, then?
HF: No. I've seen too much of it.

AS: Well, they're very lovely creatures.
HF: On these camping trips, there was always deer around, and quite often, where you got in too far, there were places where people on holidays would hire a couple of guides and go up into Canada. The first thing they'd think of is shoot a moose, up in Canada, shoot a moose, get your picture taken by it. Well when you're traveling enough around the woods, every now and then, you'll come across a carcass. And I know that some fellow who never should have owned a gun had gone up there out of season, and shot them.

AS: And wouldn't eat it, didn't take it to eat it, just left it there?
HF: Yes. They'd take a picture, you know with a gun across their arm, you know, standing with one foot on the—

AS: The mighty hunter.
HF: Yes, on a female deer.

AS: Jesus.
HF: So now you can't take a gun into Canada.

AS: Really?
HF: No.

AS: If you were going up there now, you mean you couldn't take one across the border?
HF: No, I couldn't take it. I could if I'd bought a hunting license, and had a guide to watch over me as much as do the work. Then I could go in there and hunt. I'd have to pay so much for a license, but there was too much of this wild shooting, and you can't get in with a gun now.

AS: You have been a very avid hunter, haven't you?
HF: Yes, quite a bit. All birds. I've seen too many deer, big game, I wouldn't shoot one. Somehow, they're such a part of . . . oh, our canoe trips paddle up a stream, portage over the rapids, and things, and sure enough, you're bound to see a deer standing there. Once or twice, every time you camp, just at sundown, across from your camp, across the lake, you see red deer and moose come down. They come down to the little coves where there's grass and things growing up from the bottom. And they eat there, they put their head down underwater, get them all filled, come up, they look

AS: Well, it's probably for the better, because you're right, there's probably too much of that kind of shooting going on.
HF: Oh, yes. And, you can't get away with it. I went up in a fire ranger's lookout, and the wardens didn't go up there, and just stay there. They don't have to scout the country to, find somebody traveling with a gun.

AS: How do they—?
HF: They go up there and you can look down over the country, you know, for miles and miles, and if somebody shoots, you can hear it

reverberating.

AS: Would they be able to tell where it was coming from?

HF: Yes. Right in the middle of these forest rangers tower, they go up, I don't know, 50, 60 feet. The map is right there, so that if the forest ranger ever sees smoke coming up, he can look at the map and tell just exactly where the smoke is coming from, then he knows the rivers and lakes, you know, how to get in there. So if the warden happens to be there, and hears a shot, he knows exactly where it comes from. And he don't have to chase them. If the place to go in from is a neck of the woods, or someplace, he just goes to the landing and waits for the canoe to come in, and examines if there's a gun there, why, the poacher loses his gun, and if they can prove it, big fine.

AS: I know that you have stopped writing, just finished, just recently stopped doing it. Do you find that you miss it, so far, or is it too early to . . .

HF: I don't miss it, because I've become a little bit lazy, and I feel as if I couldn't get the story across that I want to see. And I know I can't draw as fast as I did, or as accurately. I see that when I do a little sketch, like trying to get a Christmas card, or something like that. I find that I just don't—

AS: But you find, as you say, that you're slower in the drawing, and your hand isn't as accurate as it was, now it frustrates you, obviously, because you know what you want.

HF: I know that I've been good, and I couldn't stand to see amateurish work.

AS: It must have been an awfully big decision for you to stop.

HF: Well, I was getting tired. Knowing that I can't satisfy myself, with either drawing or writing, so I have nothing to worry about.

AS: You'd rather not do it, if you can't be satisfied.

HF: Yes.

AS: Do you intend to go on doing any work of any kind?

HF: Not if I can help it.

Helen: I want him to go back to doing some watercolors.

HF: Oh, I might, I might get out the colors and do a bit of sketching.

Helen: Wouldn't it be nice?

AS: It would be nice to see some fresh work, yes. Well of course, it's very recently, I believe, that you stopped doing the writing. Has it just been in the last couple of months, or so?

Helen: Well, his last one won't appear until February . . .

AS: Of 1980, isn't it?

Helen: Yes, the Sunday before the 13th. He missed it just three days of being 43 years.

AS: Is that right? Oh, my goodness. Should have gone on one more week. I guess you finished a story, probably.

HF and Helen: Yes.

AS: And stopped it at that point. Do you know yet who's going to write after you?

HF: No, I don't.

AS: I guess King Features has to decide that.

HF: I imagine the syndicate will get—

Helen: I don't think they know either

HF: —will get one of the writers out, of the out of the, where do they, the pool?

Helen: The pool, they call it, I don't know.

AS: The pool. I know Jack Murphy doesn't know yet who it's going to be either.

Helen: I don't think anybody knows.

AS: So they better hurry up and decide.

HF: I have to call Jack up on Monday, ask him if he's been treated fair.

Helen: Yes, I think King Features will really be cutting their nose off to spite their faces if they let Murphy go, because they have always said they told me, when Harold was sick when he came back from Mexico and he didn't think he was going to be able to work for a while, and then when I called Sylvan Byck to ask about it, he said, "There isn't anybody under the sun that can replace Hal. We haven't got anybody that can touch it." They've got anybody down in the other comics, you know, anybody can. So, you know, you can get by with it, for a little while. But then he said,

Right: The photo was taken at the September 2, 1967 meeting of the Burroughs Bibliophiles. In 1967, the annual meeting, or Dum-Dum, was held in conjunction with the 25th World Science Fiction Convention, or NyCon3. Both Hal Foster and Frank Frazetta were Guests of Honor, and were given the Golden Lion Award. From l-r, C. B. "Bob" Hyde, President of the Burroughs Bibliophiles, Foster, Frazetta, and Stan Vinson, Vice-President of the Burroughs Bibliophiles.

Above: Philip Wilcox (r) of Parents Magazine *presents Hal Foster with an award honoring* Prince Valiant's *contributions to education.*

"There isn't anybody that we know of." And Harold went through. He had Gray Morrow—

AS: Gray Morrow, yeah.
Helen: And who was the other?

AS: Wally Wood, I think.
HF: Wally Wood.
Helen: —and Wally Wood, and Russ Manning out in California was just dying to be Harold's assistant, but he wouldn't let go of it. He said, "This is my baby, as long as I can do it, nobody's going to touch it." Then he got to the point where he couldn't do it all in a week, and he had all of them do a page.

AS: Yeah, did Russ Manning do a page, as well?
Helen: No, I don't think he did a page, he just sent a lot of samples, and things. You never had him do a page?
HF: No, I guess not.

AS: I think I would know.
Helen: No, he wanted to go, he wanted to be taken on right then and there, and Harold wasn't willing to do it. He waited until he couldn't do it any more, and even then, it took him quite some time, a couple or three years, I guess, to make a decision. And he decided, overall, that Murphy's illustration suited *Prince Valiant* better than the other two guys. Well, I thought, my opinion doesn't amount to anything, but I thought they were too science-fiction in a way, they're good . . . The funny thing is that we get a lot of fan mail saying that Jack Murphy's drawings don't relate to the . . .

AS: Well, I don't think anybody's as good as Mr. Foster.
Helen: No, Harold told him he said, "I don't want you to copy me." He said, "Do your own thing." And it seemed like a good transition period, because everybody was getting older, so if they didn't look exactly like they did when Harold was on it. Nobody looks the same.

AS: Right. Well, now, the thing is that, Mr. Foster, you've been doing the sketches, the rough sketches for Jack Murphy haven't you, all this time?
HF: Yes, layouts.

AS: Layouts. So he would follow your composition, so that would help.
HF: And besides they're made on actual size, it's a great help, he didn't have to do anything except improve the background and copy them, but even that, the last two or three I did, they were lousy.

AS: You really think so?
HF: Yes, before this, I've initialed every rough sketch in pencil and they sell them for . . . what?
Helen: Seventy-five dollars.

AS: Yes, I was told $75.00, yes. But you didn't like the last three?
Helen: No, I had to practically force him to put his name on the last one. He said, "I'm not going to send it on. It's too lousy."
AS: What did you think?
Helen: And I said, "Well, Hal, people are walking in, asking for one of your doodlings, for heaven's sakes call it a Harold doodle if you don't want to call it anything else," and finally he did put his name on it. First, Harold had been destroying them, because there seemed no necessity to keep them, I gather, until some suggestion was made by somebody—maybe Jack Tippett, I don't know who—that they could sell those. So we had a little name, "Prince Valiant," put on top, a little strip saying "Prince Valiant," and then he signed them down at the bottom. And they immediately . . .

AS: Started selling.
Helen: Selling, yes.

AS: I can tell you, as a fan, absolutely, there'd be no question that people would want them, yeah, oh, yeah. Certainly no question about that. But it's amazing, in a way, that the pride that you have. It's not amazing, it's commendable, the pride in your work that you have. You're such a great craftsman, that if you don't feel proud of your work, you know, you just won't sign it or whatever, and it shows, really. I mean, it's pride, justifiable and necessary pride that an artist has to have. Is there some question about Jack Murphy being kept on the strip?
HF: That, I don't know. You see, we have a new general manager, that I thought was, oh, giving me the friendship, that all the others did, but except for one dinner we had together, why, I never heard a word from him. Not a word.
Helen: From who?
HF: King Features.

AS: The new general manager.
HF: What's his name? Joe . . .
Helen: Joe DiAngelo, but he is not their general manager now, he was the president of this thing, but I really think Harold was very much hurt, he didn't say anything, but I know I was. But we'd gone through five general managers. You know, 43 years, you meet quite a few. They changed, most of them died, I think the job was too much for all of them. I guess all of them died, while in the office.

2124 Oct 23

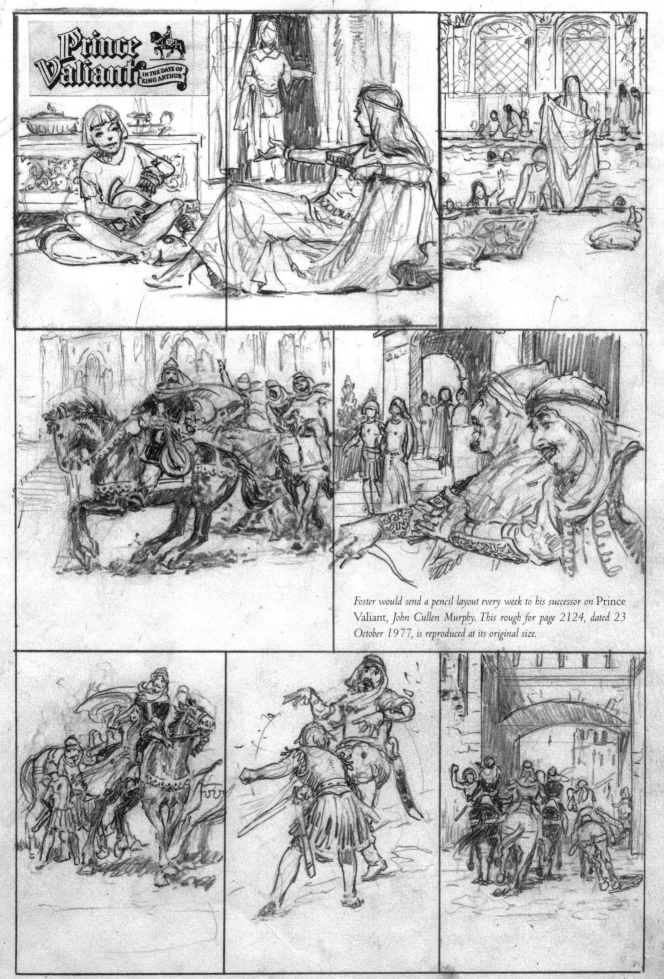

Foster would send a pencil layout every week to his successor on Prince Valiant, *John Cullen Murphy*. This rough for page 2124, dated 23 October 1977, is reproduced at its original size.

Above: Robert Wagner catching up on his reading in this 1954 promotional photo for the Prince Valiant movie.

AS: Sylvan Byck is still alive, isn't he?
Helen: No, well, he was a comics editor.

AS: Oh, I see, I'm sorry.
Helen: He was comics editor, and he's retired, of course, and has been for two or three years, and not very well, as I understand. But, from the very first, now, Harold didn't like the first head of it, Conway. But now he says he wishes to heaven that Conway was back, because when Conway meant a thing, he meant it, he told you, and things got done and so on, and so forth. But then Conway died, and then Jimmy Green came on, and Jimmy Green died, and then Belt McClaren came on, then he died in office, and then, was Kaplan the next one?
HF: Yep.
Helen: And he died in office, and then . . .

AS: The job's a killer, isn't it?
Helen: Yeah, it's a tough one. Then Joe DiAngelo came in, he was the general manager, but then he got pushed upstairs to president, you see. Then they had somebody in there whose name was Sven Svere and the only thing that we ever heard from him was that he wrote Harold a letter, and he said he'd always admired Harold's work all his life, and that he hoped that he had the pleasure of meeting him in person. It's the last and only—

AS: First and last.
Helen: First and last, now he's gone and there's another general manager.

AS: It's becoming very impersonal, isn't it?
HF and Helen: Yes.

Helen: But, when Brad Kelly was there, I suppose Harold's talked to you about him, as vice-president, he was our, oh, we said he's our fairy godfather, because we went into this business not knowing anything, you know. With *Tarzan*, we didn't have any ins with anybody. They sent it to [Harold], he drew it and sent it back, and they sent us a check, and that was just it, the entire communications we had. We didn't even know the man who wrote the stuff in New York.

AS: Right. It was much more of a job, really.
Helen: That was all it was, that's why I say we ate ape. It was a job and we ate during the Depression, and so did the other fellows in Harold's studio. But with King Features, especially after we moved to Connecticut, we were included in all the affairs. Oh, 55 miles to go into New York, we used to go in all night, stay overnight, or two nights, or anything. We were always considered a part of the King Family.

AS: Yes, is it possibly the fact that you moved down here that has anything to do with that?
Helen: No, well, they still invited us to everything, but the only thing that I can think of is that he resented us getting a lawyer. Well, now, you know that when you go into a deal like that, especially where taxes are concerned, because the IRS is going to take nearly all that King Features paid him for this.

AS: Yeah, well, things get so complicated now, you need a lawyer, don't you?
Helen: You have to have a tax lawyer, so I kept our income tax accountant, in Danbury and I called him up and told him the situation, and I said, "Any idea, Leo, you can give me about what this might cost us in taxes, and how to go about it?" And he said, "Well, I'll tell you something, for a deal like that, you need a good tax lawyer." And he said, "I know a very good one in New York. And if you would like to have him, I'll have him call you." And about 15 minutes later, this man called. And I liked the way he talked, and explained to him, and he told us he'd handled artists, and sculptors, so that he knew that branch of art.

AS: That field.
Helen: You know, how to do it. From that day, even after Joe DiAngelo called him, the first indication we had was at 10 o'clock, on a Sunday morning. He called Harold, and made him an offer, because Harold had written him, and told him, "I'm going to retire at the end of the year, I can no longer do it. So, I give you plenty of time to get a writer." See, because Jack Murphy has the contract up until the end of the year. With King, not with us, we insisted that that be a separate affair. And he called up and offered Harold, well, really, it was kind of a ridiculous sum, wasn't it, in a way? But the lawyer doesn't think we got all we should get, but Harold never ever considered selling it.
HF: Yes, I just about was going to quit.
Helen: He was just going to quit. Or give it to Jack to do.

AS: So this way, at least you're getting something out of it.
Helen: I said to Harold, "You can't give it away, Harold. King Features still owns it." They have a contract with him, still, till a year from now, 1981. He still had a contract to go. He said, "Well, I never thought about, I did forget all about it." I said, "Well, you've got all this year, and all next year to go on your three-year contract." He's the only one that's ever been given a three-year contract after he got past the age of seventy, or something. We talked it over, and I said, "Well, we might as well get something out of it," you know. We never heard another word from him. Until he called

again, and said, "Well, I was slightly out of line with the offer that I made you." Checking it out, he talked it over with the higher ups and so on, and we figured out that the price should be so much. Well, we hadn't been expecting to get anything for it, and we weren't going to fight it, and that's when I said, "Well, I guess we'd better get a lawyer." And we never have heard another word from him, either by phone or by letter, he never made either offer in writing.

AS: Did it go through, though?
Helen: Yes, he dealt with our lawyer all the way through, but never a word with us.

AS: So it is settled at any rate.
Helen: Yeah, it's been paid.
AS: It does make you feel left out, and wondering what's going on.
Helen: You would think that an outfit that has had a man with them for 43 years, and they always said that he was the only one that they never had to worry about a deadline, because he was always at least six weeks ahead. Or, they demanded nine weeks ahead and Harold always had 12 weeks done, so that if he wanted to take off a week or two, he had those pages under his desk. He never told them that.

AS: I see, so you were always way ahead.
Helen: But they never had any trouble with him. Only once did Conway send back a page, and it was one of the most beautiful pages he ever did.

AS: That's the one you told me about.
HF: Yes.
Helen: Yes, Prince Valiant in the mists and everything. And when we told Brad Kelly about it, at

Above: Foster with his knights and ladies at the 1955 Mardi Gras.

HF: The skunk comes along, and, of course, lets her have it, and she falls off the log. Shows that there's no doubt about it that she's pregnant.
Helen: Well, first they said he should never get married.
HF: Yep.
Helen: Yes, no comic hero ever got married and survived. So he married Val off and they shouldn't . . .
HF: Shouldn't have children, no.
Helen: Don't make him a family man, you know.
HF: She shouldn't, his wife shouldn't be anything but, follow him around like—what is a hero that, he went through different stars and everything and the girl followed him.

AS: Flash Gordon?
HF: Flash Gordon, yes, always with a girl.

AS: Just following around, just sort of hanging on.
HF: Yes. Well, I thought that was indecent. No fellow is going to go from planet to planet, and have his girl, especially a good-looking girl, tagging along without having some ideas.

AS: I think you're right. Very chaste, aren't they?
HF: So, of course, I had *Prince Valiant* marry the girl, so that she'd be decent, and being a decent girl, and married, she should have children. They told me that a married woman, there's no romance in a married woman and children, but—

AS: What do they know?
HF: Yes, I found out that people are not exactly what those in power in the comics think.
Helen: Haven't you noticed that since then, there have been a lot of marriages in the comics?

the time he was vice-president, he said, "Oh, Conway used to do that when he thought an artist was getting too big for his britches." And he'd take him down a peg. And he said, "If you'd have sent that page in three or four weeks later, Conway would have raved about it." So Harold was so mad about it he said, "I sat down and I did the worst, lousiest page I ever did in my life. Let him send that back." Well, of course, he didn't send that back, it was printed. Once or twice Sylvan Byck complained, because you showed Aleta pregnant, that was in the days you couldn't do those things in the comics, you know, no snakes.

AS: But you did it anyway.
HF: Yes.
Helen: Well, he made her coat a little fuller, and that's something I don't know.
HF: I shoved her relaxing in the woods, lying on a downed tree.
AS: I remember that.

AS: I know. Is this the first, really?
Helen: His was the first.

AS: That's right, I didn't realize that.
HF: And it was the first baby.
Helen: The only other one was *Jiggs and Maggie*, and everybody knew they were married.
HF: Then I had the first baby. Except for *Gasoline Alley*.
Helen: *Gasoline Alley*, but he was found on a doorstep.

AS: Yes, he wasn't exactly born, was he?
Helen: No, he wasn't born in the strip, and of course *Blondie*, Dagwood and Blondie, have always been married.
HF: Yeah.
Helen: We noticed later on, some of these characters with the girls trailing along with them, they had marriage, you know.

Johnny Cake Farm

AS SEEN BY HAL FOSTER

Helen: Well, that was a way to treat a wife, you know, throw her in a pond. He says he's always tried to do that. If he had some violence or anything like that, then for the next story, he'd try to make it light and with humor in it and everything.

AS: Well, it makes it such a delightful picture of life, instead of a one-sided, just blood and thunder all the time, it shows what life is really all about, which is so many different sides.

HF: Yes, you have to write the story the way you would compose music. You know, high notes and low notes. You have violence one week, and the next story will be the children and home, probably the adventure of one of the children. Then you can get into blood and thunder again.

Helen: But every so often you have to remember you got two girls in there, you got to weave them into a story. And then we had more comment about the twins and the things, and when she cut her hair, wore the helmet and would be the tomboy and all that sort of thing. People around here, people who had children said, "Oh, that's my daughter all over again, that's just like my daughter."

AS: Well, the strip is so true to life, isn't it? I wanted to ask you in fact, what method, if any conscious method do you use in thinking up your stories? Do you have to sit down and think, "Now what'll I do next?" or does it just come to you out of the air, or do you have a formula, or how, how did you do it?

HF: Well, you go from one adventure to another, you know you have to come down, and of course, that brings in the children, or love affair, something like that.

AS: But you never repeated yourself.

HF: No. No, but it's always been that wave . . .

AS: One of the nicest things about *Prince Valiant* has always been, well, not always, but since it happened, has been the domestic side of the strip, I've always enjoyed that, instead of taking away from the strip as I thought it might, it really added to it. Because then you have the adventure and the domestic side, which gave you humor and gave you love. And I think that these people who say that there's no romance in a family are just so wrong, and you showed how wrong they could be, because you showed how much a man and wife can love each other, and still be married and have children. It made it so human, and so nice.

Helen: Everybody was so delighted when—didn't he throw her in a pond once?

AS: I remember that one.

AS: Supposing you knew you had an adventurous one, say you had been through a family one and you knew there had to be an adventure coming up now, how did you decide, what methods did you use to write the story? How did you settle what it was going to involve?

HF: Well, those ideas have come to you.

Helen: He just picks them out of thin air, I think.

AS: There's no real process that you can explain.

HF: No, but something that you've written, say that you've had the family scene, something in there is the seed, whether it's a bit of jealousy or anything like that, or maybe the kids have come in, or . . .

Helen: Or something that you read.

HF: Yes.

Helen: It would stick in his mind, or just seeing people. When we were in Paris, and at the restaurant there, a waiter waited on us. Harold kept looking at him, and got his pencil and made a sketch of him, and said, "There's a story in that fellow's face," and he was in the script for a long time.

HF: Yes.

Helen: What did you call him, the, he was the—

HF: I don't know, but he was a fusty-looking guy, never had his hair combed, and nothing fit. So I made him a squire to Sir Gawain, Sir Gawain was always a handsome—

Helen: Served our soup with his thumb in it, you know [laughter].

AS: Oh, I see.

Helen: And then our younger son brought home a series of [photos], he was going in for photography. He's one of those young fellows that goes from one thing to another. He brought home some candid shots that he

"YOU POOR DUMB HUNS HAVE ALWAYS STARTED TROUBLE THAT YOU'VE NEVER BEEN ABLE TO FINISH!"

PRINCE VALIANT

HAL FOSTER

had taken, and he had an enlargement—a head of a girl, remember her?

HF: Yes.

Helen: And the minute he looked at her, "Oh, can I have that, Arthur?" he said, "That girl's got a story in her face," well, maybe he didn't know what the story was, but—

AS: But there's something inspiring.

Helen: That made him think of something. And he used to write down, you had a little black book that, when you'd get an idea, you'd write it down in, and sometimes, enlarge on it. So when he first did that, everything reminded him. For instance, one of our friends' mother, the lady-in-waiting—

HF: Oh, yes.

Helen: Theresa.

HF: Theresa Armstrong.

Helen: Yes, what did you call her? Oh, she had been a lady-in-waiting, and she became a queen of Spain, a queen of Sweden.

HF: Oh, I said she used to come into the room like a floundering ship.

AS: That's great.

HF: She dominated everything.

Helen: He's used lots of people, but they never knew it.

AS: But it seems like a very intuitive process rather than it being a system you have of making up stories.

HF: Yes, the story comes to you. A person's personality will write a story. You know by looking at them, that they're no hero, and they might be a little bit silly or something, and that forms a story. And it'll contrast with Val or Sir Gawain or some more heroic figure.

AS: Yeah, that would be it, I guess, you just begin to see these relationships after a while. You were talking before about the syndicate and the difficulty you're having with it now. Do you feel that the syndicates, these days, really know what they're doing with the material they're using? It seems to me that they are going so much on old methods and they don't. . . .

HF: No, I think they follow the times.

AS: Think so?

HF: [pause] Yes, they pretty well pick the best of the material that comes to them.

AS: You have confidence in their taste, even now, then?

HF: No, I think they've got such a big mass of new cartoonists struggling to get into the business, that well, if they pick the best, why, they throw the rest out, until another group of young artists come up. They should have pretty good taste in what they pick, because they have before them the kinds that succeed, and those that are failed, so they pretty well get a good idea of the public taste. Of course, the public taste changes every 10 years.

AS: You think so? Even though you weathered the changes, didn't you, for a long time?

HF: Yes.

Above: Foster takes a break to smoke a pipe in his Val-Hal-En studio in Redding. The Prince Valiant page on his drafting table is #559, 26 October 1947.

AS: I guess what I'm getting at is, the syndicates seem to have made decisions recently to cut down the size of comic strips, and I wonder whether they should have done that, because it's irreversible, now it's been done.

HF: It's been done, and they've now got more comics, and the more comics they have, and the smaller they make them, the less important they are. Now, when I was in the business, the good comics were valuable because they called attention to the newspapers. Newspapers were bought for comics, as well as anything else, so that the advertising seemed more important. Now, there's a certain dullness that goes all the way through the paper. The only bright spot is some horrible murder. And the comics amount to nothing. If the newspaper thinks these comics are of no particular value, they should throw them out.

AS: Yeah. Maybe give the spot to a few very good ones.

HF: Yes.

AS: I would agree. Where could a good illustrator hope to find work today, do you think?

HF: Well, you look through the magazines, and you'll find that they're not as important as they were 20 years ago, but there are still some good ones. You see them mostly in advertising.

AS: Ah, yes, that's right. There wouldn't be much hope in comics, I guess, for an illustrator of your type, now?

HF: Oh, yes.

Above: Hal and Helen Foster.

AS: Do you think it still could be . . .

HF: Yes, you can get the public interested in anything that's good. If the illustrations are good, why, it's one thing, and if the story's good, why, you don't need such good illustrations.

AS: You had both. You had excellent quality on both. In *Prince Valiant*, you weren't very specific about religious beliefs or anything like that. Was that done for a reason?

HF: Yes. Yes, because the religious fanatic has an awful lot of power. You may say he's a nut, or he doesn't know what he's talking about, but, just the same, so many people think they're religious, and they think that everything should be on a . . . religious connotation. Yes, I've had criticisms, when I try to stay away from religion as much as possible, and what was the one they . . . oh yes, and the Jewish question.

AS: You did deal with that at one time. I remember a story with the trader on the ship, and everyone was treating him badly because he was Jewish.

HF: Yes.

AS: So you did tackle that question, very nicely, I thought.

HF: Yes, brought him out nicely. And then I had them on shipboard, and they wanted a loan or something, so they went to the moneylenders. And they were overcharged, of course, by the moneylenders. I showed a Jew, I took the picture, took my illustration from a painting I made of Shylock, by . . . oh, it was a portrait I painted. And I made him a typical Jew moneylender, and moneylenders of ancient times were always considered kind of sneaky, and all literature plays down the Jew, so I made a copy of the picture I had painted, of Shylock, had him biting a coin. Oh, gosh, I got letters in that were, oh, really threatening.

AS: Really?

HF: Yeah, a Jewish organization. And that's the second one I've had.

AS: Second threat?

HF: I don't know what the first incident was, but it was something that was derogatory to the Jews. Of course, I should have had more sense than to make him obviously a Jew, but they were in the Levant, you know, where they're all Jews and Arabs.

AS: Well, you're trying to be historically accurate, aren't you?

HF: Yes, but I shouldn't have picked out the lousiest looking Jews, as an example.

AS: I guess that was an error in judgment. I was wondering, although you kept religion out of the strip to a great extent, whether you yourself have any particular religious feeling, whether you're involved with the church, or even think about it.

HF: No. No, I take things as they are, I believe in religion, the part that has to do with morality, and honesty, and things like that, yes. That's, well, that's not religion exactly, that's just the human traits. But I don't believe in carrying a placard or anything like that, or . . .

AS: So, it seems that the morality comes out very strongly in the strip, you did a very nice job of that, and yet it's amazing with the religious fervor that there always was in the times that you're writing about, how you managed to make it true-to-life without having to get into that. Imagine, you just always skirted around that.

HF: Well, I always think of the characters as they were in those days, but not to take here's the character, here's the bad character, here's the sainted character over here. You don't vacillate between the two.

AS: Yeah, well, everybody has more than one side to them, and you did a good job of showing that all your characters, even the best characters, have some weaknesses. Prince Valiant himself has weaknesses. And even the bad characters, at times, one of the things I've always liked was where you had a character that started out to be one of the bad characters, and then he ends up being not so bad, after all. That was always a nice trait. But, as far as religion goes, and so on, I thought with the outdooring activity you've had, you'd have something to say about God, you know, or some Almighty.

HF: No, I made it a point, right from the start, to keep away from anything like that. The fans bring in enough of it, without trying to stir them up.

AS: They always want it, I guess.

HF: Yes, every now and then, some fan reads something into your strip, and then they get into their white horse, and come galloping at me, with a lance held. They threaten me.

AS: Do you have a feeling of satisfaction also that you're leaving in the world a great body of very fine work that people for generations are going to look at?

HF: Never thought of that, no.

AS: You don't think about immortality?

HF: No.

AS: Or posterity?

HF: No. Because what I've done is what I had to do, what I enjoyed most. And if I've lost the use of one leg, and I can't remember anything, at least I can give up quietly, and . . .

AS: You feel. . .

HF: Yes, I feel repaid.

AS: That's good. You had a lot of people respond very positively to your work, a lot of fans, and friends, I suppose. You must have received a lot of mail over the years, of people saying how much they like your work.

HF: Oh, yes. Yes, it has been quite annoying. And gratifying. All these letters have to be answered.

AS: You apparently have been very good about answering, I've heard.

HF: Well, yes, I've made it a point. I figured that if they liked my work well enough to go to the trouble of writing me, and spending three cents to send a letter, well, they deserve an answer.

AS: It must have taken a lot of time.

HF: It does.

AS: Do you still get mail?

HF: Oh, yes, right up until yesterday. Now they all want my autograph, and while I'm at it, will I draw a picture of Prince Valiant?

AS: Do you do that?

HF: No.

AS: That's a lot to ask.

HF: When you get a letter asking for an illustration every day of the week, it can't be done.

AS: No, no. I didn't think you could do that. But, as you say, it's annoying, and at the same time gratifying, because you realize that people are seeing your work and liking it well enough to seek you out. It must be—

HF: Yes, that's the only thing that keeps you from ever getting too mad at them.

AS: Yes, I guess so, you realize these are fans.

HF: Yes, they spent the time.

AS: But as you say, the feeling of what you're going to be leaving behind you for years, for generations afterward, that thought hasn't particularly meant much to you.

HF: No, because when I'm gone, I won't know, and besides, I'm not doing the kind of work that lasts for future generations.

AS: You don't think so?

HF: No. Mine is a comic, during this decade or this century, and what people like

this century might not be popular in the next one, and paper doesn't wear well.

AS: This is why I would be very concerned to see some good reprints, this is why the fact that so much of your work is unavailable now, is annoying to me, and I should think, annoying to you, because I think that with it reprinted clearly, and on good paper, that a whole new generation would discover your best work.

HF: That's what I'm hoping, for these books that are being done in Austria. It's without color, and they're clean and neat, and you can read easily, but the ones that Nostalgia Press is getting out, they've got this horrible color, that is not meant to enhance the illustration of the story, it's someone that does that kind of work, does it . . .

AS: Yeah, I don't know where they got him, it's the worst possible color. Well, mustn't forget my promise to you that I will send them, if I can get them, some copies of these ones that are being published, of all places, in Tahiti, strangest place. They're very nice volumes. They're really very clear.

HF: Okay, I'd love to have it.

AS: Well, I'll definitely get you one. At least one, I think there's been three, I'll see how many I can find. I don't even have them myself yet, so I'm trying to find them. I've seen them, but I haven't got them. Coming from Tahiti, they're a bit hard to find. But I was going to say that I think that the best of any kind of work will last for generations. I think that, certainly your work is, must be among the very best comic work ever done. And, if you can even call it comics, I mean, among the best illustrations ever done, and I would predict, neither of us are going to know, but I would predict that a couple of hundred of years from now, your work will still be looked at and appreciated and respected. As I say, we're never going know, but that's my prediction, anyway, for what good it does us.

'I Must Tell King Arthur About This!'

129.

HAL FOSTER'S INDUCTION INTO
THE SOCIETY OF ILLUSTRATORS HALL OF FAME

by Brian M. Kane (2006)

Harold Rudolf Foster was inducted into the Society of Illustrators Hall of Fame at their annual President's Dinner on Thursday June 22, 2006. In attendance (pictured above l-r) were Foster biographer Brian M. Kane, Robert Hoover (Foster's great-grandson), and Murray Tinkelman (Society of Illustrators Hall of Fame Committee Chair). The following is Brian M. Kane's address to the attendees.

I would like to open with the following *fan* letter:

October 17, 1952

Dear Hal,

I got a terrific boot out of the news that the Banshees had awarded you The Lady for 1952.

Every time I look at one of your Sunday pages I wish I had led a cleaner life and devoted more time to the study of art. Each episode of *Prince Valiant* is a real masterpiece of authentic illustration and the story is so absorbing it makes the reader feel that he is a real part of it.

I marvel at the historical perfection of every detail and wonder sometimes if you weren't hiding under a drawbridge taking notes when King Arthur sent his boys on one of those colorful errands of valor and mercy.

I salute you on this happy occasion and hope that you will be around for many, many more years to add "class" to our profession. Besides all this, I like you and your gray hair and your personal outbursts against sham and pretense. Congratulations and love.

As ever,
Rube Goldberg

How many kids, and adults too for that matter, first learned about illustration from lying on the living room floor on a Sunday morning? First and foremost, Harold Rudolf Foster was a storyteller. In a beautiful concert of words and art Hal Foster created one of the greatest adventure-fantasy worlds of twentieth century art and literature. In that regard he was truly a stepson to Howard Pyle and a half-brother to the sons and daughters of the Brandywine Tradition.

Hal produced over thirty-nine-and-one-half years of weekly *Tarzan* and *Prince Valiant* Sunday pages without missing a single deadline. It is an achievement we will never see the like of again. Hal taught us how to look at the world. He taught us that every tree, rock, stream, building, animal, and person was unique. He taught us anatomy and that each character is not only distinctive but also a *real* person. Hal breathed life into his people in a way that few others could. It wasn't just that their clothing and faces were different; Hal gave them different personalities, different body language, different quirks. Hal's people were human. When they were hurt we winced, when their hearts broke so did ours. For Foster each character, each *person* was important.

I don't have to tell any of you just how influential Hal Foster's art was to the world of illustration. The love and attention he poured into every panel speaks for itself. It was an honor to be asked to speak to you tonight. Although I never met him I came to know his family and who Hal Foster was. The more I found out about him the more I respected him and in the end, for me at least, the accomplishments of Hal Foster the storyteller were only equaled by those of Hal Foster the man.

On behalf of the Foster family and myself, thank you for remembering Harold Rudolf Foster and adding his name to such a remarkable assembly of talented illustrators.

FROM PRIZEFIGHTERS TO PRINCES:
THE CLASSIC ART OF JOHN CULLEN MURPHY

by Brian M. Kane (2003)

John Cullen Murphy is one of the last great links between the Golden Age of Illustration and the modern era. He sat at the knee of Rockwell and Booth, painted portraits of generals and playwrights, served his country during the Second World War, and has entertained comics readers for over half a century with stories of prizefighters and princes. At 83, he is still producing art for the weekly Sunday *Prince Valiant* page and has no plans to retire—nor should he even consider it. For on the day he quits comics, he will have severed one of the few remaining ethereal threads that binds us to such giants as Pyle, Wyeth, Parrish, Leyendecker, Schoonover, Cornwell and Dunn. He has won the Silver Plaque for Best Story Strip from the National Cartoonists Society a record six times,[1] the Silver T Square Award for Outstanding Service to the Society, and the Elzie Segar Award for Outstanding Contributions to Cartooning, yet his pride rests not in his own artistic awards but in all of the many achievements of his eight children and seventeen grandchildren. He truly is a living legend.

"Jack" was born on May 3, 1919, in New York City to Jane (née Finn) and Robert Francis Murphy, the second of three children. The Murphys had already been living in Chicago, where Jack's father worked as the western manager for Doubleday, but Jack's mother had moved back east to be with her family until after the birth. Jack once said, "I was drawing ever since I can remember," and his parents encouraged his talent. At the age of nine, he began taking formal art classes in the cellar of The Chicago Art Institute. Every Saturday morning his father, who knew many of the writers and artists in the publishing industry, would take him on the "L" to the museum for class. Like most young boys his passion was for sports, especially baseball, and he wanted to be a sports cartoonist.

The family moved back east in 1930, to New Rochelle, New York and Murphy continued art lessons at the old Grand Central School of Art where Harvey Dunn was teaching illustration. At just seventeen the fledgling artist realized his childhood goal by selling sports cartoons

to Jim Johnston, a major sports promoter for Madison Square Garden, for $15 each. His first cartoons were for boxing matches, to publicize upcoming fights. The pugilist prints would be a foreshadowing of his first comics strip, about a boxer called Ben Bolt. While still in High School he began selling one or two sports cartoons every week to *Sport Eye*, a weekly sports magazine based in Chicago.

In the late 1930s, Murphy sold his first cover painting to *Columbia* magazine for $75.00, and in 1940, he accepted a commission to do the first of several covers for *Liberty* magazine. Also in 1940, Murphy joined the National Guard's historic 7th Infantry Regiment stationed in New York City, where his platoon commander was also his brother, 2nd Lt. Robert Francis Murphy, Jr.[2] In February 1941, his unit was switched from infantry to anti-aircraft and was sent to Camp Stewart (now Fort Stewart) near Savannah, Georgia. It was while he was stationed there that he painted his first military portrait—General Sanderford "Sandy" Jarman—and was painting him on December 8, 1941, while Jarman was redeploying troops along the East Coast. In 1942, Murphy went to Officer's Candidate School (OCS) where he earned the rank of 2nd Lt. (he would eventually become a Major). From there he was sent to the South Pacific, where he was assigned as aide-de-camp to Maj. Gen. Bill Marquat, the head of all anti-aircraft units in the South Pacific. All during the war, whether it was "a dollar a piece" head portrait for a soldier or an oil painting of General Douglas MacArthur or a spot illustration for the *Chicago Tribune* for their Sunday supplement, he continued refining his craft.

---

1. Murphy's first win for Best Story Strip was in 1971, and was a tie between *Big Ben Bolt* and *Prince Valiant*. He'd worked on both strips and won for both strips but only received one award plaque.
2. Eventually 2nd Lt. Murphy would rise to the rank of Brigadier General.

For Immediate Release

Madison Square Garden Corporation
307 West 49th Street
New York City

Above: Murphy's first paid professional work, which was commissioned to promote fights for Madison Square Garden.
Right: One of the many illustrations Murphy did for Sport Eye, the weekly sports magazine.

Brendan, a retired Navy Chief and Master Diver who works as a civilian for the Navy; Cait, a Senior Editor for *Fortune* magazine; and Mairead (Meg), who has lettered and colored *Prince Valiant* since 1988.

Without fanfare (or foreknowledge), John Cullen Murphy entered a knightly mêlée in 1970, and beat out two other contenders to become Hal Foster's handpicked artistic successor on *Prince Valiant in the Days of King Arthur*. The weekend color newspaper adventure strip has appeared worldwide for almost 70 years yet there have only been two artists to illustrate the exploits of its title character. After thirty years of labor and love, Murphy still views this slice of Camelot lore as Hal's and not his own. It is a humble wisdom that speaks more of Don Quixote than of King Arthur. Rather than being heir apparent to comics greatest throne, Murphy sees himself as a simple knight guarding a sacred trust. It is his duty, his responsibility and he has accomplished it with an elegant grace.

NOTE: The following interview was conducted by phone over several weeks, then edited together by the author.

BMK: Let's begin with how you met Norman Rockwell. It's a legendary tale, and many have probably heard it, but it was a seminal turning point in your life.
JCM: I first met Rockwell in 1934, when I was 15. I was playing baseball with some of the neighborhood kids. He drove up in his Rambler—the kind with the rumble seat—got out, and walked into the outfield towards me. He was lean and had a peculiar walk—he was pigeon-toed. He said, "My name is Norman Rockwell." And I said, "I know." I had never met him before but I'd seen pictures. He told me he was doing a *Saturday Evening Post* cover and was in a bind because his model didn't show and asked me if I'd model for him. I was a Huckleberry Finn-looking kid in those days. I said, "sure," so we got in his car and drove to my home so he could ask

After the war Murphy began looking for work wearing his uniform—they were the only clothes he had. On his first day out he found "a bunch of jobs." Metro-Goldwyn-Mayer became a major client for whom he did posters for movies like *The Yearling* and *Until the Clouds Roll By*, and portraits of such stars as Judy Garland, Frank Sinatra, Kathryn Grayson and Van Johnson. With the help of his agent Nat Feuerman, Murphy began doing work for *Esquire, Holiday, Bluebook, True, Boy's Life, Look,* and *Sport* magazine, but it was a watercolor painting for *Collier's* in 1949, of a prizefight, that would change the direction of his career. Elliott Caplin, the brother of *Li'l Abner* creator Al Capp, saw the illustration and immediately offered Murphy the artist's chair on a new strip he'd been developing about a prizefighter named Big Ben Bolt. It was an immediate and international hit.

In 1951, Murphy married Joan Byrne, and they had eight children, the oldest of which, Cullen, is Managing Editor for *Atlantic Monthly* and has written Prince Valiant's adventures since Hal Foster retired in 1980. John and Joan's other children are Mary Cullene, an Oncology Nurse at the Dana Farber Center in Boston; Siobhan, the Director of the Library in Colchester, Connecticut; Byrne, a very busy mother of five; Finn, a manager of two cashmere specialty shops in Nantucket and Greenwich;

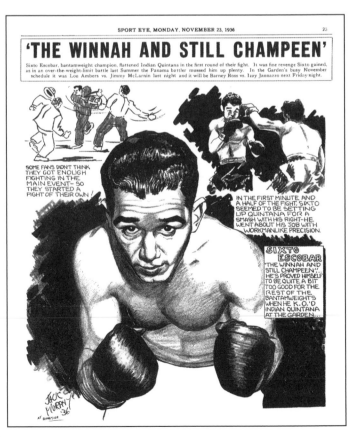

my mother for permission—you had to have permission in those days. While we were at my house my mother had me get out my sketches to show him.[3]

BMK: All of your sports cartoons?

JCM: That's right. He looked at them for a while and then my mother gave him permission. Models got $10.00 in those days. He took me to the store to buy me a sweater and a pair of shoes for the painting. After we got to his studio and he had me try on the sweater and shoes he decided he didn't like the shoes so he took off his own shoes and had me wear them.

BMK: The shoes he was wearing? Weren't they a bit big?

JCM: After the magazine came out everyone used to tell me that my feet looked too big. (laughs.) He posed me and started doing a charcoal sketch. He had the radio on—it was the second All-Star Game where Frankie Frish hit a home run. We stopped for lunch and he talked about the painting with his wife, Mary. She said, "If you feel a dog in the picture, Norman, then go ahead." After lunch he went out and borrowed a dog from the dog pound. He brought it home, gave it a sedative and posed it.

BMK: He sedated it? You couldn't do that today.

JCM: No, I guess not. Not with all the animal rights groups. He had a photographer there, I don't remember where he came from, but he took pictures of the dog.

BMK: Tell me about the Hemingway story he had you illustrate?

JCM: I use to do illustrations where Rockwell would give me a story to do. He gave me a short story by Hemingway and I had to do illustrations for it.

BMK: Which Hemingway story was it?

JCM: It was a short story called "The Killers," from the book *Men Without Women*. They made a movie from it starring Burt Lancaster. I would bring in each stage—it was like he was being another teacher. First I did a rough sketch, then a composition sketch, a full color sketch and then to the big finish. And at each stage I would bring it in and show him and he'd criticize it. I have a pencil sketch of one of Rockwell's critiques. It's the only thing I have of his.

3 Several years after their first meeting, Murphy's family moved to a house that was two doors down from Rockwell's.
4 Mead Schaffer was Norman Rockwell's neighbor in Arlington, Vermont.

Mary [Rockwell] had taken an interest in me and when the Rockwells were planning on going to Vermont in either '39 or '40 she told Norman he should let me use his studio for the summer. I had it all to myself. One time, when Norman wanted a certain table from his studio, he sent Mead Schaffer[4] to get it.

When Norman thought I was ready he sent me down to [*The Saturday Evening Post* offices in] Philadelphia to see Larry B. Kritcher. Kritcher was the art editor and he looked over my artwork. He picked out one of the paintings that had a girl in it. He told me I needed to get a real model and to make her look pretty. He said, "She's too old, she looks like your mother." I didn't tell him but I had used my mother for the girl (both laugh).

In 1941, while I was in the service stationed in Georgia, I got a telegram from Norman asking him to call collect. He'd heard I'd been working on a painting that had a serviceman in it opening a package from home and this

Below: Murphy as depicted in the Norman Rockwell painting "Starstruck." It appeared on the September 22, 1934 cover of The Saturday Evening Post.

big sergeant looking over his shoulder. Norman asked me not to try to sell it because he was working on something similar. It was just a spec piece so I was happy to withdraw it. Not long afterwards I received an orange crate full of canned goods and cheese and gourmet foods. Norman's painting became the first of the Willie Gillis series for *The Saturday Evening Post*.

After I finished OCS in '42, I went to see Norman in Arlington, Vermont. I stood in for the model of the central figure for his compositional sketch for his "Freedom of Speech" painting. I'm not in the final—he used someone else for that.

BMK: You had a great love of sports, so what made you want to become an illustrator?
JCM: When I was young I wanted to be sports cartoonist. I was good at doing caricatures. It wasn't until I met Rockwell that I thought of becoming an illustrator.

BMK: I understand tht you knew Pedro "Pete" Llanuza. When did you meet him?
JCM: I met him in 1933. He was my first idol. He was from Mexico and didn't know much about sports so he just did what the editors asked him to do. He was one of the best. He later drew *Joe Jinks*. He died too young—he was hit by a trolley car in Chicago.

BMK: You had studied under Franklin Booth at the Phoenix Institute [which has since become part of Pratt Institute] but what other pen & ink artists influenced you as a student and as a professional?
JCM: Booth mainly taught me composition. When I started *Bolt* I'd never worked in pen & ink before. I liked Gibson, Flagg, Godwin, Coll, Morgan and Henry Raleigh. I also liked Noel Sickles' work in *Life* magazine.

BMK: What was Booth like as a teacher?
JCM: Avuncular. He was a very kind, gentle man.

BMK: We've covered Rockwell and Booth so I should probably ask about some of your other teachers like Charles Chapman, Sidney Dickinson, and Walter Beach Humphrey.

JCM: I studied painting from Chapman starting in 1939—he knew Remington. I didn't start studying under Dickinson until 1960, at the Art Students' League. Humphrey was friends with Rockwell—he was another *Saturday Evening Post* cover artist. He taught me Commercial Art and lettering. Do you know Rockwell's mural "Land of Enchantment"?

BMK: Yes, I do.
JCM: Humphrey did all of the lettering on the mural. I'm in the mural as either David Copperfield or Oliver Twist along with Humphrey's two kids. It's in the New Rochelle Public Library.

BMK: So Chapman was your first painting instructor after Rockwell?
JCM: No. That would have been Lauros Phoenix, who founded the Phoenix Institute. Rockwell got a scholarship for me to the Institute through the New Rochelle Art Association. Lauros eventually became a partner with Franklin Booth at the school.

BMK: That's an impressive lineage. Do you know Everett Raymond Kinstler?[5] It seems your career paths were similar in some ways.
JCM: I've met him a few times. He's a fine artist...he was a protégé of [James Montgomery] Flagg, you know. It may be presumptuous of me but we admire each other's work.

BMK: Are there any other painters you admire?
JCM: Aaron Schickler, who painted Jacqueline Kennedy's portrait, and Bernie Fuchs. Bernie is a fine golfer. He's missing a finger, you know.

BMK: I didn't know that.
JCM: People used to say: "Imagine how good of an artist he'd be if he wasn't missing his finger." (both laugh) He once told me that when he was

---

5 Kinstler, who worked on *Zorro* as well as other comics in the 1950s, is one of the most respected portrait painters in the world. Among his commissions have been the official White House portraits of both Presidents Gerald Ford and Ronald Reagan.

studying in St. Louis that they'd used some of my pen & ink work for examples in one of his art classes.

BMK: Is there anyone else?
JCM: Frank Mullins, Bob Handville, and, of course Homer, Akins, Sargent, Sorolla...

BMK: What about Al Parker?
JCM: I never knew him personally but I admired his work. He ushered in a whole new style of illustration.

BMK: When you paint are you still influenced by Rockwell?
JCM: No, not really. Before the war I did some of the big stuff for covers but Al Parker changed the look of illustration. He made it smaller. He was an innovator. Then came Austin Briggs and later Bernie.

BMK: I know that you do portrait painting and that you did oil paintings of MacArthur, Krueger, Kenney and Eichelberger during your service time in World War II. Who else have you done?
JCM: There were several. I did Field Marshal Blamey. He was the highest-ranking Australian soldier in the army. I also did Jean MacArthur. I was painting her portrait in Lennon's Hotel in Brisbane the day MacArthur successfully reentered the Philippines.[6] We stayed friends up until her death a few years ago.

BMK: Do you still paint?
JCM: Oh yes.

BMK: Do you prefer watercolor or oil?
JCM: Oh, I can't choose.

BMK: Is there a specific brand of paint that you like to use?
JCM: Not really. I like Winsor & Newton for watercolor though.

BMK: Do you have any personal projects or commissions that you're working on right now?
JCM: I'm doing a portrait of my daughter Meg for her husband. You might say that's a commission. I've been doing portraits of literary figures like Samuel Beckett, George Bernard Shaw, Mark Twain, Thomas Mann, G.K. Chesterton... Shaw is easy to do—he's an Irishman, you know.

BMK: There's a great Shaw Festival every year in Niagara-on-the-Lake. Have you ever been there?
JCM: No, I haven't. It's in Ontario? I'll have to look that up.

BMK: I know that in addition to portraits you like to do horses, landscapes, and western scenes— All things being equal, what type of art would you be doing right now?
JCM: I like to do them all. I like the change.

BMK: Did you ever wish to do an illustrated book like Wyeth, or Dunn, or Godwin?
JCM: Well, I did do several *Reader's Digest* books, and I did three in Ireland. One was on Sean O'Casey, another was on the Abbey Theatre, and I can't remember the last one.

BMK: I never knew that. What's the one thing you haven't done that you want to do?
JCM: I don't know—not a mural, though.

BMK: Why not?
JCM: They never look as good as an artist's portrait work. Sargent's didn't. Even Cornwell's preliminaries looked better than the finished pieces. He even went to Europe to live with Brangwyn to study how to do it the right way.

6 As an aide-de-camp to a general, Murphy also did more than just paint portraits during the war. In fact, he saw a lot of combat in the South Pacific.

you decide to do comics instead of strictly illustration work or portrait painting?

JCM: I saw that most of the advertising dollars were being pulled from magazines and going into television. The strip work was steady income.

BMK: *Big Ben Bolt* was an obvious response to *Joe Palooka*, but did Caplin ever say if he took Ben Bolt's name from the 1843 poem by Thomas Dunn English?

JCM: I never really thought about *Joe Palooka* before but Al Capp was always fighting with Ham Fisher since the days he'd worked at Fisher's studio. I just thought he got the name from the song "Sweet Alice, Ben Bolt."

BMK: That's English's poem set to music.

JCM: Well, there you go—it comes full circle. Elliott liked it because it was alliterative.

BMK: Fanny Young Cory also did a single panel cartoon called *Ben Bolt* starting in 1916, did you ever get to see any of those?

JCM: No, I never did.

BMK: *Bolt* was the next-to-the-last strip accepted by William Randolph Hearst for King Features. Mort Walker's *Beetle Bailey* was the last; did you ever talk directly to Hearst about the strip?

JCM: I never met him but I did meet [Hearst's son] Junior though we never talked about the strip.

BMK: Did anyone model for Ben Bolt?

JCM: There was a model in the studio by the name of Mike Garrett who later went into the movies. I also used Willie Stribling—he was a pro boxer at the time. Later on I used Bob Mathias.

BMK: Mathias was only man to win back-to-back Olympic decathlons. Great choice.

JCM: They all had a clean-cut look to them.

BMK: You mentioned a studio—did you work for or with someone back then?

JCM: No, I always worked alone—in my own studio.

Above: A preliminary sketch of Jean MacArthur in preparation of her portrait.
Below: The only photo of Murphy (right) with Rockwell (left). Murphy's daughter, Cait, who was modeling for Rockwell at the time, is in the foreground. Circa 1969.

BMK: There's a nice mural of Rockwell's in Princeton. "Yankee Doodle."
JCM: I've seen it many times—it's in the Nassau Inn.

BMK: It's too dark in there to really get a good look at it.
JCM: They don't display it well. They don't know what they have. They don't pay mural painters what they're worth. Cornwell went broke doing them. In 1948, I did a 24-sheet billboard for Beamish Stout in Ireland and several Budweiser ads in the United States— that's as close as I got to ever doing a mural.

BMK: I want to talk about your comics work for a bit. With *Big Ben Bolt* you were approached by Elliott Caplin[7] to do the art after he'd seen a *Collier's* prizefight illustration you'd done of Willie Pep fighting Sandy Saddler for the featherweight championship. What made

---

7 Caplin, a prolific writer who scripted *Abbie an' Slats* for Raeburn van Buren, also created *The Heart of Juliet Jones* with Stan Drake in 1953, and *Broom-Hilda* with Russell Myers in 1970.

BMK: Did you follow any of the daily strips before working in the field?
JCM: I spent six years in the army so I naturally liked Caniff's work on *Steve Canyon*. I didn't follow that many strips though I liked *Terry and the Pirates*, and *Prince Valiant*. I also used to like *Little Orphan Annie* (laughs).

BMK: Did you ever talk about your work on *Big Ben Bolt* or *Prince Valiant* with Norman Rockwell?
JCM: No, I actually didn't talk with him much in those days.

BMK: Alex Raymond's brother George was your assistant on *Bolt* for a while. What did he do on the strip?
JCM: George did layouts, lettering and research for me for 15 years. When I was growing up in New Rochelle the Raymonds lived only a block away. Their brother Jim, who eventually went on to draw *Blondie* for Chic Young, was a southpaw and was the pitcher on the High School baseball team. I didn't make the cut.

BMK: Did anyone else help you with *Bolt*?
JCM: Al Williamson, Frank Giacoia, Gray Morrow and Angelo Torres all filled in for a strip or two. I never met him but Al had Carlos Garzón help him with the dailies. Stan Drake, Al Scully and Tex Blaisdell did two weeks when I had pneumonia once, and Alex Kotzky, who drew *Apartment 3G*, helped me out when I was trying to get ahead a little to go on vacation.

BMK: When you do black & white illustration do you have a favorite type of nib or ink?

Above, below, and top of the following page is a selection of Elliott Caplin and John Cullen Murphy's Big Ben Bolt *from February and March 1955. The storyline featured the title fight between Ben Bolt and Borgy Kulpin. Courtesy of the John Cullen Murphy Collection at Ohio State University's Cartoon Research Library.*

JCM: I use a Gillott 303, which are hard to come by these days. My daughter Cait, who lives in New York, gets them for me. I like to use Dr. Martin's waterproof ink, which I thin down with water so it doesn't clog the pen.

BMK: How do you approach black & white illustration? What is it that you consider first when laying out a panel or a page?
JCM: I look for the drama in the panel. It's like being a stage director. You're competing for the reader's attention so you need to get in some good blacks—some high contrast.

BMK: What would you say is your signature trademark? If someone looked at a John Cullen Murphy pen & ink piece how would they know immediately that it's yours?
JCM: I would hope it to be that the drawing's all there—the figures, the hands, the faces, the emotions. Characterization is very important. When I was doing *Ben Bolt* it was important to make the word balloons unobtrusive. The lettering didn't interfere with the art. Today I see balloons that are cutting off part of a head.

BMK: What's the hardest part of working on the strips?
JCM: Interruptions. Distractions. Phone calls. I'm inking as we're talking.

BMK: In 1964, you moved to Dublin, Ireland for two years—what prompted that move?
JCM: It was just for the fun of it. Joan and I wanted the kids to know what it was like living up in another country. We'd thought of Spain, but we stayed with one where the main language was English.

BMK: Plus you're Irish.
JCM: Yes.

137.

COUNTING OUT BORGY KULPIN IS ONLY A FORMALITY AS THE BEATEN CHALLENGER SINKS TO THE CANVAS...

BMK: Was it hard meeting deadlines and corresponding across the ocean in those days?

JCM: No, except for the time when the strips got lost in the mail. It was the only time I didn't have Photostats made. I called up Al Williamson and he redid them for me.

BMK: I'd like to ask you about what you thought of the artwork of some of the other artists who were working in the field back then. How about Milton Caniff?

JCM: I was a great admirer of his. His work was strong. He was a wonderful storyteller—it was the perfect combination of story and art. I loved his *Terry and the Pirates* and *Steve Canyon*. He was a nice person too—always willing to help.

BMK: Noel Sickles?

JCM: I admired his art too—he was a master at just drawing. He developed a style similar to Robert Fawcett.

BMK: Al Capp?

JCM: (laughs) I almost went to work for Al back in '67. I was supposed to go to Boston three days a week but he hired Bob Lubbers instead. He was irascible, contentious—a genius with characterization.

BMK: Frank Godwin?

JCM: He was one of the old masters of pen & ink. His work on *Rusty Riley* was terrific. He was a fine illustrator.

BMK: John Prentice?

JCM: Finding someone to take over *Rip Kirby* after Alex's death was hard but he did a beautiful job.

BMK: Al Williamson?

JCM: He was a true student of Alex Raymond. I liked his work very much.

BMK: Stan Drake?

JCM: He was one of the most facile, talented artists around. To think that he could work on something like *The Heart of Juliet Jones* and then turn around and do *Blondie*… wonderful stuff.

BMK: Alex Raymond?

JCM: He was a good friend. I think his best work was in the late '30s—afterwards he tightened up a bit. He had it all—impeccable drawing, great imagination, and all done in brush. He based his style on Matt Clark's Western art.

Below (l-r): Hal Foster, Helen Foster, and John Cullen Murphy.

BMK: Really?

JCM: There were two brothers, Matt and Benton Clark, who did some nice work. Benton was a painter and Matt did Westerns in mainly dry brush. He based his style on the works of Frank Hoffman. Do you know the actor, Matt Dillon?

BMK: Sure.

JCM: He's Alex's grandnephew. He's the grandson of Alex's sister Beatrice.

BMK: Okay, this may be a hard question but since you were so close to the Raymonds how were you affected by Alex's death?[9]

9 Alex Raymond died on September 6, 1956 when he drove Stan Drake's new 450 horse-power Corvette through a stop sign on a rain-slick road and crashed.

JCM: It was a shock. I had to tell George [Raymond]. Mort Walker called me, and I had to convey the news to George. Very sad. Alex loved sports cars. He made the mistake of driving Stan's car when the roads were still wet. Stan was hurt pretty bad.

BMK: Did you ever talk to Stan Drake about it?
JCM: I went to see him in the hospital—he was a mess. We talked about it then, but we never discussed it afterwards.

BMK: Okay, here's the biggie: What did you think of Hal Foster's work?
JCM: I first noticed Hal's work when I was 18. I loved it. His compositions were extraordinary. He could really do the big panels. I think he was a little weak on horses, though, and great big close-ups.

BMK: What made you decide to approach Hal in 1968?
JCM: Bolt had lost a lot of readers. By that time Elliott had left the strip and it was being written by a lot of different guys so the stories weren't that good. I'd wanted to get black people into the strip because the heyday of Jewish and Irish prizefighters was past, but the executives wouldn't do it. They thought we'd lose more readers.
BMK: This was before Cassius Clay—before Ali?

JCM: Right. I'd contributed story ideas for the strip. Early on Elliott would use them, but he became more of a producer of strips like The Heart of Juliet Jones and Broom-Hilda. He'd start the strips and then move on to something else.

BMK: When did you leave Big Ben Bolt? Was it before or after you'd started on Prince Valiant?
JCM: After. I continued with Bolt for another 3 or 4 years.

BMK: I was surprised to read in a Cartoonist PROfiles interview you had with Bill Crouch that you did some work for MAD magazine at this time too. How did that come about?
JCM: I needed the work. I did two pieces for them. The big one was "Vice President of the Year: Spiro Agnew," which was 12 pages, and I painted a "Mission Impossible" piece for the back cover.

BMK: You'd studied anatomy under George Bridgman at the Art Students League, and I know that Foster didn't care that much for Bridgman's approach. Did you have any problems reconciling the differences in styles when you first took over Prince Valiant?

Below: A Hal Foster preliminary rough and Murphy's redrawn and finished panel.

"AS COMMANDER OF THE ARMY I SHALL SEEK A TRUCE AND TRY TO SOFTEN BELLA'S DEMANDS."
VAL IS ENRAGED. "THE KING WOULD RATHER DIE UNDER TORTURE THAN SUBMIT HIS PEOPLE TO THE RAVAGES OF BELLA'S SAVAGE PIRATES! PRINCE ODO IS REGENT DURING THE KING'S ABSENCE--WHAT SAYS HE?"

Our Story: AT LAST THEY ARRIVE AT THE HUNTING GROUNDS AND CID POINTS OUT A TRAMPLED AREA. *"THE DEER COME DOWN HERE TO DRINK AT SUNDOWN. WE WILL MOOR THE BOAT A MILE DOWNSTREAM AND THE HUNTERS CAN WALK BACK AND BUILD A BLIND."*

AFTER HOURS OF WAITING UNDER THE BURNING SUN, THE COOL TWILIGHT COMES, AND WITH IT A SMALL HERD OF ANTELOPE.

VAL AND DASH READY THEIR WEAPONS, WAITING FOR THEIR QUARRY TO MOVE CLOSER. BUT THEY ARE NOT THE ONLY HUNTERS STALKING THE ANTELOPE.

WITH A BURST OF ENERGY, THE LIONESS LEAPS AND THE HERD SCATTERS IN A CLOUD OF DUST, ALMOST RUNNING OVER THE HUNTERS. THEN COMES A FRIGHTENING MOMENT WHEN THE LIONESS SEES THE HUNTERS.

NO ONE MOVES EXCEPT JASEN, WHO SLOWLY KNEELS ON THE BUTT OF HIS SPEAR AND PRESENTS IT IN FRONT OF DASH.

THEN THE LIONESS PICKS UP ITS KILL AND DRAGS IT AWAY INTO THE BUSH, AND THE HUNTERS BREATHE AGAIN.

"WHY DID YOU PROTECT ME INSTEAD OF THE PRINCE?" ASKS DASH. JASEN THINKS FOR A MOMENT. *"I GUESS IT WAS BECAUSE THE PRINCE SEEMED MORE CAPABLE OF PROTECTING HIMSELF,"* ANSWERS JASEN.

NEXT WEEK- The Storm

8-27   1855

JCM: No. I didn't know Hal didn't like Bridgman, but I didn't have any problems with the strip.

BMK: What was Bridgman like as a teacher?
JCM: Tough. He didn't have personal relationships with his students. He'd come in, look at you work, take a shammy to it, made the corrections and that was it.

BMK: Hal was giving you pencil sketches of each page every week to work from. Did you ever find working with him constricting?
JCM: No, because they were just rough guides. A few years later after I started doing the pages [Hal's wife] Helen told him, "You've got this guy doing the pages, why bother sending him layouts?" After a while Hal quit sending the layouts but continued writing the strip. I think Helen was trying to ease Hal's workload.

BMK: Your inking work is mainly with pen while Hal's was predominately with brush. Did Hal have any comments about your art or concerns about the look of the art during the transition?
JCM: No, he never said anything about my technique. His critiques were mainly about spotting blacks.

BMK: Did he give you any advice about the characters? Posture? Body language? Did he share any personal insights that are not obvious to the casual reader?
JCM: He thought I drew Val with too much emotion. He'd say: "He's a prince. He needs to be stoic."

BMK: Something that Hal could relate to coming out of a late-Victorian/ Edwardian upbringing. Was it hard for Hal to let go of *Prince Valiant*?
JCM: Very much. It was his baby.

BMK: Was it harder for him to give up Val or Aleta?
JCM: (laughs) Well, he did use Helen as a model for Aleta. Younger, of course. She was a fine lady.

BMK: When did you find out that Wally Wood and Gray Morrow had also tried out for the strip?
JCM: It wasn't until many years later when someone told me. Hal never mentioned it.

BMK: King Features' editor Sylvan Byck had written Hal in August of 1969, with samples of Gray Morrow's work. Morrow had done some *Prince Valiant* samples but was unwilling to make weekly trips from Brooklyn to visit Hal. Did you know that Gray used a Foster swipe on his tryout page?

JCM: No, I didn't know that.

BMK: Part of Panel #5 on Morrow's tryout page had been drawn by Hal only five weeks earlier. I'm sure that did not go over well with Foster.
JCM: No, I'm sure Hal didn't like that.

BMK: Your first *Prince Valiant* strip was page 1760, November 1, 1970, but you couldn't start signing your name on the page until February 17, 1980. Did it bother you that the general public didn't know you were drawing the strip for almost 10 years?
JCM: Not really. Everyone knew I was doing it.

BMK: All the cartoonists?
JCM: That's right, and even some of the fans too. Hal told me he once got a letter from a fan asking him when he'd started using Murphy on the strip?

BMK: During your time on *Big Ben Bolt* and *Prince Valiant*, did you ever help out with someone else's deadline or ghosted another strip?
JCM: No, never. I was still doing commercial work while I was doing the strips.

Below: Murphy was the Grand Marshal of the 1995 St. Patrick's Day parade in Greenwich, Connecticut.

"I've had one of the rare privileges a son can have these days, something that used to be common and now is nearly extinct—the chance to work with my Dad on a great professional enterprise. I suppose we've enjoyed some of the advantages of the old medieval guild system—pretty appropriate under the circumstances, I'd have to say. But it would have been unusual under the guild system for the master also to be the apprentice's oldest friend, which is the way it is in my case. Dad and I have been working together as artist and writer for more than a quarter of a century now, and not a day goes by when I don't think about his skill and his kindness and his smarts."

—Cullen Murphy (2002)

BMK: There are three pages that are not signed by Foster that Todd Goldberg and Carl Horak have claimed were done by another artist. Just to confirm their suspicions, do you recognize the art as your own?

JCM: No, I didn't do them. They look like Hal's, though.

BMK: But he didn't sign them. Hal never signed his name to a page he didn't do. I wonder if his son Arthur did them?

JCM: I don't think he was doing work for Hal at the time.

BMK: It might have been Tex Blaisdell, but I guess we'll never know. George Raymond helped you with the layouts on *Big Ben Bolt* and Foster initially provided you with layouts for *Prince Valiant*. Have there been any other assistants who've helped you on *Prince Valiant*?

JCM: Ben Oda did the lettering for a while. After he died my daughter Meg took it over—she also does the coloring. Frank Bolle has been helping me with layouts since 1996. Recently, Gary Gianni has assisted me on several pages.

BMK: Here's an odd piece of trivia for the readers. What was "Tic-Tac-Dough" and how did you get your studio behind the house?

JCM: I was on the TV quiz show "Tic-Tac-Dough." There was a trick to winning and I won a couple times. I came home with $5,000.00 and built my studio in the back yard.

BMK: Have any of the mythic overtones of Celtic history played a part in your development of *Prince Valiant* as a character and as a strip?

JCM: Not intentionally. Some of the stories have taken place in Ireland, but you never know what Cullen might write into the strip.

BMK: What has been the proudest achievement in your professional art career?

JCM: That I've been able to keep working all this time. I'm not the most talented person, but I always did my best. I was able to put eight kids through college.

BMK: Before we finish I just want to get back to the good Prince. How many papers is *Prince Valiant* currently in worldwide?

JCM: They keep telling me it's in 350 papers.

BMK: Other than shrinkage, what other trends have you noticed in the past 50 years of working on the strips?

JCM: Shrinkage is the worst. It's all right for gag strips but not *Prince Valiant*. The coloring is not as good as it used to be. The color they had in the papers in the early 1900s is better than what they have today.

BMK: Where do you see the future of adventure strips?

JCM: I don't know, maybe they've reached their nadir. Maybe they will come back. I'm told that there are some good strips in Europe.

BMK: You seem to have a great love for *Prince Valiant*—something that goes beyond just a steady income or a weekly paycheck.

JCM: It's my duty. I'm responsible for it.

BMK: What's the best thing about working on *Prince Valiant*?

JCM: It's something new every day. There're an infinite variety of possibilities for stories.

BMK: Granted that Hal created *Prince Valiant*, but after thirty years haven't you really made it your strip now?

JCM: No. If it's anyone's then it's more Cullen's than mine. He takes it very seriously. He spends a lot of time on it and he doesn't have a lot of time to spare.

BMK: I did some calculating and you only have a little over two years to go before you do as many pages as Hal did.

JCM: Something like that. I know I'm close.

BMK: Are you trying to break Hal's record?

JCM: I really haven't thought about it.

BMK: Let me put it this way. Once you have done as many pages as Hal did would you do one more?

JCM: Sure, why not?

JOHN CULLEN MURPHY:
GOODNIGHT FAIR PRINCE

by Brian M. Kane (2004)

A few months ago when John Cullen Murphy retired from the Sunday *Prince Valiant* strip *Scoop* and several Internet sites, and even *The Comics Journal*, announced his death. After all, he'd become such a comics mainstay that no one, not even myself, thought that he'd ever retire. After I read the first posting I called Jack and the two of us joked about it. I called him "Tom Sawyer," recited the famous quote, and remarked that serendipitously Hal Foster had lived in Reading—not far from Twain's final home. Now, less than three months later, he is gone and with his death the gossamer thread that joined all modern artists to some of the greatest illustrators and cartoonists of the early 20th century has been severed. Cornwell, Booth, Rockwell, Foster, Raymond, Caniff and so many others that he personally knew seem more distant now.

John Cullen Murphy was born in New York City on May 3, 1919, but quickly moved to Chicago where his father, Robert Francis Murphy, was the western manager for Doubleday. As a boy, Murphy attended Saturday classes at the Chicago Art Institute but it was the family's move back east to New Rochelle, NY that cemented his career as an illustrator. While still in his teens Jack met and modeled for Norman Rockwell, who became a friend and a tremendous influence on the young artist. Rockwell insisted that Murphy study under the man who taught him anatomy, George Bridgman at The Art Students League, and it was Rockwell who aided in getting Murphy a scholarship to the Phoenix Institute (which would later become part of Pratt), where he studied under Franklin Booth.

Murphy became a Second Lt. in World War II and was stationed in the South Pacific with an anti-aircraft unit as aide-de-camp to Maj. Gen. Bill Marquat. In addition to his military duties Murphy did war illustrations for the *Chicago Tribune* and painted portraits of officers, including General Douglas MacArthur and his family. After being discharged, Murphy became a successful illustrator, working for Metro-Goldwyn-Mayer and painting covers for magazines such as *Esquire, Collier's, Holiday, Sport, Reader's Digest, Look* and *Boy's Life.*

In 1949, Murphy began his career as a comic strip artist when he was approached by Elliott Caplin (Al Capp's brother) to illustrate *Big Ben Bolt*. Murphy's relationship with the successful strip lasted for over 20 years, when Murphy was chosen by Hal Foster to take over illustrating *Prince Valiant in the Days of King Arthur* in 1971. During his time as a cartoonist Murphy won the Silver Plaque for Best Story Strip from the National Cartoonists Society a record six times, the Silver "T" Square Award for Outstanding Service to the Society, and the Elzie Segar Award for Outstanding Contributions to Cartooning. Murphy's final *Prince Valiant* strip was printed on March 14th, and while his name appears on the art for the March 21st strip, that one was actually done by Murphy's successor, Gary Gianni. The addition of Murphy's name was due to a clerical error by a King Features production person who didn't get the word that Murphy had retired.

John Cullen Murphy passed away on July 2, 2004, at the age of 85, from complications resulting from a head injury he sustained in a fall a few weeks earlier. Murphy is survived by his wife, Joan Byrne Murphy; his sons Cullen, Finn and Brendan; five daughters, Mary, Cait, Siobhan Grogan, Byrne Sleeper, and Mairead "Meg" Nash; a brother, James; 18 grandchildren; and one great-grandchild.

While I talked with Jack many times by phone over the past few years I finally got to meet him at his home in Cos Cob, Connecticut last July. Both he and his wife Joan were gracious and gave me a warm welcome. I came to know *Prince Valiant* through Jack's art so it was a special moment for me to stand in the studio where my relationship with King Arthur and his knights of the round table began. His passing marks the end of an era not just for comics but for all of illustration. I would like to think that now he'll have the time to do all the paintings he still wanted to paint as he chats once more with Rockwell and Foster.

Goodnight fair prince.

LEANING AGAINST
THE BOOBY-HATCH

M/SGT
TURIACE
E DOESN'T
REALLY PLAY)

Left and Right: Two more examples of Murphy's World War II sketches.

Below: A cartoon Murphy created for the National Cartoonists Society.

Prince Valiant IN THE DAYS OF KING ARTHUR
BY HAL FOSTER

PRINCE VALIANT STRUMS
HIS GREETINGS TO THE
MEMBERS OF THE N.C.S.
AND THEIR COUNTERPARTS
IN THE PERFORMING ARTS.

JOHN
CULLEN
MURPHY

FRANK BOLLE: THE GHOST OF CAMELOT

by Bill Crouch (2008)

Frank Bolle remembers he was fixing a screen door at home in June 1996 when the phone rang. John Cullen Murphy called him "out of the blue" to ask if he did "stuff in costumes?" Bolle's answer was yes. Over the years he had drawn everything from a series of *Robin Hood* comic books to superheroes, Bible stories, horror and mystery tales.

Murphy explained he needed assistance periodically on *Prince Valiant*. He knew Frank Bolle socially from National Cartoonists Society events in Connecticut and New York City. He also knew Bolle had assisted a variety of other cartoonists including John Prentice on *Rip Kirby* and Jack Berrill on *Gil Thorp* (Bolle had covered for Berrill for eight months on *Gil Thorp*).

Frank Bolle was well known by King Features Syndicate, having drawn *Willie Winkle* for twenty years, and had taken over illustrating *The Heart of Juliet Jones* when Stan Drake left it to draw *Blondie*. Bolle also drew many issues of King's *The Phantom* comic book, and currently draws *Apartment 3G*. The timing was good for Bolle, who is a workaholic, and was finishing his commitments to *Boy's Life* magazine, for whom he produced a great deal of work from 1978-1996.

Every Tuesday about 11 a.m., Bolle would arrive at Murphy's studio, a small building behind the Murphy home in Cos Cob, Connecticut near Greenwich. Bolle would deliver the penciled page, and Murphy would critique Bolle's work and offer suggestions. Murphy hired Bolle on an "as needed" basis depending on their schedules. Bolle would be given the story and descriptions as a guide for composition and character development.

Because Bolle was also busy with other work, he soon realized it was impossible to keep all the locations, characters' costumes and physical appearances consistent without having reference. Although he began receiving repros from King of the finished art, the time difference between staying ahead of deadline and receiving them didn't help him. Thus, he

began to make photocopies of all of his pencils. That way he had a point of reference when he needed it.

While Murphy began drawing *Prince Valiant* the same size as Hal Foster's originals, over the years the reduction in size of newspaper reproduction, and the misnomer referred to as "technical improvements" in the printing of newspaper comics, resulted in smaller-sized originals. Bolle's layouts measured 14" x 20". For the *Prince Valiant* work, he used an automatic pencil with 3B lead and worked clean, without leaving a lot of sketchy lines behind. It would take him two days to lay out a *Prince Valiant* Sunday page.

"Working on *Prince Valiant* was a dream come true. Both *Val* and *Flash Gordon* were my two favorite comic strips when I was a kid," Bolle remembered. Bolle was nine-and-one-half when *Flash Gordon* premiered in January 1934, and *Prince Valiant* started three months before Bolle turned thirteen. Bolle discovered early on that he loved to draw and had natural ability to draw people and animals. During a hardscrabble childhood in Brooklyn, every scrap of paper was saved so he could draw on it. His family bought the *New York Daily News*, and the neighbors saved the comics from Hearst's *New York Journal-American* for him.

A grammar school teacher recognized Bolle's artistic talent and guided him to New York City's special High School of Music and Art. After graduating, Bolle was accepted at Pratt Institute; however, his art education was interrupted by service in the U.S. Army Air Force in World War II. After the war, Bolle graduated from Pratt and started drawing comic books. His first professional job was a seven-page *Tim Holt* cowboy story for Crown Comics.

In 2003, Bolle was honored at the San Diego International Comic-Con with a Lifetime Achievement Inkpot Award, for his work on the superhero comic book, *Dr. Solar: Man of Atom*. Over the years Bolle produced a massive amount of comic book pages. Bolle also drew and inked issues of *Flash Gordon, Buck Rogers, Rod Serling's Twilight Zone,* and *Boris Karloff's Tales of Mystery* for Gold Key, as well as stories for Warren Publishing's titles *Creepy, Eerie,* and *Vampirella.*

For *Prince Valiant,* Bolle recalls, "I was just happy to work on something I'd admired since I was a kid. It was a really nice change from all the modern soap opera stuff I'd done for syndicates. However, no one story really sticks out, as I was always busy with other work. King Arthur aged in Cullen's scripts. I had nothing to do with that except follow the script I received each week. The photocopies were really critical as I never had the script of a complete story and only received it as I was needed.

"When I visited Jack Murphy his drawing board was on one side and his daughter Meg's faced him on the other side. She watercolored the strip which was used as a color guide. The strip was photocopied in black and she would paint and number the colors. She also hand lettered the strip," remembered Bolle.

Bolle doesn't remember the dates of the first or last *Prince Valiant* pages he designed, but the last time Frank Bolle saw Jack Murphy was in the fall of 2003. By then Gary Gianni was assisting Jack Murphy. Bolle had met Gianni only once in 2003 at San Diego's Comic-Con International.

When Jack Murphy died in the summer of 2004, Bolle was vacationing in Nova Scotia, and only learned of Murphy's passing after the funeral.

Bolle assisted Murphy with layouts on *Prince Valiant* for nearly seven years. The existing photocopies of the layouts offer cartoon historians a unique insight into how the strip developed, and what changes Murphy made.

Bolle saw these photocopies as a tool to allow him to keep track of the *Prince Valiant* stories. Unfortunately, Bolle has given many chalk talks and lectures to schools and senior groups, where he gave away most of the photocopies. While this is unfortunate for cartoon historians, the few that do remain present a unique behind-the-scenes look into the production of *Prince Valiant* from the summer of 1996 to late fall 2003.

Bolle, who has loved to draw since he was a kid, is still busy illustrating and painting, and has never been without work since he started in 1946. An award-winning watercolorist, Bolle also has painted over 200 animal portraits. Several of his dog portraits were rented in 2007, by the production company filming the movie *Old Dogs* starring Robin Williams and John Travolta, for use as backgrounds. Bolle was also commissioned to paint a portrait of the canine star. For someone who was once Camelot's "ghost," Bolle continues to have a very full professional career.

Left: Frank Bolle's layouts for Prince Valiant, *page number #3412, 30 June 2002.*

Below: John Cullen Murphy's finished panel.

GARY GIANNI & MARK SCHULTZ:
THE ADVENTURES CONTINUE

by Brian M. Kane (2009)

In 2000, Gary Gianni received a call from *Prince Valiant* artist John Cullen Murphy, who was looking for an assistant. What Gianni did not realize at the time was that Murphy was also looking for his successor. In 2003, Gianni became only the third artist in *Prince Valiant's* over seventy-year history to illustrate the strip full time. The significance of that commission has not gone unnoticed by the artist.

Gianni began his career illustrating books before working on comics such as *The Shadow* and his own cult favorite series *Monstermen* (later collected as *Corpus Monstrum*). In the late 1990s, Gianni began collaborating with the British publisher Wandering Star to illustrate three books with stories written by Robert E. Howard. Beautifully produced and lavishly illustrated, *The Savage Tales of Solomon Kane, Bran Mak Morn: The Last King,* and *Conan of Cimmeria, Volume Two (1934)* all command collectors' prices. While *Prince Valiant* consumes most of his time, Gianni has been able to contribute illustrations for Pulitzer Prize-winning author Michael Chabon's novel *Gentlemen of the Road* and a return to his own series *Monstermen*.

Mark Schultz joined Gianni in the fall of 2004, taking over the writing of the strip from long-time scribe Cullen Murphy. Schultz, who had illustrated Wandering Star's *Conan of Cimmeria, Volume One (1932-1933),* is best known to comic book fans for his science fiction series *Xenozoic Tales* (a.k.a. *Cadillacs and Dinosaurs*).

Coordinating a three-way phone interview with Gary Gianni and Mark Schultz was challenging, but certainly not as arduous as the adventures of Thule's favorite prince.

BMK: Hi Gary and Mark. Mark, I don't want to slight you, but I'm going to start out with Gary because he has been on the strip longer. Just feel free to jump in whenever you want to.

MS: Sounds good.

BMK: Gary, I wanted to chronicle the events that led up to your taking over the illustrator's chair on *Prince Valiant*. Back in 2000, wasn't it King Features' assistant editor, Brendan Burford, who recommended you to King's Editor-in-Chief Jay Kennedy?

GG: Yes, that was all unbeknownst to me. It was a complete surprise when Kennedy called me and asked me if I'd consider working on the strip.

BMK: How did Brendan know of you?

GG: Previous comic book work: *The Shadow,* my own *Monstermen* series, and things that I had done before then. Mainly my comics work. However, John Cullen Murphy had the final word on choosing an artist to help him and he was not particularly interested in comic books. He wanted someone with either a newspaper strip background or illustration experience.

BMK: Tell me about your conversation with Jay?

GG: In the summer of 2000, he called, introduced himself and asked if I'd be interested in assisting John Cullen Murphy on the *Prince Valiant* comic strip. It wasn't the sort of commitment anyone could take lightly and naturally, I had a lot of questions.

Keep in mind, I never followed the strip—hadn't even seen it in 30 years. I didn't think I had the right background for the job. Jay explained that they were looking for an assistant who would be working closely with Murphy. We didn't settle anything on the initial call, I remember suggesting he get in touch with Al Williamson as a likely prospect.

I was working on other projects at the time, work I enjoyed, and the offer was set aside in my mind for a while. And then, one day, Murphy called me. He was fascinating. He personally knew many of the comic strip artists and illustrators I admired from the 1930s and '40s and his

Above: A scratchboard illustration by Gianni for Moby-Dick *(Troll Publishing, 1986). Right: Another example of Gianni's scratchboard technique. Illustration for* John Henry *(Kipling Press, 1988).*

own skills were so varied that I quickly realized that, even though I had been an illustrator for over 25 years, I might learn a lot from this man. Shortly after, I agreed to do a sample page. Jay Kennedy and Murphy were concerned about a consistent look. Newspapers are apt to drop a comic strip if they sense a change in art or writing.

BMK: Tell me about "the whole schmear."

GG: "The whole schmear." Yes, that was Murphy's answer to my question: "What specifically, do you want me to do? Help out on the backgrounds? Penciling? Some inking?"

"No," he said firmly, "I want you to do the whole schmear!"

Now, here's where I started getting nervous. You've got to keep in mind; I hadn't seen *Prince Valiant* since I was a kid! Over 35 years ago. King Features rushed out a couple of years of Murphy's run and the artist sent me a blank sheet of paper with ruled panels and an old script his son, Cullen, had written. So, I did the sample. Murphy wanted it finished in 5 days. In the end, I was dissatisfied with it, but the artist thought it was good enough. He tried to ease my fears by disabusing me of the notion I was working on the greatest American comic strip of all time, *"HAL FOSTER'S PRINCE VALIANT."* Murphy was from the old school where professionals took their work seriously but they didn't have the fanboy mentality many of us have today. The worshipful attitude can be paralyzing.

He also reassured me, if I took the job, he'd finish any aspect I wasn't comfortable with—such as faces of the main characters. I didn't even know who Aleta or Gawain were.

"This is a great opportunity for you because there isn't any illustration in the newspapers any more!" he said as a way of bucking me up.

That was it. I began ghosting the strip about once a month for about two years. There was no talk of taking over the strip myself so I didn't feel pressured.

BMK: Did you realize at the time that there were other artists trying out for the strip?

GG: I knew that Charles Vess was doing a sample (see page 38), and that you [Brian] were doing one with Al Williamson as well (see page 62). I imagine that there were other artists working on samples (see Tom Grindberg's sample on page 50), and I know Murphy had other people who were helping him out who may have had some interest in the strip (see *Frank Bolle: The Ghost of Camelot* on page 145). But I had tight deadlines myself. I was illustrating books for Wandering Star Publishers, and the *Prince Valiant* sample had to be knocked out in a couple of days so I could get back to what I considered my real job.

BMK: It has been a long time since you were a student. How did it feel to have your art so heavily scrutinized, especially by someone who was a protégé of Norman Rockwell?

GG: I didn't like it. (laughter) I hadn't felt that way in years, and I was getting to the point in my career where most of the projects I'd worked on I weren't art directed at all. To have someone just mark up what I was doing? Well, he was nice about it. He had a great sense of humor, was sensitive, and disarming—took some of the sting out of it. I remember him saying, "Don't think of my changes as corrections. I'm just an old man set in my ways." But still, I found myself second-guessing what he wanted. As a matter of fact, I still feel that way sometimes.

MS: Do you mean in terms of not wanting to be directed?

GG: Well, just in terms of looking over my shoulder, trying to maintain continuity and yet, bringing my own sensibility into play. This strip has a great history before we came on the scene and we can't ignore it.

MS: Yeah, it's always a balancing act between trying to maintain the continuity and what people expect—while working in a different format than the cartoonists that have gone before us were working in—and knowing that we have to try to put our own stamp on it rather than just trying to duplicate other people's work and therefore be second rate. So far we have had no negative reactions from King Features and no attempt to control what we are doing. I think we are careful about what we do. We haven't done anything that goes too far out on a limb, but at the same time I am more than a little surprised there hasn't been more direction coming from King.

GG: You're right there. Ultimately, King Features and the Murphys were looking for a new artist and a writer who would not need supervision.

BMK: With the Murphys it was a family affair. Between Jack, Cullen, and Meg it was really a family-run business for so long.

GG: Yeah, it was.

BMK: Gary, your inking style was clearly compatible with Murphy's. Many know that Joseph Clement Coll is one of your influences, but for the sake of the those who don't know you, who else is on your list of artistic progenitors?

GG: Oh boy, it probably runs the gamut from Rembrandt to Kirby. Reed Crandall, Franklin Booth, Charles Gibson, Orson Lowell—so many guys. The one guy who wouldn't pop off the top of my head is Hal Foster.

MS: Which actually, I think, makes you a good choice to do this strip. You've got the draftsman chops, but you're not falling into being a Hal Foster imitator. You're doing your own thing, which gives you some leeway.

GG: It does, but it short-circuits me as well because I do look at his work a lot now. His work is great reference material. Hal Foster was not a strong stylist. That's why everybody can use his artwork as reference. He drew things quite accurately, you know, his horses, his shields, and swords. Everything's very accurate and inked without too much technique. He's also a terrific cartoonist, which he isn't always given credit for.

BMK: Strangely enough, yours and Foster's paths did cross when you were entering the Chicago Academy for the Arts.

GG: Well, his artwork, not the man. I remember going into the Academy for the first day of registration, and in the office hung a huge original Hal Foster Sunday page. He was a student there in the 1920s. I wanted to be a comic book artist, so naturally I was drawn to that thing more than the great old paintings that were also hanging around the school. Little did I think that thirty years later I would be drawing the strip myself. It's funny the way life takes those twists and turns.

BMK: How did you feel when Murphy turned the strip over to you?

GG: He had been in-and-out of hospitals and in January of 2004 he was losing ground on the strip in terms of getting it out every week. He called me one afternoon, and he asked, "Are you sitting down?" His voice was shaky. "I just can't do it any more, so next week you can do it on your own. I'm turning it over to you. I've decided I'm retiring, and that I'm leaving it in capable hands."

I knew it was coming sooner or later, but I didn't think it would be quite that sudden. I thought maybe we would work together longer, or alternate weeks or something. When he said he couldn't do it any more, next week's strip was already due, I really couldn't say, "Well, let me think about it."

MS: Gary, I remember talking with you about a month leading up to that. You knew that it was

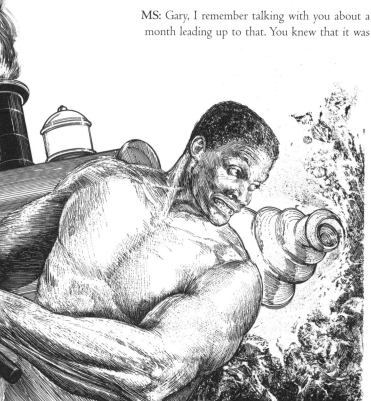

149.

"THE WIND IS UP: HARK! HOW IT HOWLS! METHINKS TILL NOW, I NEVER HEARD A SOUND SO DREARY: DOORS CREAK, AND WINDOWS CLAP, AND NIGHT'S FOUL BIRD ROOKED IN THE SPIRE SCREAMS LOUD!"

BMK: Now Gary, you and I had conversations about Jack reworking some of your art. I told you then that eventually it was going to be your strip and you would eventually be able to do what you wanted as the artist. You didn't have to follow in Jack's footsteps. You didn't have to follow in Foster's footsteps. You had to do it in your own style; the way you wanted.

GG: Sure, slowly it evolves into something more personal; how could it not? I'm not Hal Foster or John Cullen Murphy. And yet it's easier said than done. I couldn't just completely disregard all the work that had come before me. Not only that, I'm forced to work within some parameters. And this is where I differ with you, Brian. I am beholden to the last 70 years. To my mind the strip can never be totally divorced from Foster. Otherwise what's the point of continuing to call it *Hal Foster's Prince Valiant?* Maybe the next guy who draws it can create a new imprint but I can't. I'm too close to the source. Perhaps it should be discontinued altogether. Develop something completely different. But we're opening a new topic here. There is the heated debate about continuing strips once the original creator has died. There's a lot of validity to the side opposing continuation. I wrestle with it myself. I suppose we can always point to Foster's decision to allow the strip to carry on after his passing.

BMK: So what was your last conversation with Jack like?

GG: We talked over the six months between his retirement and his death in July of 2004. He called me from the hospital. He knew that I wasn't happy

going to happen sooner or later, and you seemed ambivalent about the commitment needed to do the strip full time on your own. It's a huge commitment.

GG: It *is* a huge commitment. I had a lot of things going, and yet, at the same time, I could see it was remarkable opportunity. I didn't take it lightly. I knew I couldn't do my own work *and Prince Valiant.* No. It was really a matter of one or the other. *Prince Valiant* needed complete focus and concentration. And when you look at the last seventy years of the work—those are some pretty daunting standards to try and live up to. Murphy wanted nothing to do with it from here on in. Could I possibly do *Prince Valiant* all by myself?

with how the strip was being reproduced in the newspapers. My delicate idealism was in shreds. They were digitally squashing and stretching the figures to make it fit in smaller areas, they were cutting off the panels, and dropping captions over the live art. Newspapers were completely distorting the art and I wasn't happy. Somehow, Murphy got wind of my frustrations. He called to boost my morale. "Look, you're drawing. Draw the strip for yourself. Forget about the way it's being reproduced, or how it's being colored, or the way it's being altered for different formats. There is nothing you can do about that. It's beyond your control. Just do it for yourself." We talked about fifteen minutes and I believe the torch truly passed that day. When he signed off with a frail "God Bless You." I knew it was the last time we'd speak. It took me ten minutes to put the disconnected phone down.

BMK: Tell me about your answering machine.

GG: Well, that last conversation was partially recorded by my answering machine. I listened to it several times, after he had passed away. Because of it, I remember a lot of what he said quite clearly. That's why I'm able to quote him. I remember his exact words. He said, "I'm calling from the hospital, and I have a newspaper here where *Prince Valiant* is reproduced as you drew it. It looks great; I'm going to send it to you. I wanted to call and make you feel good." And those were his exact words, "I wanted to call and make you feel good."

I don't mind sharing this private moment because it points out John Cullen Murphy's character. Here he was, as sick as he was, and he's calling me to make me feel good. Sounds melodramatic but it's true.

He was planning on painting portraits, and he was relieved to be free of the strip. I know he was dissatisfied with the way it was appearing in the newspapers as well, he referred to the problem as "shrinkage."

BMK: So tell me about the period between when Jack left and Mark came on board. What was it like working with Cullen Murphy writing the strip?

GG: Cullen was another very busy man. With as much as he had invested in *Prince Valiant*, he had other concerns as well. He was the editor-in-chief of *The Atlantic Monthly*, he was writing articles, and he was writing several books. He told me that once his dad had retired, he wasn't as interested in working on the strip either. It was the chance for him to work with his father that he enjoyed, and he had been doing it for twenty-some years. He and I worked together for about eight months. I didn't have much input on the stories he was writing. It's just as well because I had enough on my plate trying to produce the finished art. Generally, he was working five minutes to midnight as well, and I'd get a script on Monday with art due Friday. I never knew from week-to-week where he was headed with the story. This made reference gathering a problem at times. He realized this too. He could see that I would be much better off finding somebody I could work with and talk to on a regular basis. On the other hand, he was like his father. He had a great sense of humor. He never criticized anything that I had drawn. He thought it all looked fine. He was easy to work with. We talked a couple of times about Mark, and Cullen wistfully turned the reins over to him. He's gone on to other interesting projects, but I'm sure he's proud of his tenure on *Valiant* and working with his father. They were very close.

MS: How long were they on the strip together? About thirty years? Is that right?

GG: I think twenty-five. In college, Cullen was majoring in Medieval History. He knew Foster and would suggest story ideas to him. Foster was impressed and eventually, Cullen took over the full range of writing.

BMK: So Mark, tell me about how you got involved in the strip.

MS: As Gary has been talking, I've been trying to recall the timeline. Gary had started talking to me about the possibility of writing *Prince Valiant* about a year before Jack had retired. I think you knew that if Jack stepped down it was likely that Cullen would as well. You had brought up the possibility to see if I would be interested. Gary had been advocating for me behind the scenes when it became clear that after Jack had stepped down and then died, and Cullen had indicated that he was going to

be leaving the strip. Gary suggested to King that I would be a suitable replacement. At some point Jay Kennedy had indeed gotten in touch with me at Gary's urging. And Brendan Burford was familiar with my work as well.

GG: Jay knew your work from *Flash Gordon* and *Xenozoic Tales*.

MS: Right, and I'd met him at conventions. He was also associated with my old publisher, Denis Kitchen. They both had a specific interest in the underground comics. I do remember that Jay was hesitant in asking me to do this because for some reason he didn't think I would be particularly interested in writing a strip for someone else. I told him that I certainly was interested, so he asked me to submit some story proposals. I guess he had other writers doing that, as well. Between Gary's advocating for me specifically and my submitted proposals, I began writing the strip in September of that year.

GG: That sounds about right.

MS: Our first strip appeared in November.

BMK: November 21, 2004. Strip #3537.

MS: That's the one. I know I did have some contact with Cullen. As Gary indicated, Cullen was very supportive and very much behind the idea that it was time for a change, regardless of his father having left the strip. I got the feeling from him that he felt that it was time for the strip to evolve into something else. He was very nice and he sent me a pile of his texts on Medieval History and Medieval timelines to give me some framework, some background. We only had that one conversation. His final sign-off strip had that very nice last panel where he passed the torch on to us, which I thought was very gallant of him. He could have just ignored it, but he wrote, and I paraphrase, "It is time for the page to turn and a new scribe to take over."

GG: Yeah, I remember Cullen telling me he felt wistful about giving up the strip and the years spent working with his father. He did put a touching subtext into those last few weeks and he summed up the Murphy years nicely. One could read those strips and not notice it but actually, if you know the background, it adds another dimension.

MS: Absolutely.

BMK: Is there any input from King on the direction they want the strip to take?

MS: The only other voice that ever really enters into writing the strip for me right now is Gary's, and I feel we're so much on the same wavelength on what we like about storytelling and these types of stories that I've never had a situation where I sat there and thought, "Well, that's not the way I would go, but if that's what Gary wants then that's what we'll do." That's the neat thing about this. Whenever Gary brings something to the equation, and it's often, it's always something where I'll say, "That's a great direction to go in, let's do that!"

BMK: Now that you have the dinosaurs in the strip, are the Cadillacs coming any time soon?

MS: (laughing) Well, how about Brick Bradford coming back with the Time Top? Maybe we could engineer that.

Our Story:
AT CONSTANTINOPLE, A MESSAGE AWAITS ALETA FROM JUSTINIAN, NEPHEW OF THE SENILE EMPEROR JUSTIN...

HE GREETS HER WARMLY. "YOU ARE A RICH MAN," JUSTINIAN TELLS PRINCE VALIANT. "YOU HAVE ALETA AND HEALTHY CHILDREN. I HAVE AN EMPIRE BUT NO SON TO INHERIT IT." VAL LAUGHS UNEASILY. LONG AGO ALETA HAD BEEN WOOED BY THE POWERFUL REGENT.

JUSTINIAN IS EMPEROR IN ALL BUT NAME. HIS DEEDS ARE THE STUFF OF LEGEND. UNDER JUSTINIAN'S GUIDANCE, THE GENERAL BELISARIUS HAS WON BACK AFRICA AND SPAIN FROM THE BARBARIANS. AFTER A BLOODY SIEGE, EVEN ROME IS AGAIN PART OF THE "ROMAN" EMPIRE.

IT WAS JUSTINIAN WHO REBUILT THE BASILICA OF HAGIA SOPHIA. "SOLOMON, I HAVE OUTDONE YOU!" HE EXCLAIMED. HIS WIFE IS THE PROUD THEODORA. TO AN EARLIER HUSBAND SHE GAVE SONS, BUT TO JUSTINIAN SHE HAS BORNE ONLY DAUGHTERS.

"I WOULD DO ANYTHING FOR A SON," HE TELLS VAL LATER. JUSTINIAN'S DAUGHTERS WAIT UPON HIM FONDLY, BUT HE TREATS THEM WITH DRUNKEN DISDAIN. LIKE ALETA, THEODORA IS EXPECTING A CHILD. "THIS ONE MUST BE A BOY," JUSTINIAN INSISTS.

THAT NIGHT, VAL DISCOVERS AN INTRUDER IN HIS CHAMBER. THE ROGUE DEPARTS WITH A RINGING IN HIS EARS.

GG: That may be at the point where King steps in with an objection. (laughter) But even as Cullen stepped into the wings the time had come for a new approach. Things can't stay the same. I would be dissatisfied repeating what had been done over and over again. As we move on from here, Mark and I would like to push it further. I'm not quite sure how but with the shrinking format and the general demise of the newspaper industry, not to mention the changing taste of the reader, the strip must evolve.

BMK: How do the two of you brainstorm on story ideas?

GG: You want to start that, Mark?

MS: I'll start that. It's pretty collaborative. I'll come up with a basic general arc of a story idea, say for instance: Val goes adventuring into Pictland and meets the Loch Ness Monster. Then I'll ask, "What do you think, Gary? Is that something you'd be interested in drawing?" Now I don't think Gary has ever said, "Nah, I don't want to do that. Let's do something else." But Gary will take the idea and say, "Hey, well what if we do this?" and I'll say, "That's a good idea. We can head in that direction." And then that makes me think of something else. The story bounces back and forth between us and it evolves into something with meat on it, some real character development.

GG: I've worked with other writers before on comic strips and comic books, and that doesn't always work out well. It helps when two people are of the same mind.

MS: If I have one advantage as a writer that a lot of other comic strip writers don't have it's that I draw, and I story-tell through cartooning as well.

GG: I'm glad you mentioned that, Mark, because you know what will and won't work. You know what can and can't be drawn. There are times when writers have asked for a sequence which is impossible to put down in one panel.

MS: Right.

GG: You have a great sense of that because you are an illustrator and comic artist as well.

MS: You would think that more writers in comics would have a visual sense because it is a visual medium, but many don't. Some people can't imagine that you can't have a single panel where you have a character get out of bed, strap on his sword, run out the door, and point into the sky. That's a full strip right there, involving several panels. You need more than one panel to show successive actions, but some people just don't get that.

GG: With *Valiant* it's more difficult. Being a Sunday-only page, and being so small, we have a limited space to get a story across.

MS: It becomes a real challenge to bring the reader up to speed on what's happened the previous week, advance the plot, do a little character

development, or a little bit of humor involving what we know about the characters, and then wrap it up in the last panel and end with somewhat of a cliffhanger so that the reader will want to come back next week. That's a lot to fit into the little amount of space we have.

GG: There have been times where Mark's pulled off a genuine coup. He's cleverly written a couple of weeks where the strip is not only self-contained, but engaging enough to be "continued next week."

MS: It's important to realize that Gary writes too, and he could be writing this strip himself if he chose to eat up even more of his life. He could be writing this perfectly well.

BMK: I don't think Julie (Gary's wife) would like that too much.

MS: (Laughing) No, I don't think so. It allows me to be involved in the strip, so I'm just as happy that he chooses to just do the art. I will get on a roll and have the basic story arc worked out. Then I'll give Gary a series of plots, a week-by-week breakdown of what has to happen. Sometimes I'll get carried away with a certain sequence or a certain scene, like a battle scene that goes on for several weeks, and Gary will say, "Mark, don't you think we need to break this up a little bit? Maybe we can interject one week's worth of character development, for a breather." Or he might suggest a real change-up in attitude if we've been pretty serious for a while. He'll suggest, "Let's try to go for a little more humor this week." To me it's always good to have the perspective of someone else who knows storytelling.

BMK: Foster did that a lot.

MS: Yeah, absolutely. He did a great balance of the epic stuff and the character-oriented material, and that's what we try to do.

GG: We keep referring back to Foster, don't we? He should be rediscovered by every generation and now Fantagraphics is printing great, new volumes of Foster's original material. Even fans who are familiar with the art will be impressed.

MS: And it's so rich as you go over it, and you see things from different perspectives. You appreciate different aspects of his work. That I think is the goal of anyone: to have that kind of richness in their work, but Foster absolutely did achieve it.

Left: Gary Gianni's Prince Valiant *tryout page.*
Right: Gary Gianni (l) with Sid Weiskirch (r) at the Skokie Public Library, Skokie Illinois. Sid has been a tireless promoter of the Prince Valiant *strip in the Chicago area for many years, giving lectures and displaying his collection at all of the area's public libraries.*

BMK: I sent both of you samples of the original color engraver's proofs that will appear in this book, and in the new editions by Fantagraphics. I've seen all of the pages they're shooting from, which is about ninety-five percent of Foster's run, and my God, the line work is so delicate. Every reprint up until now has been so blotchy. These proof sheets really give you a whole new perspective on Foster's craft.

We've gotten a bit off track. I want to get back to the collaborative process. Now, Mark, when do you write the final script?

MS: First, I give Gary a little plot breakdown of a weekly strip. I usually send plots to him in a group of five or six weeks, sometimes a few more, so he can see a little bit in advance.

These are just basic breakdowns of how many panels I see the strip being, what needs to happen in each panel, and maybe a little snippet of the dialogue just to give Gary an idea if the strip is humorous or serious or dramatic or whatever. Then Gary takes it and decides how he wants to divide the panels. If he has another idea of how to stage the scene we'll discuss that.

GG: It might be worth inserting one of those pages. Even if it's just a one-by-one inch example of what your breakdowns look like.

BMK: Can you get one to me to include with the interview?

MS: Yeah, I can shoot one out to you easily. But Gary also does a little thumbnail breakdown based on what I'd initially written and then sends it back to me. It's from that breakdown that I write the text, the actual narrative and dialogue that will appear, and then Gary takes that and based on the completed art he will edit it down to what will fit in the drawn panels.

BMK: Is it possible for me to get the entire process of breakdowns, thumbnails, and final art to put in the book?

MS: No problem (see pages 157-159 for the entire process).

BMK: I'll let the two of you decide which one you want to appear. I'd rather that come from you, as creators. Whichever one the two of you think shows the process best.

MS: Maybe the one with the dragon throwing the man off the back of his head because Gary took what I broke down and divided the panels up even further. It really illustrates how the strip evolves.

BMK: That would be wonderful. I want you both to answer my next question individually. For each of you, what has been the most rewarding aspect about working on the strip?

MS: I get a kick every week when I get an envelope from American Color, which is the company that does the formatting for the strip. They send me a black & white proof of the strip, and it's the first chance I get to see Gary's completed art with the lettering in place. That is always such a kick, to get to see what I started visualizing, what I had in mind, and how it evolved, how it turns out. Sometimes what we start out with is a very different idea than what it evolves into. I am also lucky enough that my local paper carries *Prince Valiant*, and that's exciting too, although the excitement is modulated by the depressing size and the variable printing that it comes in every week. I'm looking at this week's *Prince Valiant* right now, and below it is *Marvin*, *Fred Basset*, *The Lockhorns*, and *Andy Capp*, and it is so unique compared to those other strips. And this is a great week, because it features a huge panel with the lizard dragon creature coming over the battlements of Camelot. Gary sets the creature up with a great silhouette. It just grabs your attention. You could see it from across the room and still read it perfectly well. It really jumps off the page as compared to the other strips, which are done very contemporary, very simplified bigfoot cartooning.

BMK: Looking forward in the strip, King Arthur's abdication of the throne was a thinly veiled reference to John Cullen Murphy's retirement. According to legend, since King Arthur never gave up his kingdom, will he be returning to the throne anytime soon?

MS: I'm going to vacillate on that because I don't want to tip our hand in any direction. I will say that I don't want us to become beholden to any

kind of preexisting Arthurian legend. It should stand on its own. The story is Prince Valiant's. Maybe at some point it will be worth bringing Arthur back. But just because the subtitle reads "In the days of King Arthur" doesn't carry any particular weight in my mind.

GG: I agree. First and foremost this strip is a fantasy. Some readers appreciate more historical accuracy but with the strip reduced in size we're forced to take a broader approach with the storytelling.

BMK: Have you started thinking of a storyline leading up to 2012 and the seventy-fifth anniversary?

MS: (laughter) It never entered my mind. I don't think in terms of those things.

GG: I remember editor Jay Kennedy telling me that King Features tries to downplay the significant milestones of older comic strips. You don't want to proclaim that fact too loudly. Of course, anyone reading this is obviously an aficionado but for the most part, general newspaper readers don't care about the legacy aspect. They want their newspaper fresh, timely and topical. Here we are fawning over it, but the majority of people aren't interested in Hal Foster or what happened a month ago in *Prince Valiant*. Their only interest might be "Let's see what Prince Valiant's doing today" and that's the reality of it. If Mark and I can attract a reader to peruse *today's* strip amongst all the other distractions—I'll feel we've done our job successfully.

BMK: I think that one of the key elements about the tenure of the two of you is that you have made it a Prince Valiant strip again. For a long time it

had become about everybody else. It had become about Arn, or Nathaniel, or anyone except Val. There were battle scenes where Val and Gawain were crouching down, hiding behind a boulder, which was not Val at all. He had become old, but he has become younger, vibrant, and vital since the two of you have taken over.

MS: Well, thanks! The one thing that Gary and I discussed was to return the strip to Prince Valiant—to make him the center of the story again. I think the Murphys, with good reason, had decided to look at different characters. They had written *Prince Valiant* for an awful long time, and I think they earned the right to develop other characters.

GG: Even Kennedy liked the idea that it had fostered the image of being a family-oriented strip, and that it resonated a certain empathy with the readers because they could connect with the characters.

MS: That's a good point. We do try to maintain a balance, though, because I think it is important. A lot of people do relate to this, whether it's conscious or not, as being something of their own lives. In a big, epic, medieval, fantasy strip it's important to have something of contemporary home life to make it somewhat relatable. That's where doing little family bits now and then is valuable. We do try to keep that in there and we try to remind each other at certain times to put it in there.

GG: That sort of stuff is a lot more subtle than a giant lizard thing coming over a castle wall. (laughter) You might not believe it but it's much more difficult to draw family squabbles, comedic moments and tender domestic scenes.

BMK: And you don't have the page size to do what Foster did.

GG: Quite frankly, even if I had the page size, I still wouldn't be able to do that. It's a convenient excuse to use on my behalf, but Foster's and Murphy's stuff looks great at any size.

BMK: How many days do you work on the strip, Gary?

GG: It's about four days.

BMK: I don't think many people realize that you do not color the strip, and that you have no control over that.

GG: I have a minimal amount of input on the coloring. I make suggestions, but the page must be colored on the computer. I'm not technically proficient in that area and the

THEY HAVE COME ACROSS AN INTRIGUING VESSEL AND ARE STUDYING ITS SAIL. SUDDENLY FOOTSTEPS ARE HEARD IN A DARKENED DOORWAY. "WHO GOES THERE?" VAL DEMANDS AS HE DRAWS THE 'SINGING SWORD.' THE FOOTSTEPS MOUNT A STAIRWAY.

Opposite: A Prince Valiant *panel as drawn by Gary Gianni. After Gianni completed each assignment, John Cullen Murphy would make copies and write notes to his sucessor.*

Left: The panel as it appeared in print with all of John Cullen Murphy's artistic changes.

3756

2-1-09

color shifts drastically from the monitor screen to newsprint. I'm always just as surprised to see the colors as the reader is on Sunday morning.

BMK: Who does the coloring on the strip?

GG: Tom Roberts.*

MS: He also does the lettering, which is computer generated, but he has to fit it in with the image.

GG: He's caught a few inconsistencies in the art and the dates; sometimes we get the dates mixed up. And he's also had to correct my art scans, which is a big job.

MS: Sometimes I get the names of the characters mixed up and he catches that.

BMK: So he's the colorist, letterer, and proofreader?

MS: And chief bottle washer. (laughter)

BMK: Any last words, Mark?

MS: I think that covers it. Just writing the strip I refer back a lot to the Murphys and Foster just to get myself stoked, or to figure out a different way of telling something, or developing a character.

BMK: I should ask you who your writing influences are?

MS: Again, first and foremost, I look back to Foster, and even though we can't tell his type of stories and do what he did, it's still his rhythm; his sense of humor, his touch with the characters is always in my mind. The Murphys carry that honor as well. Prose writers like Robert E. Howard and Edgar Rice Burroughs are always going to be a big influence on the type of adventure stories I choose to tell.

BMK: I think that's a wrap. Thank you gentlemen for taking the time out of your busy schedules. I really appreciate it!

MS: You're welcome, Brian.

GG: You're welcome. You guys have a good day!

Opposite: When Gary Gianni's mother passed away late in 2008, Mark Schultz gave his partner some time off by filling in with this Prince Valiant *page. It is page 3756, 1 February 2009.*
Above: Mark Schultz.
Below: The plot to Prince Valiant *page 3776.*
Overleaf: The following two pages display Gianni's rough layouts for page 3776 (l), and the finished inked page (r).

Prince Valiant 3776

BEFORE THE BEASTMEN CAN REACH THE MONSTER'S EYES, IT SHAKES THEM OFF LIKE FLEAS, WITH A MASSIVE HEAVE. THE BEASTMEN GO A FLYING!

VAL DASHES OVER TO WHERE THE SEMI-STUNNED NUDDER LAYS.
VAL: "HOW DO YOUR PEOPLE STOP THESE ABOMINATIONS?!"

NUDDER SHRUGS: "WE DON'T. MOSTLY WE JUST HIDE WHEN THEY COME, ALTHOUGH MANY OF US DIE. HOW DO YOUR PEOPLE STOP THEM?"

VAL SPUTTERS AS HE REALIZES NUDDER DOESN'T REALIZE THIS PARTICULAR CREATURE ISN'T NATIVE:
"WE DON'T! WE... THEY DON'T LIVE HERE! THIS ONE FOLLOWED US FROM YOUR ISLAND! WHY DOES IT WANT YOU?!"

NUDDER PUTS IT TOGETHER: "OH! THEM, NOT US IT WANTS!
SHE WANTS HER SEED RACK. SHE WANTS EGG GAWAIN STOLE FROM HER!

NEXT: WHITHER GAWAIN?

---

*This is not the same Tom Roberts who wrote the recent biography on Alex Raymond.

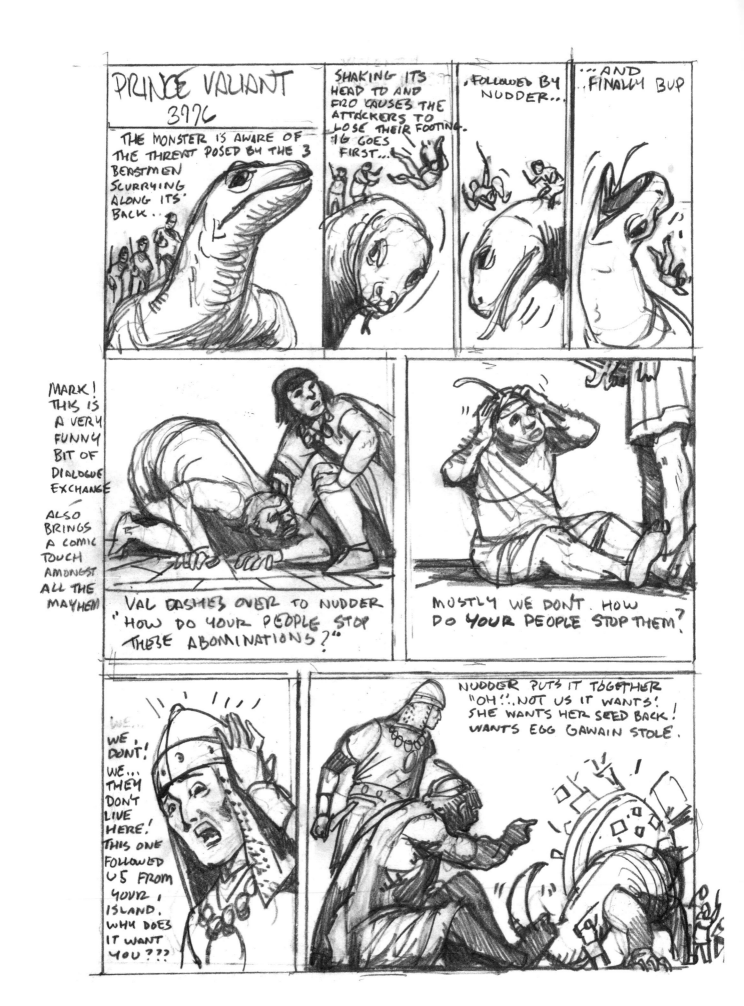

PRINCE VALIANT
3976

THE MONSTER IS AWARE OF THE THREAT POSED BY THE 3 BEASTMEN SCURRYING ALONG ITS BACK...

SHAKING ITS HEAD TO AND FRO CAUSES THE ATTACKERS TO LOSE THEIR FOOTING. 1G GOES FIRST...

...FOLLOWED BY NUDDER...

...AND FINALLY BUP

MARK! THIS IS A VERY FUNNY BIT OF DIALOGUE EXCHANGE

ALSO BRINGS A COMIC TOUCH AMONGST ALL THE MAYHEM

VAL DASHES OVER TO NUDDER "HOW DO YOUR PEOPLE STOP THESE ABOMINATIONS?"

MOSTLY WE DONT. HOW DO YOUR PEOPLE STOP THEM?

WE... WE DONT! WE... THEY DONT LIVE HERE! THIS ONE FOLLOWED US FROM YOUR ISLAND. WHY DOES IT WANT YOU???

NUDDER PUTS IT TOGETHER "OH!"...NOT US IT WANTS! SHE WANTS HER SEED BACK! WANTS EGG GAWAIN STOLE.

HAL FOSTER'S — GIANNI AND SCHULTZ

Prince Valiant

Our Story:

THE COURAGEOUS BEASTMEN MAKE FOR THEIR MARAUDING FOE'S EYES...

...BUT THE BRUTE IS NOT SO DUMB...

...AND DISMISSES THE THREE...

...ONE BY ONE.

VAL DASHES TO NUDDER, WHO HAS FALLEN NEAREST HIM: *"HOW DO YOUR PEOPLE STOP THESE ABOMINATIONS?"*

NUDDER SHRUGS, GROGGILY. *"MOSTLY WE DON'T. MOSTLY WE HIDE, AND PRAY TO THE SKY GODS. HOW DO YOU PEOPLE STOP THEM?"*

"WE DON'T! WE..." VAL SPUTTERS. *"THEY DON'T LIVE HERE! THIS CREATURE FOLLOWED FROM YOUR ISLAND! WHY DID IT FOLLOW YOU?"*

3976

SUDDENLY, NUDDER HAS A REVELATION. *"OH! NOT US SHE WANTS! SHE WANTS HER SEED BACK! WANTS EGG GAWAIN STOLE!"*

NEXT: Wither Gawain?

Gianni 6-21-09

159.

The Friends of Hal Foster Society is a non-profit organization that was founded in 2002 in Foster's hometown of Halifax, Nova Scotia, Canada by Eric Comeau and Calum Johnston. The purpose of *Hal's Pals*, as it is affectionately nicknamed, is to bring attention to Foster's artistic achievements. The current *Crusade* focuses on raising money to erect a life-sized, bronze statue of Prince Valiant, similar to the one pictured above, in a park in downtown Halifax. Proceeds from the sale of this book will go to Hal's Pals to aid in making the statue a reality. To make a charitable donation, or to find out about how you can help, please mail all correspondences to: The Friends of Hal Foster Society, 5262 Sackville Street, Halifax, Nova Scotia, Canada B3J 1K8.